Journal of Biblical Literature

Volume 137
2018

GENERAL EDITOR
ADELE REINHARTZ
University of Ottawa
Ottawa, ON K1N 6N5

A Quarterly Published by
SBL Press

JOURNAL OF BIBLICAL LITERATURE

EDITORS OF THE JOURNAL
General Editor: ADELE REINHARTZ, University of Ottawa
Managing Editor: JONATHAN M. POTTER, Society of Biblical Literature
Editorial Assistant: CAITLIN J. MONTGOMERY, Society of Biblical Literature

EDITORIAL BOARD

ELIZABETH BOASE, Flinders University
HELEN BOND, University of Edinburgh
JO-ANN A. BRANT, Goshen College
TONY BURKE, York University
DAVID M. CARR, Union Theological Seminary
RICHARD J. CLIFFORD, Boston College
KELLEY COBLENTZ BAUTCH, St. Edwards University
COLLEEN CONWAY, Seton Hall University
TOAN DO, Australian Catholic University
KATHY EHRENSPERGER, University of Potsdam
GEORG FISCHER, Leopold-Franzens-Universität Innsbruck
PAULA FREDRIKSEN, Hebrew University of Jerusalem
WIL GAFNEY, Brite Divinity School
FRANCES TAYLOR GENCH, Union Presbyterian Seminary
SHIMON GESUNDHEIT, Hebrew University of Jerusalem
MARK GOODACRE, Duke University
MARTIEN A. HALVORSON-TAYLOR, University of Virginia (Charlottesville)
RACHEL HAVRELOCK, University of Illinois at Chicago
ELSE K. HOLT, Aarhus Universitet
DAVID G. HORRELL, University of Exeter
CAROLINE E. JOHNSON HODGE, College of the Holy Cross
JONATHAN KLAWANS, Boston University
JENNIFER KNUST, Boston University
BRUCE W. LONGENECKER, Baylor University
MICHAEL A. LYONS, Simpson University
DANIEL MACHIELA, McMaster University
JOHN W. MARSHALL, University of Toronto
NAPHTALI MESHEL, Hebrew University of Jerusalem
CHRISTINE MITCHELL, St. Andrew's College, University of Saskatchewan
KENNETH NGWA, Drew University
KEN M. PENNER, St. Francis Xavier University
PIERLUIGI PIOVANELLI, University of Ottawa
MARK REASONER, Marian University
THOMAS RÖMER, Collège de France and University of Lausanne
DALIT ROM-SHILONI, Tel Aviv University
JEAN-PIERRE RUIZ, St. John's University (New York)
SETH L. SANDERS, University of California, Davis
KONRAD SCHMID, University of Zurich
WILLIAM M. SCHNIEDEWIND, University of California, Los Angeles
ABRAHAM SMITH, Perkins School of Theology, Southern Methodist University
JOHANNA STIEBERT, University of Leeds
JOHN T. STRONG, Missouri State University
D. ANDREW TEETER, Harvard Divinity School
MATTHEW THIESSEN, McMaster University
STEVEN TUELL, Pittsburgh Theological Seminary
CECILIA WASSEN, Uppsala University
EMMA WASSERMAN, Rutgers University
LAWRENCE M. WILLS, Episcopal Divinity School

The Society of Biblical Literature is a constituent member of the American Council of Learned Societies. *President of the Society:* Brian K. Blount, Union Presbyterian Seminary, Richmond, VA 23227; *Vice President:* Gale A. Yee, Episcopal Divinity School, Cambridge, MA 02138; *Chair, Research and Publications Committee:* M. Patrick Graham, Candler School of Theology, Atlanta, GA 30322; *Executive Director:* John F. Kutsko, Society of Biblical Literature, 825 Houston Mill Road, Suite 350, Atlanta, GA 30329.

The *Journal of Biblical Literature* (ISSN 0021–9231) is published quarterly by the Society of Biblical Literature, 825 Houston Mill Road, Suite 350, Atlanta, GA 30329. The annual subscription price is US$55.00 for members and US$220.00 for nonmembers. Institutional and online rates are also available. For information regarding subscriptions and membership, contact: SBL Press, 825 Houston Mill Road, Suite 350, Atlanta, GA 30329. Phone: 866-727-9955 (toll free) or 404-727-9498. E-mail: sblservices@sbl-site.org. For information concerning permission to quote, editorial and business matters, please see the first issue of the year, p. 2. Periodical postage paid at Atlanta, Georgia, and at additional mailing offices. POSTMASTER: Send address changes to SBL Press, 825 Houston Mill Road, Suite 350, Atlanta, GA 30329. Copyright © 2018 by the SBL Press.

JBL is indexed in the following resources:

Arts and Humanities Citation Index
Scopus
ATLA Religion Database
Religious and Theological Abstracts
New Testament Abstracts (ATLA)
Old Testament Abstracts (ATLA)
Periodicals Index online (Proquest)
European Reference Index for the Humanities

PRINTED IN THE UNITED STATES OF AMERICA

"My Father, My Father! Chariot of Israel and Its Horses!" (2 Kings 2:12 // 13:14): Elisha's or Elijah's Title?

KRISTIN WEINGART
kristin.weingart@uni-tuebingen.de
University of Tübingen, 72074 Tübingen, Germany

Among the prophetic narratives in the book of Kings, the stories about the "men of God" Elijah and Elisha are by far the most elaborate. Elijah and Elisha are presented as closely connected; they even carry the same title: "chariot of Israel and its horses." In 2 Kgs 2:12 Elisha cries out to Elijah using the appellation; later the Israelite king expresses his despair at Elisha's death (2 Kgs 13:14) by addressing him in the same way. In the current narrative sequence, the title is one of the features that present Elisha as the successor of Elijah. Second Kings 2 depicts Elijah's ascent to heaven in a fiery chariot and explains why Elijah carries the title. While no similar explanation is given in the case of Elisha, the tradition history of the images shows that the title is more easily connected with the Elisha narratives than with the Elijah stories. Elisha is seen as a supporter of various Israelite kings in military conflicts, and the Elijah narratives show a dependency on the Elisha material. It is likely, therefore, that the title "chariot of Israel and its horses" originated in the Elisha tradition and was later transferred to Elijah. Accordingly, 2 Kgs 2 was intended not only to present Elijah as Elisha's predecessor but also to provide an explanation why Elijah carries the title.

According to Hermann Gunkel, an essential characteristic of Old Testament narratives is that "they almost exclusively depict what is perceived by the senses, only what one can see and hear. The inner life…, the spiritual life, though existing and—how highly!—developed in ancient Israel, expresses itself only indirectly; it is hidden behind deeds and words."[1] Second Kings 2:1–18 provides a striking example of Gunkel's assessment: Elijah and his disciple Elisha are walking together.

[1] Hermann Gunkel, *Geschichten von Elisa*, vol. 1 of *Meisterwerke hebräischer Erzählungskunst* (Berlin: Curtius, 1922), 6: "Denn alle urtümliche Erzählungskunst und so auch diejenige Israels stellt zunächst nur dasjenige, was sich den Sinnen bietet, dar, nur das, was man sehen und hören kann. Das innere Leben ist … auch schon damals vorhanden und in Israel – wie reich!

When Elijah asks Elisha to stay behind, the latter refuses. When he tries to shake him off through a strenuous hike, ascending four thousand feet from Gilgal to Bethel only to descend these four thousand feet again toward Jericho in the Jordan Valley, Elisha follows along. When the prophets of Bethel and Jericho try to discourage him, he silences them and walks on.² Without any explicit characterization, Elisha appears to the reader as loyal to his master, as persevering in his attachment to him, and as an independent spirit among the prophetic circles they encounter on their way.³

What is true for the story as a whole also applies to a singular feature. When Elisha sees Elijah riding up to heaven in a fiery chariot drawn by fiery horses, he calls him: אבי אבי רכב ישראל ופרשיו, "My father, my father! Chariot of Israel and its horses!" The same title is used again by the Israelite king Joash when he cries out in despair and addresses the dying Elisha in 2 Kgs 13:14. In order to distinguish the men of God from ordinary people, Joash and Elisha employed a powerful and expressive image.

The pictorial quality of the title and a certain indeterminateness facilitated its applicability to both Elijah and Elisha, although their profiles, as presented in the respective prophetic narratives in 1 Kgs 17–2 Kgs 13, differ considerably. From the perspective of literary and/or tradition history, however, two questions arise: where did the title originate, and with which prophetic figure was it initially associated? I will argue that the title רכב ישראל ופרשיו ("chariot of Israel and its horses") has its origins in the Elisha tradition and was only secondarily applied to Elijah, a process in which the succession narrative in 2 Kgs 2:1–18 played a decisive role. Accordingly, the following analysis will (I) address the function of 2 Kgs 2:1–18 within the Elisha cycle, (II) discuss the usage of the title's imagery in its different attestations within the Elijah and Elisha narratives, and (III) present some conclusions regarding the stories of Elijah and Elisha as well as their respective traditions.

I. Second Kings 2:1–18 within the Elisha Cycle

Second Kings 2:1–18 has been convincingly described as a succession narrative.⁴ There can be no doubt that it aims to legitimize Elisha as the rightful successor of Elijah. A number of narrative features confirm this function:

– entwickelt. Aber es spricht sich nur mittelbar aus; es verbirgt sich hinter den Handlungen und Worten."

²As Marvin A. Sweeney correctly points out, the threefold repetition also heightens the narrative suspense (*I and II Kings: A Commentary*, OTL [Louisville: Westminster John Knox, 2007], 272).

³See Martin Rehm, *Das zweite Buch der Könige: Ein Kommentar* (Würzburg: Echter, 1982), 39; Iain W. Provan, *1 and 2 Kings*, NIBCOT (Peabody, MA: Hendrickson, 1995), 172.

⁴See, e.g., Hans-Christoph Schmitt, *Elisa: Traditionsgeschichtliche Untersuchungen zur*

1. Elisha's perseverance and loyalty enable him to witness Elijah's last miracle, the dividing of the Jordan,[5] and his ascent to heaven in a chariot of fire.

2. Elisha inherits two-thirds of Elijah's spirit, which corresponds, according to Deut 21:17, to the share of the firstborn. This is the traditional and widely accepted explanation,[6] but other options have recently been suggested. Nachman Levine points to an understanding of פי שנים prevalent in midrashic exegesis of 2 Kgs 2:9: Elisha receives a "double portion" of the spirit and therefore performs twice as many miracles as Elijah.[7] Ruth Sauerwein argues that the author of 2 Kings is playing with the ambiguity of the term: he wants to characterize the relation between Elijah and Elisha as one of a father and his firstborn but knows at the same time that Elisha will surpass Elijah in his miracles.[8] Wesley J. Bergen, on the other hand, assumes that פי שנים means that Elisha receives only a part of the spirit of Elijah, which suggests that "Elisha is likely to be less powerful than Elijah."[9] In light of the overall intention of the story to present Elisha on a par with Elijah—he is not only capable of exactly repeating Elijah's miracle (2:14) but is also equally venerated by the בני הנביאים ("sons of the prophets")—any attempt to play one off against the other does not seem to fit its narrative profile. Therefore, the traditional

---

vorklassischen nordisraelitischen Prophetie (Gütersloh: Mohn, 1972), 102; Susanne Otto, *Jehu, Elia, und Elisa: Die Erzählung von der Jehu-Revolution und die Komposition der Elia-Elisa-Erzählungen*, BWANT 152 (Stuttgart: Kohlhammer, 2001), 222.

[5] The crossing of the Jordan is reminiscent of Josh 3, which is of course also associated with Gilgal, the first station of Elijah's and Elisha's itinerary (2 Kgs 2:1), but the differences in the imagery between Josh 3 and 2 Kgs 2 should not be neglected. According to Josh 3:15, when the bearers of the ark reached the river, the water from upstream stopped flowing while the water downstream continued toward the Dead Sea until the Israelites could cross on dry ground (see, e.g., Joachim J. Krause, *Exodus und Eisodus: Komposition und Theologie von Josua 1–5*, VTSup 161 [Leiden: Brill, 2014], 208–9). In 2 Kgs 2, Elijah divides the water, and it stands like two walls on both sides (v. 8). This picture is much closer to the priestly account in Exod 14, although it uses a different vocabulary (e.g., בקע and יבשה in contrast to חצה and חרבה in 2 Kgs 2). Nevertheless, the miracle is often seen as a feature connecting Elijah with Moses, an analogy that is much stronger in the Elijah stories themselves (e.g., 1 Kgs 18:20–40 and Exod 7:8–20 or 1 Kgs 19:8 and Exod 3; see Georg Fohrer, *Elia*, ATANT 31 [Zurich: Zwingli, 1957], 55–58; Robert P. Caroll, "The Elijah-Elisha Sagas: Some Remarks on Prophetic Succession in Ancient Israel," *VT* 19 [1969]: 400–415; or Nachman Levine, "Twice as Much of Your Spirit: Pattern, Parallel and Paronomasia in the Miracles of Elijah and Elisha," *JSOT* 85 [1999]: 25–46, esp. 35–37).

[6] See Kurt Galling, "Der Ehrenname Elisas und die Entrückung Elias," *ZTK* 53 (1956): 129–48, esp. 140; Alexander Rofé, "The Classification of the Prophetical Stories," *JBL* 89 (1970): 427–40, esp. 437, https://doi.org/10.2307/3263449; Ernst Würthwein, *Die Bücher der Könige*, 2 vols., ATD 11 (Göttingen: Vandenhoeck & Ruprecht, 1984), 2:275.

[7] Levine, "Twice as Much," 25–34.

[8] Ruth Sauerwein, *Elischa: Eine redaktions- und religionsgeschichtliche Studie*, BZAW 465 (Berlin: de Gruyter, 2014), 24.

[9] Wesley J. Bergen, *Elisha and the End of Prophetism*, JSOTSup 286 (Sheffield: Sheffield Academic, 1999), 63.

understanding of a transition from a father to his firstborn who takes over the rights and responsibilities of the father remains the most plausible one.

3. As an outward token of his prophetic authority, Elisha also receives Elijah's mantle and is able to repeat the latter's miracle with it. Henceforward, Elisha is the legitimate successor of Elijah, the new איש האלהים ("man of God") and leading authority among the prophets, who, like a choir in the Attic drama, acknowledge his new role by bowing down to him (2:15).[10] The title "chariot of Israel and its horses" is an additional feature fulfilling the same narrative aim. After being used as an epithet for Elijah in 2 Kgs 2, its next appearance, in 2 Kgs 13, as a title for Elisha gives the impression that it is just one more feature that Elisha took over from his master.

Remarkably, the strongest and most vivid picture in the story, namely, the ascent to heaven in a fiery chariot, is connected to Elijah but not to Elisha. Nevertheless, the narrative design and the connections to other Elisha narratives justify a view of the story as an integral part of the Elisha cycle:[11]

a. Second Kings 2:1a functions as a summarizing prolepsis removing the narrative suspense from the ascension of Elijah.[12] The reader's attention is

---

[10] Verses 16–18 are usually seen as a later addition. The main arguments were provided already by Gunkel, *Geschichten von Elisa*, 14: (1) In verses 3 and 5, the sons of the prophets talk about Elijah's ascension, but in verses 16–18 they do not know what happened. (2) According to verse 7, fifty men stand by the Jordan, but in verse 16, there seems to be a larger group, because fifty among them go to search for Elijah. According to Gunkel, the addition's purpose is to confirm that Elijah was indeed taken away and that no grave is to be found. A great majority of commentators follows Gunkel's reasoning (e.g., Rofé, "Classification of the Prophetical Stories," 438; Würthwein, *Die Bücher der Könige*, 276; Schmitt, *Elisa*, 105–6; Sauerwein, *Elischa*, 22); Rehm does not see enough evidence (*Das zweite Buch der Könige*, 29); Sweeney emphasizes the literary function of the verses in 2 Kgs 2 (*I and II Kings*, 274).

[11] Joachim Conrad tried to argue that 2 Kgs 2:1–18 constitutes an Elijah story ("2 Kön 2,1–18 als Elija-Geschichte," in *"Wünschet Jerusalem Frieden": Collected Communications to the XIIth Congress of the International Organization for the Study of the Old Testament, Jerusalem 1968*, ed. Matthias Augustin and Klaus-Dietrich Schunck, BEATAJ 13 [Frankfurt am Main: Lang, 1988], 263–71). To support his view, he reversed an older argument by Gunkel (*Geschichten von Elisa*, 14–15) and Galling ("Der Ehrenname Elisas," 142), who proposed that 2 Kgs 2 was built on an older Elijah legend. According to Conrad, 2 Kgs 2 turned an older Elisha episode into an Elijah story (266–67).

Burke O. Long refrains from a final decision, stating that "the story has to do as much with Elijah as Elisha" (*2 Kings*, FOTL 10 [Grand Rapids: Eerdmans, 1991], 29), but most commentators simply treat 2 Kgs 2 as an Elisha story (for further arguments, see, e.g., John Gray, *I and II Kings: A Commentary*, 2nd rev. ed., OTL [London: SCM, 1980], 466–67; Rofé, "Classification of the Prophetical Stories," 436–37; or Hartmut N. Rösel, "2Kön 2,1–18 als Elija- oder Elischa-Geschichte," *BZ* 59 [1991]: 33–36).

[12] Gunkel, *Geschichten von Elisa*, 4: "Den Gipfel des Ganzen freilich kann dieser Satz nicht darstellen: diesen würde ein guter Erzähler sich nicht selber so im Anfang und gar im Nebensatze vorweggenommen haben"; cf. Rofé, "Classification of the Prophetical Stories," 436. For Galling,

consequently drawn to the circumstances of the ascension and especially to Elisha's behavior in the event. Elisha is mentioned in verse 1 as well, but his fate remains completely open. The account focuses on Elisha, and he does the unexpected when he refuses to leave Elijah despite the obviously aimless wandering about from the Jordan Valley up to the Ephraimite hills and down again.

The geography of the chapter has puzzled many commentators. The text itself gives no reason for the sequence of places visited by Elijah and Elisha; in verses 2, 4, and 6, Elijah simply informs Elisha that YHWH is sending him to their next destination. A. Graeme Auld sees Elijah and Elisha "retracing in reverse some of Israel's first steps in its land."[13] Many commentators note a concentric or chiastic structure in 2 Kgs 2.[14] The chiasm (Gilgal–Bethel–Jericho–Jordan–Jericho–Bethel), however, is broken by verse 25, which sends Elisha not back to Gilgal but onward to Mount Carmel and Samaria. While some see in the structural break a narrative signal that the transition from Elijah to Elisha is not as smooth as it seems and does mark a change in prophetic activity,[15] others opt for a redaction-critical explanation and find in verse 25 one or two later additions.[16] But there is no need to ascribe verse 25 to a later hand. Rather, 2 Kgs 2:25 as well as the itinerary in 2 Kgs 2 functions as a compositional device within the Elisha cycle (see below).

A special problem is the use of ירד in 2 Kgs 2:2 for the way from Gilgal to Bethel. Since Bethel is situated at a considerably higher altitude than Gilgal in the Jordan valley, "going down" is hardly a fitting description for the four-thousand-foot climb. Many commentators try to solve the problem either by identifying "Gilgal" in 2 Kgs 2 with a site different from the place in the Jordan Valley or by assuming a wider meaning of ירד. The former was already proposed by Otto Thenius, who identified "Gilgal" in 2 Kgs 2 with a site called *Jiljîlia* situated in Ephraim.[17] The latter was suggested by G. R. Driver, who understood ירד also as

---

the heading "betrays too much"; he therefore sees it as a post-Deuteronomistic addition ("Der Ehrenname Elisas," 139). He is followed, for example, by Würthwein, *Die Bücher der Könige*, 274; Schmitt, *Elisa*, 102; and Sauerwein, *Elischa*, 17. In light of the focus on Elisha and the narrative function of verse 1a, however, it is best described as a prolepsis; on this literary technique, see Jean Louis Ska, "Sommaires proleptiques en Gn 27 et dans l'histoire de Joseph," *Bib* 73 (1992): 518–27.

[13] A. Graeme Auld, *I and II Kings*, Daily Study Bible (Philadelphia: Westminster, 1986), 154.

[14] See Hermann-Josef Stipp, *Elischa–Propheten–Gottesmänner: Die Kompositionsgeschichte des Elischazyklus und verwandter Texte, rekonstruiert auf der Basis von Text- und Literarkritik zu 1 Kön 20.22 und 2 Kön 2–7*, ATSAT 24 (St. Ottilien: EOS, 1987), 57, 264; and Joel S. Burnett, "'Going Down' to Bethel: Elijah and Elisha in the Theological Geography of the Deuteronomistic History," *JBL* 129 (2010): 281–97, here 288–90, https://doi.org/10.2307/27821019.

[15] Bergen, *Elisha and the End*, 67.

[16] See, e.g., Schmitt, *Elisa*, 76–77; Stipp, *Elischa–Propheten*, 57.

[17] Otto Thenius, *Die Bücher der Könige*, KEH (Leipzig: Hirzel, 1873), 270–71; Thenius is followed, e.g., by Gray, *I and II Kings*, 474; and Mordechai Cogan and Hayim Tadmor, *II Kings: A New Translation*, AB 11 (Garden City, NY: Doubleday, 1988), 31.

"going southwards."[18] Yet this does not solve the geographical problem of 2 Kgs 2, because in order to reach Bethel from Gilgal, one must travel in a northwestern direction. A more plausible solution has been offered by Joel S. Burnett, who notes that עלה לבית אל ("going up to Bethel") could suggest an intention to worship there, which, in light of the Deuteronomistic critique of the Bethel cult and later anti-Bethel polemic, could have been perceived as problematic.[19] It could well be that וירדו בית אל is the result of an early scribal correction attempting to correct a theologically objectionable expression.

It is also Elisha who talks to the local prophets; when alluding to Elijah's ascension, Elisha stress its consequences: "YHWH will take *your* master from *your* head today" (2:5). Furthermore, the story ends not with Elijah's ascension but with Elisha and his authority and leadership among the prophets.[20]

b. Second Kings 2 shares a characteristic feature of other Elisha stories: בני הנביאים, the "sons of the prophets." They are a group of people gathered around the man of God who are not professional prophets.[21] They obviously belong to a lower class of society, are threatened by creditors (2 Kgs 4:1–7), and are prone to suffer from hunger (4:42–44) or to be deeply disturbed by the loss of a borrowed axe head (6:1–7). In contrast, the Elijah stories never mention a comparable group of followers.

c. The most decisive evidence for the view that 2 Kgs 2:1–18 belongs to the Elisha stories lies in its compositional function. It not only introduces and characterizes the main protagonist but also sets the geographical stage for the following narratives. Elisha and Elijah visit Gilgal, Bethel, Jericho, and the Jordan; Elisha returns to Jericho. Besides the narrative function in characterizing Elisha, the itinerary of 2 Kgs 2 also marks the main locations of Elisha's activities in the following

---

[18] G. R. Driver, "On עלה 'went up country' and ירד 'went down country,'" *ZAW* 28 (1957): 74–77. Somewhat similarly, James A. Montgomery suggested "that the verb may have been used from the writer's geographical standpoint" (James A. Montgomery and Henry Snyder Gehman, *A Critical and Exegetical Commentary on the Books of Kings*, ICC [Edinburgh: T&T Clark, 1960], 353–54).

[19] Burnett, "'Going Down' to Bethel," 293–97; see 283–85 for Burnett's critical appraisal of different proposals. For anti-Bethel polemic, see, e.g., 1 Kgs 13 and Erhard Blum, "Die Lüge des Propheten: Ein Lesevorschlag zu einer befremdlichen Geschichte (1Kön 13)," in *Textgestalt und Komposition: Exegetische Beiträge zu Tora und Vordere Propheten*, ed. Wolfgang Oswald, FAT 69 (Tübingen: Mohr Siebeck, 2010), 319–38. The assumption, however, that an anti-Bethel polemic was already intended in 2 Kgs 2 (as Burnett suggests) seems questionable in light of the matter-of-fact way in which the Elisha stories describe his going up there (2:23), and considering the northern provenience and early date of the stories (see Otto, *Jehu, Elia, und Elisa*, 220–37, esp. 236, 237).

[20] Rofé, "Classification of the Prophetical Stories," 436.

[21] Schmitt offers an extensive discussion of the prophetic groups that appear in the Elisha stories, as well as their forms of organization and relation to the official cult (*Elisa*, 162–72).

stories: he goes to Bethel in 2:23, reaches Gilgal in 4:38, and returns to the Jordan in 6:2. In addition, five more places are explicitly named in the stories: Shunem (4:8), Mount Carmel (4:25), Dothan (6:13), Samaria (6:19–20), and Damascus (8:7, 9).[22] These places do not turn up in the itinerary of 2 Kgs 2:1–18, but two of them appear in 2:25.[23] The verse only names places Elisha had passed through and does not provide any further information; it has obviously no other purpose than to complete Elisha's itinerary.[24] According to verse 25, he moved from Bethel to Mount Carmel and back to Samaria. So, verse 25 explicitly names two of the sites that will appear later on, but at the same time it explains Elisha's passing through Shunem, which lay on one of the routes to the west, as well as his coming to Dothan, which was situated on the way from Mount Carmel via Shunem to Samaria.[25]

---

[22] Some episodes are implicitly localized: in 2 Kgs 2:19, העיר ("the city") refers back to Jericho; the widow of 4:1–7 seems to live in Samaria, because no change of place is indicated. Second Kings 3 and 5 give no specific details regarding Elisha's abode, while 6:32 assumes that he dwells in Samaria. Whether 3:4–27, chapter 5, and 6:24–7:20 belonged to an older collection of Elisha stories is doubtful. Otto pointed out the various parallels between 2 Kgs 3* and 1 Kgs 22 and between 2 Kgs 6–7* and 1 Kgs 20; she convincingly argued that these stories originated in earlier collections of war narratives and were only secondarily inserted into the Elisha cycle, which by then was already part of a Deuteronomistic History (*Jehu, Elia, und Elisa*, 211–18, 252). Second Kings 5 presents the Aramean Naaman as a non-Israelite YHWH worshiper and thus deals with a situation that was highly controversial in postexilic times; it is a later addition to the Elisha stories as well (see Volker Haarmann, *JHWH-Verehrer der Völker: Die Hinwendung von Nichtisraeliten zum Gott Israels in alttestamentlichen Überlieferungen*, ATANT 91 [Zurich: TVZ, 2008], 132–67).

[23] Damascus (2 Kgs 8:7–15) remains an exception. Here, Elisha acts on extraterritorial ground and also differently from his usual activities in the political sphere—not as the savior of Israel and a fighter against the Arameans but as a collaborator of the Aramean usurper Hazael, not as a miracle worker but rather as a diviner predicting the future. The episode is obviously connected to 1 Kgs 19:15–16. If Stipp (*Elischa*, 476–77) and Otto (*Jehu, Elia, und Elisa*, 233–34) are correct in assuming that the episode was not part of an early Elisha collection, this could explain why Damascus is lacking in the geographical picture of 2 Kgs 2.

[24] Schmitt correctly points out that 2:25 prepares Elisha's stays in Samaria and on Mount Carmel, but he sees the verse as the result of redactional work and not as a compositional feature (*Elisa*, 76–77). Accordingly, he has to assign verse 25a and b to different hands because the episodes, which are integrated through verse 25 (2 Kgs 3 and 2 Kgs 4:8–38), belong to different strata in his model of the literary history of the Elisha material. Stipp (*Elischa*, 443–45, 474), Otto (*Jehu, Elia, und Elisa*, 224), and Sauerwein (*Elischa*, 32) accept Schmitt's view despite their different redaction-historical models. They all share the assumption that Samaria in 2:25b exclusively refers to the events of 2 Kgs 3:4–27 and that this connection prompted the creation of the verse. Since 2 Kgs 3 is a later addition to the Elisha story, this would indeed call for an exclusion of 2:25b. If, however, 2:25 as a whole (and together with 2:1–6) outlines in a more general way the area of Elisha's activities, mentioning Samaria does not create any problem but fits with the places (Shunem, Dothan) he visits later on. Moreover, in 2 Kgs 6:19–20, Elisha is explicitly said to be in Samaria.

[25] For the Israelite road system, see David A. Dorsey, *The Roads and Highways of Ancient*

The itinerary clearly functions as a structural device connecting the different Elisha stories and integrating them into a greater composition.[26] This means that 2 Kgs 2, by naming these places, also fulfills a compositional task;[27] it is not an independent narrative but was composed as an opening piece for the greater literary context of a collection of Elisha stories.[28]

II. The Title "Chariot of Israel and Its Horses"

The title רכב ישראל ופרשיו evokes images of weaponry used predominantly in military operations or in big-game hunting.[29] The following discussion will focus on the title's literary representations and their dependencies more than on tradition-historical aspects.[30]

Israel, ASOR Library of Biblical and Near Eastern Archaeology (Baltimore: Johns Hopkins University Press, 1991), esp. 98–100 and 119–24 regarding Shunem and Dothan.

[26] The compositional function of the itinerary was stressed also by Otto, *Jehu, Elia, und Elisa*, 224, 235.

[27] The recognizable double function of the itinerary in 2 Kgs 2:1b–6 refutes the frequent attempts to exclude 2:2–6 from the episode and to regard these verses as a secondary addition (see, among many others, Würthwein, *Die Bücher der Könige*, 274; Schmitt, *Elisa*, 102–4 [both are discussed critically by Stipp, *Elischa*, 58–61]; Sauerwein, *Elischa*, 19). Formulaic language and repetitions, which, doubtlessly, characterize 2:2–6, are hardly sufficient indications of redactional activity (against Sauerwein, *Elischa*, 19).

[28] The literary history of the Elisha cycle cannot be dealt with here; for different proposals that have been put forward, see, e.g., Schmitt, *Elisa*; Stipp, *Elischa*; Otto, *Jehu, Elia, und Elisa*; and, recently, Sauerwein, *Elischa*. Despite their different views on the origin of the stories, the degree of redactional activity to be detected in them, and the ways the Elisha stories found their way into the book of Kings, these scholars agree that diverse Elisha materials were collected and integrated at a certain stage into an "Elisha biography" (Otto, *Jehu, Elia, und Elisa*, 220–39; Sauerwein, *Elischa*, 116–22) or, in analogy to the *vitae* known, for example, in Christian medieval hagiography, in an Elisha *vita* that not only contained accounts of his miraculous deeds but held in view "the *whole life* of the holy man; i.e., they have a *biographical drive*" (Rofé, "Classification of the Prophetical Stories," 436; emphasis in original).

[29] On the use and impact of chariots, see the recent study by Robin Archer, "Chariotry to Cavalry: Developments in the Early First Millennium," in *New Perspectives on Ancient Warfare*, ed. Garret G. Fagan and Matthew Trundle, History of Warfare 59 (Leiden: Brill, 2010), 57–79. As different translations show, it is not quite clear whether פרש refers primarily to the horses or to the driver. The semantics of the word allow both possibilities. The question was discussed thoroughly already by Galling, "Der Ehrenname Elisas," 131–35, who in this case argued convincingly for an understanding as "horses." In addition to the reasons Galling provided, we can add that the imagery of the title is used in 2 Kgs 2 and 6 (see below) and that both texts mention fiery horses (2:11, 6:17). Here, פרש was obviously understood as referring to horses, not drivers.

[30] Textual-historical aspects can only be mentioned. Variants in the ancient versions were recently discussed by Matthieu Richelle, "Élie et Élisée, auriges en Israël: Une métaphore militaire oubliée en 2 R 2,12 et 13,14," *RB* 117 (2010): 321–36. Richelle points to the Vetus Latina and argues

The supposition that the title evokes primarily military connotations does require some justification, because the iconographic feature of a heavenly chariot is certainly not limited to the Elijah and Elisha stories. The chariot is a common attribute of several ancient Near Eastern manifestations of the storm god.[31] The root רכב is even directly applied to Baal in the divine epithet *rkb. ʿrpt*, "Rider of Clouds,"[32] which has its biblical echoes in the picture of YHWH riding a storm chariot (e.g., Pss 18:11, 77:19).[33]

There are strong indications, however, that the application of the title to Elisha and Elijah does not build on the storm-god imagery. The chariot of the storm god is usually made of clouds (not fire) and is drawn by bulls or dragons.[34] It is a symbol of cosmic power or accompanies the theophany of its rider and, as such, is exclusively associated with gods and not human actors.[35] The biblical imagery differs. In the title רכב ישראל ופרשיו, Elisha and Elijah are addressed as the chariot, not as its riders.[36] Thus, their power is likened to the effects of the vehicle, which is easily connected to the devastating effect of war chariots in battle.

The "rider"—which here probably implies the beneficiary of the chariot's power—is Israel. In this regard, the title differs fundamentally from Hab 3, probably the most blatant adaptation of the chariot and storm god imagery in the Hebrew Bible. There the rider is YHWH, who steers the chariot into a cosmic battle (v. 8).

---

that רכב in 2 Kgs 2:12 as well as 13:13 originally referred to the military title *auriga* ("charioteer") and not to a chariot. While it might be correct that the Vetus Latina reflects such an interpretation of the title, as in the case of the horses (see preceding note), the narrative context (2:11, 6:17) betrays an understanding of רכב as "chariot" or "chariotry."

[31] This was already pointed out by Galling, "Der Ehrenname Elisas," 144–45.

[32] See *KTU* 1.2 IV:8, 29; 1.4 III:11, 18, V:60 and many more from the Ras Shamra texts.

[33] Mark S. Smith, *The Early History of God: Yahweh and the Other Deities in Ancient Israel*, 2nd ed (Grand Rapids: Eerdmans, 2002), 81–82; Alberto R. W. Green, *The Storm-God in the Ancient Near East*, BJSUCSD 8 (Winona Lake, IN: Eisenbrauns, 2003), 258–80.

[34] For the iconography of the storm god, see the classic study by A. Vanel, *L'iconographie du dieu de l'orage dans le Proche-orient ancien jusqu'au VIIᵉ siècle avant J.-C.*, CahRB 3 (Paris: Gabalda, 1965), or the material collected by Green, *Storm-God*.

[35] Another heavenly chariot is that of the sun god, which is known from Neo-Babylonian (and Greek) mythology. The cultic veneration of Bunene, the chariot driver of Shamash is attested in the inscriptions of Nabonidus (see Hanspeter Schaudig, *Die Inschriften Nabonids von Babylon und Kyros' des Großen samt den in ihrem Umfeld entstandenen Tendenzschriften: Textausgabe und Grammatik*, AOAT 256 [Münster: Ugarit-Verlag, 2001], 2.4 I 30.31 [p. 359]; 2.4 II [p. 359]; 2.9 II [p. 387]; 2.11 III 51 [p. 406]). Second Kgs 23:11 also mentions cultic installations known as מרכבות השמש ("chariots of the sun") in Jerusalem. Recourse to these mythic concepts in order to explain the title "chariot of Israel" faces the same obstacles as the case of the storm god.

[36] In 2 Kgs 2, Elijah eventually rides the chariot. He is not depicted as actually driving it, however, but rather as being transported in it. In 2 Kgs 13, he is addressed with the title chariot and horses.

Finally and decisively, as will be shown below, the Elisha texts using the title or its imagery strongly suggest a military connotation.

Second Kings 13:14

Second Kings 13:13–19 recounts the last deed of Elisha during his lifetime. The Elisha cycle will end in 13:20–21 with a story about the miraculous power of his dead bones. In 13:13–19, Elisha is about to die and is visited by King Joash. The king does not utter any specific plea or question; he only cries and addresses Elisha respectfully as אבי, "my father," and uses the title רכב ישראל ופרשיו. Elisha instructs Joash to perform two symbolic acts: shooting arrows toward the east and striking the ground with arrows. Both actions symbolize victory over the Arameans.

The short episode presents Elisha as a capable helper in a time of military threat. This also explains the king's despair over Elisha's imminent death. Second Kings 13:13–19 belongs to a group of Elisha stories that portray him in close contact with the Israelite king and present him as a savior who prevents a seemingly inevitable military defeat. Other examples are 2 Kgs 6:8–23 or the revealing remark in 2 Kgs 4:13, where Elisha offers the hospitable woman in Shunem his advocacy before the king or the captain of the host. The title רכב ישראל ופרשיו functions as a condensed appraisal of Elisha's role and power;[37] consequently, no detailed elaboration is needed. When he is addressed with this title, Elisha knows that help is needed, and he knows which kind. He reacts accordingly.

The manner in which 2 Kgs 13:13–19 is narrated clearly shows that the title "chariot of Israel" and its applicability to Elisha are known not only to the main characters in the story but also to the intended readers. The title's military profile and its connection to the miraculous powers of Elisha do not need any further explanation. The mere mention of the title suffices to justify the interaction between the king and the man of God and to make it plausible for the audience.

Second Kings 6:15–17

Second Kings 6:8–23 does not use the title "chariot of Israel," but verses 15–17 are strongly connected to its imagery. The story describes a military threat of the Arameans, who repeatedly try to ambush the Israelites but are tricked by Elisha. The story plays on the superior knowledge of Elisha in contrast to the blindness of the Arameans, who are ridiculed to the point that when they actually come to fight, they are given a feast in Samaria and sent home.

Within the story, verses 15–17 form a somewhat curious episode: Elisha's

---

[37] See Würthwein, *Die Bücher der Könige*, 365: "Der Ehrenname … macht evident, daß es eine Tradition über Elischa gab, die ihn als Helfer in den Aramäerkriegen feierte und ihn in seinen paranormalen Fähigkeiten dem Wert einer Streitmacht gleichstellte." See also Galling, "Der Ehrenname Elisas," 135–42, 146–48; Schmitt, *Elisa*, 176.

servant sees the man of God surrounded by horses and chariots of fire outnumbering the Aramean troops. This episode, however, has no bearing on the overall story. Neither the chariots nor their strength is needed for the resolution of the conflict; they are not even seen by any other protagonist. Moreover, the servant simply disappears from the stage. This episode does not seem to have any narrative function, and most commentators view the verses as a later addition to the story.[38] They see the purpose of the episode as attempting to strengthen Elisha's connection to the title רכב ישראל ופרשיו by developing a picture that draws upon its imagery.[39]

Second Kings 2:11

Second Kings 2 is the only text that contains the title as well as the image of a fiery chariot and fiery horses. Both are applied to Elijah. While the title, with its military connotations, fits well with Elisha's activities, this not the case with Elijah. The stories about Elijah in 1 Kgs 17–19, 21 and 2 Kgs 1 present him as an unrelenting fighter for YHWH and against the worship of other gods, while the Israelite king Ahab and his wife are the main antagonists. These stories do not feature any military campaign, and Elijah never helps to defeat Israel's enemies or appears as a supporter of the Israelite king—quite the contrary.[40] It has long been noted, therefore, that the title רכב ישראל ופרשיו is more appropriately applied to Elisha than to

---

[38] Commentators disagree, however, regarding the extent of the addition. Stipp proposes verses 15–17 (*Elischa*, 332–35); Galling includes verse 14 and parts of verse 18 in addition to verses 15–17 ("Der Ehrenname Elisas," 136–37); Schmitt (*Elisa*, 91–93), Würthwein (*Die Bücher der Könige*, 305), Volkmar Fritz (*Das zweite Buch der Könige*, ZBK.AT [Zurich: TVZ, 1998], 34), Harald Schweizer (*Elischa in den Kriegen: Literaturwissenschaftliche Untersuchung von 2 Kön 3; 6,8–23; 6,24–7,20*, SANT 37 [Munich: Kösel, 1974], 215–19, 261–65), and Sauerwein (*Elischa*, 68–69) also add verse 20 (or parts thereof). The allocation of verses 18*, 20* to the addition is usually based on the assumption of a secondary theologization of the story indicated, for example, by Elisha's prayer in verse 18. The argument was initially presented by Schmitt, who identified a redactional layer, the "Jahwebearbeitung," which introduced theological motifs into the miracle stories about Elisha because these originally displayed little interest in theological matters (e.g., *Elisa*, 93, 126–27). The problem with this argument is that it easily runs the risk of circular reasoning if—as in the case of 2 Kgs 6:18, 20 (see the critical evaluation of Galling and Schmitt in Stipp, *Elischa*, 332–35)—reliable literary indications are lacking.

[39] See Gray, *I and II Kings*, 516. Interestingly, 2 Kgs 6:17 also mentions the element of fire, which connects this picture with 2 Kgs 2. It is not necessary to assume with Galling ("Der Ehrenname Elisas," 137) that a "mythischer Untergrund des Ehrennamens Elisas" comes into play here; rather, it seems that the author of 6:15–17 knew 2:11 and intended to offer a further parallel between Elisha and Elijah. Second Kgs 6* might have suggested itself as a fitting place for the use of the title for Elisha not only because the situation involved a military threat but also because, as in 2 Kgs 13:14, Elisha is addressed as אבי by an Israelite king (a fact noted also by Sweeney, *I and II Kings*, 274; and Sauerwein, *Elischa*, 97).

[40] Even if one assumes some traces of storm-god chariot imagery in the title, it would be hard to explain why Elijah of all people should have carried such an epithet, given his highly

Elijah.⁴¹ The lack of fit in the case of Elijah renders it highly improbable that the title was ascribed independently to both figures.

As I proposed at the beginning of the article, 2 Kgs 2:1–18 is a compositional text written as an introductory piece for the Elisha stories—probably before their insertion into the DtrH.⁴² It was composed in light of older Elisha stories, and it helped to transform them into a comprehensive Elisha cycle by foreshadowing Elisha's itinerary and by presenting Elisha as the legitimate successor of Elijah. The title "chariot of Israel and its horses" has strong links to Elisha's activities but does not show a similar connection to Elijah's; it is likely, therefore, that the title was taken from the Elisha tradition and transferred to Elijah in order to create another link between the two characters. The scene depicted in 2 Kgs 2 makes possible the application of the title's imagery to Elijah.⁴³

The stage is set at the beginning of the story when the "sons of the prophets" somewhat enigmatically announce that Elijah "will be taken away from your [Elisha's] head" (היום יהוה לקח את אדניך מעל ראשך) in verses 3 and 5.⁴⁴ The narrative is further developed in verse 11, where the fiery horses and the chariot take Elijah from Elisha and carry him away in a whirlwind (סערה). In this way, the pictorial components of the title are connected with Elijah, offering a vivid description of his ascension. The metaphoric meaning of the title, however, remains a loose end: riding up in a chariot of fire does not really make Elijah a "chariot" like Elisha, that is, an equally powerful protector and savior of Israel. Nevertheless, the story achieves its end in presenting the title רכב ישראל ופרשיו as yet another element (besides the mantle, the miracle, and so on) of continuity between Elisha and his predecessor Elijah.

---

critical attitude toward the worship of Baal (e.g., 1 Kgs 18:19–40) as well as the polemic against applying storm-god characteritics to YHWH (1 Kgs 19:11).

⁴¹ This view was held already by Gunkel, *Geschichten von Elisa*; see also Rehm, *Das zweite Buch der Könige*, 33, 133; Gray, *I and II Kings*, 472; Würthwein, *Die Bücher der Könige*, 275; Schmitt, *Elisa*, 103; Otto, *Jehu, Elia, und Elisa*, 222. Sauerwein shares this opinion but sees the connection only at a later redactional level in 2 Kgs 2 (*Elischa*, 18). For Fritz, the title originates with Elijah, but he does not offer any explanation (*Das zweite Buch der Könige*, 73).

⁴² On the inclusion of the Elisha (and Elijah) stories in the DtrH, see the discussion in Otto, *Jehu, Elia, und Elisa*, 259–63; Hermann-Josef Stipp, "Ahabs Buße und die Komposition des deuteronomistischen Geschichtswerks," *Bib* 76 (1995): 471–97; and Erhard Blum, "Die Nabotüberlieferung und die Kompositionsgeschichte der Vorderen Propheten," in Oswald, *Textgestalt und Komposition*, 356–74.

⁴³ Gray alluded to this possibility (*I and II Kings*, 476). When the title's origin is attributed to the Elijah tradition, it is usually understood as deriving from the way the ascension is described. For example, Walter Brueggemann argues that the "phrasing [of the title] is triggered by the vision of v. 11" (*1 and 2 Kings*, SHBC [Macon, GA: Smyth & Helwys, 2000], 297; cf. Fritz, *Das zweite Buch der Könige*, 13). Yet, since its origins are connected to the Elisha tradition, as shown above, this solution becomes problematic.

⁴⁴ Cf. Long, *2 Kings*, 26.

III. The Literary and Tradition History of Elisha and Elijah

In the canonical version of the book of Kings, Elijah is presented as Elisha's master and predecessor, not only in terms of chronology but also in terms of their activities and theological impact. As Hermann-Josef Stipp and Erhard Blum have shown, however, there are features in the Elijah stories that are best explained as building on and using older Elisha narratives as a template. The most striking example is the case of 1 Kgs 17 and 2 Kgs 4, where the Elijah story of the widow in Zarephath and her son is developed out of the two stories in 2 Kgs 4, the miracle of the oil and the rich woman in Shunem. In 1 Kgs 17, one can still see the friction caused by the combination of these two stories, for example, the fact that the poor widow in 1 Kgs 17, who is close to starving, suddenly owns a house that even features a second floor (עליה) where the resurrection of the child takes place just as in 2 Kgs 4.[45] With regard to their literary shape, therefore, the Elisha stories could be older than the Elijah stories.[46] On the other hand, the Elisha stories betray a familiarity with and a veneration of the man of God Elijah, whom they present as Elisha's master. The Elijah narratives also presuppose this knowledge in their intended readers; otherwise a story like 2 Kgs 2:1–18 would lose its point. In the case at hand, the history of tradition and the history of Hebrew Bible literature show an almost chiastic relationship.

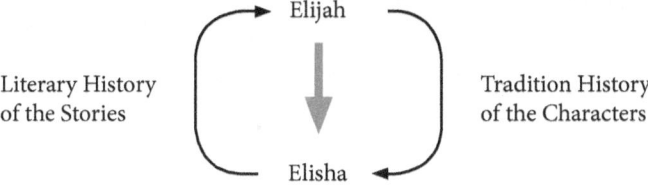

Literary History
of the Stories

Elijah

Elisha

Tradition History
of the Characters

---

[45] Stipp, *Elischa*, 451–57; Erhard Blum, "Der Prophet und das Verderben Israels: Eine ganzheitliche historisch-kritische Lektüre von 1 Regum XVII–XIX," *VT* 47 (1997): 277–92, here 280.

[46] For 1 Kgs 21 a relatively late date was proposed already by Alexander Rofé, "The Vineyard of Naboth: The Origin and Message of the Story," *VT* 38 (1998): 89–104. First Kings 17 is not to be divided from chapters 18–19*, for which it functions as an exposition. Moreover, there is an important narrative thread that links 17:7–24 to the following chapters: the widow in Zarephath (located in the vicinity of Sidon) functions as a positive counterpart to the Sidonian princess Jezebel not only in her support for Elijah but also in her faith in him and even in the acknowledgment that the fate of her son must have been prompted by some sin against YHWH (v. 18).

Blum, pointing to the theological issues in the Elijah stories (reflection on the tasks and impact of the prophets vis-à-vis YHWH's judgment and the catastrophe of Israel) argues for a postexilic date of 1 Kgs 17–19 ("Der Prophet und das Verderben Israels," 277–92).

he case of the title "chariot of Israel and its horses," which—as I argue here—originated in the Elisha tradition and was secondarily applied to Elijah, is an early example of this phenomenon.

By applying Elisha's title רכב ישראל ופרשיו to Elijah and constructing a scenic realization of its imagery in 2 Kgs 2, the composers of the Elisha cycle created an extremely powerful motif. Ironically, a story originally aimed at stressing the importance of Elisha succeeded even more in enhancing the reputation of Elijah. The motif of Elijah's ascension to heaven shaped the later perception and reception of Elijah up to the New Testament and beyond.

The Authorship of Ezra and Nehemiah in Light of Differences in Their Ideological Background

NISSIM AMZALLAG
nissamz@post.bgu.ac.il
The Ben-Gurion University in the Negev, Beer Sheba 84105, Israel

The books of Ezra and Nehemiah differ in their definition of the repatriates from Babylon, the boundaries of the in-group, the appellations of God, the celebration of the Sukkot festival, the status of the priests, the prestige bestowed on Ezra, and the attitude toward the foreign Yahwistic singers (Ezrahites) who took part in musical worship at the Jerusalem temple. The intersection of all these differences reveals the contrasting ideological backgrounds of these two books. In Ezra, the returnees from Babylon and their religious elite (priests, Levites, and prophets) constitute the nucleus preserved by YHWH from destruction from which Israel as a whole is expected to regenerate. Both this view of the repatriates as the sole legitimate remnant and its ideological consequences are challenged in Nehemiah. These differences are perceptible not only when the first-person narrative sections in Ezra and Nehemiah are compared (the so-called Ezra and Nehemiah memoirs) but also in the third-person narration segments. These positions are consistent throughout Ezra and Nehemiah, leading to the conclusion that the two books were composed and/or edited by two distinct authors who expressed contrasting views on the theological importance of the Babylonian exile.

A lengthy tradition, promoted by the Septuagint, the Masoretes, the Talmud (b. B. Bat. 15a), and many medieval commentators, pairs the books of Ezra and Nehemiah.[1] The opposing view, however, has also long been defended. Origen

The anonymous reviewers are gratefully thanked for their useful advices, comments, and observations, which substantially contributed to the maturation of the thesis and arguments presented in this work.

Biblical quotations are from the ESV with some minor modifications.

[1] In the MT, the notes normally expected at the end of Ezra (indicating the number of verses, the midpoint of the volume, and so on) appear toward the end of Nehemiah. The pairing of the books is reflected in the continuity of ancient exegesis between the end of Ezra and the beginning of Nehemiah. See Loring W. Batten, *A Critical and Exegetical Commentary on the Books of Ezra*

(185–254 CE) considered Ezra and Nehemiah two separate entities; the editors of the Vulgate concurred. Some ancient Jewish exegetes also expressed doubts about the common authorship of Ezra and Nehemiah, as reflected in the separation of the two books in the earliest printed editions of the Masoretic Bible.[2] This timeworn question has not been fully resolved. Today, most scholars assume that the books of Ezra and Nehemiah, in their final form, should be treated as a single literary entity.[3] Some, however, still subscribe to the opposite premise.[4]

The question is not easy to resolve. For example, the repetition of the list of returnees in Ezra 2 and in Neh 7:6–72 is both treated as confirmation of the literary unity of these two books and employed by those who advocate for independent authorship on the grounds that a single author would not have inserted the same list twice.[5] Similarly, the abrupt end of Ezra 10 supports the assumption that the narration should continue with Neh 1, whereas the fact that Neh 1:1 reads like the beginning of a stand-alone opus is evoked in defense of the hypothesis of separate authorship. Further, the explicit mention of Ezra the priest in the book of Nehemiah (8:1–13; 12:1, 13, 26, 33, 36) promotes the idea of the literary unity of

---

and Nehemiah, ICC (Edinburgh: T&T Clark, 1913), 1; Hugh G. M. Williamson, *Ezra, Nehemiah*, WBC 16 (Waco, TX: Word, 1985), xxi; Kyung-Jin Min, *The Levitical Authorship of Ezra-Nehemiah*, JSOTSup 409 (London: T&T Clark, 2004), 22; Elelwani B. Farisani, "The Composition and Date of Ezra-Nehemiah," *OTE* 17 (2004): 208–30, esp. 216.

[2] Daniel Bomberg edition, 1525. See F. Charles Fensham, *The Books of Ezra and Nehemiah*, NICOT (Grand Rapids: Eerdmans, 1982), 1; Williamson, *Ezra, Nehemiah*, xxii. According to Christian D. Ginsburg, Ezra and Nehemiah were first separated in the Venice Rabbinic Bible of 1517 (*Introduction to the Massoretico-Critical Edition of the Hebrew Bible* [London, 1897], 933–34, quoted by Eran Viezel, "Ezra katav sifro veyahas shel divrey ha-yamim … On the author of Chronicles in Bava Batra 15a," *JSQ* 16 [2009]: 243–54, esp. 244).

[3] Among the many scholars who defend this opinion, we may cite Tamara Cohn Eskenazi, *In an Age of Prose: A Literary Approach to Ezra-Nehemiah*, SBLMS 36 (Atlanta: Scholars Press, 1988), 11–14; Williamson, *Ezra, Nehemia*, xxxiii–xxxv; Judson R. Shaver: "Ezra and Nehemiah: On the Theological Significance of Making Them Contemporaries," in *Priests, Prophets, and Scribes: Essays on the Formation and Heritage of Second Temple Judaism in Honour of Joseph Blenkinsopp*, ed. Eugene Ulrich et al., JSOTSup 149 (Sheffield: JSOT Press, 1992), 76–86, esp. 85; Lester L. Grabbe, *Ezra-Nehemiah*, OTR (London: Routledge, 1998), 94–105. For a review of modern scholars who defend this opinion, see Min, *Levitical Authorship*, 22–30.

[4] See David Kraemer, "On the Relationships between the Books of Ezra and Nehemiah," *JSOT* 59 (1993): 73–92, esp. 75–76; James C. VanderKam, "Ezra-Nehemiah or Ezra and Nehemiah?," in Ulrich et al., *Priests, Prophets, and Scribes*, 55–75, esp. 64–66; Edwin M. Yamauchi, "Ezra and Nehemiah," in *The Expositor's Bible Commentary*, ed. Tremper Longman III and David E. Garland, rev. ed. (Grand Rapids: Zondervan, 2010), 4:337–568, here 368; Andrew E. Steinmann, *Ezra and Nehemiah*, ConcC (St. Louis: Concordia, 2010), 12–21; Bob Becking, *Ezra, Nehemiah, and the Construction of Early Jewish Identity*, FAT 80 (Tübingen: Mohr Siebeck, 2011), 5–6, 27.

[5] For example, Eskenazi assumes that "the repeated list of returnees, Ezra 2 and Neh 7,6–72, literally frames this section. This major repetition represents the major character, provides continuity for the section as a whole, and unifies the events in between" (*Age of Prose*, 39).

the two books, but the evidence that two distinct *I*-voices exist—Ezra's in Ezra and Nehemiah's in Nehemiah—suggests that each is independent of the other. Finally, similar themes imply the unity of the two books, but the importance of social reforms in Nehemiah (5:14–19), a topic overlooked in Ezra, invites their treatment as distinct literary entities.[6] Some of these problems are resolved by scholars who identify the section evoking the period of Zerubbabel–Jeshua (Ezra 1–6) as a first opus and the story of Ezra and Nehemiah (Ezra 7–Nehemiah 13) as a second one.[7] Other issues, however, remain unsolved.

The question of the authorship of Ezra and Nehemiah is complicated by the possibility that the two works were originally separated and later unified in content and/or style by an editor. The coexistence in both of a first-person voice alongside a third-person narration may reflect the integration by the narrator of true autobiographical fragments (the Ezra and Nehemiah memoirs, or even a collection of biographical sources[8]) into a third-person narration.[9] In this case, authorship encompasses editing the biographical fragments and composing a narration that

---

[6] Min revived the controversy concerning the authorship of Ezra and Nehemiah as follows: "In conclusion, while it is true that the introductory words in Neh 1,1 probably indicate an editorial perception of a different original author for the subsequent source material, there is insufficient evidence to suppose that this reflects either genuinely different authorship or a quite separate composition" (*Levitical Authorship*, 26). VanderKam, however, acknowledges, "It is evident that the linguistic data alone are insufficient for demonstrating whether the same or different authors penned these works" ("Ezra-Nehemiah," 58).

[7] See, e.g., Williamson, *Ezra, Nehemiah*, xxv; Michael W. Duggan, *The Covenant Renewal in Ezra-Nehemiah (Neh 7:72b–10:40): An Exegetical, Literary, and Theological Study*, SBLDS 164 (Atlanta: Society of Biblical Literature, 2001), 80–83, 166; Lisbeth S. Fried, "The ʿAm haʾareṣ in Ezra 4:4 and Persian Imperial Administration," in *Judah and the Judeans in the Persian Period*, ed. Oded Lipschits and Manfred Oeming (Winona Lake, IN: Eisenbrauns, 2006), 123–45, esp. 78–79.

[8] See Williamson, *Ezra, Nehemiah*, xxiv–xxviii. Similarly, Titus Reinmuth identifies in the Nehemiah Memoir a narrative relative to the city wall construction (*Mauerbau-Erzählung*, in Neh 1:1–4:17, 6:1–7:5, 12:27–43) and memorial composition (*Nehemia-Denkschrift*, in Neh 5:1–19, 13:4–31) (*Der Bericht Nehemias: Zur literarischen Eigenart, traditionsgeschichtlichen Prägung und innerbiblischen Rezeption des Ich-Berichts Nehemias*, OBO 183 [Freiburg: Universitätsverlag; Göttingen: Vandenhoeck & Ruprecht, 2002]).

[9] For references and argumentation about the existence of these "memoirs," especially that of Nehemiah, as reflected in the personal accounts in Neh 1:1–2:30, 4:1–7:5, 12:31–43, and 13:6–31, see Mark J. Boda, "Redaction in the Book of Nehemiah: A Fresh Proposal," in *Unity and Disunity in Ezra-Nehemiah Redaction, Rhetoric, and Reader*, ed. Mark J. Boda and Paul L. Redditt, HBM 17 (Sheffield: Sheffield Phoenix, 2008), 25–54, esp. 25. The purported Ezra memoirs are found in Ezra 7–10. According to Christiane Karrer, the memoirs comprise Ezra 7:6a–c, 7:28b–d, 8:15–34, 9:1–10:44, and Neh 8:1–18 (*Ringen um die Verfassung Judas: Eine Studie zu den theologisch-politischen Vorstellungen im Esra-Nehemia Buch*, BZAW 308 [Berlin: de Gruyter, 2001], 240). According to Grabbe, Ezra and Nehemiah encompass three distinct sources, the Jeshua-Zerubbabel tradition, the Ezra tradition, and the Nehemiah tradition, which were gathered and integrated in a whole literary entity by an editor (*Ezra-Nehemiah*, 102, 187).

embodies them.[10] A final author may have adapted the literary style, language, and themes of the narrative (the third-person voice) to the singularities of the biographical (first-person) segments if they predated the third-person material. The ideological background of the author—the person who selected the relevant events, guided their interpretation, and organized them into a coherent narrative—is nevertheless expected to remain constant throughout the whole opus. Accordingly, if the books of Ezra and Nehemiah (or at least their third-person narration) are the work of a single author, one would expect to find a similar approach both toward the community, its identity, and its theology and toward foreigners. The question, then, is whether singularities in the text of Ezra and Nehemiah are able to reflect substantial discrepancies in their authors' ideological backgrounds.

I. The In-Group and Its Appellations in Ezra and Nehemiah

The Concept of "Remnants"

The term פליטה ("remnant") occurs four times in Ezra, all in Ezra 9 (vv. 8, 13–15). In this chapter, Ezra explicitly addresses the community of repatriates (v. 4) and explains that they are the remnant preserved by YHWH "to give us a secure hold within his holy place" (v. 8) and to reconstruct the temple and the city of Jerusalem (v. 9). This exclusiveness of the status of remnant, reserved for those who had been exiled to Babylon, explains why the reconstruction of the temple in Ezra is to be performed solely by the returnees from this exile (4:3). It also clarifies the background of the prohibition of intermarriage with nonrepatriate women (Ezra 9–10).[11]

The term פליטה is also found once in the book of Nehemiah: "that Hanani, one of my brothers, came with certain men from Judah. And I asked them concerning the Judeans, the remnant [הפליטה] who remained from the exile [אשר נשארו מן השבי], and concerning Jerusalem" (1:2). The expression אשר נשארו מן השבי is generally translated as denoting the "people who had survived the exile," a feature

---

[10] Many scenarios of composition of this narrative layer have been proposed. Farisani writes: "We conclude that the composition of the text of Ezra-Nehemiah took place in two stages. The first stage was the writing, in 440 BC and 432 BC, of the Ezra and Nehemiah memoirs respectively. The second stage was the compilation of the memoirs, with addition of several sources by the final author" ("Composition and Date," 228). This explanation may account for why Ezra treats the Torah mainly as a code of sacrificial practices whereas Nehemiah approaches it as a book used for teaching the people through public readings. The same reasoning may explain the social dimension specifically expressed in Nehemiah.

[11] Ezra considers such intermarriage a sin that rekindles divine anger against the initially preserved remnant (= the sons of exile): "Would you not be angry with us until you consumed us, so that there should be no remnant, nor any to escape?" (Ezra 9:14b).

that extends the definition of פליטה in Ezra 9 to Nehemiah.¹² This expression, however, may also refer to those *others* than the exiled who survived.¹³ Hanani's answer confirms this interpretation: "And they said to me: the survivors [הנשארים] who had survived the exile [נשארו מן השבי] there in the province [שם במדינה] are in great trouble and shame. The wall of Jerusalem is broken down, and its gates are destroyed by fire" (Neh 1:3). This verse specifically refers to those who had survived the exile *in Judea* (שם במדינה).¹⁴ Consequently, the term פליטה may reflect contrasting realities in Ezra (those who had been exiled to Babylon) and in Nehemiah (those who survived in Judea after the fall of the Judean kingdom).

Sons of Exile

The appellation "sons of exile" (בני הגולה) is extensively used in Ezra to denote the community that coalesces around Jerusalem and its temple (4:1; 6:16, 19–20; 8:35; 10:7, 16). In this book, the exile is not viewed as a stigma, a sign of divine rejection and punishment. Rather, the status of a chosen remnant, preserved by YHWH for reconstruction of the temple, the city, and even the people of Israel as a whole, transforms this community into the exclusive heir of the ancient Israelite tradition. The prestige of such a status is emphasized in the book of Ezra by the evidence that everyone who disobeys the instructions of Ezra and the leaders is threatened with exclusion from the community of the "sons of exile" (Ezra 10:7–8),¹⁵ meaning that "sons of exile" is a desired status. This appellation is used to separate the repatriates from all the local populations, who are commonly designated as "peoples of the land" (עמי הארץ).¹⁶

---

[12] See, e.g., Dalit Rom-Shiloni, *Exclusive Inclusivity: Identity Conflicts between the Exiles and the People Who Remained (6th–5th Centuries BCE)*, LHBOTS 543 (New York: Bloomsbury T&T Clark, 2013), 36.

[13] It has been suggested that, in Neh 1:2, פליטה alludes obliquely to the remnants living in Judea irrespective of their exilic or indigenous origin. See Karrer, *Das Ringen um die Verfassung Judas*, 151–53; Rainer Albertz, "Purity Strategies and Political Interests in the Policy of Nehemiah," in *Confronting the Past: Archaeological and Historical Essays on Ancient Israel in Honor of William G. Dever*, ed. Seymour Gitin, J. Edward Wright, and J. P. Dessel (Winona Lake, IN: Eisenbrauns, 2006), 199–206, esp. 202. Even in this case, however, a difference is observed relative to the book of Ezra, in which the remnant community is strictly limited to the repatriates.

[14] This interpretation of פליטה in Neh 1:2 as designating the remnants of the Judean population not taken into captivity is defended by Wilhelm Rudolph, *Esra und Nehemia samt 3. Esra*, HAT 20 (Tübingen: Mohr Siebeck, 1949), 104–5; Joseph Blenkinsopp, *Ezra-Nehemiah: A Commentary*, OTL (London: SCM, 1989), 207; Williamson, *Ezra, Nehemiah*, 169–70.

[15] Ezra 10:7–8: "And a proclamation was made throughout Judah and Jerusalem to all the returned exiles [בני הגולה] that they should assemble at Jerusalem. And that if anyone did not come within three days, by order of the officials and the elders all his property should be forfeited, and he himself banned from the congregation of the exiles [מקהל הגולה]" (Ezra 10:7–8).

[16] See Antonius H. J. Gunneweg, "עם הארץ—A Semantic Revolution," *ZAW* 95 (1983): 437–40; Jonathan E. Dyck, "The Ideology of Identity in Chronicles," in *Ethnicity and the Bible*, ed.

The definition of the community as "sons of exile" is absent from Nehemiah. Even the term גולה alone, repeatedly invoked in Ezra (6:16, 21; 9:4; 10:6, 8), is only exceptionally encountered in Nehemiah (see table 1).[17] Rather, the extensive use of "people" (עם) in Nehemiah in comparison with Ezra (table 1) indicates that this term becomes a substitute for "sons of exile" in designating the community.[18]

TABLE 1. Comparison of the Appellations of Community in Ezra and Nehemiah

	גולה		Israel		People (עם)		
	Total occurrences	Community[19]	Total occurrences	Community[20]	Total occurrences	Community	Foreigners[21]
Ezra	12	7	32	21	23	11	7
Nehemiah	1	0	22	21	53	43	9

יהודים

The appellation יהודי is absent from Ezra, whereas it occurs ten times in Nehemiah.[22] This difference is especially interesting in view of the use of this term in Kings and Jeremiah as a general designation of the inhabitants of the Judean kingdom.[23] The same meaning is observed in Nehemiah, where יהודים evokes both the Judeans who remained in the land after the others were exiled (Neh 1:2; 4:6;

Mark G. Brett, BibInt 19 (Leiden: Brill, 1996), 89–116, esp. 100; Peter R. Bedford, "Diaspora: Homeland Relations in Ezra-Nehemiah," *VT* 52 (2002): 147–65, esp. 149, 152, 158; John Kessler, "Persia's Loyal Yahwists: Power Identity and Ethnicity in Achemenid Yehud," in Lipschits and Oeming, *Judah and the Judeans in the Persian Period*, 91–121, esp. 108. Concerning the recent controversy about the meaning of this expression, see John Tracy Thames Jr., "A New Discussion of the Meaning of the Phrase ʿam hāʾāreṣ in the Hebrew Bible," *JBL* 130 (2011): 109–25, https://doi.org/10.2307/41304190.

[17] The only exception is Neh 7:6, where the land of Babylon whence the returnees are coming back is called "the captivity of exile" (משבי הגולה). According to Juha Pakkala, however, the list is in its original form in Ezra 2 and thereafter was recopied in Neh 7:6–72 (*Ezra the Scribe. The Development of Ezra 7–10 and Nehemiah 8*, BZAW 347 [Berlin: de Gruyter, 2004], 137–40).

[18] Bedford observes, "As an example, Ezra identifies 'foreigners'/'enemies' whose origins lie both outside (Ezr. iv) and inside (Ezr. ix) Judah, whereas in Neh. all 'foreigners'/'enemies' seemingly have origins outside the homeland (e.g., Neh ii 10, 19; iii 33–35; iv 1–2; xiii 1–9)" ("Diaspora," 149).

[19] Designated as בני הגולה or קהל הגולה.

[20] Designated as כל ישראל, עם ישראל, בני ישראל, זרע ישראל, or even simply ישראל.

[21] This designation includes the mention of עם in a foreign context together with the mention of עם הארץ or עמי ארצות.

[22] Neh 1:2; 2:16; 3:33–34; 4:6; 5:1, 8, 17; 6:6; 13:23.

[23] 2 Kgs 16:6; 25:25; Jer 32:12; 34:9; 38:19; 40:11–12; 41:3; 43:9; 44:1; 52:28, 30.

5:1, 8), the repatriates (Neh 3:33–34 mentions the יהודים who rebuilt the city wall), and both groups together (Neh 2:16, 5:17, 6:6, and 13:23).[24] Here again, the use of יהודים in Nehemiah introduces mixing between the repatriates and the indigenous population.

The three differences in terminology between Ezra and Nehemiah are interrelated. Defining the repatriates as the *only* remnant of Israel (Ezra) implies an appellation ("sons of exile") that distinguishes them from all other populations, including their brethren who "survived the exile in Judea." This means that the differences in terminology in Ezra and Nehemiah indicate changes in the definition of the in-group, restricted in Ezra to returnees from the Babylonian exile (and then avoiding the term יהודים) but including all Judeans in Nehemiah (thus avoiding the denomination "sons of exile"). This distinction confirms the difference in meaning of פליטה, the remnant, strictly restricted to the sons of exile in Ezra but designating the survivors of the fall of the kingdom in Nehemiah. It also explains why the existence of a nonexilic Judean population is scrupulously silenced in Ezra, which systematically describes the homeland as empty of Judeans, devastated, inhospitable, and inhabited by a foreign, hostile and/or impure population.[25]

II. Attitude toward Foreigners

One should expect the aforementioned differences in the definitions of the in-group to affect this group relationship with foreigners and its ability to integrate them.

Integrity of the In-Group in Ezra and Nehemiah

Intermarriage between alien women and sons of exile is vigorously condemned in Ezra 9–10. The appellation of the in-group not only as a remnant (פליטה, Ezra 9:8, 13–15) but even as "holy seed" (זרע הקדש, Ezra 9:2) emphasizes the nature of such sin: exogamy by members of the in-group counteracts the divine plan deduced from the allegory of the good and bad figs (Jer 24:5–10)—the separation of those chosen for the regeneration of Israel (good figs = sons of exile) from the destruction-minded Judeans (bad figs = those who remained in the land).[26] The description at the beginning of Ezra (1:1–2) of the return from the Babylonian exile

---

[24] Albertz deduces that, in Nehemiah, "the term יהודים comprises all people of Judean origin.... The Nehemiah Memoir does not distinguish between the Babylonian exiles (הגולה) and those who remained at home" ("Purity Strategies," 202).

[25] Ezra 3:3; 4:16; 6:21; 9:2, 11–12; 10:10–11.

[26] The allegory does not necessarily carry this view in its original meaning. According to Peter Ross Bedford, this metaphor originally attempted to counteract the claim of nonexiled Judeans interpreting the exile as curse and divine rejection (*Temple Restoration in Early Achaemenid Judah*, JSJSup 65 [Leiden: Brill, 2001], 56).

as the fulfillment of Jeremiah's prophecy supports the interpretation of intermarriage with women from the in-group, a notion including the Judeans who remained in the land, as a sin against YHWH (Ezra 9:4).[27]

The interdiction of intermarriage with foreign women is also expressed in Neh 13:23–30. In this text, however, the prohibition pertains to the *Judeans* (יהודים) as a whole: "In those days also I saw the Judeans [היהודים] who had married women of Ashdod, Ammon, and Moab" (Neh 13:23). It therefore includes the nonexiled Judeans, who are treated as foreigners in Ezra 9. This difference is confirmed by the designation of the out-group in both. In Ezra 9:1, two types of foreigners are mentioned: (1) distant nations, defined as Ammonites, Moabites, Egyptians, and Amorites; and (2) peoples named Hittites, Perizzites, and Jebusites. This anachronistic reference to Canaanites is used to condemn intermarriage with people living in the midst of the sons of exile, that is, nonexiled people from Judea, without mentioning their genuine identity. In Neh 13:23, in which the prohibition applies to the Judeans as a whole, the second category (the so-called Canaanites) has obviously disappeared, so that the interdiction concerns marital alliances only with women of non-Judean origin: Philistines, Ammonites, and Moabites.[28]

Beyond these changes, the motivation for the prohibition of intermarriage differs in Ezra and Nehemiah. In Ezra, the injunction is meant to prevent the disappearance of the so-called holy seed preserved by YHWH through the Babylonian exile. Nothing similar is invoked in Nehemiah, where the ban on intermarriage is motivated by the wish to preserve the Judean national identity, religious beliefs, and cultural markers: "And half of their children spoke the language of Ashdod, and they could not speak the language of Judah, but only the language of each people" (Neh 13:24).[29]

Trends in the Integration Process

An examination of the census in Ezra 2 reveals that all the people included in the community do not fit the in-group definition in Ezra. For example, the list includes the נתינים and sons of Solomon's servants of explicit foreign origin

---

[27] See Bedford, "Diaspora," 154, and the references therein; and Daniel L. Smith-Christopher, "Between Ezra and Isaiah: Exclusion, Transformation and Inclusion of the 'Foreigner' in the Post-Exilic Biblical Theology," in Brett, *Ethnicity and the Bible*, 117–42, esp. 123–24.

[28] It is noteworthy that the Edomites do not appear on this list, even though many Edomites inhabited southern Judea in Nehemiah's time. This is the first indication that the Edomites from southern Judea and the Negev (thereafter designated as Idumeans) are not considered foreigners in Nehemiah.

[29] See Smith-Christopher, "Between Ezra and Isaiah," 123, 127. Wolfgang Oswald concluded that, in Neh 13:23–30, "the assembly of the exiles as a corporate body does not exist; the problem is not exiles vs. natives, rather, the opposition is Judeans vs. Ashdodites" ("Foreign Marriages and Citizenship in Persian Period Judah," *JHebS* 12 [2012], art. 6, pp. 1–17, here 4, https://doi.org/10.5508/jhs.2012.v12.a6).

(vv. 43–58).³⁰ The people from Pahath-moab (v. 6) are probably a group of Israelite origin that did not experience the exile.³¹ The integration of "foreigners" (nonexiled Judeans and people from other nations) is even mentioned during the first celebration of Passover after reconstruction of the temple of Jerusalem: "It [the Passover sacrifice] was eaten by the people of Israel who had returned from exile, and also by everyone who had joined them and separated himself from the uncleanness of the peoples of the land to worship YHWH, the God of Israel" (Ezra 6:21).³² This verse indicates that those who agreed to follow the way of life, religious practices, and theology of the sons of exile could be members of that community. Where women are concerned, such consent is an implicit consequence of marriage with a repatriate. This may explain the practice of intermarriage among the sons of exile and even their religious elite (Ezra 9:2, 10:18–24). Consequently, the prohibition of intermarriage and the isolation of the postexilic community reported in Ezra 9–10 should be considered a novelty, the sealing of the boundaries of the in-group that existed in Ezra's time.

An opposite trend is observed in Nehemiah, where a southern expansion of the boundaries of Yehud, ignored in Ezra, is mentioned for the first time (Neh 11:25–31). This implies the sudden accommodation in the in-group of a population that had not experienced the Babylonian exile.³³ Most villages in the newly "annexed" area are situated in southern Judea and the Negev, an area later identified as Idumea due to the immigration of an Edomite/Seirite population after the fall of Edom.³⁴ By implication, it seems that an Edomite/Seirite population in these

---

³⁰ Bob Becking, "Ezra's Re-enactment of the Exile," in *Leading Captivity Captive: 'The Exile' as History and Ideology*, ed. Lester L. Grabbe, JSOTSup 278 (Sheffield: Sheffield Academic, 1998), 40–61, esp. 45.

³¹ Benjamin Mazar, "The Tobiads," *IEJ* 7 (1957): 229–38, esp. 232.

³² Most scholars and translators agree with this interpretation. See, e.g., J. M. Myers, *Ezra, Nehemiah: Introduction, Translation, and Notes*, AB 14 (Garden City, NY: Doubleday, 1965), 54; David J. A. Clines, *Ezra, Nehemiah, Esther: Based on the Revised Standard Version*, NCBC (Grand Rapids: Eerdmans, 1984), 97; Fensham, *Ezra and Nehemiah*, 96; Blenkinsopp, *Ezra-Nehemiah*, 132–33; Williamson, *Ezra, Nehemiah*, 36, 85; Sara Japhet, "People and Land in the Restoration Period," in *Das Land Israel in biblischer Zeit: Jerusalem-Symposium 1981 der Hebräischen Universität und der Georg-August-Universität*, ed. Georg Stecker, GTA 25 (Göttingen: Vandenhoeck & Ruprecht, 1983), 103–25, esp. 116; Anna L. Grant-Henderson, *Inclusive Voices in Post-exilic Judah* (Collegeville, MN: Liturgical Press, 2002), 122; Peter H. W. Lau, "Gentile Incorporation into Israel in Ezra-Nehemiah?," *Bib* 90 (2009): 356–73, esp. 364–65; Joseph Fleishman, "An Echo of Optimism in Ezra 6:19–22," *HUCA* 69 (1998): 15–29, esp. 19–20. Some scholars reject this integrative interpretation and the eventual integration of foreigners in the book of Ezra. See Matthew Thiessen, "The Function of a Conjunction: Inclusivist or Exclusivist Strategies in Ezra 6.19–21 and Nehemiah 10.29–30?," *JSOT* 34 (2009): 64–79; Pieter M. Venter, "Congruent Ethos in the Second Temple Literature of the Old Testament," *HvTSt* 67 (2011): 1–13, esp. 8–9.

³³ Oded Lipschits, "Literary and Ideological Aspects of Nehemiah 11," *JBL* 121 (2002): 423–40, esp. 429–30, https://doi.org/10.2307/3268154.

³⁴ See Charles E. Carter, *The Emergence of Yehud in the Persian Period: A Social and*

regions was integrated into the province of Yehud in the time of Nehemiah.[35] This interpretation is confirmed by the mention, in Neh 11:24, of a "son of Zerah" named Pethahiah, who was appointed administrator of the southern territory mentioned in Neh 11:25–31.[36] By inference, some barriers of the in-group, at least concerning people of Edomite origin, were lowered in Nehemiah's time.

Attitude toward Foreign Singers

In Ezra 2, a group of singers (משררים), the sons of Asaph (v. 41), is included in the census of the returning exiles totaled in verse 64. This group is mentioned between Levites (v. 40) and temple gatekeepers (v. 42) and probably includes the cultic singers who performed at the Jerusalem temple. This collective is referenced again in the final verse (v. 70) relating to the temple clergy: "Now the priests and the Levites, ומן־העם, and the singers, the gatekeepers and the נתינים lived in their towns; and all the rest of Israel, in their towns." The separation—priests and Levites on one side and singers, gatekeepers, and נתינים on the other—remains obscure as long as the locution ומן העם is interpreted as "and some of the people," a reference to laypeople dwelling in villages attributed to the clergy.

If laypeople are truly quoted here, we expect them to be mentioned *before* or *after* the members of the Jerusalem staff (as in the census list), but in no way should they interrupt the listing. This problem disappears when the *vav* in the preposition ומן is interpreted as a *vav explicativum*.[37] In this manner, the expression ומן העם in Ezra 2:70a designates *those belonging to the people*, so that it introduces a distinction

---

Demographic Study, JSOTSup 294 (Sheffield: Sheffield Academic, 1999), 82; Amos Kloner, "The Identity of the Idumeans Based on Archaeological Evidence from Maresha," in *Judah and the Judeans in the Achemenid Period: Negotiating Identity in an International Context*, ed. Oded Lipschits, Gary N. Knoppers, and Manfred Oeming (Winona Lake, IN: Eisenbrauns, 2011), 563–73.

[35] J. Gordon McConville, "Ezra-Nehemiah and the Fulfilment of Prophecy," *VT* 36 (1986): 205–24, esp. 222; Richard A. Horsley, "The Expansion of Hasmonean Rule in Idumea and Galilee: Toward a Historical Sociology," in *Studies in Politics, Class and Material Culture*, vol. 3 of *Second Temple Studies*, ed. Philip R. Davies and John M. Halligan, JSOTSup 340 (Sheffield: Sheffield Academic, 2002), 134–65, esp. 145.

[36] The affiliation of this newly integrated population to the sons of Zerah and the sudden mention of sons of Perez (Neh 11:4), together with the Edomite ascendency of the sons of Zerah, confirm the integration of an Edomite population in Yehud at the time of Nehemiah. See Nissim Amzallag, *Esau in Jerusalem: The Rise of a Seirite Religious Elite in Zion at the Persian Period*, CahRB 85 (Pendé: Gabalda, 2015), 103–6.

[37] The use of the *vav explicativum* in Biblical Hebrew is explained in detail in Bill T. Arnold and John H. Choi, *A Guide to Biblical Hebrew Syntax* (Cambridge: Cambridge University Press, 2003), 147; Ronald J. Williams, *Williams' Hebrew Syntax*, rev. and exp. John C. Beckman, 3rd ed. (Toronto: University of Toronto Press, 2007), 154; David W. Baker, "Further Examples of the *waw explicativum*," *VT* 30 (1980): 129–36, esp. 134; Thiessen, "Function of a Conjunction," 71–72.

among the temple staff between the groups of "pure Israelite origin" (priests and Levites) and those of mixed/foreign extraction (singers, gatekeepers, and temple servants/נתינים). This interpretation is consistent with the Israelite origin of the priests and Levites of the community (priests of dubious origin being excluded from the service; see Ezra 2:61–62) and with the foreign extraction of the נתינים[38] and of some of the gatekeepers (the foreign group of sons of Obed-Edom).[39] Accordingly, the gathering of the singers with the gatekeepers and the נתינים has two possible explanations: (1) some Asaphites were not of Israelite ethnic origin; or (2) all the Asaphites belonged to the "holy seeds" but were not the only singers who served in the temple. The latter eventuality is supported by the mention in Ezra 2:65 of another pool of anonymous male and female singers. That this group is not included in the total count of the sons of exile (v. 64) reveals their exclusion from the community. Their participation in the musical worship at Jerusalem, however, is suggested by their appellation as משררים, a term reserved in the Bible exclusively for the musical worship of YHWH.[40]

In Neh 7, these anonymous male and female משררים are listed (v. 67) after the complete census of the community is reported (v. 66). A difference with the Ezra census list, however, is observed in the final verse: "Now lived the priests, the Levites, the singers [משררים] and the gatekeepers, that is, from the people [ומן העם], and the נתינים and all Israel in their towns" (Neh 7:72a). Exactly as in Ezra 2, the foreign origin of some of the gatekeepers and especially of the singers is not denied in Neh 7 (see vv. 66–67). In contrast to Ezra 2:70, however, this does not prevent their being fully integrated into the religious elite of the community (Neh 7:72).[41]

The small difference between Ezra 2:70 and Neh 7:72 in the position of the locution ומן העם is generally treated as no more than an insignificant scribal error.

---

[38] The foreign origin of the נתינים is revealed by their non-Israelite names. See Menahem Haran, "The Gibeonites, the Nethinim and the Sons of Solomon's Servants," *VT* 11 (1961): 159–69, esp. 164–66.

[39] In 1 Chronicles, the gatekeepers are described as a heterogeneous collective that includes Levites from prestigious clans (26:19–26), singers from the clan of Korah (26:1), and the sons of Obed-Edom (15:24–25, 16:38, 26:4–8), who are explicitly of foreign origin. See Nancy Tan, "The Chronicler's Obed-Edom: A Foreigner and/or a Levite?," *JSOT* 32 (2007): 217–30; Juan M. Tebes, "The Edomite Involvement in the Destruction of the First Temple: A Case of Stab-in-the-Back Tradition?," *JSOT* 36 (2011): 219–55, esp. 243.

[40] In the Hebrew Bible, the term משרר is encountered only in Ezra (2:41, 65, 70; 7:7; 10:24), Nehemiah (7:1, 44, 67, 72; 10:29, 40; 11:22–23; 12:28, 29, 42, 45, 46, 47; 13:5, 10) and Chronicles (1 Chr 6:18; 9:33; 15:16, 19, 27; 2 Chr 5:12, 13; 13:13; 20:21; 29:28; 35:15). In all these instances, apart from mentions of the foreign singers (Ezra 2:65, Neh 7:67), the term refers unambiguously to cultic singers who were appointed to the Jerusalem temple.

[41] The integration of the foreign singers into the Israelite ethnos in Neh 7:72a introduces an inconsistency relative to their first mention as foreign singers in Neh 7:67. For this reason, we may conclude that Ezra 2:70a is the original wording, which was modified in Neh 7:72a.

The modification that it introduces, however, is corroborated by another positive change in the attitude toward these foreign singers in Nehemiah. In this book, a group of cultic singers distinct from the sons of Asaph and ignored in Ezra is also mentioned: the sons of Jeduthun (Neh 11:17). Identification of the anonymous foreign singers (Ezra 2:65 // Neh 7:67) of controversial status with the sons of Jeduthun/Ethan is confirmed by the following considerations:

- The involvement of the sons of Jeduthun (as well as their brothers, the sons of Heman) in musical worship is ignored in preexilic writings. These clans are, however, mentioned in 1 Chr 25:1–6 together with the sons of Asaph, confirming their participation in musical worship at the temple in the postexilic period.
- In 1 Kgs 5:11, the sons of Jeduthun and of Heman are considered foreign (Zerahite) poets and singers.[42] Their first mention as Levites appears in postexilic writings (Neh 11:17; 1 Chr 25:1–6), a feature suggesting their Levitization during the Persian period.
- The enumeration of 200 foreign singers in Ezra 2:65 (and of 245 singers in Neh 7:67) closely approximates that of the sons of Jeduthun and of Heman (240) who served at the Jerusalem temple.[43]
- The census list refers to male and female foreign singers. The only mention in the Bible of female singers serving in musical worship of YHWH appears in 1 Chr 25:5–6 and concerns the "daughters" of Heman.[44]

The identification of the anonymous cultic singers in the census list with the sons of Ethan/Jeduthun and Heman (= the Ezrahites) confirms an essential difference between the book of Ezra, which excludes them, and the books of Nehemiah and Chronicles, which fully integrate them into the religious elite. This trend corroborates the integration of the Edomite population (identified as "sons of Zerah") promoted in Neh 11:25–31.

---

[42] Three clans of sons of Zerah are identified in the Bible: Judahite (Num 26:20, 1 Chr 2:4, 27:11), Simeonite (Num 26:13, 1 Chr 4:24), and Edomite (Gen 36:13, 1 Chr 1:37). Some scholars assume that all these clans originated in Edom. See Robert H. Pfeiffer, "Edomitic Wisdom," *ZAW* 44 (1926): 13–25, esp. 14–15; Ernst A. Knauf, "Zerah," *ABD* 6:1080–81.

[43] From 1 Chr 25:2–5 we learn that only four of the watches of twelve singers each belonged to the sons of Asaph. Thus, all twenty other watches of twelve singers each (= 240 singers) belonged to the two congregations (Heman and Jeduthun) who are amalgamated as sons of Zerah.

[44] See 1 Chr 25:5–6: "All these were the sons of Heman the king's seer, according to the promise of God to exalt him, for God had given Heman fourteen sons and three daughters. They were all under the direction of their father in the music in the house of YHWH with cymbals, harps, and lyres for the service of the house of God. Asaph, Jeduthun, and Heman were under the order of the king" (1 Chr 25:5–6).

III. YHWH and His Worship

Naming the Deity

Preferential names for the deity are evidenced in some biblical texts. The appellation *YHWH* is the only name for the deity encountered in Obadiah. A strong preference for this name is evinced in Zechariah (133 of 144 occurrences); Genesis, however, favors alternatives (165 uses of YHWH of 402 mentions of God). In the Psalter, too, the preferential use of Elohim (אלהים) in some songs (the so-called Elohistic Psalter, Pss 42–83, sometimes extended to Pss 84–89[45]) and of YHWH in others, irrespective of their themes or functions, reflects preferences for one appellation over the other among psalmists.[46] For this reason, a comparison of the way the deity is named in Ezra and in Nehemiah may be useful in determining whether the two books were written by the same hand or school. Since the name YHWH is avoided in the Aramaic sections of the Bible, the Aramaic sections of Ezra have not been taken into consideration in this analysis.[47] Comparison of the appellations of the deity in Nehemiah and in the Hebrew sections of Ezra reveals significant differences (see table 2).[48]

- *Diversity.* Only two appellations of God—YHWH and Elohim—are encountered in the Hebrew parts of Ezra, whereas four names occur in Nehemiah: YHWH, Elohim, El, and Eloah.
- *The name YHWH.* A similar frequency of use of the names YHWH and Elohim (about 40 to 45 percent each) is observed in the Hebrew parts of the

---

[45] See Laura Joffe, "The Elohistic Psalter: What, How and Why?," *SJOT* 15 (2001): 142–69, esp. 149.

[46] For example, R. G. Boling observes that, in the parallelism of divine names, YHWH is generally quoted first (Elohim being used in the reiteration) in the Yahwistic Psalter, whereas the inverse is observed in the Elohistic Psalter ("Synonymous Parallelism in the Psalms," *JSS* 5 [1960]: 221–55, esp. 242, 248).

[47] The deity is uniformly called אלה (with or without an emphatic א) in the Aramaic sections of Ezra (forty-three occurrences: Ezra 4:24; 5:1–2, 5, 8, 11–17; 6:3, 5, 7–10, 12, 14, 16–18; 7:12, 14–21, 23–26). The very same phenomenon is observed in the book of Daniel, in which the God is constantly called אלה (fifty-one occurrences) in the Aramaic sections. In contrast, the name YHWH is encountered in the Hebrew section of Daniel (9:2, 4, 8, 10, 13–14, 20); this confirms the existence of a bias in appellation of the deity in foreign languages. Other changes in point of view are noticed between the Hebrew and Aramaic parts of Ezra and Daniel. See Bill T. Arnold, "The Use of Aramaic in the Hebrew Bible: Another Look at Bilingualism in Ezra and Daniel," *JNSL* 22.2 (1996): 1–16, esp. 7–8. Accordingly, the absence of Aramaic in Nehemiah itself emphasizes ideological differences between these two books.

[48] The almost identical number of mentions of God (ninety-two in the Hebrew sections of Ezra, ninety-one in Nehemiah) makes such a comparison especially effective.

book of Ezra. In contrast, the author of Nehemiah clearly minimizes the use of YHWH, which is invoked in only 18.6 percent of the cases.

- *The God of Israel.* The deity is sometime called "God of the fathers" or "God of Israel" in Ezra (14 percent of instances).[49] These appellations are *never* encountered in Nehemiah.

Table 2. Names of God in Ezra, Nehemiah, and the Memoir and Nonmemoir Sections

[The category *God of Israel/fathers* comprises both the occurrences of "God of Israel" (אלהי ישראל) and "God of fathers" (אלהי אבות), God of Abraham, God of Isaac, and God of Jacob. The percentage values that follow are calculated on the basis of the total number of occurrences of these divine names in the book (first column of data).]

		Total mentions	YHWH		Elohim		El		Eloah		God of Israel /fathers	
			Value	%	Value	%	Value	%	Value	%	Value	%
Ezra	Total	92	37	40.2	42	45.6	0	0	0	0	13	14.1
	Non-memoirs[50]	48	26	54.1	15	31.2	0	0	0	0	7	14.5
	Memoirs[51]	44	11	25.0	27	61.3	0	0	0	0	6	13.6
Nehemiah	Total	91	17	18.6	70	76.9	3	3.3	1	1.1	0	0
	Non-memoirs[52]	69	16	23.1	50	72.4	2	2.89	1	1.44	0	0
	Memoirs[53]	22	1	4.5	20	90.9	1	4.5	0	0	0	0

The appellations of the deity have been examined separately in the first-person (the so-called memoir) and the third-person narration voices in Ezra and Nehemiah. In Ezra, the deity is called *God of Israel/fathers* at the same frequency in both. A small difference is nevertheless observed: whereas the appellation *Elohim* is preferred in the "memoirs," the deity is called *Elohim* and *YHWH* equally in the

---

[49] In parallel, the designation אלה ישראל occurs in the Aramaic sections of Ezra (5:1, 6:14, 7:15).
[50] Ezra 1:1–7:26.
[51] Ezra 7:27–10:44.
[52] Neh 4:18–5:19, 7:6–12:26, 12:44–13:31.
[53] Neh 1:1–4:17, 6:1–7:5, 12:27–43.

narration (see table 2). Also in Nehemiah, the appellation YHWH is more frequently encountered in the narration than in the memoirs, where it is almost completely excluded. Beyond this similar trend, a comparison of the narration sections in Ezra and Nehemiah shows that *YHWH* (54.1%) is preferred over *Elohim* (31.2%) as the deity's name in Ezra, whereas the latter name (72.4%) is preferred in Nehemiah (see table 2).

To evaluate the significance of these differences concerning authorship, a similar analysis is performed for the two books of Samuel, the two books of Kings, and the two books of Chronicles. It reveals that the use of the names of God is very similar within each pair of books (table 3). Variations in the use of the deity's three main appellations (YHWH, Elohim, God of Israel/fathers), quantified for all the pairs of compared books, discloses a similarly low level of variance between the two books of Samuel, of Kings, and of Chronicles (table 4). This result contrasts with the strong variance existing in the books of Ezra and of Nehemiah, which is observed even in the third-person narration segments. From table 4, we may conclude that the pairs of Samuel, Kings, and Chronicles were written/edited by the same hand or by authors who belonged to the same group or school. In contrast, the high level of variance observed between Ezra and Nehemiah in the uses of the name of God suggests not only different authorship but also different approaches to the deity.

TABLE 3. Comparison of the Names of God in the Two Parts
of the Books of Samuel, Kings, and Chronicles

[The category *God of Israel/fathers* comprises both the occurrences of "God of Israel" (אלהי ישראל) and "God of fathers" (אלהי אבות), God of Abraham, God of Isaac, and God of Jacob. The percentage values that follow are calculated on the basis of the total number of occurrences of these divine names in the book (first column of data).]

		Total mentions	YHWH		Elohim		El		Eloah		God of Israel /fathers	
			Value	%	Value	%	Value	%	Value	%	Value	%
Samuel	1	421	320	76.0	83	19.7	1	0.2	0	0	17	4.0
	2	212	153	72.1	50	23.5	5	2.3	0	0	4	2.0
Kings	1	364	257	70.6	88	24.1	0	0	0	0	19	5.2
	2	375	277	73.8	86	22.9	0	0	1	0.2	11	2.9
Chronicles	1	293	175	59.7	101	34.4	0	0	0	0	17	5.8
	2	587	384	65.4	155	26.4	0	0	1	0.1	47	8.0

TABLE 4. Comparative Fluctuation in the Appellation of God between Ezra and Nehemiah, and between 1 and 2 Samuel, 1 and 2 Kings, and 1 and 2 Chronicles

[For each appellation (YHWH, Elohim, God of Israel/fathers), the fluctuation between two biblical sources is calculated as the ratio (×100) between the standard deviation and the average for the values determined in tables 2 and 3.]

		YHWH	Elohim	God of fathers/ Israel
Ezra versus Nehemiah	Whole books	51.9	36.1	141.4
	Nonmemoir segments	56.7	56.2	141.4
1 Samuel versus 2 Samuel		3.7	12.4	47.0
1 Kings versus 2 Kings		3.1	3.6	40.0
1 Chronicles versus 2 Chronicles		6.4	18.6	22.4

The Sukkot Festival

In both Ezra and Nehemiah, the long list of repatriates (Ezra 2, Neh 7:6–72) is followed by an account of the celebration of the Sukkot festival (Ezra 3:4–5, Neh 8:13–18). One would expect the celebration of Sukkot in Ezra and Nehemiah to be as similar as are the respective census lists (Ezra 2:1–70 and Neh 7:6–72). In Ezra 3, the Sukkot festival focuses on sacrifices, and the description corroborates the celebration of this festival in the other sources (Lev 23:33–43, Num 29:12–39, and 2 Chr 8:13).[54] The specific mention of the sacrifices performed "as written, day by day" in Ezra 3:4–5 even corroborates the daily instructions delineated in Num 29:12–39.[55]

The celebration of Sukkot in Nehemiah, however, is markedly different.[56] The sacrificial aspect is ignored. The departure from the pentateuchal tradition is revealed here by the fact that the Israelites are instructed to build booths and, especially, to gather branches on the first day of the festival (Neh 8:15).[57] This contrasts with Lev 23:35, which stresses that every form of labor is strictly forbidden

---

[54] The Sukkot festival is also mentioned in Deut 13:13–15; 31:10; and Zech 14:16, 18–19, but without detailing the way it was celebrated.

[55] Grabbe, *Ezra, Nehemiah*, 17.

[56] Kraemer, "On the Relationships," 84; Pakkala, *Ezra the Scribe*, 133.

[57] In Leviticus, this sacrificial instruction (Lev 23:36–37) is accompanied by the directive of "sitting/dwelling in booths" (סכה) throughout the seven days of the festival (v. 42). Omitted by all the other sources, this commandment is probably not restricted to the Leviticus source, because the name *Sukkot*, designating the booths, is acknowledged in all the other biblical quotations of this festival.

on this day.⁵⁸ The novelty is even confirmed by the specific mention, in Neh 8:17, that the Sukkot festival has never been celebrated in such fashion from the days of Joshua the son of Nun.⁵⁹

The Priests' Status

Long before Ezra himself is first mentioned, the book of Ezra accords a prominent status to the priests. Their initiative in restoring the altar and renewing the sacrifices (Ezra 3:3) presents them as leaders of the community, the initiators of Israel's postexilic rebirth. The portrayal of priests in Nehemiah is different. They take part in reconstructing the city wall (Neh 3:1), but their standing in this endeavor is no different from that of any other clan or guild (Neh 3:2–32). In no way do they initiate or lead the reconstruction. Additional indications confirm the priests' loss of prestige in Nehemiah.

The supplication ceremony. A ceremony composed of collective supplications, fasting, and mourninglike rituals is reported in Neh 9:1–5. It is conducted solely by the Levites (9:4); the participation of the priests is curiously ignored, even though their delegates probably participated in the congregation's blessing of YHWH (9:5).⁶⁰ If so, the Levite religious leadership is clearly promoted in Nehemiah at the expense of the priestly leadership. In Ezra, in contrast, the Levites are minor clergy only.

The dedication ceremony. The change in the priests' status is confirmed by examination of their involvement in the ceremony marking the completion of the Jerusalem city wall (Neh 12:27–43). Most of the seventeen-verse account of the ceremony is devoted to the musical performance. Only four verses (vv. 30, 35, 41, 43) refer to the priests and their functions. There, too, the priests are hardly described as leaders. Verse 30 reports their purification of the city wall and gates, but the Levites are mentioned as fulfilling this function in conjunction with them. Thereafter (vv. 35, 41), the priests do not conduct the procession but merely follow it with trumpets. This contrasts with the ceremony related in Ezra 3:10–11, in which the priests sound trumpets and are mentioned first, suggesting that they conducted it. The last mention of the priests in Neh 12:43, immediately following the completion of the musical part of the dedication ceremony (v. 42), does refer explicitly to

---

⁵⁸ Pakkala points to further differences between the mention of the Sukkot festival in Neh 8:13–18 and Lev 23:33–43, such as the lack of exact dating in Nehemiah, or the appellation of the festival (*Ezra the Scribe*, 163).

⁵⁹ See Neh 8:17: "And all the assembly of those who had returned from the captivity [השבים מן השבי] made booths and lived in the booths, for from the days of Jeshua the son of Nun to that day the people of Israel had not done so. And there was very great rejoicing."

⁶⁰ The singular use of the jussive (ויברכו), a typical impersonal mood, in urging the congregation to bless YHWH suggests that the identity of those in the congregation (the priests) is intentionally silenced.

their sacrificial duties. Surprisingly, however, the sacrificial contributions are gathered amid popular rejoicing instead of constituting the holy part of the ceremony: "And they offered great sacrifices that day and rejoiced, for God had made them rejoice with great joy; the women and children also rejoiced. And the joy of Jerusalem was heard far away" (v. 43).[61] By means of this literary artifice, it seems that, in contrast to the book of Ezra, the author of Nehemiah intentionally diminished the ritual importance of both the priests and the sacrifices, elevating instead the musical performance conducted by the singers/Levites.

IV. Ideological Divergences between Ezra and Nehemiah

Each dissimilarity identified above concerns a specific point. If all of them are interconnected, however, their intersection reflects essential differences in the ideologies that conditioned the redaction and/or editing of Ezra and Nehemiah.

The Babylonian Repatriates as Remnants in Ezra

The *remnant* (פליטה) is essentially the entity that ensures continuity. In Ezra, this remnant is identified *exclusively* with the Babylonian repatriates. Therefore, the author interprets their deportation from Judah as a positive event, the intentional preservation of a chosen group by YHWH even as he expressed his destructive wrath, from which the people as a whole is expected to regenerate. The theological importance of the exile transpires from the parallel stressed in Ezra between the return of the repatriates and the exodus. This is revealed by reminiscences in Ezra 1:4 about the silver and gold that the Israelites removed from Egypt (Exod 11:2, 12:35–36).[62] The reference to the land of Judea as the site of impure practices (Ezra 6:21) and the anachronistic Canaanite terminology used in Ezra 9:1 (Canaanite, Hittites, Perizzites, Jebusites) clearly introduce a parallel between the return of the sons of exile and the Israelite conquest of Canaan.[63]

The return from exile is interpreted as the fulfillment of Jeremiah's prophecies

---

[61] This feature contrasts with the central importance of sacrifices in the ceremony of inauguration of the Jerusalem sacrificial area by David (2 Sam 24:24–25), and of the Jerusalem temple (1 Kgs 8:62–66). It is also noteworthy that musical celebrations are not mentioned in these sources. The transportation of the ark of YHWH to Jerusalem is an inauguration ceremony accompanied by musical performance and dance (2 Sam 6:12–19). But even in this case, this musical dimension is intimately mixed with sacrifices (vv.13–15). Nothing similar is observed in the inauguration ceremony evoked in Nehemiah.

[62] See Melody D. Knowles, "Pilgrimage Imagery in the Returns in Ezra," *JBL* 123 (2004): 57–74, esp. 57–58, https://doi.org/10.2307/3268549. According to Knowles, even the dates and duration of Ezra's journey (Ezra 7–8) refer to the exodus (60).

[63] See Bedford, "Diaspora," 150–53.

in the opening sentence of Ezra (1:1).⁶⁴ This includes the metaphor promoting the Judeans deported to Babylon (the good figs, Jer 24:5) at the expense of their brethren who remained in Judah (the rotten figs, Jer 24:8, 26:17) and are doomed to perdition.⁶⁵ From such a perspective, the deportation to Babylon of the Jerusalemite religious elite promoted, and even strengthened, the legitimacy of its leadership.⁶⁶ This representation obviously has many consequences. First, it confers legitimacy on the preexilic religious traditions of the exclusive election of Israel, leading to YHWH's appellation as *God of Israel* (table 2). Furthermore, it conduces to the repatriates' definition as "holy seeds" (Ezra 9:2), from which the whole of Israel is expected to regenerate, and implies that Israel should beware of all foreign influence and even intermarriage with Judeans who remain in the land (Ezra 9:1, 12, 14). This explains why the presence of remaining (nonexilic) Judeans is omitted in Ezra, why even the designation "Judean" (which amalgamates the sons of exile with the remaining population) is avoided, and why this local Judean population is assimilated with the Canaanites who inhabited the land before the Israelite conquest. It even explains the exclusion from the community of the foreign Yahwistic singers (sons of Zerah) who have been appointed to the Jerusalem temple (Ezra 2:65, 70).

The Nonexiled Judeans as Remnants in Nehemiah

In Nehemiah, the appellation of the nondeported Judeans as *remnants* reflects the idea that this population is the core around which Judah/Israel will regenerate. Consequently, the Babylonian exile is deprived of its positive dimension. Rather, it is approached as the quintessential expression of divine punishment for sins.⁶⁷ Accordingly, the remaining Judeans become the in-group escaping the divine curse of the exile. This explains why the appellation of the in-group as "sons of exile" is

---

⁶⁴ This linkage is especially relevant in view of the concentration of the term גולה (up to 80 percent of the forty-two biblical occurrences) in only three books: Jeremiah (28:6; 29:1, 4, 16, 20, 31; 46:19; 48:7, 11; 49:3), Ezekiel (1:1; 3:11, 15; 11:24, 25; 12:3, 4 [2x], 7, 11; 25:3), and Ezra (1:11; 2:1; 4:1; 6:16, 19–21; 8:35; 9:4; 10:6–8, 16). The other occurrences are found in 2 Kgs 24:15–16, Amos 1:15, Nah 3:10, Zech 6:10, 14:2, Esth 2:6, Neh 7:6, and 1 Chr 5:22.

⁶⁵ See McConville, "Ezra-Nehemiah," 216; Becking, *Ezra, Nehemiah*, 30. Joseph Blenkinsopp observes how Jeremiah's fig metaphor became a dominant negative image in some postexilic writings (*Judaism, the First Phase: The Place of Ezra and Nehemiah in the Origins of Judaism* [Grand Rapids: Eerdmans, 2009] 44). According to McConville, reminiscences in Jer 31 dealing with the remnant of Israel may also be identified in Ezra 7–9 ("Ezra-Nehemiah," 215–17).

⁶⁶ According to the book of Ezra (2:36, 41; 6:16; 7:6–7), the priests and Levites affiliated with the temple in Jerusalem belonged exclusively to the group defined as sons of exile. The leadership of such a religious elite, among which Ezra is numbered, is unchallenged.

⁶⁷ See, e.g., Deut 28:32, 36, 41; 2 Kgs 17:20–23; Isa 20:4–6. Even in Jeremiah, portrayal of the positive dimension of the Babylonian exile is counterbalanced by negative views expressed in 46:19; 48:7, 11–12; and 49:3.

excised in Nehemiah. This also explains the loss of prestige of the religious elite, whose deportation becomes ostensible evidence of its (relative) depreciation by YHWH. Indeed, the priestly leadership is tacitly but clearly criticized in Nehemiah. This emerges in the lengthy recapitulation of Israelite history, from its origins to postexilic times, in Neh 9:6–37. This text separates the preexilic history (vv. 6–31) from the community's deplorable situation in the present (vv. 32–37). It is noteworthy that, beyond the responsibility of the Israelites at large (vv. 32–33), the leaders are specifically reproached for sinning against YHWH (vv. 34–35). The mention of the king obviously refers to the preexilic period. The insertion of this criticism into the second part (vv. 32–37), however, explicitly extends it to the priests and especially to the prominent ones who constitute the elite of the postexilic community.[68] This may explain the decline in prestige of the priestly elite in the book of Nehemiah, as well as the opposition to Nehemiah of *all* the prophets (Neh 6:14) and even of the great priest (Eliashib and his lineage, Neh 13:4–9, 28–29).[69]

The antagonism between the postexilic theology and the ideology promoted in Nehemiah is confirmed by further singularities. The first is the distance from the Israelite preexilic traditions expressed in Nehemiah. This singularity is reflected by the changes in celebration of the Sukkot festival and by the breakdown of the ideology of substitution of Esau/Edom by Jacob/Israel as the people of YHWH promoted by the Israelite theology. This latter point finds an expression in the integration of a population of non-Israelite origin (the Edomites inhabiting southern Judah and the Negev; see Neh 11:25–31), in the reference to Abraham as the common founding father of the "people of YHWH" (Neh 9:7), in the disappearance of the specific appellation of YHWH as "God of Israel" in Nehemiah. This is confirmed by the integration of the (foreign) Ezrahite singers, the sons of Heman and of Jeduthun, into the staff of the Jerusalem temple, a feature evoked for the first time in Neh 7:72 and 11:17 and thereafter confirmed in 1 Chr 25–26.[70]

These considerations reveal that the differences identified between the books of Ezra and Nehemiah are not random. Rather, all of them should be regarded as consequences of an essential difference between the books of Ezra and Nehemiah concerning the theological significance of exile.

---

[68] The only group among the elite that the preamble excuses from its critique is the Levites, who are totally omitted in verses 34–35. This difference between Ezra and Nehemiah in regard to the Levites has long been stressed in scholarship. Jacob L. Wright, for example, concludes: "Therefore, while we cannot deny that in several passages Nehemiah displays sympathies for the Levitical guild, these texts appear to be the work of anonymous authors writing in Nehemiah's name" (*Rebuilding Identity: The Nehemiah-Memoir and Its Earliest Readers*, BZAW 348 [Berlin: de Gruyter, 2005], 207).

[69] The opposition of Eliashib, the high priest, is reflected also in his absence from the list of priests (Neh 10:2–9) who sign the charter promoted by Nehemiah.

[70] See Amzallag, *Esau in Jerusalem*, 77–120.

V. Differences in Authorship of Ezra and Nehemiah

Insofar as the books of Ezra and Nehemiah are a series of independent documents that were later gathered, compiled, and reworked by a narrator/editor into a coherent literary text, as some scholars presume (see above), the narrator/editor may have had to gather sources (the first-person narration) with a distinct ideological background into a common opus. Consequently, an author who wished to safeguard the prestige of both Ezra and Nehemiah may have chosen to adapt his/her narration to the ideological background of the different sources of the first-person narration.[71] This argument may explain, at least partly, why the narration supports the view of Ezra first and of Nehemiah thereafter without providing any justification. It cannot, however, justify contradictions inherent in the mention of the *same* reality in Ezra and Nehemiah. For example, a narrator may evoke the progressive downgrading of the priests' status in the early Persian period to explain the differences between the first-person expressions of Ezra and of Nehemiah. Such a narrator, however, is not expected to exploit the figure of Ezra to denote such an evolution.

The intriguing appearance of Ezra in Neh 8 and his explicit mention alongside Nehemiah in 8:9 is a central argument in favor of the amalgamation of the books of Ezra and Nehemiah, or at least parts of them. Many scholars even deduce that Neh 7:72b–8:12 originally belonged to the account of Ezra in Ezra 7–10.[72] In such a case, one would expect to find Ezra portrayed in a similar fashion in both works, even though the single writer adapted his/her prose to the different ideologies carried by the Ezra and Nehemiah memoirs. But this is not the case. Ezra is presented in Ezra 7 as the descendant of "Aaron the high priest" (v. 5), a prestigious origin that legitimizes his supreme sacrificial functions. He is also characterized as a scribe skilled in the laws of Moses (v. 6) and thoroughly versed in YHWH's Torah (v. 10a), teaching it to the masses (v. 10b). These attributes are summarized in v. 11b, which describes Ezra as "a man learned in matters of the commandments of YHWH and his statutes for Israel." This representation, together with the power accorded to Ezra by King Artaxerxes (v. 21), justifies his unchallenged status as leader of the whole community (v. 25).

---

[71] Karrer even suggests that the ideology of the final editor is somewhat intermediate between the positions expressed by the Nehemiah and Ezra sources, especially concerning the sociopolitical structure of the postexilic community (*Ringen um die Verfassung Judas*, 284–378).

[72] For details about this opinion, see, e.g., Håkan Ulfgard, *The Story of Sukkot: The Setting, Shaping, and Sequel of the Biblical Feast of Tabernacles*, BGBE 34 [Tübingen: Mohr Siebeck, 1998], 124); Pakkala, *Ezra the Scribe*, 167–77; Titus Reinmuth, "Nehemiah 8 and the Authority of Torah in Ezra-Nehemiah," in Boda and Redditt, *Unity and Disunity*, 241–62, here 261; Boda, "Redaction in the Book of Nehemiah," 27. Though this assumption is stressed by Becking (*Ezra, Nehemiah*, 46), it is challenged by the cohesiveness of Neh 8 with the adjacent chapters.

Nehemiah 8 reports a ceremony in which Ezra reads the Torah to the assembly (vv. 2–3). In verses 1–12, however, the community, rather than Ezra, is the focus of attention. It is the community that, in verse 3, takes the initiative by asking Ezra to read the Torah.[73] No longer, however, does Ezra comment on its contents. In Nehemiah, this instructional function is ceded to the Levites (v. 7),[74] who not only explain the Torah to the people but also read it publicly instead of (or in parallel with) Ezra the priest (v. 8). Immediately afterward (v. 9), it is Nehemiah, and not Ezra, who addresses the people. Thereafter (v. 11), this role is granted to the Levites.[75] The figure of Ezra overcomes in the book of Nehemiah the same decline in prestige that affects all the other priests. For this reason, the differences between the two books in their portrayal of Ezra argue in favor of their separate authorship.

Further observations concur with this conclusion. Differences in the uses of the name of God may hardly be considered a means of illustrating changes because this characteristic of the text is invisible in a superficial reading; only a numerical analysis reveals it. Therefore, it reflects differences in the perception of the deity between the one who composed the book of Ezra and the writer behind the book of Nehemiah. Similarly, contrasting claims are observed in the two books. A first one concerns the status of the foreign singers, excluded from the community in Ezra 2:70 and integrated into it in Neh 7:72. Such antagonism cannot in any way be attributed to evolution of the status of these singers, because the two lists are expected to reflect exactly the same reality. In light of evidence for integration of Edomite foreigners in the book of Nehemiah, the small but highly significant textual change in Neh 7:72 relative to Ezra 2:70 cannot be dismissed as a meaningless scribal error. Rather, it probably denotes a radical change in the reference to these foreign singers—apparently an intentional modification introduced in Nehemiah to antedate the integration of foreign cultic singers into the religious elite and to attribute it to the ancient leadership of the postexilic community.

Finally, the use of the term פליטה in opposite senses in Ezra 9 and in Neh 1 is totally unexpected if both chapters are elaborated by the same hand. The definition of פליטה at the very beginning of Nehemiah is of crucial importance for stressing

---

[73] Duggan, *Covenant Renewal*, 85–86. Duggan even concluded that, in Neh 8, "Ezra's comportment tends to diminish his supremacy on the others. He functions as the servant who responds to the people's desire for the law (8:1). Even on the platform, he stands in the midst of laymen (8:4)" (121).

[74] Ibid., 100. Duggan stressed this secondary role of Ezra in regard to the Levites: "Moreover, the use of additional verbs and phrases indicates that the Levites engage in more complex activity than did Ezra in mediating the law to the people. Not only do they (like Ezra) read from the book of the law; they also read "distinctly" [מפרש], presenting the meaning [שום שכל], thereby helping the people understand [מבינים] the law."

[75] Kraemer observes, "The Ezra remembered in Ezra is not the Ezra known in Nehemiah. In Ezra, Ezra is a priest, a man concerned with the cult and its purity, while in Nehemiah he is a scribe, a man of the book who is entirely unconcerned with the Temple or sacrifices" ("On the Relationships," 83).

its ideological singularity. The fact that the term פליטה is not necessary for understanding the meaning of Neh 1:2 (in light of the redundant mention of the survivors among the remaining Judeans in Neh 1:2–3) even suggests that it is intentionally introduced here to announce a drift in the ideological background of this book in regard to the postexilic theology in general and the book of Ezra in particular.

VI. Consequences concerning the Ezra–Nehemiah Relationships

The Literary Linkage as a Stratagem

The substantial differences in ideological background between Ezra and Nehemiah (in both their memoir and their narration segments) imply that these two books cannot be approached as a single opus. Concurrently, however, the many parallels and literary linkages between them may easily justify their being gathered in one single literary entity, as most modern scholars argue. These contrasting conclusions may be combined if one interprets many of the elements that link Nehemiah to Ezra as a literary stratagem introduced by the author of Nehemiah in order to minimize opposition in the postexilic community to the reforms promoted in this book. This point is now examined.

The old census list. The completion of the Jerusalem city wall (Neh 7:1–3) is immediately followed by Nehemiah's initiative to repopulate the city (v. 4). The process begins with a census (7:5a), is followed by the gathering of the in-group in Jerusalem (8:1), and concludes with the mention of those whom Nehemiah designates to dwell within the city (11:4–24). The insertion of the earlier list of returnees (7:6–73) in the midst of this process appears to have no practical function because almost nothing in 11:4–24 is reminiscent of the names or families of returnees mentioned in the earlier list.[76] Furthermore, the ancient list of returnees is mentioned only *after* Nehemiah's initiative of a new census: "Then my God put it into my heart to assemble the nobles and the officials and the people for registration by affiliation [להתיחש]. And I found the book of the affiliation [יחש] of those who came up at the first, and I found written in it" (Neh 7:5). Finally, nothing alludes to any subsequent use of the earlier list by Nehemiah.

The reinsertion in Neh 7:6–73 of the list of returnees from Ezra 2, however, fulfills three other essential functions: (1) it creates an illusion of continuity between the initial community of repatriates and the in-group, whose boundaries have been totally redefined by Nehemiah; (2) it positions Nehemiah's initiative for repopulating Jerusalem in continuity with the actions of the previous leaders of the

---

[76] The name of three priest ancestors (Jedaiah, Pashhur, and Immer, in Neh 11:10, 12–13 respectively) may, however, be identified on the list of returnees (Neh 7:39–41).

community; and (3) the reiteration of the list of returnees in Ezra 2 and Nehemiah 7 produces a giant *inclusio* that unifies all events from the beginning of the construction of the temple (Ezra 3) to the completion of the Jerusalem city wall (Neh 7:1–3). Therefore, it creates the illusion of literary unity in the books of Ezra and Nehemiah.[77]

Reconstruction of Jerusalem. When Nehemiah is read immediately after Ezra, its first six chapters, centering on the reconstruction of the Jerusalem city wall, give a clear impression of the extension, and even the completion, of the temple reconstruction work reported in Ezra 3–6.[78] Separate reading of the first Nehemiah chapters, however, yields a different picture. Here, the community leaders are explicitly accused of sinning (Neh 1:5–7) and of neglecting the reconstruction of Jerusalem (2:13–15).[79] This accusation is amplified by the avoidance, at the beginning of Nehemiah, of all mention of the reconstruction of the temple, the successful achievement of the previous community leaders that Ezra praises so explicitly.[80] The presentation of Nehemiah as an extension of Ezra, therefore, makes it possible to debunk the previous leadership and its ideology and to reframe such virulent criticism as the appearance of continuity in policy.

Recruitment of Ezra in Nehemiah. Ezra, the leader who explicitly defends the Israelite tradition symbolized by the laws of Moses (Ezra 7:6), is recruited in Neh 8 to promote new religious practices. In Neh 12:27–43, the persona of Ezra is again exploited to sponsor the reformation of musical worship and enhance the Levites' role at the expense of the priests, whereas nothing in the book of Ezra supports such a premise.[81] These uses of the persona of Ezra in Nehemiah reinforce the illusion of literary continuity between the two books and quench the community's resistance to the profound changes promoted in Nehemiah. Two other famous figures from the past, Joshua the son of Nun and Zerubbabel, are similarly recruited, the former to legitimize the reformation of the Sukkot festival (Neh 8:17) and the latter to reform the Levites' status and reward (Neh 12:47).

---

[77] Such a structural *inclusio* generated by repetition of the census list (Ezra 2 and Neh 7) has served as a main argument for approaching Ezra and Nehemiah as a single opus. See Tamara Cohn Eskenazi, "The Structure of Ezra-Nehemiah and the Integrity of the Book," *JBL* 107 (1988): 641–56, esp. 646–47, https://doi.org/10.2307/3267626.

[78] Eskenazi, *Age of Prose*, 38.

[79] The impression is strenghtened by Nehemiah's defiance of the postexilic officials: "I told no one what my God had put into my heart to do for Jerusalem" (Neh 2:12).

[80] This silence contrasts with the mention, in Neh 2:16, of the priests who were appointed to the temple.

[81] The appending of the concluding verses (Neh 12:44–47) indicates that the ceremony marked not only the completion of the city wall but the integration of the foreign (Ezrahite) singers into the community and, especially, the reform that systematized the remittances of taxes by the community. See Amzallag, *Esau in Jerusalem*, 111–12.

Parallel ending. The books of Ezra and Nehemiah have similar endings, in which the leaders inveigh against intermarriage (Ezra 10, Neh 13:23–30). Here again, such a nontrivial parallel looks like a stratagem in Nehemiah: (1) it establishes textual continuity between Nehemiah's reforms and Ezra's policy, despite the difference between the two approaches toward intermarriage, consequent on differences in the definition of the in-group;[82] (2) it dissimulates the conflict between Nehemiah and the priests over the Levite status and income reform (Neh 13:4–13, 30) from the conflict between Nehemiah and priests involving intermarriage (Neh 13:28–30); and (3) it reinforces the literary relationship between Ezra and Nehemiah, leading to the possibility of treating the two books as a single opus.

These four examples reveal a deliberate literary mimicry of the book of Ezra in Nehemiah that was probably introduced in order to neutralize the opposition of the postexilic community. The treatment of the entire book of Nehemiah as an extension of Ezra even represents the ultimate achievement of such a stratagem.

Diachronic and Historical Considerations

The question of precedence of Ezra or Nehemiah is a matter that has been debated for more than a century.[83] In view of the mimicry stratagem identified here, we may conclude—assuming that these two figures are historical—that Ezra's mission truly precedes Nehemiah's. It also seems clear that the book of Ezra already existed, at least in nearly final form, at the time the book of Nehemiah was composed.[84]

Many scholars treat the documents identified as the Nehemiah memoir as

---

[82] See Becking, *Ezra, Nehemiah*, 103–7. Some scholars assume that Neh 13 is no more than an appendix to the book. For an overview, see Gary E. Schnittjer, "The Bad Ending of Ezra-Nehemiah," *BSac* 173 (2016): 32–56. This premise does not, however, challenge the present conclusion. It merely invites us to interpret Neh 13 as a chapter added later to reinforce the linkage with the book of Ezra.

[83] On the basis of the identification of the king mentioned in Ezra 7:7–8 as Artaxerxes I, scholars have dated Ezra's arrival in Jerusalem at 458/457 BCE (or 428/427 BCE for others), shortly before the advent of Nehemiah. Others, identifying the same king as Artaxerxes II, argue that Ezra reached Jerusalem in 398/397 BCE, several decades after Nehemiah's mission. Yet other scholars assume that Ezra reached Jerusalem a short time after Nehemiah did and that they worked together to promote the rehabilitation of the Israelite tradition and the reconstruction of the city. For an overview of these opinions, see Edwin M. Yamauchi, "The Reverse Order of Ezra/Nehemiah Reconsidered," *Them* 5 (1980): 7–13; Aaron Demsky, "Who Came First, Ezra or Nehemiah? The Synchronistic Approach," *HUCA* 65 (1994): 1–19.

[84] This conclusion contrasts with the idea that the Ezra and Nehemiah memoirs were redacted by Ezra and Nehemiah, or in close relation with them, in the second half of the fifth century BCE and the composition of Ezra-Nehemiah as a single opus about a century later, as is defended by many scholars. For a review of this opinion, see Farisani, "Composition and Date," 225–28; Albertz, "Purity Strategies," 199.

exercises in apologia and self-glorification, hence of little historical value.⁸⁵ In fact, the mimicry stratagem identified here confirms that some elements of the Nehemiah memoir and even of the narrative sections are guided by literary considerations rather than historical purposes.⁸⁶ Such a stratagem, however, also strengthens the historical value of the claims and events that Nehemiah reports in a discreet tenor concealed behind an ostensible continuity with the Ezra mission. More generally, it also pleads for the historicity of Nehemiah's reforms in enlarging the in-group, transforming the cult, and transcending the theology defended by the sons of exile.

VII. Conclusion

Although the opinion of common authorship of Ezra and Nehemiah is well accepted today, this study identifies differences between these books in the definition of the in-group, its religious identity, its elite, and its attitude toward foreigners. These contrasting positions are not equal in status and legitimacy. Whereas the opinions defended in Ezra are congruent with the exilic and early postexilic tradition, the underlying ideological background of the book of Nehemiah challenges some of these fundamentals. This conclusion is corroborated by the hostility to Nehemiah among the religious elite.⁸⁷ This conflict is probably responsible for the prudence of the author of Nehemiah and the difficulty encountered by ancient

---

⁸⁵ See John Bright, "The Date of Ezra's Mission to Jerusalem," in *Yehezkel Kaufmann Jubilee Volume: Studies in Bible and Jewish Religion*, ed. Menahem Haran (Jerusalem: Magnes, 1960), 70–87, here 86: "Nehemiah, on the other hand, intended his memoirs as a personal apologia not as a history of the contemporary Jewish community; he was concerned exclusively with what he himself had done." Sigmund Mowinckel treats these fragments as a commemoration of Nehemiah's deeds (*Studien zu dem Buche Ezra-Nehemia*, 3 vols., SNVAO.HF 3 [Oslo: Universitetsforlaget, 1964], 2:63). Willy Schottroff finds similarities between segments of the Nehemiah memoir and West Semitic votive or dedicatory inscriptions ('*Gedenken' im alten Orient und im Alten Testament: Die Wurzel zākar im semitischen Sprachkreis*, WMANT 15 [Neukirchen-Vluyn: Neukirchener Verlag, 1964], 218). Joseph Blenkinsopp finds parallels with Egyptian autobiographical votive inscriptions ("The Mission of Udjahorresnet and Those of Ezra and Nehemiah," *JBL* 106 [1987]: 409–21, https://doi.org/10.2307/3261065). See also David J. A. Clines. "The Nehemiah Memoir: The Peril of Autobiography," in *What Does Eve Do to Help? And Other Readerly Questions to the Old Testament*, JSOTSup 94 (Sheffield: JSOT Press, 1990), 124–64.

⁸⁶ Some of these features may even be anachronistic. For example, according to Israel Finkelstein, the list in Neh 3 corresponds better to the geopolitical situation in the Hasmonean period than to that in the Persian era ("The Historical Reality behind the Genealogical Lists in 1 Chronicles," *JBL* 131 [2012]: 65–83, esp. 75, https://doi.org/10.2307/23488212).

⁸⁷ According to Blenkinsopp, "The Nehemiah memoir gives the impression of enemies on every side" (*Judaism, the First Phase*, 111). The opposition to Nehemiah, expressed both by all the prophets of the community (Neh 6:10–14) and by Eliashib, the high priest (Neh 13:7–8) confirms this. The many additional novelties relative to the Israelite tradition that are identifiable in Nehemiah (introduced mainly to promote the Levitization of the Edomites who have been

exegetes and modern scholars in identifying the ideological underpinnings of this book.

Scholars have suggested that the various opinions developed in Ezra and Nehemiah reflect a debate within the community about the nature of "genuine Yahwism."[88] Conflicts about the nature of the in-group and its receptiveness to aliens have even been identified through comparison of some postexilic texts.[89] The results reported in this study confirm the validity of these assumptions. They even suggest that the root of this conflict is to be found in the theological interpretation of the Babylonian exile—a positive event for some (preservation of a holy seed for regenerating the whole people) and a negative one for others (a state of sin that affects the religious and political elite in the main). The last-mentioned point opens a new horizon for interpretation of the book of Nehemiah, emancipated from the prism of the book of Ezra, and also of other biblical writings that carry a similar ideology.

---

appointed to the Jerusalem temple) also corroborate this point. See Amzallag, *Esau in Jerusalem*, 97–120, 145–60.

[88] Becking, *Ezra, Nehemiah*, 46.

[89] See Venter, "Congruent Ethos," 11–12.

New from Mohr Siebeck

Journeys in the Roman East: Imagined and Real
Edited by Maren R. Niehoff
2017. XI, 440 pages (CRPG 1).
ISBN 978-3-16-155111-6 cloth
eBook

Seeing the God
Image, Space, Performance, and Vision in the Religion of the Roman Empire
Edited by Marlis Arnhold, Harry O. Maier, and Jörg Rüpke
2018. 300 pages (est.) (CRPG).
ISBN 978-3-16-155721-7 cloth (June)
eBook

Eva Cancik-Kirschbaum / Jochem Kahl
Erste Philologien
Archäologie einer Disziplin vom Tigris bis zum Nil
Unter Mitarbeit von Klaus Wagensonner
2018. XVI, 471 pages.
ISBN 978-3-16-155425-4 sewn paper
eBook

Ephesos
Die antike Metropole im Spannungsfeld von Religion und Bildung
Hrsg. v. Tobias Georges
2017. XII, 448 pages (COMES 2).
ISBN 978-3-16-152635-0 cloth
eBook

Reinhard Feldmeier
Hermann Spieckermann
Menschwerdung
2018. 440 pages (est.) (TOBITH).
ISBN 978-3-16-155776-7 sewn paper (May)
eBook

The Physicality of the Other
Masks from the Ancient Near East and the Eastern Mediterranean
Ed. by Angelika Berlejung and Judith E. Filitz
2018. X, 570 pages (ORA 27).
ISBN 978-3-16-155513-8 cloth
eBook

Izaak J. de Hulster
Figurines in Achaemenid Period Yehud
Jerusalem's History of Religion and Coroplastics in the Monotheism Debate
2017. XV, 225 pages (ORA 26).
ISBN 978-3-16-155550-3 cloth
eBook

Rüdiger Lux
Ein Baum des Lebens
Studien zur Weisheit und Theologie im Alten Testament
Hrsg. v. Angelika Berlejung u. Raik Heckl
2017. VIII, 377 pages (ORA 23).
ISBN 978-3-16-155377-6 cloth
eBook

Reettakaisa Sofia Salo
Die judäische Königsideologie im Kontext der Nachbarkulturen
Untersuchungen zu den Königspsalmen 2, 18, 20, 21, 45 und 72
2017. XV, 389 pages (ORA 25).
ISBN 978-3-16-155338-7 cloth
eBook

Information on Mohr Siebeck eBooks:
www.mohr.de/ebooks

Mohr Siebeck
Tübingen
info@mohr.de
www.mohr.de

Concluding the Book of Job and YHWH: Reading Job from the End to the Beginning

TROY W. MARTIN
martin@sxu.edu
Saint Xavier University, Chicago, IL 60655

Penitentialist, consolationist, and existentialist interpretations of Job read the concluding words of Job 42:2–6 as spoken by Job and then struggle to explain how these words form a coherent conclusion to the book. In this article, the narrative frame in 42:1, 7 is applied to its immediate context and understands Job as speaking the words in verses 2–4 but YHWH as uttering the statements in verses 5–6. Job's prosecutorial declaration in verse 4 that he will ask the questions and that YHWH will answer him signals the shift of speakers and allows Job to have his day in court. YHWH's announcement in verse 6a of the withdrawal of his case against Job marks an end to the legal proceedings, and his profound expression of repentance in dust and ashes in verse 6b provides redress for his unjust treatment of Job, which requires vindicating Job (42:7–9) and making restitution (42:10–17). This new perspective allows these final words in 42:2–6 to provide a coherent conclusion to the major issues in the book.

Job's interpreters generally agree that Job 42:2–6 represents the conclusion of the book and expend enormous effort trying to understand Job's final words as a coherent conclusion.[1] This effort results in a myriad of disagreements about what

I dedicate this article to my mother, LaValta Ruth Martin, and to Sr. Essie Gary, Rabbi Charles D. Isbell, and Prof. Jon D. Levenson, all of whom taught me how to read the Hebrew Bible. Avis Clendenen, Charles Gibson, Jeffrey Stackert, and John Burnight have been helpful conversation partners in the writing of this article, a version of which was presented at the 2016 Annual Meeting of the Midwest Region of the Society of Biblical Literature. I am grateful to those in attendance including JoAnn Scurlock, Richard H. Beal, Lowell K. Handy, Amie D. Littrell, and Lucas M. Weethee. Except where noted, the translations are either my own or from the RSV.

[1] Samuel E. Balentine, *Job*, SHBC (Macon, GA: Smyth & Helwys, 2006), 693; Edwin M. Good, *In Turns of Tempest: A Reading of Job with a Translation* (Stanford, CA: Stanford University Press, 1990), 375; David J. A. Clines, *Job*, 3 vols., WBC 17, 18A, 18B (Nashville: Nelson, 1989–2011), 3:1218; Jan P. Fokkelman, *The Book of Job in Form: A Literary Translation with Commentary*, SSN 58 (Leiden: Brill, 2012), 313; Tremper Longman III, *Job*, BCOTWP (Grand Rapids: Baker Academic, 2012), 448.

299

Job was attempting to say, "ranging from a statement of regret and repentance to a declaration of being consoled or of contempt of humanity … up to an expression of hope for being comforted after his death."[2] Carol A. Newsom even argues that these ambiguities are intentional to produce "ironic dissonance rather than coherency."[3] Such a "polyphonic" or "polysemous" conclusion to the book may satisfy postmodern relativism and inclusiveness. Any conclusion, however, that does not address the book's major issues will fail to satisfy at least some readers.[4] A satisfying conclusion may be in the eye of the beholder, but reading the book from the end to the beginning once again can provide a coherent alternative to the solutions already proposed.[5]

I. A Coherent Conclusion

Each interpreter tries to present an understanding of Job's final words as a coherent conclusion but does so by substituting a problem that differs from the one described in the book.[6] Penitentialists, who understand Job's final words as an expression of repentance, identify the problem as some defect in Job's character, such as sin, self-righteousness, hubris in challenging God, or lack of knowledge.[7]

---

[2] Thomas Krüger, "Did Job Repent?," in *Das Buch Hiob und seine Interpretationen: Beiträge zum Hiob-Symposium auf dem Monte Verità vom 14.–19. August 2005*, ed. Thomas Krüger et al. ATANT 88 (Zurich: TVZ, 2007), 217–29, here 217, 219.

[3] Carol A. Newsom, "The Book of Job: Introduction, Commentary, and Reflections," NIB 4:317–637, here 636.

[4] For *polyphonic*, see Carol A. Newsom, "Job," WBC, 208–15, here 209. For *polysemous*, see William Morrow, "Consolation, Rejection, and Repentance in Job 42:6," *JBL* 105 (1986): 211–25, here 223, https://doi.org/10.2307/3260390. For critique of postmodern approaches, see Charles Muenchow, "Dust and Dirt in Job 42:6," *JBL* 108 (1989): 597–611, here 598–99, https://doi.org/10.2307/3267182; Clines, *Job*, 3:1223; and Krüger, "Did Job Repent?," 222–23.

[5] This reading participates in a growing trend in Joban studies that understands the book as "a legal altercation between God and Job." See F. Rachel Magdalene, *On the Scales of Righteousness: Neo-Babylonian Trial Law and the Book of Job*, BJS 348 (Providence, RI: Brown Judaic Studies, 2007), 1–12; quotation from 2.

[6] James L. Crenshaw, "Job," in *The Oxford Bible Commentary*, ed. John Barton and John Muddiman (Oxford: Oxford University Press, 2001), 331–55, here 333. For the various approaches, see Mark Larrimore, *The Book of Job: A Biography*, Lives of Great Religious Books (Princeton: Princeton University Press, 2013), passim.

[7] For sin or self-righteousness, see John Chrysostom, *Comm. Job* 42:6, in *Job*, ed. Manlio Simonetti and Marco Conti, ACCSOT 6 (Downers Grove, IL: InterVarsity Press, 2006), 218; John E. Hartley, *The Book of Job*, NICOT (Grand Rapids: Eerdmans, 1988), 537. For hubris, see Longman, *Job*, 450; John D. W. Watts, John J. Owens, and Marvin E. Tate Jr., "Job," in *The Broadman Bible Commentary*, ed. Clifton J. Allen et al. (Nashville: Broadman, 1971), 4:22–151, here 149; Norman C. Habel, *The Book of Job: A Commentary*, OTL (Philadelphia: Westminster, 1985), 577. For lack of knowledge, see Michael V. Fox, "Job the Pious," *ZAW* 117 (2005): 351–66; Fox, "Reading

Whatever the subject of Job's repentance, penitentialist readings require that he in the end admit his defect and submit "to a power infinitely greater than himself" by uttering, "I repent in dust and ashes."[8]

Interpreters who see no defect in Job's character react strongly to penitentialist readings. For example, Jan P. Fokkelman says, "Therefore it is cuckoo in 42:6 to present a Job who buckles under pressure and to make him moan words that are totally unfounded and completely contrary to his character and personality." Fokkelman points out that the narrator (1:1, 22; 2:10), YHWH (1:8, 2:3, 42:7), and even Job himself (6:10, 24–30; 7:20; 9:14–24; 10:1–7; 12:1–6; 16:17; 23:10–12; 27:1–6; 29:11–25; 31:1–40) affirm that Job has done no wrong and that he is not even wrong in his assessment of God or the situation.[9] Job is blameless, as everyone in the book affirms except his friends, who are clearly wrong (42:7–9). A repentant Job cannot be the meaning of his final words, "for this is what his friends have been urging" but Job has been resisting all along.[10] These friends need repentance and expiatory sacrifices, but Job requires neither (42:7–8).[11] Francis I. Andersen says that if Job repents, "the whole story would collapse."[12] Penitentialist readings of Job's final words, therefore, do not provide a coherent conclusion for many scholars.

Seeking a more adequate conclusion, others propose that the deficiency is in the situation of mourning rather than in Job's character. For example, Dale Patrick argues that the preposition על with the verb נחם ("to repent") in 42:6 never designates the place of repentance but always refers to the object of repentance from which the penitent turns.[13] He rejects the traditional translation that Job repents "in dust and ashes" in favor of Job's repenting "of dust and ashes," explaining that this verse "expresses Job's intention of abandoning the posture of mourning." Others support this interpretation by pointing out that the verb נחם and its word group elsewhere in the book always refer to comfort, comforting, or consolation (2:11; 6:8–10; 7:13–14; 15:11; 16:2; 21:2, 34; 29:25; 42:11).[14] Thomas Krüger admits that

---

the Tale of Job (Job 1,1–2,13 + 42,7–17)," in *A Critical Engagement: Essays on the Hebrew Bible in Honour of J. Cheryl Exum*, ed. David J. A. Clines and Ellen van Wolde (Sheffield: Sheffield Phoenix, 2012), 145–62.

[8] Jon D. Levenson, *The Book of Job in Its Time and in the Twentieth Century*, The Le Baron Russell Briggs Prize Honors Essays in English 1971 (Cambridge: Harvard University Press, 1972), 1–2.

[9] Fokkelman, *Book of Job in Form*, 317.

[10] Good, *In Turns of Tempest*, 376.

[11] David A. Lambert, "The Book of Job in Ritual Perspective," *JBL* 134 (2015): 557–75, here 558, https://doi.org/10.15699/jbl.1343.2015.2878.

[12] Francis I. Andersen, *Job: An Introduction and Commentary*, TOTC 14 (Downers Grove, IL: InterVarsity Press, 1976), 315.

[13] Dale Patrick, "The Translation of Job XLII 6," *VT* 26 (1976): 369–71; L. J. Kaplan notes that Maimonides earlier proposed a consolationist reading ("Maimonides, Dale Patrick, and Job XLII 6," *VT* 28 [1978]: 356–58).

[14] Krüger, "Did Job Repent?," 223–24. Clines (*Job*, 3:1220) cites others who have a similar

the use of this verb in 42:6 could be an exception, but he does not think so.¹⁵ Most recently, David A. Lambert proposes that Job 42:6 describes "the renunciation of a ritual stance of mourning" as Job abandons his dust and ashes, drops his protest, and reintegrates into normal society.¹⁶ According to a consolationist reading, therefore, this verse marks the end of Job's mourning.

Not everyone is convinced, however, that such a reading of Job's final words adequately concludes the book. The most serious challenge is that Job's mourning does not end with verse 6 since his siblings and acquaintances come later to comfort and console him (42:11). Even some of those who adopt a consolationist reading recognize that it "contains one of the biggest surprises of the book."¹⁷ David J. A. Clines explains, "We have not been prepared by the course the book has taken to witness Job's abandoning his case against God. His arguments have been so cogent, his passion so sincere, that it is almost unthinkable that at the end of the day he should merely withdraw from the lawsuit."¹⁸ Clines perceptively recognizes that a consolationist reading of Job's final words leaves many of the issues raised in the book unresolved, and the reason for Job's abandoning his mourning is not entirely clear.

Some attempt to provide a reason. Fokkelman proposes that Job is consoled when he sees God.¹⁹ One wonders, however, how seeing the God who has caused him such pain would be consoling to Job rather than contributing even more to his perplexity. Ellen van Wolde attributes Job's consolation to a realization of his limited insight and his adopting YHWH's point of view.²⁰ The major problem with these proposals is that Job's mourning is occasioned by YHWH's prosecution of him (Job 1–2), and Job's final words, according to consolationist readings, do not mark an end to that prosecution. As long as the prosecution continues, Job cannot be consoled, and consolationist readings of Job's final words do not provide an entirely consistent conclusion to the book.

Even less coherent are existentialist readings that locate the problem neither in Job's defective character nor in Job's situation of mourning but rather in the nature of existence itself. J. Gerald Janzen proposes that Job changes his mind about his human condition while Edwin M. Good asserts that what Job abandons is the

---

understanding, including Ina Willi-Plein, "Hiobs Wiederruf?—Eine Untersuchung der Wurzel נחם und ihrer erzähltechnischen Funktion im Hiobbuch," in *Essays on the Bible and the Ancient World: Isac Leo Seeligmann Volume*, ed. Alexander Rofé and Yair Zakovitch, 3 vols. (Jerusalem: E. Rubinstein, 1983), 3:273–89; and Daniel J. O'Connor, "The Comforting of Job," *ITQ* 53 (1987): 245–57.

¹⁵ Krüger, "Did Job Repent?," 224.
¹⁶ Lambert, "Book of Job," 559, 572.
¹⁷ Clines, *Job*, 3:1222.
¹⁸ Ibid.
¹⁹ Fokkelman, *Book of Job in Form*, 318.
²⁰ Ellen van Wolde, "Job 42:1–6: The Reversal of Job," in *The Book of Job*, ed. W. A. M. Beuken, BETL 114 (Leuven: Leuven University Press, 1994), 223–50, here 250.

"entire structure of the world" in terms of guilt and innocence.²¹ James L. Crenshaw notes that "repenting of a world where repentance plays no role is hugely ironic."²² Indeed, many of these existentialist readings understand Job's final words as ironic or sarcastic.²³ John B. Curtis asserts, "With biting sarcasm and hostility Job declares it useless to try to talk to a god who is so concerned with great matters (like cosmology) that he does not even recognize that the small problems (like the suffering of the innocent) exist."²⁴ Curtis proposes that Job's final words represent a total rejection of an omnipotent deity who ignores "the complaints of a mere man."²⁵ Norman C. Habel thinks that Job exposes God "as a blind force and blustering orator who is threatened by Job's insights" and that an innocent Job repents just to mollify this God. According to Habel, Job's final words are "his final act of defiance," as he resists God even while speaking tongue in cheek.²⁶ Since they involve deconstruction of reality, rejection of God, or human defiance, these existentialist approaches to Job's conclusion seem odd for a book that takes so seriously the human condition of suffering and the divine–human relationship.²⁷

Nor do these readings of Job's final words provide a fitting conclusion to the major problem raised by the book. The book's plot is initiated and sustained by YHWH's prosecution of Job (chapters 1–2). YHWH's prosecution prompts Job to counter with a prosecution of his own as he demands to present his case against YHWH (13:3–19, 16:21, 23:1–17), who has treated him unjustly (2:3; 9:17, 22; 19:6; 29:1–31:40).²⁸ In whichever way the final words of Job in 42:2–6 are read, they should at a minimum provide an occasion for Job to present his case before YHWH,

---

²¹ J. Gerald Janzen, *Job*, IBC (Atlanta: John Knox, 1985), 6–57; Good, *In Turns of Tempest*, 377; Good, "The Problem of Evil in the Book of Job," in *The Voice from the Whirlwind: Interpreting the Book of Job*, ed. Leo G. Purdue and W. Clark Gilpin (Nashville: Abingdon, 1992), 50–69, here 68.

²² James L. Crenshaw, *Reading Job: A Literary and Theological Commentary*, Reading the Old Testament (Macon, GA: Smyth & Helwys, 2011), 159.

²³ For the former expression, see Good, *In Turns of Tempest*, 377. For the latter, see Habel, *Book of Job*, 577; Leo G. Purdue, *Wisdom and Creation: The Theology of Wisdom Literature* (Nashville: Abingdon, 1994), 180.

²⁴ John B. Curtis, "On Job's Response to Yahweh," *JBL* 98 (1979): 497–511, here 507, https://doi.org/10.2307/3265665.

²⁵ Ibid., 511. See also Leslie S. Wilson, *The Book of Job: Judaism in the 2nd Century BCE; An Intertextual Reading*, SJ(L) (Lanham, MD: University Press of America, 2006), 201–2.

²⁶ Habel, *Book of Job*, 577.

²⁷ See André LaCocque, "The Deconstruction of Job's Fundamentalism," *JBL* 126 (2007): 83–97, https://doi.org/10.2307/27638421. See the response to LaCocque by Philippe Guillaume, "Dismantling the Deconstruction of Job," *JBL* 127 (2008): 491–99, https://doi.org/10.2307/25610135.

²⁸ Edward L. Greenstein describes the proceedings as suit and countersuit ("A Forensic Understanding of the Speech from the Whirlwind," in *Texts, Temples, and Traditions: A Tribute to Menahem Haran*, ed. Michael V. Fox et al. (Winona Lake, IN: Eisenbrauns, 1996), 241–58, here 247.

they should designate the end of YHWH's prosecution of Job, and they should redress YHWH's unjust treatment of Job. Whatever else a coherent conclusion for the book may encompass, some resolution of these three main issues seems absolutely necessary. Although penitentialist, consolationist, and existentialist readings arrive at very different conclusions about Job's final words, they nevertheless all subscribe to a consensus that Job speaks all the words in 42:2–6 with perhaps an occasional quotation of God. This consensus needs rethinking if a coherent conclusion is to be found in the final words in 42:2–6.

II. A New Perspective

Interpretations of 42:2–6 rarely give full import to the narrative frame in 42:1, 7. Even though 42:1 introduces Job as the speaker, some interpreters designate verse 3a and verse 4 as YHWH's words that Job quotes even though the text provides no markers indicating a quotation.[29] For example, Fokkelman renders verse 3a as "[You said,] 'Who is this who obscures counsel without knowledge?'" Similarly, he translates verse 4 as "[You said,] 'Hear now for I am the one who will speak; I will ask you and you will let me know.'"[30] The quotation marker "You said" is not in the Hebrew text, although many translators add it since YHWH speaks similar words in 38:2–3 and 40:7.[31] Consequently, almost all translations place the words in verses 3a and 4 in quotation marks. Some others omit these words altogether as marginal glosses that have made their way into the text.[32] Interpretations that do not attribute all of the words in 42:2–4 to Job but rather eliminate verses 3a and 4 or see them as quotations do not give full import to the frame in 42:1.[33]

---

[29] For examples, see Andersen, *Job*, 314; Jeffrey Boss, *Human Consciousness of God in the Book of Job: A Theological and Psychological Commentary* (London: T&T Clark, 2010), 212; Janzen, *Job*, 251; Longman, *Job*, 424; Watts, Owens, and Tate, "Job," 148; James A. Wharton, *Job*, WeBC (Louisville: Westminster John Knox, 1999), 173; Claus Westermann, *The Structure of the Book of Job: A Form-Critical Analysis* (Philadelphia: Fortress, 1981), 125–26. See also Robert Gordis, *The Book of Job: Commentary, New Translation, and Special Studies*, Moreshet Series 2 (New York: Jewish Theological Seminary of America, 1978), 491, 573; and Mayer Gruber, "Job," in *The Jewish Study Bible*, ed. Adele Berlin and Marc Zvi Brettler (Oxford: Jewish Publication Society, 2004), 1499–1562, here 1561.

[30] Fokkelman, *Book of Job in Form*, 191, 193.

[31] Edward Ho cogently argues that such unmarked quotations are unlikely in a work that carefully places explicit markers elsewhere ("In the Eyes of the Beholder: Unmarked Attributed Quotations in Job," *JBL* 128 [2009]: 703–15, here 705, 714–15, https://doi.org/10.2307/25610215).

[32] Marvin H. Pope, *Job: Introduction, Translation, and Notes*, AB 15 (New York: Doubleday, 1973), 347–48; H. H. Rowley, *The Book of Job*, NCB (Grand Rapids: Eerdmans, 1983), 265. For a list of other versions, including the NAB, that omit 42:3a or 42:4, see Clines, *Job*, 3:1206 n. 4.a.

[33] Michael V. Fox notes that supposing unmarked attributed quotations can easily serve to mask or eliminate interpretive difficulties ("The Identification of Quotations in Biblical Literature,"

Similarly, interpreters do not give full import to the second part of this frame in 42:7, which reads, "And it happened after YHWH said these words to Job."[34] Now Job 42:1 clearly indicates that Job begins speaking, but 42:7 just as clearly states that God has just finished speaking. According to these verses, Job must have stopped speaking somewhere between verses 2 and 6 and God must have begun speaking. Not a single interpreter, however, understands verse 7 in this way. Some separate this verse from the preceding because verse 6 is poetry while verse 7 is prose and because the portrayal of Job in the poetic sections starkly contrasts with the prose sections.[35] Many understand the prose epilogue in 42:7–17 as well as the prologue in 1:1–2:13 as later additions that obviate the need to interpret verse 7 in relation to verse 6.[36] The majority, however, make little or no reference at all to the relationship of verse 7 to the preceding but simply ignore the explicit force of this verse in its immediate context.[37]

An exception is van Wolde, who comments, "It is odd that verse 7, which immediately follows this answer by Job, reports 'After YHWH had spoken these words to Job' … it is strange that it says that YHWH spoke, while Job has just been speaking." She explains that verse 7 points back to YHWH's speech from the storm "as if verses 1–6 have not taken place."[38] The obvious problem for her explanation is that verses 1–6 have "taken place" and cannot be so easily dismissed. Influenced by van Wolde, Clines comments on verse 7, "There is a strange opening to this narrative … for it is Job who has most recently been speaking. It is as if the Yahweh

---

ZAW 92 [1980]: 416–31, here 423). Ho ("In the Eyes," 705–6) agrees but then points out that even Fox himself resorts to such quotations because he cannot otherwise explain Job 42:3a, 4.

[34] One exception is the work of Manfred Oeming and Konrad Schmid, *Job's Journey: Stations of Suffering*, Critical Studies in the Hebrew Bible 7 (Winona Lake, IN: Eisenbrauns, 2015), 98–99, but they relate 42:7 to all of verses 2–6 rather than just to verses 5–6.

[35] Watts, Owens, and Tate, "Job," 150. The cantillation marks indeed shift from poetic in verse 6 to regular in verse 7, and the parasha petuha at the end of verse 6 clearly indicates that verse 7 begins a new section that should be placed on a new line. All of these marks, however, as well as the shift in Job's character do not preclude the narrative frame in verse 7 from referring to the poetic speech in verse 6.

[36] For examples, see Gordis, *Book of Job*, 573; and Edward L. Greenstein, "Job," in *The Jewish Study Bible*, 2nd ed., ed. Adele Berlin and Marc Zvi Brettler (Oxford: Oxford University Press, 2014), 1490. In contrast, Frank Crüsemann thinks that the poet himself inserted the oldest kernel of the narrative frame (Job 1:1–5, 13–22; 42:11–17) into his original work ("Hiob und Kohelet: Ein Beitrag zum Verständnis des Hiobbuches," in *Werden und Wirken des Alten Testaments: Festschrift für Claus Westermann zum 70. Geburtstag*, ed. Rainer Altertz et al. [Göttingen: Vandenhoeck & Ruprecht, 1980], 373–93, here 383–84). Westermann (*Structure of the Book*, 7) and others argue that the prose parts are essential to the book.

[37] Naphtali H. Tur-Sinai (Harry Torczyner) interprets 42:7 as a reference to what God said in chapter 18, which has been misplaced (*The Book of Job: A New Commentary*, rev. ed. [Jerusalem: Kiryat Sefer, 1967], 577–79). No manuscript evidence, however, supports his conjecture. See the critique of Tur-Sinai by Westermann, *Structure of the Book*, 19 n. 6.

[38] Van Wolde, "Job," 238.

of v 7 is ignoring what Job has said in his speech in vv 2–6."³⁹ Curiously, Clines blames YHWH for ignoring the explicit import of verse 7, but the blame must surely remain on those interpreters who refuse to relate verse 7 to its immediate context. Even though there is a growing trend in Job studies to read the book as a whole as being composed of a prose prologue and epilogue with poetic dialogue in between, interpreters persist in ignoring the explicit import of verse 7.⁴⁰ Allowing for the full import of 42:1 and 42:7 by applying this frame to its immediate context leads to a new perspective on the final words in 42:2–6. This perspective interprets the passage as a crisp dialogue between two litigants, Job and God, who battle it out in a rapid-fire exchange of words, and this reading provides a more coherent conclusion to the book than any proposed thus far.

III. Job's Final Words to YHWH (42:2–4)

According to 42:1, Job begins speaking in verse 2 with a direct response to YHWH's previous speeches from the storm (38:2–40:2, 40:7–41:26). The first speech emphasizing YHWH's omnipotent execution of his cosmic plans leaves Job silent with little to say in response (40:4–5).⁴¹ The second speech, however, focuses on YHWH's justice in executing his plans as YHWH asks a key question, "Will you even impugn my justice, deem me guilty so you can be innocent?"⁴² This question raises the pivotal issue in the litigation between Job and YHWH. The second speech, however, does not then address this issue directly but rather questions whether Job or YHWH has the power to bring the cosmos into line. Considering the Behemoth (40:15–24) and Leviathan (40:25–41:26), the obvious answer is only YHWH can do so.

Job appropriately begins his final words and responds in 42:2 to these two speeches by saying, "I know that you can do all things and that no scheme of yours is impossible."⁴³ Throughout the book, Job never questions YHWH's power, which is perfectly obvious to him as he experiences YHWH's destructive might in the loss

---

³⁹ Clines, *Job*, 3:1231. See also William D. Reyburn, *A Handbook on the Book of Job*, UBS Helps for Translators (New York: United Bible Societies, 1992), 774.

⁴⁰ See Fox, "Job the Pious," 351–66; Fox, "Reading the Tale," 145–62; Lambert, "Book of Job," 559; Yair Hoffman, "The Relation between the Prologue and the Speech-Cycles in Job: A Reconsideration," *VT* 31 (1981): 160–70; Rick D. Moore, "The Integrity of Job," *CBQ* 45 (1983): 17–31; Alan Cooper, "Reading and Misreading the Prologue to Job," *JSOT* 46 (1990): 67–79; and C. L. Seow, *Job 1–21: Interpretation and Commentary*, Illuminations (Grand Rapids: Eerdmans, 2013), 27–29.

⁴¹ Crenshaw, *Reading Job*, 149, 152.

⁴² Ibid. The translation is Crenshaw's.

⁴³ The noun מזמה can refer to a wicked plan or scheme (Job 21:27; Jer 11:15), and this meaning is appropriate to the context of this legal proceeding as Job casts aspersions on his rival litigant who has plotted to destroy him. See van Wolde, "Job," 239; and Clines, *Job*, 3:1205 n 2.b.

of his family, fame, fortune, and health. In Job's opinion, these legal proceedings have no need to waste any more time demonstrating this point since both litigants agree about YHWH's unrestrained power.[44]

Job's problem is not with YHWH's absolute power to control the cosmos but rather with YHWH's injustice toward him in particular.[45] YHWH's responses to Job from the storm (38:1–41:34) thus miss the point of Job's complaint.[46] After listening carefully to YHWH's responses, Job acknowledges his divine absolute power (42:2) but asks in 42:3a, "Who is this that hides counsel for lack of knowledge?" Words similar to these were spoken already by Elihu (35:16) and by YHWH (38:2) to state that Job's or perhaps Elihu's words have missed the point of the case.[47] Consequently, 42:3a is often considered a quotation of one or the other of these earlier utterances.[48] According to the new perspective, however, these words should be understood as Job's and not YHWH's or Elihu's. Edouard Dhorme and Edward Ho certainly take them that way.[49] In his final utterance (42:3a), therefore, Job throws these words back at YHWH to impugn YHWH as the one who has missed the point of the case by following a line of argumentation that merely defends divine power to rule the cosmos without specifically addressing YHWH's unjust treatment of Job.[50]

In his final utterance, Job succinctly states his problem. Because YHWH has hidden counsel and has not communicated in his two speeches the knowledge Job needs to understand his situation (42:3a), Job says, "I reported *your* disastrous deeds in respect to me and I do not understand *them* and I do not know *how you could do them to me*" (42:3b).[51] This translation is obviously interpretive but makes

---

[44] Interestingly, the *ketiv* might indicate a second person in reference to YHWH while the *qere* is first person in reference to Job. Taken together, therefore, both the uncorrected and the corrected text indicate that the knowledge of YHWH's omnipotence is known or agreed upon by both litigants, YHWH and Job.

[45] Gruber, "Job," 1555.

[46] Newsom, "Job," 208.

[47] Ludwig Köhler describes this strategy as a common feature of ancient legal proceedings (*Hebrew Man: Lectures Delivered at the Invitation of the University of Tübingen, December 1–16, 1952* [London: SCM, 1953], 161).

[48] On the ambiguity of the antecedent, see Clines, *Job*, 3:1095; and Crenshaw, *Reading Job*, 148.

[49] E. Dhorme, *A Commentary on the Book of Job* (1967; repr., Nashville: Nelson, 1984), 645; Ho, "In the Eyes," 711–14.

[50] Edward J. Kissane interprets the notion of darkening or hiding counsel in 38:2 and 42:3a in reference to previous statements that "tend to mislead" the hearers or "to lead them away from the true solution of the problem" (*The Book of Job: Translated from a Critically Revised Hebrew Text with Commentary* [Dublin: Browne & Nolan, 1939], 264 n. 2). See also Crüsemann, "Hiob," 379–80.

[51] Clines identifies the Hebrew term rendered as "reported" as a legal term in reference to a legal deposition, and he points out that Job said in 31:37 he would make his deposition if he were granted a hearing before YHWH (*Job*, 3:1204, 1211).

good sense of the grammar in the context of this legal proceeding. First, נפלאות, translated as "disastrous deeds," is the only explicitly stated object for all three verbs. Second, the disastrous deeds are clearly those of God and should be specified by the pronoun *your* added in the translation. Third, ממני can mark a number of relationships, and many translations render this preposition with its pronominal object as a comparative and translate "things too wonderful for me" (ASV, KJV, NAB, NASB, NIV, and RSV). The context, however, indicates that the divine deeds are not just those in general but those specifically pertaining to Job.[52] For these reasons, Job's words in 42:3b are best rendered, "I reported *your* disastrous deeds in respect to me and I do not understand *them* and I do not know *how you could do them to me.*"

This translation of 42:3b emphasizes that Job's problem is specifically with YHWH's disastrous deeds, which are usually called "wondrous deeds" in many other passages. These deeds are understood as positive by almost all interpreters. Thus, the Hebrew people celebrate YHWH's plagues against Egypt as wondrous deeds (Exod 3:20). As the beneficiaries of these deeds, the Hebrews deem them constructive wonders. From the Egyptians' point of view, however, these plagues are disastrous evils. Their water supply turns to blood, their crops are destroyed, their livestock perish, their bodies erupt in painful lesions, and the oldest son in each home dies. The Hebrews also celebrate YHWH's wondrous deeds in driving out the inhabitants of Canaan (Exod 34:10–11). For these inhabitants, however, YHWH's deeds are a terrifying experience of genocide. YHWH's wondrous deeds thus cut two ways. For the beneficiaries, they are truly *wondrous*; for the victims, however, they are disturbingly *disastrous* (cf. Dan 8:24). When recounting these deeds in respect to himself, Job often complains that YHWH counts him as an enemy (Job 13:24; 16:9; 19:11; cf. 27:7; 33:10). For Job, YHWH's deeds are not wondrous but disastrous.

Job's friends are convinced that whether one is the beneficiary or the victim of these deeds is determined by one's behavior. Job disagrees with them because he is righteous and yet has suffered the full weight of YHWH's disastrous deeds. Job finds no comfort or explanation for his situation in the doctrine of rewards and punishments but faces the terrifying prospect that YHWH acts and humans have no control over whether they will be the beneficiaries or the victims of these acts. Job thus testifies that he does not understand YHWH's deeds and he does not know them (42:3b).

What can Job mean by this testimony (42:3b)? He certainly knows YHWH's deeds well enough to recount them (42:3a), and he knows that YHWH can do them without any constraints (42:2). He has personally experienced them first hand in the loss of his family, fortune, fame, and health. What Job does not know is how to explain them and, more particularly, how YHWH could make his faithful devotee

---

[52] Cf. Westermann, *Structure of the Book*, 126–27.

the victim of these deeds. Job's particular problem is how to make sense of YHWH's deeds as they relate to him.

After succinctly stating his problem (42:3), Job now demands an answer of YHWH. Job insists, "Listen now, and I shall speak. I shall question you, and you will answer me" (v. 4). Scholars typically attribute these words to YHWH or eliminate them from the text altogether. Habel, however, argues persuasively that the words in verse 4 should not be omitted because "the verbal modifications in this verse as compared to 38:3 and 40:7 evidence that it is not a scribal repetition."[53] Like many other interpreters, Habel then explains verse 4 as a quotation of these two earlier statements of YHWH. This explanation, however, does not account for why Job would quote YHWH at this point or what such a quotation would mean.[54]

If spoken by Job as a direct prosecutorial challenge to YHWH, however, these words make good sense. Good perceptively observes, "If 42:4a is not a quotation of Yahweh but is Job's speaking in his own right, he may be seizing the opportunity to take the initiative in the trial as he had wished to do in chapter 13."[55] John E. Hartley also suggests that these words are "part of the formulaic request for a legal hearing."[56] Clines indeed places verse 4 in the genre category of "legal disputation," and he notes that the terms *listen, speak, question,* and *answer* all belong in a legal setting.[57] As Clines correctly perceives, the language of verse 4 often finds expression in legal proceedings as it is spoken by a litigant who takes the offensive and demands that the other litigant defend his or her actions. Words similar to these were spoken by YHWH from the storm in 38:3 and 40:7 when he came to prosecute Job and demanded, "Gird up your loins like a man. I shall question you and you will answer me."[58] The reference to girding up your loins as a man clearly indicates that YHWH is addressing Job in 38:3 and 40:7. This reference to a man, however, is lacking in 42:4 because Job now takes the offensive and initiates his prosecution of YHWH.[59]

Unless Job speaks the prosecutorial words in 42:4, Job never receives what he has demanded throughout the book.[60] Repeatedly, Job complains that YHWH has forced him into court and is prosecuting him even though he is innocent (9:1–35,

---

[53] Habel, *Book of Job*, 576. Similarly, Gordis, *Book of Job*, 492.
[54] Hartley, *Book of Job*, 536.
[55] Good, *In Turns of Tempest*, 372; Kissane, *Book of Job*, 292.
[56] Hartley, *Book of Job*, 536.
[57] Clines, *Job*, 3:1211.
[58] Magdalene understands the book of Job as an account of a legal proceeding and describes these questions as "an important rhetorical strategy" used by YHWH in the legal proceedings (*On the Scales*, 248–49). Greenstein says that they "sustain the juridical tenor of the proceedings" and are "precisely the language we would expect of a litigant drawing testimony out of a witness in cross-examination" ("Forensic Understanding," 253).
[59] Crenshaw, *Reading Job*, 157. Although he thinks Job is quoting God, Crenshaw nevertheless comments, "Because Job has listened to Yahweh for some time, he may ask for the same courtesy."
[60] Ho, "In the Eyes," 714.

10:1–22, 14:1–6, 16:1–22, 19:22, 27:1–6, 30:16–23). Job then wants to put YHWH on trial for treating him so unjustly (13:3–19, 16:21, 23:1–17).[61] Job states, "I have prepared my case; I know I shall be vindicated" (13:18). Job says, "I would present my case before him … and be delivered from my judge" (23:4, 7). Unless Job speaks the prosecutorial words in 42:4, he never gets to present his case before YHWH, and the book of Job ends on a disappointingly incomplete note.

In addition to the command to gird up his loins like a man, another significant difference between YHWH's prosecutorial words in 38:2 and 40:7 as contrasted with Job's in 42:4 is that YHWH's declaration "I shall ask the questions" is actually followed by questions while Job's is not.[62] This anomaly points to Job's being interrupted and indicates that the following words in 42:5–6 are an abrupt outburst of YHWH, as often happens in ancient as well as modern legal proceedings. One has only to think of the case of the two prostitutes who appear before Solomon with each claiming the live son as hers and the dead son as belonging to the other. The two women keep interrupting one another shouting, "No, the live one is mine, and the dead one yours" (1 Kgs 3:22). Job's prosecutorial declaration "I shall ask the questions, and you will answer me" is followed not by Job's questioning but by YHWH's outburst at long last answering Job's pressing question.

The riveting moment in this trial, indeed the climax of the book, is reached as YHWH finally takes the stand to defend his gross mistreatment of his faithful devotee. Understood as Job's prosecutorial challenge to YHWH, the words in 42:4 thus consummate Job's desire to place YHWH on trial and consequently provide one of the three requirements for a coherent conclusion for the book. These words, however, also signal a transition between Job's speech in verses 2–4 and YHWH's speaking in verses 5–6 and obviate the need for an introductory formula for YHWH's reply. Indeed, the lack of such a formula for verses 5–6 juxtaposes the repartee between these two litigants, intensifies YHWH's outburst, and effectively heightens this poignant courtroom scene when the two finally come head to head over the real issue of this case. Job's persistence finally pays off, and YHWH answers Job—but not as Job or anyone else could have predicted.

IV. YHWH's Final Reply (42:5–6)

YHWH responds in 42:5, "I had heard of you by the hearing of the ear, but now my eye sees you." These words contrast the less reliable information obtained from hearsay with the much more reliable information acquired from direct

---

[61] Larrimore, *Book of Job*, 2; Edward L. Greenstein, "Truth or Theodicy? Speaking Truth to Power in the Book of Job," *PSB* 27 (2006): 238–58, here 249; Greenstein, "When Job Sued God," *BAR* 38.3 (2012): 55–57; Greenstein, "Forensic Understanding," 241–58.

[62] Crenshaw, *Reading Job*, 157.

observation.⁶³ YHWH's response refers to the beginning of the book, when the satan accuses Job of not being a true devotee but rather of serving YHWH only for benefits (1:9–11). YHWH has no comeback to the accusation but instructs the satan to prosecute Job (1:12). In the beginning, YHWH has incomplete knowledge and has heard of Job only from hearsay but lacks the relational experience with Job to say, "Now my eye sees you."⁶⁴ After YHWH's prosecution of Job, YHWH now sees Job for who he really is. Job is a tried and true, faithful devotee, and he has proven himself by maintaining his integrity throughout all his afflictions.

YHWH's response continues in 42:6, and "perhaps no verse has occasioned more discussion than this one."⁶⁵ Krüger notes, "The semantic ambiguity of Job 42:6 results mainly from the ambiguity of the two verbs in this verse and of the overarching syntax of the two sections constituted by them."⁶⁶ Krüger then lists three possible translations of the verb אמאס in 42:6a:

1. I reject (or despise) dust and ashes.
2. I reject (or despise) my former thoughts and statements.
3. I dissolve (or melt away)—in the sense of dying away or perhaps giving up.⁶⁷

The first two possibilities as contrasted with the third point to a disagreement among interpreters as to whether the verb אמאס is from the root מאס ("to reject" or "to despise") or from the root מסס ("to melt" or "to dissolve").⁶⁸ Of the two roots, the former is more appropriate to legal proceedings and thus more likely in the context of the dispute between YHWH and Job.⁶⁹

The first two possibilities for translating the transitive verb אמאס emphasize the need to specify a direct object for this transitive verb.⁷⁰ Although Krüger provides objects for this verb in his translation, the Hebrew text does not, and this ellipsis opens the door to numerous suggestions. The Septuagint translator supplies

---

⁶³ Dhorme, *Commentary on the Book of Job*, 646; Pope, *Job*, 348; Robert Gordis, *The Book of God and Man: A Study of Job* (Chicago: University of Chicago Press, 1969), 305; Gordis, *Book of Job*, 491.

⁶⁴ Gordis (*Book of Job*, 491), Hartley (*Book of Job*, 536), Newsom ("Book of Job," 629–30), Pope (*Job*, 348), and Watts, Owens, and Tate ("Job," 149) all see a contrast in this verse while Clines (*Job*, 3:1205, 1216–17) construes the two verbs as coordinate.

⁶⁵ Longman, *Job*, 449–50; Fokkelman, *Book of Job in Form*, 317.

⁶⁶ Krüger, "Did Job Repent?," 213.

⁶⁷ Ibid., 218. See also Morrow, "Consolation, Rejection," 211–12 and Newsom, "Book of Job," 629.

⁶⁸ For a discussion of these roots, see Clines, *Job*, 3:1207–8. For arguments favoring the root מאס, see Morrow, "Consolation, Rejection," 213–15.

⁶⁹ Pope, *Job*, 349.

⁷⁰ Of course, the verb could be intransitive as Janzen (*Job*, 251) and Boss (*Human Consciousness*, 212) think, or it could be reflexive as Hartley (*Book of Job*, 537) and Longman (*Job*, 424, 499) understand.

ἐμαυτόν ("myself") in reference to Job, as does Gordis, while others understand Job to be rejecting his previous argumentative words and questions or to be rejecting even God.⁷¹ A recent trend construes the prepositional phrase עַל־עָפָר וָאֵפֶר ("upon dust and ashes") at the end of the verse as the object of the verb אמאס and thus understands Job to be rejecting dust and ashes.⁷² This construal of the syntax would be more persuasive if the preposition were ב or מן or if the words "dust and ashes" were in the accusative without a preposition. Nevertheless, all of these suggestions arise from attributing the verb אמאס to Job.⁷³ According to the new perspective, however, YHWH says this verb, and its unstated object must be derived from the legal case YHWH is prosecuting against Job.

Although he views these words as Job's, Habel nevertheless reasons, "If, however, we recognize the legal framework of Job's response, then a clue as to the object of the verb *mʾs* may be found in 31:13, where Job asserts that he did not 'dismiss/reject' the case (*mišpāṭ*) of his manservant." Habel then applies his observation to the verb אמאס in 42:6a and states, "The implied object in the present context, therefore, would appear to be Job's case against God, which he 'dismisses/retracts.'"⁷⁴ Habel thus identifies Job's legal case as the object of the verb אמאס and understands this verb to be expressing Job's dismissing his case. Similarly, Fokkelman understands Job to be giving up his legal case and simply saying, "I quit."⁷⁵ Clines also interprets Job's words as withdrawing "his lawsuit against Yahweh," and Sylvia Huberman Scholnick likewise sees 42:6 as a "retraction of Job's lawsuit."⁷⁶

Moving the insight of these scholars from Job as the speaker to the new perspective in which YHWH is the speaker means that YHWH's uttering the word אמאס announces the withdrawal of his case against Job. No direct object need be stated in the context of this legal proceeding because all a litigant need declare in the course of the proceedings is אמאס, and the case is over.⁷⁷ YHWH initiated these proceedings, and only YHWH can determine when his prosecution is at an end. This single-word declaration tersely brings to a close the legal proceedings that have driven the action of the entire book since the beginning, and this announcement

---

⁷¹ Gordis, *Book of Job*, 491. For Job's rejecting his arguments, see Lester J. Kuyper, "The Repentance of Job," *VT* 9 (1959): 91–94. For a list of others who follow Kuyper's suggestion, see Morrow, "Consolation, Rejection," 217 n. 21. For Job's rejecting his questions, see Balentine, *Job*, 692; and for Job's rejecting God, see Curtis, "On Job's Response," 504.

⁷² Patrick, "Translation of Job XLII 6," 369–71. See also Good, *In Turns of Tempest*, 376.

⁷³ For further critique, see Clines, *Job*, 3:1218–19.

⁷⁴ Habel, *Book of Job*, 576.

⁷⁵ Fokkelman, *Book of Job in Form*, 317.

⁷⁶ Clines, *Job*, 3:1218–19. Sylvia Huberman Scholnick, "The Meaning of *MIŠPAṬ* in the Book of Job," *JBL* 101 (1982): 521–29, here 521, https://doi.org/10.2307/3260896.

⁷⁷ Köhler explains, "Before the legal assembly the speech and counterspeech continue back and forth until one party has nothing more to say" (*Hebrew Man*, 159–60). YHWH has reached this point and is the defeated litigant. Contra Greenstein ("Forensic Understanding," 253) and Magdalene (*On the Scales*, 259–62), who think Job is defeated.

thus provides the second of the three constituents for a coherent conclusion by marking the end of YHWH's prosecution of Job.

Just as he listed three possibilities for translating the first verb אמאס in 42:6a, Krüger also lists three possibilities for the second verb נחמתי in the second half of this verse. He states that all of the following translations seem possible for 42:6b:

1. I regret (or am sorry because of) —
   a. dust and ashes
   b. my former thoughts and statements—in dust and ashes
2. I console myself —
   a. about dust and ashes
   b. in dust and ashes
3. I repent in dust and ashes.[78]

Krüger states that the semantics of the verb נחמתי cannot decide among these translations since this verb encompasses all three notions of being sorry, consoling oneself, and repenting. Interpreters are then forced to rely on their understanding of the context, and, not surprisingly therefore, no agreement has been reached about the meaning of this verb.[79] As long as interpreters remain committed to reading נחמתי as spoken by Job, they will likely remain deadlocked over the meaning of this verb without any apparent means of resolution.

The new perspective that understands נחמתי as spoken by YHWH, however, allows for a resolution. The meaning "console myself" is the least likely of the three possibilities listed by Krüger since the book does not describe YHWH as a sufferer in need of consolation. Options 1 and 3 therefore remain the most likely, and these two options are not completely incompatible since sorrow is often an emotion that accompanies repentance.[80] Nevertheless, the third option provides a more coherent conclusion to the book since YHWH is the one in the relationship who needs to repent, for YHWH is the only one who has mistreated the other relational partner—although a repentant YHWH can then demand repentance from Job's three friends for their wrongdoing as well (42:7–9).

Whereas Job's righteousness is upheld throughout the book, YHWH behaves unjustly and even indicts himself by saying to the satan, "Job still steadfastly maintains his integrity although you incited me to destroy him without cause" (2:3).[81]

---

[78] Krüger, "Did Job Repent?," 218. See also Morrow, "Consolation, Rejection," 211–12; and Newsom, "Book of Job," 629.

[79] Greenstein illustrates this lack of agreement by rejecting all other translations and then translating, "I take pity on wretched humanity" ("Job," 1555). See also Greenstein, "The Problem of Evil in the Book of Job," in *Mishneh Todah: Studies in Deuteronomy and Its Cultural Environment in Honor of Jeffrey H. Tigay*, ed. Nili Sacher Fox, David A. Glatt-Gilad, and Michael J. Williams (Winona Lake, IN: Eisenbrauns, 2009), 333–62, here 358–60.

[80] Morrow, "Consolation, Rejection," 216 n. 17.

[81] Greenstein, "Problem of Evil," 241–42.

Destroying someone without cause is an admission of unjust behavior. Job certainly accuses YHWH of injustice for wounding him without cause (9:17) and for destroying the innocent and the guilty together (9:22). Job states emphatically, "YHWH has wronged me" (19:6). Job's last words to his friends describe in detail his righteous life and friendship with YHWH, who has for no reason become his enemy (29:1–31:40).[82] In this relationship, YHWH has acted unjustly and needs to repent.[83]

The dialogues between Job and his friends further confirm the need for YHWH's repentance. Job's three friends, Eliphaz, Bildad, and Zophar, all defend YHWH's justice and insist that Job must have sinned for YHWH to destroy him as he did. Eliphaz (4:7) asks Job, "Whoever perished who was innocent?" Job challenges Eliphaz to show him where he has sinned (6:24), but Eliphaz cannot. Bildad insists that YHWH does not pervert justice but judges justly (8:3) and that, if Job were upright, YHWH would defend him (8:5–7). Job responds that YHWH has indeed wounded him without cause (9:17), declared him guilty even though he is not (9:20), and destroyed the innocent and the guilty together (9:22). Job does not agree with Bildad that YHWH judges justly. Zophar defends YHWH by saying that the punishment Job has received from YHWH is less than Job's guilt deserves (11:4). Job disagrees and answers Zophar by saying that he is prepared to argue his case and innocence before YHWH (13:3).

Job's three friends astutely realize that, if Job is righteous, YHWH cannot be, for YHWH is punishing Job without cause. Job resolutely maintains his righteousness, and his three friends finally fall silent (32:1). At the end of the book, YHWH determines who is right and says to Eliphaz, "My wrath is inflamed against you and your two friends because you have not spoken the truth about me as my servant Job has" (42:7). YHWH disagrees with Job's three friends that YHWH has acted justly toward Job. Instead, YHWH agrees with Job that YHWH is in the wrong.[84] The dialogues between Job and his friends thus further confirm YHWH's need of repentance.

One additional feature supports understanding YHWH's repentance in 42:6b. Just after this expression of repentance, YHWH makes twofold restitution to Job (42:10–17). In the Covenant Code, twofold restitution is stipulated for someone who unjustly deprives another of property. Exodus 22:4 reads, "If something he

---

[82] Crüsemann, "Hiob," 375.

[83] Several passages indicate that God does not or cannot repent (Num 23:19, Ps 110:4, Jer 4:28, Ezek 24:14, Zech 7:14–15). Just as many or more passages, however, affirm God's repenting (Gen 6:6–7; Exod 32:7–14; 2 Sam 24:16; Ps 90:13; Jer 18:7–8; 18:10; 26:3, 13, 19; 42:10; Amos 7:3, 6; Jonah 3:10). Considering this ambiguity, Joel (2:14) and the king of Nineveh (Jonah 3:9) appropriately ask, "Who knows whether God will repent?" This ambiguity is reflected in 1 Sam 15:29, which reads, "The Glory of Israel will not lie or repent, for he is not a human that he should repent." Just a few verses later, however, YHWH repents for having made Saul king (1 Sam 15:35). These passages thus affirm that God does repent and that repentance is not impossible for God. The notion of God's repenting in Job 42:6b is therefore neither impossible nor unusual.

[84] Greenstein, "Truth or Theodicy?," 256–57.

stole is actually found alive in his possession, he shall repay double." YHWH replaces Job's fortunes twofold, restores children to Job, and gives Job a long and healthy life (42:10–17). If YHWH had acted justly toward Job, YHWH would have no need to make these reparations. YHWH's restitution is therefore a legal admission that he had unjustly murdered Job's children, stolen his property, and afflicted him with illness. Of all this injustice toward Job, YHWH repents in 42:6b.

YHWH does not merely repent and make restitution, but YHWH repents עַל־עָפָר וָאֵפֶר ("in dust and ashes"). Some interpreters reject the locative understanding of this prepositional phrase since the preposition עַל with the verb נחם elsewhere forms an idiom expressing some action or intention of which YHWH repents or changes his mind (e.g., Jer 18:8, 10). Charles Muenchow argues, however, that everywhere this idiom occurs, "the object of the preposition is a noun denoting a mental construct (thought, plan, idea), never a physical object" such as dust and ashes.[85] He further argues, "By placing the *athnach* where they did, the Masoretes clearly did not see in 42:6 an instance of the ... idiom, and the judgment of the Masoretes on this point is sound."[86] Muenchow points out the unique use of this prepositional phrase in 42:6b with a physical object and consequently argues for the locative sense. He further adduces the role of dust and ashes in gestures of repentance in support of a locative understanding. When the king of Nineveh repents, for example, he sits in ashes (יֵשֶׁב עַל־הָאֵפֶר; Jonah 3:6), and Muenchow sees a similar locative sense for the prepositional phrase in Job 42:6b.

Even though a unique instance, a locative understanding of this prepositional phrase with the verb נחם in Job 42:6b best fits the context.[87] YHWH's unjust actions against Job have driven Job to sit in ashes (2:8) and to feel as though he had become dust and ashes (30:19). YHWH now takes his place next to Job on the ash heap (42:6). YHWH's unjust actions have driven them both to the same place of diminution, but in this place of diminution, Job hears YHWH's expression of repentance for treating him unjustly. In this context, the relational function of the verb נחם plays a significant role in enabling Job to turn from being a combative litigant and to rise from the ash heap and resume a positive relationship with YHWH. The relational function of this verb is clearly seen in the interplay between the verbs נחם ("repent") and שוב ("turn") in passages such as Jer 18:7–11, where a change of direction by one relational partner results in a change in the other as well, and so

---

[85] Muenchow, "Dust and Dirt," 609–10 n. 53.

[86] Ibid. Van Wolde, however, understands the *athnah* as indicating that the prepositional phrase provides the object for both verbs in 42:6 ("Job," 244). Since the *athnah* does not separate the preposition from the verb in the idiom, Muenchow's observation is sound that 42:6 is different because the *athnah* indicates a separation. His explanation is therefore preferred.

[87] YHWH's repentance in dust and ashes is indeed unique to the Hebrew Bible, but so is YHWH's act of restitution to someone for mistreating them. Both of these unique actions emphasize the profound depth and the genuineness of YHWH's repentance.

it is with Job when he hears YHWH's expression of repentance.[88] YHWH's repentance and subsequent restitution make it possible for them both to exit the ash heap and resume their relationship. In the end, their relationship is more than in the beginning (42:12).[89]

YHWH's words in 42:5–6 are indeed the high point and crucial moment in this trial. On the basis (עַל־כֵּן; 42:6) of his new insight provided by the legal proceedings and his now seeing Job for who he really is (42:5), YHWH announces to Job, "I withdraw *my prosecution of you* and repent in dust and ashes" (42:6). In these legal proceedings, YHWH retracts and capitulates and decides not to continue his prosecution or to mount any further defense. During the proceedings, YHWH had asked Job (40:8), "Will you indeed put me in the wrong? Will you condemn me that you may be justified?" YHWH perceives the clear alternative that either Job or YHWH is just but that both cannot be. In the end, YHWH withdraws his case and recognizes Job as the righteous litigant. YHWH accepts the verdict that he is unjust, and he takes responsibility for treating Job unjustly. YHWH owns stretching forth his hand to destroy Job without cause (2:3), repents in dust and ashes (42:6), and makes the necessary legal restitution (42:10–17).

V. Job and Ludlul Bēl Nēmeqi: A Comparative Analogy

Support for this new perspective in reading Job 42:1–7 may be found in the Babylonian poem of the righteous sufferer that is entitled Ludlul Bēl Nēmeqi.[90] The author of Job certainly could have been familiar with this "well-known, widely-diffused, and highly valued poem."[91] Although the poem is generally dated several centuries before the exilic or postexilic dating of Job, more than "fifty tablets or fragments, dating to the first half of the first millennium BCE, from seven different ancient cities preserve its text."[92] Some of these tablets indicate that this poem was used in the training of scribes and thus was part of the scribal curriculum. Amar Annus and Alan Lenzi contend that during the first millennium BCE, "every advanced scribe would have read sections of *Ludlul* just as every high school student reads Shakespeare today." Other tablets of this poem from royal and scholarly libraries "confirm the poem's learned origins and social capital for cultural and

---

[88] God's complete change of mood is rapid, but such is the nature of repentance. For example, see the swift and total change of the Ninevites to Jonah's terse message (Jonah 3:1–10).

[89] Oeming and Schmid, *Job's Journey*, 101.

[90] JoAnn Scurlock first pointed me to the analogy of Ludlul, and Richard H. Beal kindly provided me with the text and English translation of this poem.

[91] Amar Annus and Alan Lenzi, *Ludlul Bēl Nēmeqi: The Standard Babylonian Poem of the Righteous Sufferer: Introduction, Cuneiform Text, and Transliteration with a Translation and Glossary*, SAACT 7 (Winona Lake, IN: Eisenbrauns, 2010), ix.

[92] Ibid.

political elites."[93] Both spatially and temporally, the Joban author could have had access to this poem, and Jacob Kaaks comments, "*Ludlul* ... was certainly the model for the Book of Job."[94]

The structure of Ludlul is largely a monologue and differs so significantly from Job's dialogical structure that any direct literary influence cannot be posited. Both texts, however, reflect a similar theme; both approach the problem of human suffering by focusing on a single person who is described as righteous.[95] In Ludlul, the righteous devotee Subsi-mesre-Sakkan endures the loss of status, wealth, and health as does Job. His suffering is blamed on falling afoul of the deity but for no apparent sin. His restoration is attributed to a turn or change in the deity's attitude and affections toward him, and this similarity between the two works has some bearing on the interpretation of Job 42:5–6.

The poem Ludlul begins with these lines:

> I will praise the lord of wisdom, the cir[cumspect] god
> Angry at night but relenting at daybreak.
> Marduk, the lord of wisdom, the circumspect god,
> Angry at night but relenting at daybreak. (Ludlul, I 1–4)[96]

These lines set the tone for the entire poem and present a deity of contrasts. Marduk may cause his righteous devotee pain and suffering for a time but then relents or repents and makes a decided turn to restore his devotee. Marduk is the god "who in his anger is irresistible, his fury a flood, but his mind turns back, his mood relents" (Ludlul, I 7–8). Similar perhaps to Job 42:5, this change in Marduk is attributed to his noticing or seeing his devotee, who exclaims, "He [Marduk] frowns: the divine guardian and protective spirit withdraw; he takes notice: his god turns back to him whom he had rejected" (I 15–16). After Marduk takes notice, he restores divine protection to his devotee, who testifies, "[He who] struck me, Marduk, restored me (lit., raised up my head)" (IV 10–11). This restoration is attributed to a change in Marduk toward his devotee, who explains, "After the heart of my lord was st[ill], the min[d of] merciful Marduk was app[eased]. After [he accept]ed my prayer ... his [bene]volent attention was sweet" (III 51–54).[97]

By applying 42:1, 7 to its immediate context, we encounter in the book of Job a similar God of contrasts. YHWH prosecutes his righteous devotee mercilessly but then takes notice or sees him (ראתך; 42:5). After this reference to YHWH's seeing, the very next words at the beginning of 42:6 are על־כן, which "even more

---

[93] Ibid.

[94] Jacob Kaaks, *Job and the God of Babylon: Theo-Politics, the Covenant and the Fall of Marduk* (Delft: Eburon, 2011), 36.

[95] Ibid. Kaaks, however, points out that Shubsi-mesre-Shakkan "assumes he has done something wrong, perhaps without realizing it" while "Job considers himself righteous."

[96] Annus and Lenzi, *Ludlul Bēl Nēmeqi*, 31.

[97] Ibid., 31, 42, 39.

than ל־כן marks the causal relation of what went before and what follows."⁹⁸ YHWH's seeing Job with his eye for who Job really is *causes* YHWH to have a change of heart, mind, and attitude toward Job. On the basis of this seeing, YHWH withdraws (אמאס) his case against Job and relents or repents (נחמתי) in dust and ashes (42:6). This change in YHWH prompts him to make restitution and restore the fortunes of Job (42:10, 12–17). YHWH's "turn" or "repentance" enables Job "to turn" and to be comforted by his family and friends (42:11), something Eliphaz, Bildad, and Zophar were unable to accomplish when the God-of-Contrasts was in prosecutorial rather than conciliatory mode. Reading Job from this new perspective points to some striking similarities between this book and Ludlul, the Babylonian poem of the righteous sufferer and his relationship with a god of contrasts, and these similarities support reading Job according to this new perspective.

VI. Conclusion

The final enigmatic words in Job 42:2–6 are indeed by all accounts the climax and conclusion of the book and almost require the modern interpreter to read this book from the end to the beginning and back again. These words allow Job to present his case before YHWH; they mark an end of YHWH's prosecution of Job; and they redress YHWH's unjust treatment of Job. In doing so, they tie up the loose ends of the narrative and provide a sense of closure to the book as a whole.

Job's prosecutorial declaration in 42:4 depicts Job as having his day in court to prosecute YHWH for injustice. Job's words in 42:4 thus supply the first constituent of a coherent conclusion for the book. YHWH's word of response in 42:6a that tersely announces the withdrawal of his case against Job satisfies the second constituent of such a conclusion by ending the litigation. Finally, YHWH's words in 42:6b that present YHWH as repenting in dust and ashes supply the third and final constituent of a coherent conclusion by redressing his mistreatment of Job. YHWH's vindication of Job in 42:7–9 and his making the necessary legal restitution in 42:10–17 further emphasize the profound depth and earnestness of YHWH's repentance. The legalities at an end and justice restored, the book concludes with the two no longer as combative litigants but as once again faithful devotee and benevolent deity.⁹⁹

---

⁹⁸ Van Wolde, "Job," 248. See also, Fokkelman, *Book of Job in Form*, 317.

⁹⁹ Köhler states that the "sole endeavor" of the legal assembly "is to settle quarrels" and that the most important matter is the safeguarding of community and justice (*Hebrew Man*, 156, 165). In the end, the trial of Job achieves all of these.

Wolf and Lamb as Hyperbolic Blessing: Reassessing Creational Connections in Isaiah 11:6–8

JOSHUA J. VAN EE
jvanee@wscal.edu
Westminster Seminary California, Escondido, CA 92027

Isaiah 11:6–8 is commonly interpreted as an allusion to a creation paradise characterized by peace among the animals. In this article I offer three arguments to counter such an allusion. First, a blessing that depicts cosmic changes does not fit well with the royal prophecy in verses 1–5, which focus on judicial changes. Based on parallel texts found elsewhere in the Hebrew Bible and the ancient Near East, this-worldly blessings are expected in the context of a royal prophecy. Second, there are no creational texts in the Hebrew Bible or the ancient Near East similar enough in their descriptions to form the background for an allusion in Isa 11:6–8. I will evaluate the various parallels cited by commentators and question their relevance. Third, the imagery of Isa 11:6–8 does not fit with a creational animal peace theme. A close reading indicates that these verses focus on security for human interests, not animal peace in general, with the wild animals described as domesticated, not just peaceful. Further, there is no indication of a return to vegetarianism for humans. Thus, I suggest that the focus of the imagery is not on a restored creation but on the absence of divinely implemented curses. It is a portrayal of blessedness through the removal of the curse of devouring animals. In contrast to similar blessings elsewhere in the Hebrew Bible, the animals themselves are not removed. Instead, in a unique hyperbolic turn, the animals formerly feared by humans are described as domesticated, providing a poignant image of safety and security for Israel.

The reader of Isa 11:6–8 is confronted by a crux: how to interpret dangerous wild animals that are not behaving in a dangerous or wild manner. The description does not match the world as we know it, and so we are compelled to decide if it is figurative or a realistic description of a different time or state of the world. It is no surprise that commentators throughout the centuries have not agreed on a solution.

In this article, I will engage with the various interpretations offered, situating my own hyperbolic view among them. The question in which I am most interested, however, concerns the source of the imagery. Many (if not most) modern commentators interpret Isa 11:6–8 as alluding to a creation paradise of animal peace, a time before predation and hostility among the animals and between animals and humans. Thus, they argue that the motif of animal peace in these verses is at least partially based on descriptions of a creation paradise. In the analysis below, I will question this broad consensus and then offer an alternative source for the imagery: the blessing and curse tradition in which harm from animals is a punishment and safety is a reward.

Before proceeding, it is helpful to state briefly my views on the composition of Isa 11:6–8 in the larger context of verses 1–9. First, I am not convinced that any part of verses 1–9 is clearly exilic or postexilic. The reasons given for dating verses 1–5 after the exile—the stump imagery, the connection between the spirit of YHWH and the king, and the language—are inconclusive.[1] Issues involving verses 6–9 will be discussed later. Nevertheless, such a position is not essential for my main argument about the source of the imagery and thus is not a focus of this essay. Second, I will argue for the coherence of verses 1–9. There is therefore no reason to posit diverse origins. This unity is more important to my main argument, although again not essential.

I. Allegorical Interpretations

For present purposes, it is helpful to distinguish allegorical and nonallegorical interpretations of Isa 11:6–8. A number of ancient Christian commentators identify the various animals with different types of people that are brought together in the church.[2] A few modern scholars interpret the animal imagery as a depiction of the new peaceful relations of people generally or of the nations with Israel.[3] Some interpretations are better described as semiallegorical since they understand the

---

[1] For helpful comments on these issues, see Hans-Jürgen Hermisson, "Zukunftserwartung und Gegenwartskritik in der Verkündigung Jesajas," *EvT* 33 (1973): 54–77, here 61–63; J. Vermeylen, *Du prophète Isaïe à l'apocalyptique: Isaïe, I–XXXV, miroir d'un demi-millénaire d'expérience religieuse en Israël*, 2 vols., EBib (Paris: Gabalda, 1977–1978), 1:270, 273; Hans Wildberger, *Isaiah 1–12: A Commentary*, trans. Thomas H. Trapp, CC (Minneapolis: Fortress, 1991), 466–70; Paul D. Wegner, *An Examination of Kingship and Messianic Expectation in Isaiah 1–35* (Lewiston, NY: Mellen, 1992), 232–33, 263–65; Christopher R. Seitz, *Isaiah 1–39*, IBC (Louisville: John Knox, 1993), 96–98.

[2] E.g., Eusebius of Caesarea, Jerome, Chrysostom, Gregory the Great (see Steven A. McKinion, ed., *Isaiah 1–39*, ACCSOT 10 [Downers Grove, IL: InterVarsity Press, 2004], 105–8).

[3] Martin Rehm, *Der königliche Messias im Licht der Immanuel-Weissagungen des Buches Jesaja*, ESt NF 1 (Kevelaer: Butzon & Bercker, 1968), 216–18; Marjo C. A. Korpel, "The Messianic King: Isaiah 10:33–11:10," in *Enigmas and Images: Studies in Honor of Tryggve N. D. Mettinger*, ed. Göran Eidevall and Blaženka Scheuer, ConBOT 58 (Winona Lake, IN: Eisenbrauns, 2011), 147–59, here 151–54; Seitz, *Isaiah 1–39*, 106–7.

imagery as referring to animals but argue that it primarily implies a similar change in people.[4]

In general, allegorical interpretations do not involve an allusion to a primeval animal peace; instead, the imagery is connected with the use of animals elsewhere in the Hebrew Bible to designate people and nations.[5] In the context, peace among humans fits well as a blessing for the reign of a coming king (vv. 1–5), although it needs to be reconciled with the description of the king smiting the wicked (v. 4).[6] Some commentators claim that verse 9 clarifies the author's allegorical purpose since the lack of harm and destruction is founded upon the knowledge of YHWH, something not applicable to animals.[7]

Nevertheless, the major shortcoming of an allegorical interpretation is that it fails to explain the content of the imagery—the interactions of the dangerous wild animals with both domesticated animals and humans. If the various animals represent humans or nations, why do human figures also appear in these verses? In a biblical allegory, we would expect a contrast between wild and domestic animals or between animals and humans, not both.[8] Thus, most recent commentators rightly argue for a nonallegorical interpretation, although with a number of variations.

---

[4] Ronald E. Clements, "The Wolf Shall Live with the Lamb: Reading Isaiah 11:6–9 Today," in *New Heaven and New Earth: Prophecy and the Millennium; Essays in Honour of Anthony Gelston*, ed. P. J. Harland and Robert Hayward, VTSup 77 (Leiden: Brill, 1999), 83–99, here 99; Bernd Janowski, "Der Wolf und das Lamm: Zum eschatologischen Tierfrieden in Jes 11,6–9," in *Eschatologie—Eschatology: The Sixth Durham-Tübingen Research Symposium; Eschatology in Old Testament, Ancient Judaism and Early Christianity (Tübingen, September 2009)*, ed. Hans-Joachim Eckstein, Christof Landmesser, and Hermann Lichtenberger, WUNT 272 (Tübingen: Mohr Siebeck, 2011), 3–18, here 15; J. J. M. Roberts, *First Isaiah: A Commentary*, Hermeneia (Minneapolis: Fortress, 2015), 180.

[5] E.g., Isa 14:29, 59:5, Jer 2:15, 4:7, 23:1–4, 50:17–19, Ezek 19:1–7, 34:1–22, Nah 2:12–14.

[6] See Seitz, *Isaiah 1–39*, 106–7. For more on the connection of royal prophecy and blessing, see the discussion of context below.

[7] Rehm, *Der königliche Messias*, 216–17. For more on verse 9, see below.

[8] Franz Feldmann, *Das Buch Isaias übersetzt und erklärt*, 2 vols., EHAT 14 (Münster: Aschendorff, 1925–1926), 1:157; Heinrich Gross, *Die Idee des ewigen und allgemeinen Weltfriedens im Alten Orient und im Alten Testament*, 2nd ed., TThSt 7 (Trier: Paulinus-Verlag, 1967), 92; E. Zenger, "Die Verheissung Jesaja 11,1–10: Universal oder partikular?," in *Studies in the Book of Isaiah: Festschrift Willem A. M. Beuken*, ed. Jacques van Ruiten and Marc Vervenne, BETL 132 (Leuven: Leuven University Press, 1997), 137–47, here 140; Wildberger, *Isaiah 1–12*, 481; cf. n. 5. Pace Rehm, *Der königliche Messias*, 217 n. 102; Korpel, "Messianic King," 151. Additionally, Gene M. Tucker argues that elsewhere in Isa 1–39 symbolic language is more clearly identified, e.g., 5:1–7 ("The Peaceable Kingdom and a Covenant with the Wild Animals," in *God Who Creates: Essays in Honor of W. Sibley Towner*, ed. William P. Brown and S. Dean McBride Jr. [Grand Rapids: Eerdmans, 2000], 215–25, here 218).

II. Nonallegorical Interpretations

Nonallegorical interpretations can be organized into three groups based on whether they interpret the imagery as realistic and whether they argue for a creation paradise allusion. The first interpretation is of paradise restored. The author of Isa 11:6–8 is, to one degree or another, alluding to a time before hostility and predation among animals and humans and is predicting a return to that state, including a real dietary change in carnivorous animals.[9] The second approach also argues for an allusion to a primeval time of animal peace but states that it is not to be interpreted realistically. Instead, commentators describe the images as "figurative," "poetic," "hyperbolic," or "utopian," not giving exact details but illustrating the peaceful character of the new state.[10]

The third, which includes my own view, is a nonrealistic interpretation like the second. It does not, however, connect the imagery with a creation paradise but finds its source elsewhere.[11] John J. Collins, for example, states, "Isa. 11 is a prophecy of the restoration of the Davidic monarchy to its full glory. Never mind that the

---

[9] For an ancient Christian example, see Gregory of Elvira (see McKinion, *Isaiah 1–39*, 107–8). Among modern examples, see Lea Mazor, "Myth, History, and Utopia in the Prophecy of the Shoot (Isaiah 10:33–11:9)," in *Sefer Moshe: The Moshe Weinfeld Jubilee Volume; Studies in the Bible and the Ancient Near East, Qumran, and Post-Biblical Judaism*, ed. Chaim Cohen, Avi Hurvitz, and Shalom M. Paul (Winona Lake, IN: Eisenbrauns, 2004), 73–90, here 77–80; George Buchanan Gray, *A Critical and Exegetical Commentary on the Book of Isaiah: I–XXVII*, ICC (New York: Scribner's Sons, 1912), 213–14, 218–20; John Watts, *Isaiah 1–33*, WBC 24 (Waco, TX: Word, 1985), 175; Gross, *Die Idee des ewigen und allgemeinen Weltfriedens*, 92–93; Hermisson, "Zukunftserwartung und Gegenwartskritik," 59; Vermeylen, *Du prophète Isaïe*, 1:275; Richard Bauckham, *Living with Other Creatures: Green Exegesis and Theology* (Waco, TX: Baylor University Press, 2011), 125–26.

[10] Wegner, *Examination of Kingship*, 258; Wildberger, *Isaiah 1–12*, 480–81; John Skinner, *The Book of the Prophet Isaiah, Chapters I–XXXIX*, CBC (Cambridge: Cambridge University Press, 1896), 98; G. Johannes Botterweck, "זְאֵב," TDOT 4:6–7; Brevard S. Childs, *Myth and Reality in the Old Testament*, SBT 27 (Naperville, IL: Allenson, 1960), 67; Odil Hannes Steck, "'… ein kleiner Knabe kann sie leiten': Beobachtungen zum Tierfrieden in Jesaja 11,6–8 und 65,25," in *Alttestamentlicher Glaube und Biblische Theologie: Festschrift für Horst Dietrich Preuss zum 65. Geburtstag*, ed. Jutta Hausmann and Hans Jürgen Zobel (Stuttgart: Kohlhammer, 1992), 104–13, here 107; Zenger, "Die Verheissung Jesaja 11,1–10," 147.

[11] Tucker argues that verses 1–5 and 6–9 are idealized descriptions dependent on the Davidic and Zion traditions, respectively ("Peaceable Kingdom," 218–19, 225). Wegner interprets verses 6–9 as figurative and states that the origin may be "either from the paradise myths or royal ideology" (*Examination of Kingship*, 258). See also Feldmann, *Das Buch Isaias*, 157; Jason M. Silverman, "Yes We Can (Hyperbolize)! Ideals, Rhetoric, and Tradition Transmission," *JBRec* 1 (2014): 263–84, here 277.

wolf did not lie down with the lamb in the time of David or Solomon. This is an idealized description of a this-worldly kingdom."[12]

To evaluate these interpretations, especially the proposed allusion to a creational animal peace, I will focus on three main issues: the immediate context of the passage, the alleged parallels for the imagery, and the content of the imagery itself.

Context

There are numerous issues concerning the larger context of Isa 11:6–8, but here I will address the most relevant: its relation to Isa 11:1–5. The issues surrounding verse 9 will be touched on later. Verses 1–5 contain the well-known description of a coming Davidic king, endowed with the spirit of YHWH, whose righteous reign will lead to just judgments for the poor and oppressed and the destruction of the wicked. Then, without transition, animal imagery appears in verse 6. What is the connection?

It is best to take verses 6–8 as a blessing. The notion that a king's righteous reign will lead to blessings for himself, his land, and his people is seen elsewhere in the Hebrew Bible and the ancient Near East.[13] There are even parallels to Isa 11:1–8 in a group of ancient Near Eastern "prophecies" that tie together a king's righteous reign and the blessedness accompanying it.[14] Thus many commentators argue that the king's righteous reign described in verses 1–5 leads to the peace in verses 6–8.[15] Targum Jonathan makes the connection explicit by an addition at the beginning of verse 6: "In the days of the Messiah of Israel shall peace increase in the land."[16]

What is debated is whether a blessing about animal peace, especially when understood realistically, fits a royal prophecy. Some commentators admit that the

---

[12] John J. Collins, "The Eschatology of Zechariah," in *Knowing the End from the Beginning: The Prophetic, the Apocalyptic and Their Relationships*, ed. Lester L. Grabbe and Robert D. Haak, JSPSup 46 (London: T&T Clark, 2003), 74–84, here 76. Elsewhere, however, Collins speaks of "paradisiac motifs" in Isa 11 ("Models of Utopia in the Biblical Tradition," in *"A Wise and Discerning Mind": Essays in Honor of Burke O. Long*, ed. Saul M. Olyan and Robert C. Culley, BJS 325 [Providence, RI: Brown Judaic Studies, 2000], 51–67, here 51).

[13] The connection between righteousness and prosperity is certainly not unusual in Isaiah or in the Hebrew Bible in general; see esp. Isa 1:19–20, 32:17. On the blessedness of Solomon's reign for his people, see 1 Kgs 4:20, 5:5 (Eng. 4:25).

[14] Five works are generally included in this group: the Marduk Speech, Grayson and Lambert's Text A (Albert K. Grayson and Wilfred G. Lambert, "Akkadian Prophecies," *JCS* 18 [1964]: 7–30, here 12–16), the Shulgi Speech, the Uruk Prophecy, and the Dynastic Prophecy. Cf. "The Prophecies of Neferti," trans. Miriam Lichtheim (*COS* 1.45:106–10) and the letter of Adad-shuma-usur (*ANET*, 626–27).

[15] Wildberger, *Isaiah 1–12*, 467–68; Watts, *Isaiah 1–33*, 175; Tucker, "Peaceable Kingdom," 217.

[16] Bruce D. Chilton, *The Isaiah Targum*, ArBib 11 (Wilmington, DE: Glazier, 1987), 28.

combination is unique and somewhat surprising, since the more expected animal blessing would be the elimination of dangerous animals found elsewhere.[17] Many commentators, however, reason that it accords with the paradigm of royal rule having an effect on the natural world, including the animals.[18]

Nevertheless, others rightly question such reasoning. In the Hebrew Bible and the ancient Near East, descriptions of a coming king's reign can include blessings in nature related to fertility and peace; however, nowhere else are they accompanied by allusions to a time of primordial animal peace. The blessings listed are this-worldly.[19] To have adequate rain or an abundance of crops is one thing; lions eating straw is another. Thus, a number of commentators conclude that verses 6–8 are a later addition.[20]

While I appreciate their arguments, redaction is not the only or the best solution. Instead, a figurative understanding of the imagery would address their concerns regarding a this-worldly blessing. For example, interpreting the imagery as hyperbole would fit with the common use of hyperbolic rhetoric in the Hebrew Bible and the ancient Near East, especially concerning kingship.[21] This argument from context does not eliminate a possible allusion to a time of creational animal peace since the author could be using the image in a nonrealistic manner or doing something entirely unique. Nevertheless, context should carry some weight.

Parallels

If Isa 11:6–8 is an allusion to a time at creation characterized by animal peace, where do we find a description of such a creational state? It is possible that these verses are the only extant evidence for such a motif, but that is not the usual argument. Outside of Isa 65:25, scholars acknowledge that a return to a paradise of animal peace is found nowhere else in the Hebrew Bible.[22] But more importantly, some commentators note that we do not find very close parallels to Isa 11:6–8 in creation texts in the Hebrew Bible or in the ancient Near East.[23] The parallels

---

[17] Botterweck, *TDOT* 4:7; Skinner, *Isaiah, Chapters I–XXXIX*, 98; Karl Löning and Erich Zenger, *To Begin With, God Created—: Biblical Theologies of Creation* (Collegeville, MN: Liturgical Press, 2000), 177; cf. Lev 26:6; Isa 35:9; Ezek 34:25, 28.

[18] Wildberger, *Isaiah 1–12*, 479–80; Wegner, *Examination of Kingship*, 257–58; Watts, *Isaiah 1–33*, 175.

[19] For Hebrew Bible examples, see Isa 9:5–6 (Eng. 6–7), 32:1–8, Jer 23:5–6, 33:14–16, Ezek 34:23–31, 37:15–28, Amos 9:11–15, Mic 5:1–5 (Eng. 2–6), Zech 9:9–10. For the ancient Near Eastern material, see the texts and literature in n. 14. One key in the analysis of these texts is a recognition of hyperbole, as discussed below.

[20] Hermisson, "Zukunftserwartung und Gegenwartskritik," 59–61; Vermeylen, *Du prophète Isaïe*, 1:275–76; Steck, "'… ein kleiner Knabe,'" 107; Janowski, "Der Wolf und das Lamm," 12–13.

[21] Wilfred G. E. Watson, *Classical Hebrew Poetry: A Guide to Its Techniques*, JSOTSup 26 (Sheffield: JSOT Press, 1984), 317.

[22] Vermeylen, *Du prophète Isaïe*, 1:275.

[23] Feldmann, *Das Buch Isaias*, 157; Rehm, *Der königliche Messias*, 215–16; Botterweck,

suggested are not as close and helpful as claimed. It is beyond the scope of this article to provide a thorough analysis of each of the texts commonly cited; a few relatively brief comments will suffice to question their relevance.[24]

Hebrew Bible

For the Hebrew Bible, commentators point to the granting of plants for food in Gen 1:29–30 as an implicit indication of original vegetarianism and thereby animal peace,[25] but this provision does not necessarily prohibit what is not mentioned. Most commentators recognize that these verses are not meant as an exhaustive list of what every creature eats—nothing is given to the fish—and thus argue that other nonmeat items like milk and honey are not forbidden.[26] Why then should we assume that meat is forbidden, especially since elsewhere in the Hebrew Bible it is viewed as a blessing?[27]

Genesis 1:29–30 grants humans and land animals the general right to use plants for their benefit with one purpose made explicit—as food. Humankind's relationship with animals is regulated earlier in v. 28. The verbs used, כבש ("subdue")[28] and רדה ("rule"), involve a level of conflict and coercion that is at odds with an absolutely peaceful relationship and grant humans the right to use animals for their benefit,[29] including the common use of animals as a food source.[30]

Some commentators argue that the explicit provision of animals for food in

---

TDOT 4:7; Tucker, "Peaceable Kingdom," 219; Bendt Alster, "Dilmun, Bahrain, and the Alleged Paradise in Sumerian Myth and Literature," in *Dilmun: New Studies in the Archaeology and Early History of Bahrain*, ed. Daniel T. Potts, BBVO 2 (Berlin: Reimer, 1983), 39–74, here 52–58; Bernard Frank Batto, "Paradise Reexamined," in *The Biblical Canon in Comparative Perspective*, ed. K. Lawson Younger Jr., William W Hallo, and Bernard F. Batto, Scripture in Context 4 (Lewiston, NY: Mellen, 1991), 34–50.

[24] For a more extensive discussion of the evidence, although in an earlier form, see Joshua J. Van Ee, "Death and the Garden: An Examination of Original Immortality, Vegetarianism, and Animal Peace in the Hebrew Bible and Mesopotamia" (PhD diss., University of California, San Diego, 2013), 12–33, 50–111, 116–53, 193–278, 335–58.

[25] Gray, *Book of Isaiah: I–XXVII*, 219; Hermisson, "Zukunftserwartung und Gegenwartskritik," 59 n. 14; Vermeylen, *Du prophète Isaïe*, 1:275; Mazor, "Myth, History, and Utopia," 78.

[26] John Skinner, *A Critical and Exegetical Commentary on Genesis*, 2nd ed., ICC (1930; repr., Edinburgh: T&T Clark, 1969), 34.

[27] For example, in Deut 12 the eating of meat is part of the blessed bounty of the promised land (vv. 6–7, 15, 17–18, and 20–22); cf. Rehm, *Der königliche Messias*, 215.

[28] Based on the parallel wording in Num 32:22, 29; Josh 18:1; and 1 Chr 22:18; the command to subdue the earth is best taken as metonymy, to subdue those dwelling on the earth, that is, the animals (Samuel Luzzatto, *The Book of Genesis: A Commentary by ShaDal*, trans. Daniel A. Klein [Northvale, NJ: Aronson, 1998], 26; Jakob Wöhrle, "*Dominium terrae*: Exegetische und religionsgeschichtliche Überlegungen zum Herrschaftsauftrag in Gen 1,26–28," *ZAW* 121 [2009]: 171–88, here 174).

[29] Wöhrle, "*Dominium terrae*," 173–76.

[30] Luzzatto, *Book of Genesis*, 27; Manfred Weippert, "Tier und Mensch in einer menschenarmen Welt: Zum sog. *dominium terrae* in Genesis 1," in *Ebenbild Gottes—Herrscher über die Welt*:

Gen 9:3 indicates that meat was forbidden in 1:29–30.³¹ In response, it is important to note, first, that the context of 9:3 does not indicate a change in human–animal relations. The statements in 9:2 are the positive counterparts of the commands in 1:28 since establishing fear and dread is what is necessary for subduing and ruling.³² Additionally, there is no record elsewhere of the introduction of hostility among animals and between animals and humans.³³

Second, Gen 9:3 does not make a temporal comparison between the provision of vegetation and animals (e.g., using "previously" and "now"). Instead, the comparison is best taken as an "agreement in manner or norm" with the end of the verse indicating the point of the comparison—the extent of the provision ("as green plants, I give to you all [animals]").³⁴ In an Israelite context of dietary laws that declared some animals unclean, it is easy to see why such a comparison is needed. Genesis 9:3 is not introducing a new right but, in connection with verses 4–6, is emphasizing the distinction between proper and improper bloodshed as a way to deal with the violence that caused the flood.

Furthermore, proposed connections between Isa 11 and creation texts that would strengthen the case for an allusion are unconvincing. Some scholars argue for a link between the snakes mentioned in Isa 11:8 and the snake in Gen 3, showing that the enmity between humans and snakes ordained in Gen 3:15 will be reversed.³⁵ There are no linguistic ties between the two texts, however, to indicate an allusion; Isa 11:8 mentions two specific types of poisonous snakes, while Gen 3 uses the generic נחש.³⁶ The inclusion of snakes among other fearsome animals in Isa 11:6–8 is easily understood in light of the dangers they posed. Other, less-promising connections have been proposed with Isa 11:9 and creation texts in the Hebrew Bible.³⁷

Studien zu Würde und Auftrag des Menschen, ed. Hans-Peter Mathys, BThSt 33 (Neukirchen-Vluyn: Neukirchener Verlag, 1998), 35–55, here 54.

³¹ Skinner, *Genesis*, 34; Gross, *Die Idee des ewigen und allgemeinen Weltfriedens*, 85.

³² For example, YHWH promises that Israel will be able to conquer the Canaanites because he will place fear and dread of Israel upon them (Deut 11:25). See also Michael A. Fishbane, *Biblical Interpretation in Ancient Israel* (Oxford: Clarendon, 1985), 318; Wöhrle, "Dominium terrae," 181.

³³ Rehm, *Der königliche Messias*, 215–16. There is no reason to take the enmity of Gen 3:15 as applying to all animals.

³⁴ *IBHS* 11.2.9b

³⁵ Mazor, "Myth, History, and Utopia," 77; Löning and Zenger, *To Begin With*, 175–76; Gray, *Book of Isaiah: I–XXVII*, 220.

³⁶ Cf. Isa 65:25, where a proposed connection with Gen 3:14 is based on stronger linguistic ties.

³⁷ For examples, see Mazor, "Myth, History, and Utopia," 83–84; Bauckham, *Living with Other Creatures*, 126; Vermeylen, *Du prophète Isaïe*, 1:275 n. 2; Zenger, "Die Verheissung Jesaja 11,1–10," 145; Janowski, "Der Wolf und das Lamm," 13–15.

Finally, many scholars appeal to Isa 11:6–8 in their analysis of creation texts in the Hebrew Bible. Somewhat circularly, they argue that Isa 11:6–8 is alluding to the creation state, and they then use its imagery to interpret creation texts, saying that it makes explicit the primeval animal peace motif that is implicit elsewhere.[38] Thus, the imagery of wolf and lamb has cast a long shadow, especially in the study of the early chapters of Genesis.

Mesopotamia

Passages in two Sumerian works are often cited as evidence of a similar primeval animal peace motif. First, lines 1–30 of Enki and Ninhursaga use a list of negations to describe the land of Dilmun in an early time. Since a number of harmful or unpleasant elements are listed as not present, the text has been viewed as a description of an idyllic paradise before predation, sickness, and maybe even death.[39] Yet, in light of the use of negation elsewhere, the inclusion of nonharmful elements on the list, and the structure of the list, this section is best interpreted as a description of an unformed world where all of normal life, both the pleasant and the unpleasant, is absent. Additionally, in the following section of the text another element missing is fresh water, something essential for a supposed paradise.[40]

Second, lines 136–155 in Enmerkar and the Lord of Aratta contain a description of a time when there were no dangerous animals—that is, when humans had no equal—and when all people spoke one language. It has been interpreted as a primeval paradise of animal peace.[41] Nevertheless, the passage is describing not an ancient period near the time of creation but the postdiluvian time of Enmerkar, which is characterized by conflicts and other nonparadisiacal elements.[42] In addition, the lack of rivals for humans seems to indicate an instability in the cosmos since an unbounded humanity was destined to anger the gods. Thus, it is not an

---

[38] E.g., Benno Jacob, *Das erste Buch der Tora: Genesis* (1934; repr., New York: Ktav, 1974), 62; Claus Westermann, *Genesis: A Commentary*, trans. John J. Scullion, 3 vols. (Minneapolis: Augsburg, 1984–1986), 1:164–65.

[39] Samuel Noah Kramer and John R. Maier, *Myths of Enki, the Crafty God* (Oxford: Oxford University Press, 1989), 23.

[40] P. Attinger, "Enki et Ninḫursaĝa," *ZA* 74 (1984): 1–52, here 33–34; Batto, "Paradise Reexamined," 38–40; Alster, "Dilmun, Bahrain," 58; Dina Katz, "Enki and Ninhursaĝa, Part One: The Story of Dilmun," *BO* 64 (2007): 568–89, here 577–79.

[41] Kramer and Maier, *Myths of Enki*, 88.

[42] Lines 136–155 have often been wrongly interpreted as the content of a spell of Nudimmud that is speaking of the distant past or future. Instead, these lines are a narrative aside that gives needed background information about the time of Enmerkar. See Catherine Mittermayer, *Enmerkara und der Herr von Arata: Ein ungleicher Wettstreit*, OBO 239 (Göttingen: Vandenhoeck & Ruprecht, 2009), 57–62. Another text (UET 6.61) uses what seems to be almost identical language to characterize a time before the flood and is connected with a description of humans in a precivilized state, living like animals (Thorkild Jacobsen, "The Eridu Genesis," *JBL* 100 [1981]: 513–29, here 516–17 n. 7, https://doi.org/10.2307/3266116).

idyllic time but a time before the present, well-ordered world in which wild animals, along with other means, control human propagation.[43]

A few commentators identify an animal peace motif in the depiction of Enkidu living with the animals in the Akkadian Gilgamesh Epic.[44] Enkidu's original animal-like state, however, does not mean that there was peace among the animals in general or even between Enkidu and all animals, especially since conflicts with lions are mentioned elsewhere.[45] Instead, Enkidu is modeled after descriptions of early humans who lack the gifts (and attendant hardships) of civilization.[46]

In the interpretation of these Mesopotamian texts, supposed biblical parallels have often played a crucial role. Commenting on the search for a creation paradise in Sumerian literature, Dina Katz asks, "If not for the biblical source, would we look for a Sumerian paradise?"[47] The dominant motifs in Mesopotamian literature of primeval humans as animal-like and created for toil are at odds with an original paradise, at least for humankind.[48]

Greece and Rome

In Greco-Roman literature, descriptions of a golden age characterized by vegetarianism and animal peace are often cited as parallels to the biblical descriptions.[49] It is doubtful, however, whether these examples are illustrative of older, broader cultural motifs and thus relevant to Isa 11:6–8. In the oldest extant depiction of the golden age, Hesiod's portrayal of the golden race (*Op.* 109–120), there is no mention of vegetarianism or animal peace. While these traits may be compatible with his descriptions of self-producing fields and human ease and peace, they are not in view since the contrast is with the human–human violence and cultural toils of the current iron race.[50]

---

[43] Similarly, Thorkild Jacobsen reasons that a unified and proliferating human race with one language would eventually irritate Enlil and bring about disastrous results, as in the flood traditions ("The Spell of Nudimmud," in *Sha'arei Talmon: Studies in the Bible, Qumran, and the Ancient Near East Presented to Shemaryahu Talmon*, ed. Michael A. Fishbane, Emanuel Tov, and Weston W. Fields [Winona Lake, IN: Eisenbrauns, 1992], 403–16, here 414–16). Note that Enki in his rebuke of Enlil after the flood says that Enlil should have used wild animals (lions and wolves) to control the human population instead of the flood (Gilgamesh XI.188-191).

[44] Wildberger, *Isaiah 1–12*, 479–80; Wegner, *Examination of Kingship*, 258 n. 257.

[45] Gilgamesh II.60, 237–238.

[46] A. R. George, *The Babylonian Gilgamesh Epic: Introduction, Critical Edition, and Cuneiform Texts*, 2 vols. (Oxford: Oxford University Press, 2003), 450.

[47] Katz, "Enki and Ninhursaĝa," 579.

[48] Alster, "Dilmun, Bahrain," 54–55; Batto, "Paradise Reexamined," 33–34, 57–58.

[49] The earliest examples come from Empedocles (ca. 492–432 BCE) frag. 130 (cf. frags. 136-137) and Plato (ca. 427–347 BCE), *Pol.* 271d–e (cf. *Leg.* 782c–d).

[50] Luc Dequeker, "'Green Herbage and Trees Bearing Fruit' (Gen. 1:28–30; 9:1–3): Vegetarianism or Predominance of Man over the Animals," *Bijdr* 38 (1977): 118–27, here 125; Bodo Gatz, *Weltalter, goldene Zeit und sinnverwandte Vorstellungen*, Spudasmata 16 (Hildesheim: Olms,

Instead, primitive vegetarianism and animal peace were introduced into Greco-Roman thought in connection with the vegetarianism of a number of philosophers, from Empedocles in the fifth century BCE to Porphyry in the third century CE. Vegetarianism was a radically new and countercultural ideal, arising in the sixth and fifth centuries BCE from the Orphic and Pythagorean belief in metempsychosis, the transmigration of souls, making meat eating a form of cannibalism.[51] The tie between the golden age and vegetarianism and animal peace originated later in philosophical polemics for vegetarianism and then spread in the culture more generally.[52]

The most often-mentioned Greco-Roman parallel to Isa 11:1-8 is Vergil's *Eclogue* 4 (ca. 37 BCE) since it combines a royal prophecy with peaceful animal imagery.[53] Some have even suggested that the description is dependent on Isa 11:6-8 as mediated through Sib. Or. 3:788-795.[54] The imagery in Vergil, however, is not as close a parallel as claimed since the dangerous animals seem to be removed, not transformed as argued below for Isa 11:6-8.[55]

Imagery

The most important criterion in evaluating an allusion to a creational animal peace is whether it actually fits with what is described in Isa 11:6-8. To examine this issue more thoroughly, I will provide a translation and analysis of the text.

Translation: Isaiah 11:6-8

6. Then the wolf will sojourn with the lamb, and the leopard with the kid will lie down, then the calf and the lion will feed together, and the young boy will be leading them.

1967), 165–66. Note that the parodies of the golden age by the fifth-century BCE comic poets did not portray the golden age as vegetarian. See Telecleides, *Amphictyons*, and Pherecrates, *Metalles*, both in Athenaeus, *Deipn.* 6.268-269; cf. Lucian, *Sat.* 7.

[51] Gatz, *Weltalter, goldene Zeit*, 165–74; Stephen T. Newmyer, *Animals in Greek and Roman Thought: A Sourcebook*, Routledge Sourcebooks for the Ancient World (New York: Routledge, 2011), 97–110; Marcel Detienne, "Culinary Practices and the Spirit of Sacrifice," in *The Cuisine of Sacrifice among the Greeks*, trans. Paula Wissing (Chicago: University of Chicago Press, 1989), 5–7.

[52] Robert Parker, *Polytheism and Society at Athens* (Oxford: Oxford University Press, 2005), 189–90; Gordon Lindsay Campbell, *Strange Creatures: Anthropology in Antiquity* (London: Duckworth, 2006), 43. There is no evidence for belief in a primitive animal peace among the Orphics or Pythagoreans, and the evidence that Pythagoras taught primitive vegetarianism comes from much later in Ovid (43 BCE-17/18 CE), *Metam.* 15.96-110.

[53] Cf. Horace, *Epod.* 16 (ca. 29 BCE); Einsiedeln Eclogues 2.35-37 (mid-first century CE).

[54] Bauckham, *Living with Other Creatures*, 127 n. 35.

[55] Jan N. Bremmer, *The Rise and Fall of the Afterlife: The 1995 Read-Tuckwell Lectures at the University of Bristol* (New York: Routledge, 2002), 124, 184 n. 105.

7. Then the cow and the bear will graze, together their young will lie down, and the lion as the ox will eat straw.
8. Then the suckling will play by the hole of the cobra, and upon the young of the viper the weaned will extend his hand.

Notes: Isaiah 11:6–8

Verse 6, "will feed together": The MT (and probably also 4QIsa^c, frag. 6) has a nominal clause with a list of three animals ending with ומריא, "and fatted calf," while 1QIsa^a (ימרו) and the LXX (βοσκηθήσονται) contain a verb. A verbal form of מרא appears nowhere else in the Hebrew Bible but is found in Ugaritic, Akkadian, and Arabic.[56] Both readings are intelligible, but the verb is preferable since it best fits the context (all the other animal groupings are pairs with an expressed verb) and its rarity could explain the MT use of the more common noun.

Verse 7, "will graze": Since the MT reading does not emphasize any unity or tie between the cow and bear, some commentators propose taking the verb from the root רעה, used to describe the association or friendship of people, and repointing it as a *niphal* or emending it to a *hithpael*.[57] Another possibility is to follow the reading in 1QIsa^a ורבצו, "and they will lie down," taking יחדו ("together") with the first colon, since in the MT the second colon of verse 7 is the only one in verses 6–8 that does not begin with a ו conjunction. A third possibility is that a second יחדו dropped out of the first colon by haplography, maybe with a conjunction: יחדו ויחדו (cf. LXX which has ἅμα, "together," in all three cola of v. 7). Since the idea of grazing fits the context and is supported by the LXX, I favor retaining the MT, with the idea of unity present by backward gapping.[58]

Verse 8, "the young": The meaning of MT מאורת is unclear. Based on the LXX translation κοίτην ("lair") and the parallel with חר ("cave") earlier in the verse, some emend the text to מערת ("cave"). Others assume a connection with אור ("light") and thus argue for "lighthole" or some gleam coming from the snake that attracts the child, possibly its eyes.[59] Most convincing is F. Perles, who relates מאורת to Akkadian *mûru*, "young animal," a meaning that fits well in verse 8 and coheres with the mention of other young animals in verses 6 and 7.[60]

Verse 8, "will extend his hand": A few commentators have sought to emend the MT reading יָדוֹ הָדָה into a single imperfect verbal form (יְתָדֶּה, "to trip about," or יְדַהְדֶה, "to throw pebbles") since the perfect is unexpected in context and the root is a *hapax legomenon* without clear cognates.[61] The verb, however, could either be repointed as a participle הֹדֶה in parallel with נֹהֵג in verse 6 or read as an imperfect יְהַדֶה with 4QIsa^c (haplography of simi-

---

[56] *HALOT*, s.v. "מרא."

[57] *BHS*; Wildberger, *Isaiah 1–12*, 462.

[58] Cf. the suggestion that יחדו is "an *apokoinu* construction" (Roberts, *First Isaiah*, 178).

[59] Gray, *Book of Isaiah: I–XXVII*, 220.

[60] F. Perles, "Übersehenes akkadisches Sprachgut im Alten Testament," *JSOR* 9 (1925): 126–28, here 126–27.

[61] Gray, *Book of Isaiah: I–XXVII*, 221; Joseph Reider, "Etymological Studies in Biblical Hebrew," *VT* 2 (1952): 113–30. here 115.

larly shaped letters; cf. LXX). The meaning "to stretch out, extend" is derived from context but is not far removed from Arabic and Syriac "to guide."[62]

Analysis

To interpret the imagery of Isa 11:6–8, it is essential to note which animals are described, where they are, and what they are doing. The imagery in verse 6 is taken from the pastoral life of the shepherd. Even though the young boy is not called a shepherd, his leading (נהג) of the animals and their lying down (רבץ) indicate his role.[63] In addition, the three herbivores described are traditional herd animals, although only the young are mentioned—the lamb, kid, and calf—those especially vulnerable to attacks by wild animals.[64]

What is unusual is the presence of predators, wild animals normally feared by shepherds, that are not acting as predators. The young boy is not fighting these dangerous animals to protect his flock.[65] Instead, the verbs used progressively increase the tie between the wild animals and the domesticated herd: first sojourning, then lying down, and finally a communal meal. Yet the most surprising development is that the boy is leading all of these animals. His flock now includes wolves, leopards, and lions; the predators have become domesticated.[66]

The imagery in verse 7 is taken from the realm of the larger animals that were usually kept closer to the village and used for labor. In ancient Israel, especially in a small village, large cattle were primarily kept as draft animals, both males and females.[67] When not working, large cattle would be taken out to graze but most likely not as far as the flocks and herds. They were fed straw when working the fields or being cared for in the village.[68]

This domestic scene, however, is now populated by bears and lions. A bear

---

[62] *HALOT*, s.v. "הדה"; Frederick E. Greenspahn, *Hapax Legomena in Biblical Hebrew: A Study of the Phenomenon and Its Treatment since Antiquity with Special Reference to Verbal Forms*, SBLDS 74 (Chico, CA: Scholars Press, 1984), 111, 202; cf. the common idiom שלח יד, "to send out a hand."

[63] For נהג, see Exod 3:1, Pss 78:52, 80:2; for רבץ, Ps 23:2, Song 1:7, Isa 13:20, Jer 33:12, Ezek 34:14–15; Watts, *Isaiah 1–33*, 173.

[64] For כבש, see Isa 5:17, Hos 4:16; for גדי, Gen 27:9, Song 1:8; for עגל, Isa 27:10. Although כבש can be a general term for sheep, in combination with גדי and עגל it is best taken as the young of the flock. Note that these terms do not mean that the animals are small since they may be full grown and still considered young.

[65] The age of the boy may imply his inability to fight off such predators, although David's youth is also highlighted when he describes fighting lions and bears (1 Sam 17:33–37).

[66] Others who argue that following the shepherd indicates that the wild animals are now domesticated include Mazor, "Myth, History, and Utopia," 79; and Bauckham, *Living with Other Creatures*, 126.

[67] Oded Borowski, *Every Living Thing: Daily Use of Animals in Ancient Israel* (Walnut Creek, CA: AltaMira, 1998), 42, 74, 121–25.

[68] Note the contrast between grazing animals and working animals in Isa 30:23–24.

and her cub are eating and lying down beside a cow and her calf, two protective mothers at ease with each other. And, shockingly, the lion is found eating straw. Here the theme of domestication becomes most explicit since the lion is not eating straw *with* the ox but *like* an ox. The focus is not on peace with a domesticated animal but acting like one.[69]

Thus, the imagery in verse 7 is about more than what bears and lions do—or do not—consume. As the wild animals in verse 6 were not only eating with the domesticated ones but also becoming like them, following the shepherd boy as a part of the flock, something similar is implied in verse 7. The bear and lion not only graze and eat straw like cattle; they also serve the one who feeds them (e.g., pulling the plow).

The imagery in verse 8 is taken from even closer to the village, maybe inside its confines. The text describes the realm of mothers with their young children, going about the business of the day. What is new, however, is that the most defenseless of children, those nursing or newly weaned, are depicted as playing with impunity by the holes of the most dangerous snakes. In fact, if my reconstruction of the text is correct, the image is of children playing not only near the holes of snakes but even with their young. The imagery is again one of domestication as the poisonous snakes behave like pets.[70]

It is helpful to emphasize three conclusions about verses 6–8. First, what is described is not a lack of hostility in the animal world at large. Note that nonpredatory wild animals are not mentioned. The point is not whether wolves are at peace with deer, whether lions stop chasing gazelles. The focus is on animal threats to humans and their interests, more specifically, the dangers to an Israelite villager. The dangerous animals are no longer harming humans or the domesticated animals on which humans depend for their livelihood. The frequent mention of the young and vulnerable emphasizes this point. Further, verse 8 does not deal with animal–animal peace since it mentions only serpents and young children.[71] Thus, the peace between wolf and lamb is not primarily about the relations of those two animals. The point is whether wolves are attacking the shepherd's flock and thereby hurting his interests.[72] The geographical areas mentioned highlight this point. As argued

---

[69] Steck argues that this comparison indicates that the wild animals are now acting like domesticated animals ("'... ein kleiner Knabe,'" 111–12).

[70] Similarly, some commentators state that the children are playing with the snakes although without further argumentation (Mazor, "Myth, History, and Utopia," 77, 79; Seitz, *Isaiah 1–39*, 106).

[71] Using the same reasoning but more briefly, other commentators likewise argue that the focus is on human security and not a general animal peace. See Skinner, *Isaiah, Chapters I–XXXIX*, 98; Tucker, "Peaceable Kingdom," 217; Bauckham, *Living with Other Creatures*, 125. Steck adds that the human focus is seen in the fact that the predatory animals mentioned are those used elsewhere by God to punish Israel ("'... ein kleiner Knabe,'" 110–11). I will address that topic below.

[72] Whether verses 6–8 imply a general animal peace relates to the purpose and rhetoric of

above, the imagery moves throughout the regions used by an Israelite villager, from the boy leading flocks in the pasture to the babies in the village.[73] Thus, Isa 11:6–8 deals with areas of human activity; the wilderness is not the concern.

Second, verses 6–8 describe something beyond a simple lack of hostility. As mentioned above, the dangerous animals are portrayed not only as peaceful or even tame but as domesticated. They are acting not as nonpredatory wild animals, like a deer, but as animals under human care and control. They join the flock, feed at the trough, and play with children.[74]

Third, the imagery of Isa 11:6–8 is based on normal life for an average rural Israelite. It is describing village life in which flocks and herds are being kept, assumedly, for all their usual purposes. There is no mention, explicit or otherwise, of a vegetarian diet for humans.[75] The only change is the level of peace and security that the villagers now experience in their relationship with formerly dangerous and wild animals.

All three of these conclusions reveal key differences between the imagery in Isa 11:6–8 and usual descriptions of a creational animal peace. Thus they cast much doubt on a possible allusion. It could be that the author has significantly altered the theme of primeval animal peace for his purposes, but that is certainly not the simplest explanation.

III. A Hyperbolic Blessing

In light of the various issues raised above, I propose a nonallegorical way to understand Isa 11:6–8 that accords with the description, fits the context of the royal prophecy, and also provides an alternative source for the imagery. The author has taken the standard blessing regarding devouring animals and given it a unique hyperbolic spin.[76] Thus, the source of the imagery is not a paradise of animal peace but the blessings and curses found in the ancient Near East, the Hebrew Bible, and even elsewhere in Isaiah.

I am not alone in relating Isa 11:6–8 to blessings and curses. Some commentators connect these verses with particular blessings and curses in the Hebrew Bible,

---

the passage. A general animal peace is assumed by those advocating a realistic change but is not necessary if the imagery is in some way figurative.

[73] Watts emphasizes the village setting for verses 6–8 as a whole (*Isaiah 1–33*, 175).

[74] Second Baruch 73:6 alludes to Isa 11:6–8 and emphasizes the theme of domestication or dominion: "And the wild beasts will come from the wood and serve men, and the asps and dragons will come out of their holes to subject themselves to a child" (trans. A. F. J. Klijn, *OTP* 1:645).

[75] Some commentators argue that a human vegetarian diet is implied; however, their reason for doing so is anchored not in the text but in its assumed allusion to a creation paradise (see, e.g., Bauckham, *Living with Other Creatures*, 126).

[76] The terminology of devouring animals comes from the categorization of curses in Delbert R. Hillers, *Treaty-Curses and the Old Testament Prophets*, BibOr 16 (Rome: Pontifical Biblical Institute, 1964), 54–56.

although they still root the imagery in a creational animal peace.[77] Others relate all the blessings in the Hebrew Bible regarding devouring animals to a primeval animal peace, failing to see the common elements in the blessing-and-curse tradition.[78] In what follows, I am not arguing for dependence on specific passages but for a connection with the blessing-and-curse tradition in general, of which these texts are representative examples.

Threats from wild animals were a part of life in ancient Israel. Settlements may push the animals back, but they were always on the fringe, seeking to return.[79] In the Hebrew Bible and the ancient Near East, however, animals are not viewed simply as a natural threat; they are portrayed as instruments of divine curses or punishment.[80] Examples can be found throughout the Hebrew Bible, often involving snakes, lions, and bears.[81] Jeremiah 5:6 contains a list of animals very similar to Isa 11:6–7, "Therefore a lion from the forest will strike them down. A wolf from the wilds will devastate them. A leopard is watching their cities. Everyone who goes out of them will be torn in pieces, because their transgressions are many, their apostasies are great."

Curses often have a corresponding blessing in the Hebrew Bible, and many blessings are the positive alternative to the curse, for example, defeating your enemies instead of being defeated.[82] Other blessings are stated as the absence of the curse, for example, no one making you tremble;[83] and sometimes there is a more fundamental transformation, for example, peace with your former enemies.[84] For devouring animals, the positive alternative of humans striking wild animals is

---

[77] Steck states that the wild animals listed in Isa 11:6–8 are those YHWH used to punish Israel, specifically as described in Jer 5:6 and Amos 5:19. Thus, Isa 11:6–8 is a cancellation of God's promise to punish Israel with the wild animals as in Lev 26:22 ("'… ein kleiner Knabe,'" 110–12). Vermeylen relates Isa 11:6–8 to the blessing regarding animals in Ps 91:13 (*Du prophète Isaïe*, 1:275–76). Clements says that Isa 11:6–8 is an elaboration of YHWH honoring animals in Isa 43:20 ("Wolf Shall Live," 92).

[78] Wegner, *Examination of Kingship*, 257–58; cf. Gross, *Die Idee des ewigen und allgemeinen Weltfriedens*, 85–87. In contrast, Hillers excludes Isa 11:6–8 as an example of a blessing regarding devouring animals since he interprets it as an allusion to a creation paradise (*Treaty-Curses*, 56–57 n. 40); cf. n. 88 below.

[79] The danger posed by too much unsettled land lies behind Deut 7:22.

[80] Hillers, *Treaty-Curses*, 54–56; Tucker, "Peaceable Kingdom," 222–24. A related notion is the restraint of chaotic forces by the gods in the ancient Near East, including control of the wild animals, for example, Erra and Ishum I.84–86. Humans, especially the king, play a role as they keep the gods favorably disposed and thus diligent in their restraint of chaos.

[81] E.g., Lev 26:22, Num 21:6, Deut 32:24, 1 Kgs 13:26, 20:36, 2 Kgs 2:24, 17:25, Isa 15:9, Jer 8:17; cf. Sefire Treaty I.A.30–32; Esarhaddon's treaty with Baal, King of Tyre IV.6–7.

[82] E.g., Lev 26:7–8, Deut 28:7.

[83] E.g., Job 11:19, Jer 30:10, Mic 4:4.

[84] E.g., Isa 2:1–4, 19:24–25.

occasionally found as a blessing.[85] More often the absence of the curse, the removal of wild animals, is used as a blessing.[86] A more fundamental transformation is seen in a few places; for example, in Hos 2:20 (Eng. 18) a covenant is made with the animals that results in security for humans.[87]

For Isa 11:6–8, another common variation is most important. Blessings and curses often include not only the realistic but also the hyperbolic.[88] For example, the blessing on crops in Deut 11:14 is somewhat mundane, "He will give the rain for your land in its season, the early rain and the later rain, that you may gather in your grain and your wine and your oil."[89] In comparison, Amos 9:13, which is connected with a royal prophecy like Isa 11:6–8, contains a hyperbolic form, "'Behold, days are coming,' declares YHWH, 'when the plowman will overtake the reaper and the treader of grapes the sower of seed; the mountains will drip sweet wine, and all the hills will flow.'" Especially note that the final clause employs a metaphor, speaking of wine as water to exaggerate its abundance.[90]

In Isa 11:6–8, the author has created a hyperbolic form of the blessing related to devouring animals. Humankind's fear of predators and the damage they can inflict on humans and their livelihood will be no more. Yet, instead of describing the removal of these wild animals from the land, as seen elsewhere, the prophet goes further. He portrays a world in which dangerous wild animals act domesticated: wolves join the flock, lions serve as oxen, and young vipers are played with like puppies. To be more precise, it is best to describe Isa 11:6–8 as a metaphoric hyperbole. The author uses the characteristics associated with domesticated animals to describe wild carnivores—a metaphor—as a way to exaggerate the extent of the change in the animal world, a hyperbole. As with all hyperboles, there is nothing about the form itself that identifies it as such. Instead, it is the simple

---

[85] E.g., Ps 91:13. A narrative example would be the empowerment of Samson to kill an attacking lion (Judg 14:6). The Testaments of the Twelve Patriarchs record a similar notion of subduing the wild animals (T. Iss. 7:7; T. Naph. 8:4, 6; T. Ben. 3:4–5; 5:2; cf. Bauckham, *Living with Other Creatures*, 121–24).

[86] E.g., Lev 26:6; Isa 35:9; Ezek 34:25, 28.

[87] That verse 20 (Eng. 18) is a reversal of the curse is seen in the context since in verse 14 (Eng. 12) the beasts of the field are used to punish Israel (Tucker, "Peaceable Kingdom," 223–24). A narrative example, although temporary, would be God's shutting of the lions' mouths in Dan 6:23. Cf. Job 5:22–23, where the righteous are said to be protected by God from all harm, including wild animals.

[88] See Robert Alter, *The Art of Biblical Poetry* (New York: Basic Books, 1985), 156. Some commentators fail to appreciate the use of hyperbole and instead connect everything beyond normal to paradise, e.g., Antonine DeGuglielmo, "The Fertility of the Land in the Messianic Prophecies," *CBQ* 19 (1957): 306–11, here 310; Childs, *Myth and Reality*, 66.

[89] Cf. Lev 26:4–5, which is exceedingly bountiful but may still be possible.

[90] Related is the common metaphoric hyperbole "a land flowing with milk and honey" (e.g., Exod 3:8; cf. *KTU* 1.6 III 6–7, 12–13).

incongruity between what is depicted and the normal state of the world. Wild animals do not act like domesticated ones; nevertheless, that is how the prophet portrays the future peace as he seeks to comfort and inspire. This imagery would have resonated with the author's audience since almost every Israelite was familiar with the agricultural way of life and most were involved in it daily.[91]

This interpretation accords well with verses 1–5, which answers the concerns raised about the unity of verses 1–8. What is described need not be understood as otherworldly; it is prophetic, not apocalyptic.[92] The fears of an Israelite villager are removed not by a change in nature—carnivores becoming herbivores—but by a changed relationship. Devouring animals will no longer be used as a divine sanction because of the new reign of righteousness inaugurated by the coming king. Hyperbolic rhetoric and blessings in nature are common in the Hebrew Bible and the ancient Near East concerning kingship. What is unique about Isa 11:6–8 is the particular hyperbolic form of the blessing regarding devouring animals.

Relating verses 6–8 to blessings and curses also helps clarify verse 9 and its relationship to verses 1–8.[93] My translation of verse 9 is as follows: "They will not harm and they will not destroy on all my holy mountain because the land will have become filled with the knowledge of YHWH as the waters cover the sea." Many commentators argue that the subject of the verbs רעע ("to harm") and שחת ("to destroy") cannot be the animals since the reason given is the knowledge of YHWH filling the land.[94] When understood as a blessing, however, the lack of harm is brought about not by a change in the animals themselves but by YHWH, who is no longer using them to punish Israel. The change has occurred in the people of Israel, whose land is no longer filled with injustice but with the knowledge of YHWH.

When the lack of harm is understood as a blessing, its limitation to "my holy mountain" is clarified. The imagery is not about the universal nature of wild animals but about their relations to YHWH's people in his land.[95] Thus, the extent of the blessing, הר קדשי ("my holy mountain"), and the extent of the knowledge of YHWH, הארץ ("the land"), both refer to the land of Israel.[96]

In other words, Isa 11:9 functions as a concluding statement, tying together verses 1–5 and 6–8 as cause and effect although listed in reverse order.[97] Verse 9a

---

[91] Philip J. King and Lawrence E. Stager, *Life in Biblical Israel*, LAI (Louisville: Westminster John Knox, 2001), 8. Cf. the less fantastic and yet still hyperbolic image of everyone sitting under his or her own vine and fig tree, which shares the ideal of agricultural security with Isa 11:6–8 (1 Kgs 5:5 [Eng. 4:25], Mic 4:4, Zech 3:10, 1 Macc 14:12, cf. 2 Kgs 18:31 // Isa 36:16).

[92] Collins, "Eschatology of Zechariah," 75.

[93] On the priority of Isa 11:9 to Isa 65:25b and Hab 2:14, see Wegner, *Examination of Kingship*, 251; Vermeylen, *Du prophète Isaïe*, 1:276; Korpel, "Messianic King," 153–54.

[94] Feldmann, *Das Buch Isaias*, 157; Gray, *Book of Isaiah: I–XXVII*, 224.

[95] Steck, "'… ein kleiner Knabe,'" 111.

[96] Gray, *Book of Isaiah: I–XXVII*, 224; cf. Exod 15:17, Ps 78:54, Jer 31:23.

[97] Wildberger, *Isaiah 1–12*, 467, 481; Tucker, "Peaceable Kingdom," 217; Wegner, *Examination of Kingship*, 251.

states the intent of the imagery in verses 6–8, the lack of harm and destruction. Verse 9b describes what will be true under the king's righteous rule of verses 1–5, the knowledge of YHWH will fill the land as the waters cover the sea, that is, fully. The future perfect מלאה in v. 9b, "will have become filled," makes the causal connection clear in that the filling precedes the lack of harm.[98]

IV. Conclusions

Interpreting Isa 11:6–8 as a hyperbolic form of the blessing regarding devouring animals has ramifications beyond the text itself. As a hyperbole, it is obvious that the details of the imagery—domestication of the predatory animals, peace between predatory and domestic animals, and a vegetarian diet for predatory animals—were never expected to find a literal fulfillment. But it also means that these features were not necessarily viewed as ideals, indicating something wrong with the present state of the world. The author uses these elements to illustrate security for humans, not what he or the Hebrew Bible in general understood as a better world.[99]

More to the point here, Isa 11:6–8 is not an example of *Endzeit* equals *Urzeit*. I have sought to sever the connections often made in both directions between these verses and creation texts. Creational motifs should not be assumed in Isa 11:6–8, and the imagery of verses 6–8 should not be read back into creation texts.

---

[98] 1QIsa[a] reads תמלאה, which seems to be a combination of the perfect and imperfect forms. The ת is probably secondary to match the other verbs in context or the *niphal* imperfect in the parallel passage in Hab 2:14. It is best to follow the MT and interpret it as a future perfect (Wildberger, *Isaiah 1–12*, 462).

[99] Cf. the similar conclusion of Tucker, "Peaceable Kingdom," 219.

New and Recent Titles

POVERTY, LAW, AND DIVINE JUSTICE IN PERSIAN AND HELLENISTIC JUDAH
Johannes Unsok Ro
Paperback $38.95, 978-1-62837-206-9   318 pages, 2018   Code 062635
Hardcover $53.95, 978-0-88414-286-7 E-book $38.95, 978-0-88414-285-0
Ancient Israel and Its Literature 32

PERCHANCE TO DREAM
Dream Divination in the Bible and the Ancient Near East
Esther J. Hamori and Jonathan Stökl, editors
Digital open-access, 978-0-88414-287-4
https://www.sbl-site.org/publications/Books_ANEmonographs.aspx
Paperback $34.95, 978-1-62837-207-6   232 pages, 2018   Code 062824
Hardcover $49.95, 978-0-88414-288-1   Ancient Near East Monographs 21

INFANCIA Y LEGALIDAD EN EL PRÓXIMO ORIENTE ANTIGUO DURANTE EL BRONCE RECIENTE (CA. 1500–1100 A. C.)
Daniel Justel
Digital open-access, 978-0-88414-279-9
https://www.sbl-site.org/publications/Books_ANEmonographs.aspx
Paperback $55.95, 978-1-62837-203-8   420 pages, 2018   Code: 062825
Hardcover $75.95, 978-0-88414-280-5   Ancient Near East Monographs 20

SUPPLEMENTATION AND THE STUDY OF THE HEBREW BIBLE
Saul M. Olyan and Jacob L. Wright, editors
Paperback $30.95, 978-1-946527-05-9   240 pages, 2018   Code 140361
Hardcover $45.95, 978-1-946527-07-3 E-book $30.95, 978-1-946527-06-6
Brown Judaic Studies 361

INTERMEDIATE BIBLICAL HEBREW GRAMMAR
A Student's Guide to Phonology and Morphology
Eric D. Reymond
Paperback $44.95, 978-1-62837-189-5   354 pages, 2018   Code 060395
Hardcover $59.95, 978-0-88414-250-8 E-book $44.95, 978-0-88414-249-2
Resources for Biblical Study 89

SBL Press • P.O. Box 2243 • Williston, VT 05495-2243
Phone: 877-725-3334 (toll-free) or 802-864-6185 • Fax: 802-864-7626
Order online at www.sbl-site.org/publications

Reading "House of Jacob" in Isaiah 48:1–11 in Light of Benjamin

CAT QUINE
catherine.quine@nottingham.ac.uk
University of Nottingham, Nottingham NG7 2RD, United Kingdom

Isaiah 48:1–11 has been described as a difficult passage because of a perceived discord between its harsh tone and the message of comfort espoused elsewhere in Isa 40–55. This article analyzes this passage with regard to four groups of arguments: proposals of a Judahite origin for the text, the archaeological evidence for settlement continuity in the Benjaminite region in the Neo-Babylonian period, the development and use of the patriarchal traditions in the sixth century, and studies of hidden polemic. Drawing these together, I propose that the address to the house of Jacob in Isa 48:1–2 can be understood as referring to a sixth-century Judahite community in the Benjaminite region, perhaps in the vicinity of Bethel.

Isaiah 48:1–11 comprises a series of harsh statements against the house of Jacob that have caused some difficulty for interpreters. Some scholars see no issue with the content of these verses and note pejorative statements directed at Jacob-Israel elsewhere in chapters 40–48. Others, however, attempt to harmonize the section with other material in chapters 40–55 by attributing particular phrases to later redactors. These efforts suggest that some uncertainty about the provenance of these verses persists.[1] The origin of Isa 40–55 as a whole has been widely debated, but in recent years strong arguments have been made in favor of a Judahite origin

---

This research was undertaken with funding from Midlands3Cities AHRC Doctoral Training partnership. Thanks are due to my supervisor, Dr. C. L. Crouch, for her assistance with earlier drafts of this paper and to the anonymous reviewers for their helpful comments.

[1] See the table of redactional proposals in A. Schoors, *I Am God Your Saviour: A Form-Critical Study of the Main Genres in Is. XL–LV*, VTSup 24 (Leiden: Brill, 1973), 285, table 6; and more recent comments in Chris Franke, *Isaiah 46, 47, and 48: A New Literary-Critical Reading*, Biblical and Judaic Studies 3 (Winona Lake, IN: Eisenbrauns, 1994), 173–244, here 271. John Goldingay and David Payne note that verses 1, 12, and 20 all start new sections within the chapter, each building on previous verses (*A Critical and Exegetical Commentary on Isaiah 40–55*, 2 vols., ICC (London: T&T Clark, 2006), 2:116. Due to considerations of space, I will deal only with 48:1–11, though a broader range of verses will be taken into account in a future research project.

for the core material of the text.² I accept these proposals and combine them with textual and archaeological evidence from Judah in the sixth century, in order to approach Isa 48:1–11 in light of issues that may have arisen in a Judahite context at this time.³

In section I, I look briefly at the arguments regarding a Judahite origin for Isa 40–55.⁴ In section II, I consider the archaeological evidence for settlement continuity and growth in the Benjaminite region in the sixth century, before commenting specifically on the situation of Bethel.⁵ In section III, I examine Jacob's association with Bethel in light of recent studies regarding the development and use of the Jacob and Abraham traditions in the exilic period. Finally, in section IV, I return to Isa 48:1–11 and analyze it on the basis of the preceding sections, proposing to read the "house of Jacob" in light of a sixth-century community in the Benjaminite region of Judah, most likely in the vicinity of Bethel. In this interpretation, Isa 48:1–11 may be shown to be in keeping with the prophet's rhetoric elsewhere in chapters 40–55 and in accord with theological and rhetorical developments in other exilic texts. By focusing on Bethel and raising the probability of other

---

²See Moses Buttenwieser, "Where Did Deutero-Isaiah Live?," *JBL* 38 (1919): 94–112, https://doi.org/10.2307/3259155. See also, e.g., Hans M. Barstad, *The Babylonian Captivity of the Book of Isaiah: "Exilic" Judah and the Provenance of Isaiah 40–55* (Oslo: Novus, Instituttet fur sammenlignende kulturforskning, 1997); Barstad, *A Way in the Wilderness: The "Second Exodus" in the Message of Second Isaiah*, JSSMS 12 (Manchester: Manchester University Press, 1989); Lena-Sofia Tiemeyer, *For the Comfort of Zion: The Geographical and Theological Location of Isaiah 40–55*, VTSup 139 (Leiden: Brill, 2011); Tiemeyer, "Geography and Textual Allusions: Interpreting Isaiah XL–LV and Lamentations as Judahite Texts," *VT* 57 (2007): 367–85; M. Goulder, "Deutero-Isaiah of Jerusalem," *JSOT* 28 (2004): 351–62.

³All dates given in this article are BCE.

⁴In this article, "Isa 40–55" refers to the core material in these chapters; it is not a claim for the unity of chapters 40–55 as a whole. For observations of redactional levels and editorial developments within Isa 40–55, see, e.g., Jürgen van Oorschot, *Von Babel zum Zion: Eine literarkritische und redaktionsgeschichtliche Untersuchung*, BZAW 206 (Berlin: de Gruyter, 1993); Rainer Albertz, *Israel in Exile: The History and Literature of the Sixth Century BCE*, trans. David Green, SBLStBL 3 (Atlanta: Society of Biblical Literature, 2003).

⁵In this article, "Benjamin" refers to the cities north of Jerusalem that survived the Babylonian destruction of Jerusalem in 586. The region of Benjamin seems to have had fairly fluid borders for most of its existence; consequently, the exact relationship between Benjamin and Judah after the fall of the northern kingdom, and thereafter in the seventh–fifth centuries, is as yet unclear. Notable works on the subject include Klaus-Dietrich Schunck, *Benjamin: Untersuchungen zur Entstehung und Geschichte eines israelitischen Stammes*, BZAW 86 (Berlin: Töpelmann, 1963); Schunck, "Benjamin," *ABD* 1:671–73; Philip R. Davies, "The Trouble with Benjamin," in *Reflection and Refraction: Studies in Biblical Historiography in Honour of A. Graeme Auld*, ed. Robert Rezetko, Timothy H. Lim, and W. Brian Aucker, VTSup 113 (Leiden: Brill, 2007), 93–111; Davies, "The Origin of Biblical Israel," in *Essays on Ancient Israel in Its Near Eastern Context: A Tribute to Nadav Na'aman*, ed. Yairah Amit et al. (Winona Lake, IN: Eisenbrauns, 2006), 141–49; Benjamin D. Giffone, *"Sit at My Right Hand": The Chronicler's Portrait of Benjamin in the Social Context of Yehud*, LHBOTS 628 (London: Bloomsbury T&T Clark, 2016).

Yahwistic shrines and communities within Judah, I demonstrate the likelihood of intracommunal strife within the Yahwistic community in the sixth century. With regard to the book of Isaiah, this intracommunal strife does not begin with the returnees from Babylon in Isa 56–66 but, in all likelihood, was present at any time when the interpretation of the true Israel was up for discussion.

I. An Anonymous Prophet in Exilic Judah

The difficulty of identifying the location of Isa 40–55 has provoked interest from scholars since the nineteenth and early twentieth centuries.[6] Hans Barstad's *Babylonian Captivity* demonstrates well the weaknesses in arguments claiming, or assuming, a Babylonian origin for the text.[7] More recently, Lena-Sofia Tiemeyer's monograph *For the Comfort of Zion*, has furthered considerably the case for a Judahite origin of Isa 40–55.[8] She systematically works through the text, demonstrating both where the text appears to betray a Judahite provenance and, equally importantly, where the theology or content of the verses might be closer to a Judahite perspective than a Babylonian one despite the absence of explicit information.[9] In a separate study, Tiemeyer laid out six reasons in favor of a Judahite author, including observations regarding the flora and fauna referred to in Isa 40–55, the pervading focus on Jerusalem and corresponding lack of focus on Babylon (except Isa 47), and the seeming geographical orientation behind statements such as "go forth from Babylon, flee from Chaldea" (Isa 48:20).[10] On the basis of the trees listed in Isa 44, Simon J. Sherwin has also argued for a western origin of the text, and the comments of Robert Koops and Michael Zohary on the trees mentioned elsewhere in Isa 40–55 (41:18; 44:4, 14; 55:13) are also instructive on this point.[11] A Judahite

---

[6] E.g., Bernhard Duhm, *Das Buch Jesaja*, HAT 3.1 (Göttingen: Vandenhoeck & Ruprecht, 1902), 336; Heinrich Ewald, *Die jüngsten Propheten des Alten Bundes mit den Büchern Barukh und Daniel*, vol. 3 of *Die Propheten des alten Bundes* (Göttingen: Vandenhoeck & Ruprecht, 1868), 30–31; Rudolf Kittel, "Cyrus und Deuterojesaja," ZAW 18 (1898): 149–62; Buttenwieser, "Where Did Deutero-Isaiah Live?"; William H. Cobb, "Where Was Isaiah XL–LXV Written?," JBL 27 (1908): 48–64, https://doi.org/10.2307/3260071; John A. Maynard, "The Home of Deutero-Isaiah," JBL 36 (1917): 213–24, https://doi.org/10.2307/3259227; Menahem Haran, "The Literary Structure and Chronological Framework of the Prophecies in Is. xl–xlviii," in *Congress Volume: Bonn 1962*, VTSup 9 (Leiden: Brill, 1963), 127–55, esp. 150–55; R. Abma, "Travelling from Babylon to Zion: Location and Function in Isaiah 49–55," JSOT 74 (1997): 3–28. See also the works referred to in n. 2 above.

[7] Barstad, *Babylonian Captivity*, esp. 59–75.

[8] Tiemeyer, *For the Comfort of Zion*, esp. 131–329.

[9] Ibid., esp. 132–53.

[10] Tiemeyer, "Geography and Textual Allusions," 369.

[11] Simon J. Sherwin, "In Search of Trees: Isaiah XLV 14 and Its Implications," VT 53 (2003): 514–29; Robert Koops, *Each according to Its Kind: Plants and Trees in the Bible* (Reading: United

location has also been suggested by recent studies on the patriarchal traditions in the exilic period. C. A. Strine has highlighted Ezekiel's polemic against those who remained in the land of Judah and claimed it for themselves, which they expressed via recourse to the promise of the land to Abraham (Ezek 33:23; cf. 11:15).[12] Tiemeyer also notes the use of the Abraham traditions in a range of exilic and early postexilic texts, including Isa 40–55 (Ezek 33:23, Isa 41:8, 51:2, 62:16, Neh 9:7–8).[13] The polemic against Babylon and its gods in Isa 46:1–2 and chapter 47 should also be taken into consideration; most scholars date the core material of Isa 40–55 shortly prior to the fall of Babylon in 539, on account of the references to Cyrus and the manner in which the prophet predicts the conquering of Babylon. Although Cyrus was gaining momentum during this time, it is unclear that a prophet could so openly mock Babylon and, in particular, the Babylonian gods, while Babylon was still in control of the exiled groups. With regard to the exiles in Babylon, Strine observes a correlation between proximity and polemic; in his view, Ezekiel says covertly against Babylon what Isa 40–55 can say overtly. This contrast suggests that the authors differed in time period as well as location.[14] In this context it seems more reasonable to view the overt polemic against Babylon in Isa 40–55 as originating in Judah, rather than among the Babylonian exiles.

II. Sixth-Century Judah and Benjamin

Having briefly outlined the reasoning for approaching Isa 40–55 as a Judahite text, I next consider some aspects of the historical reality of sixth-century Judah and Benjamin that would have influenced its author and formed the background against which the text was written. To this end, I will give more attention to Benjamin than has been typical of previous studies of Isa 40–55. In recent years scholarship has increasingly begun to focus on the role of Benjamin in the formation of Israelite identity and traditions in the exilic period, which seems a sensible development given that the Benjaminite region became preeminent in Judah during this time. If we are to argue for a Judahite Isa 40–55, then the role of Benjamin should be taken into account. Jill Middlemas has proposed the phrase "templeless Judah" to refer to the land of Judah in the exilic period, in order to acknowledge

---

Bible Societies, 2012); Michael Zohary, *Plants of the Bible: A Handbook* (Cambridge: Cambridge University Press,1982).

[12] C. A. Strine further argues that Ezekiel polemicizes against a combined Abraham-Jacob tradition and contends that there is a polemic against Jacob in a case of "hidden identity" in Ezek 35–36 (*Sworn Enemies: The Divine Oath, the Book of Ezekiel and the Polemics of Exile*, BZAW 436 [Berlin: de Gruyter, 2013], 177–215, here 193–211).

[13] Lena-Sofia Tiemeyer, "Abraham—A Judahite Prerogative," *ZAW* 120 (2008): 49–66.

[14] Strine, *Sworn Enemies*, 257–58.

the existence of the nonexiles who remained in the land.[15] Yet, in view of my purpose here, that is, to raise the possibility that Isa 40–55 was aware of other Yahwistic cult sites functioning in the sixth century, it would be inappropriate to use the term "templeless Judah." Therefore I refer to the land of Judah during the Neo-Babylonian period using the terms "exilic," or "sixth century."[16] In the past twenty years or so, archaeological and historical scholarship has sought to rectify the previous unfortunate lacuna in studies regarding this period.[17] Through these recent works, it has become clear that, although the areas around Jerusalem and, more centrally, in the Shephelah, suffered destruction or decline immediately after 586, the regions north of Jerusalem, particularly around Mizpah and Gibeon, did not.[18] Regarding the region of Benjamin, Oded Lipschits observes that

> no evidence emerges of destruction at the beginning of the sixth century, apart from the razing of parts of Tell el-Ful. At all the excavated sites evidence of continuity of settlement exists between the seventh and sixth centuries, and of their existence throughout the time of Babylonian rule, until the last third of the sixth century.[19]

The material culture of the population that remained in Benjamin was continuous with that of the pre-586 settlements, such that archaeologists have been unable to identify any change between early sixth-century and mid-sixth-century pottery.[20]

---

[15] Jill Middlemas, *The Troubles of Templeless Judah*, OTM (Oxford: Oxford University Press, 2005).

[16] Given the multiplicity of exiles and exilic communities, the breadth of the term *exilic* can be somewhat difficult when one wishes to speak specifically about a particular time, region, or group in the ancient Near East in the eighth–fifth centuries. Where possible in this article, therefore, I have endeavored to use the wordier but occasionally more accurate term *sixth century*. *Exilic* is used when a broader term is required.

[17] E.g., Oded Lipschits, "Demographic Changes in Judah between the 7th and 5th Centuries BCE," in *Judah and the Judeans in the Neo-Babylonian Period*, ed. Oded Lipschits and Joseph Blenkinsopp (Winona Lake, IN: Eisenbrauns, 2003), 323–76; Lipschits, "The History of the Benjaminite Region under Babylonian Rule," *TA* 26 (1999): 155–90; Erhard Gerstenberger, *Israel in the Persian Period: The Fifth and Fourth Centuries B.C.E.*, trans. Siegfried S. Schatzmann, SBLBE 8 (Atlanta: Society of Biblical Literature, 2011); Joseph Blenkinsopp, "Benjamin Traditions Read in the Early Persian Period," in Lipschits and Blenkinsopp, *Judah and the Judeans in the Neo-Babylonian Period*, 629–47.

[18] E.g., Gösta W. Ahlström, *The History of Ancient Palestine from the Palaeolithic Period to Alexander's Conquest*, JSOTSup 146 (Sheffield: JSOT Press, 1993), 806–7; J. Maxwell Miller and John H. Hayes, *A History of Ancient Israel and Judah* (Philadelphia: Westminster, 1986), 426.

[19] Lipschits, "History of the Benjaminite Region," 179.

[20] Ibid., 179–80; cf. Oded Lipschits, "Shedding New Light on the Dark Years of the 'Exilic Period': New Studies, Further Elucidation and Some Questions regarding the Archaeology of Judah as an 'Empty Land,'" in *Interpreting Exile: Displacement and Deportation in Biblical and Modern Contexts*, ed. Brad E. Kelle, Frank Ritchel Ames, and Jacob L. Wright, AIL 10 (Atlanta: Society of Biblical Literature, 2011), 57–90, esp. 66–68.

Administrative continuity has also been noted at Ramat Raḥel, Mizpah (Tell en-Naṣbeh) and Gibeon (el-Jib). These observations of continuity are unsurprising, given that Jeremiah 40–41 narrates the transition of government from Jerusalem to Mizpah under Gedaliah, and other narratives indicate that people were already leaving Jerusalem for the Benjaminite region prior to the fall of the city (e.g., Jer 37:11–15).[21]

In this light, the lack of any mention of the Benjaminite cities in Isa 40–55 and Ezekiel is striking. Ezekiel portrays Judah as a desolate and ruined land as part of his polemic against those who remained there.[22] Interestingly, Isa 40–55 does the same, though it is not generally considered polemical. In chapters 40–55, the only two cities specifically mentioned are Jerusalem and Babylon, while all other cities, and the land of Judah, are portrayed as ruined and desolate (cf. 42:22; 43:28; 44:26; 47:6; 49:8, 19; 51:3; 54:3). The prophet's focus on the restoration of Jerusalem is usually assumed to explain the emphasis on Judah's ruin. If chapters 40–55 are considered to be a Judahite text, however, then the omission of Mizpah, Gibeon, Bethel, or any functioning Benjaminite city is noteworthy.

I turn next to a discussion of Bethel, which both illuminates these preceding comments on Judah and Benjamin in the Neo-Babylonian period and also moves the discussion forward into the realms of tradition and polemic.

Bethel

Since 1838, Bethel has been identified with Beitin and, notwithstanding David Livingston and John Bimson's alternative proposal of el-Bireh, the majority of scholars hold to this view.[23] Beitin was excavated by James L. Kelso in 1954, 1957, and 1960 after an initial sounding by W. F. Albright in 1927 and the first campaign by Albright and Kelso in 1934.[24] The excavations provided evidence of a long

---

[21] Middlemas, *Templeless Judah*, 41–46; Jeffrey R. Zorn, "The Levant during the Babylonian Period," in *The Oxford Handbook of the Archaeology of the Levant c. 8000–332 BCE*, ed. Margreet L. Steiner and Ann E. Killebrew (Oxford: Oxford University Press, 2014), 825–41, here 829; Zorn, "Naṣbeh, Tel en-," *NEAEHL* 3:1098–1102; Davies, "Origin of Biblical Israel," 141–49; Hans M. Barstad, "After the 'Myth of the Empty Land': Major Challenges in the Study of Neo-Babylonian Judah," in Lipschits and Blenkinsopp, *Judah and the Judeans in the Neo-Babylonian Period*, 3–21, here 6–11; Albertz, *Israel in Exile*, 82–90; Jason Radine, *The Book of Amos in Emergent Judah*, FAT 2/45 (Tübingen: Mohr Siebeck, 2010), 185.

[22] Ezek 12:15–20, 15:7–8, 33:23–29.

[23] John J. Bimson and David Livingston, "Redating the Exodus," *BAR* 13 (1987): 40–53, 66–68; David Livingston, "Location of Biblical Bethel and Ai Reconsidered," *WTJ* 33 (1970): 20–44; Livingston, "Further Considerations on the Location of Bethel at el-Bireh," *PEQ* 126 (1994): 154–59; cf. Jules Francis Gomes, *The Sanctuary of Bethel and the Configuration of Israelite Identity*, BZAW 368 (Berlin: de Gruyter, 2006), 2–7.

[24] See W. F. Albright, "The Kyle Memorial Excavation at Bethel," *BASOR* 56 (1934): 1–15; James L. Kelso, "The Second Campaign at Bethel," *BASOR* 137 (1955): 5–10; Kelso, "Excavations

history of occupation and use of the site, from the Chalcolithic through to the Byzantine period but found no evidence of an Iron Age temple. In 2009, Israel Finkelstein and Lily Singer-Avitz reanalyzed the reports and finds from these excavations.[25] They noted the difficulty of assigning the pottery vessels to an original context and, in any case, found that most of the loci were mixed.[26] Finkelstein and Singer-Avitz did, however, note that much of the pottery the excavators had identified as sixth century BCE had come from loci marked on the excavation plans as Iron I. This, combined with the small evidence for Persian-period activity, led them to conclude that Bethel was most likely very small in the Neo-Babylonian–Persian periods.[27] Finkelstein and Singer-Avitz note that the lack of destruction layers in the first half of the seventh century makes dating difficult but points to the lack of "unambiguous evidence" for Neo-Babylonian or Persian-period settlement to suggest that Bethel was in a state of decline at this time.[28] It is important to note, however, that much of Beitin is covered by modern buildings. The fact that the excavators found no evidence of the temple suggests that the main settlement was either beneath or outside modern Beitin and remains unexcavated.[29] In this case, absence of evidence cannot entirely prove absence of historical settlement. Though appreciated, the efforts of Finkelstein and Singer-Avitz to reevaluate the Bethel material do little to challenge the prevailing view that, while the archaeology of Bethel is inconclusive, textual considerations suggest that habitation at Bethel continued in the exilic period.[30]

Contrary to Finkelstein's view that Bethel was in decline from the seventh century, Lipschits's survey of demographic changes in Judah and Benjamin suggests that the decline of the Benjaminite region, including Bethel, began toward the end of the sixth century rather than at the beginning.[31] Although the finds from Bethel are scant for the sixth–fifth centuries, the fact remains that Bethel is in close proximity to Mizpah and Gibeon, the former of which became the new administrative center of the region and experienced some measure of prosperity; for the latter there is evidence of settlement continuity and growth and continued production

---

at Bethel," *BASOR* 19 (1956): 36–43; Kelso, "The Third Campaign at Bethel," *BASOR* 151 (1958): 3–8; Kelso, "The Fourth Campaign at Bethel," *BASOR* 164 (1961): 5–19; Kelso, *The Excavation of Bethel 1934–1960*, AASOR 39 (Cambridge: American Schools of Oriental Research, 1968).

[25] Israel Finkelstein and Lily Singer-Avitz, "Reevaluating Bethel," *ZDPV* 125 (2009): 33–48.
[26] Ibid., 36.
[27] Ibid., 40–43.
[28] Ibid., 43–45.
[29] See Nadav Na'aman, "Beth-Aven, Bethel and Early Israelite Sanctuaries," *ZPDV* 103 (1987): 13–21.
[30] So, e.g., Joseph Blenkinsopp, "Bethel in the Neo-Babylonian Period," in Lipschits and Blenkinsopp, *Judah and the Judeans in the Neo-Babylonian Period*, 93–107, here 93–94; Blenkinsopp, "Benjamin Traditions," 643; Lipschits, "Shedding New Light," 66–67, 83; Gomes, *Sanctuary at Bethel*, 59–111.
[31] Lipschits, "Demographic Changes," 347–51.

of wine.³² Blenkinsopp has argued strongly for the likelihood of a Yahwistic sanctuary operating either at Mizpah or Bethel in the sixth century in view of this social and political shift toward the Benjaminite sites.³³ He notes that in the incident recorded in Jer 41:4–8 the pilgrims are presented as approaching Mizpah en route to the "house of Yahweh"; Jerusalem is never mentioned. Given that it would be implausible to think that the pilgrims were unaware of Jerusalem's destruction, Blenkinsopp argues that the pilgrims were traveling to a sanctuary in the vicinity of Mizpah, whether Bethel or otherwise.³⁴ Middlemas agrees that a cult center at Bethel likely functioned during the period when Mizpah was at the center of administration during the exile.³⁵

Jules Francis Gomes and Philip Davies also argue that Bethel continued in the Neo-Babylonian period and played an important part in forming Israelite identity at this time.³⁶ Gomes highlights the importance of the fact that Bethel appears prominently in the various redactions of both the Abraham and Jacob traditions. He notes further that, through the reception of the promises of land and descendants to Jacob and Abraham, Bethel became the locus of two of the most important promises in ancient Israelite society—promises that made the Bethel cult and its community the inheritors of the land.³⁷

Ernst Axel Knauf also has concluded that Bethel played an important role in the sixth century when, by virtue of its continued existence when the Jerusalem temple was destroyed, its rivalry with Jerusalem was at its highest. He suggests that it may even have provided an obstacle to the rebuilding of Jerusalem.³⁸ It seems, therefore, that there is some agreement that Bethel probably survived the Babylonian destructions of 586 and continued to function in some form during the sixth century.

Silence as Polemic

Despite the circumstantial evidence, it is clear that neither Bethel nor any community around or in Bethel is explicitly mentioned in the sixth-century biblical

---

³² Ibid., 347–48; Lipschits, "History of the Benjaminite Region," 172–79.

³³ Blenkinsopp, "Bethel in the Neo-Babylonian Period," 96–98; Blenkinsopp, "The Judean Priesthood during the Neo-Babylonian and Achaemenid Periods: A Hypothetical Reconstruction," *CBQ* 60 (1998): 25–43; see also Middlemas, *Templeless Judah*, 133–34; Scott M. Langston, *Cultic Sites in the Tribe of Benjamin: Benjaminite Prominence in the Religion of Israel*, AmUStTR 200 (New York: Lang, 1998), 100.

³⁴ Blenkinsopp, "Bethel in the Neo-Babylonian Period," 98–99.

³⁵ Middlemas, *Templeless Judah*, 134–44.

³⁶ Gomes, *Sanctuary at Bethel*, esp. 14, 59, 71–76; Philip R. Davies, *The Origins of Biblical Israel*, LHBOTS 485 (London: T&T Clark, 2007), 159–71.

³⁷ Gomes, *Sanctuary at Bethel*, 67, 70, 86–99.

³⁸ Ernst Axel Knauf, "Bethel: The Israelite Impact on Judean Language and Literature," in *Judah and the Judeans in the Persian Period*, ed. Oded Lipschits and Manfred Oeming (Winona Lake, IN: Eisenbrauns, 2006), 291–351.

texts. Yet the postexilic texts suggest that habitation at the site did continue, even if it was reduced significantly from what it was in previous centuries.[39] It thus seems that the silence of certain biblical writings, particularly Ezekiel, Isa 40–55, Lamentations, and Jeremiah, may have been part of a deliberate effort to downplay the importance or existence of Bethel.[40]

The possibility of hidden, or implicit, polemic as a rhetorical strategy has been noted in other biblical texts of this period in several studies.[41] Yairah Amit highlights the story of Micah the Levite in Judg 17 as an example of hidden polemic against Bethel, observing that the story of Micah is full of place-names, but the location of Micah's house is identified only as in the hill country of Ephraim; the city is not named.[42] Given the prevalence of other place-names and on the basis of textual indicators, she concludes that the unnamed city is Bethel and argues that Bethel is singled out for polemic due to its potential to act as an alternative to Jerusalem.[43] Amit argues that, in previous years when Jerusalem was stronger, there was no issue of condemning Bethel outright because Jerusalem could be held up as a better alternative. In the exilic period, however, when Bethel continued as a ritual center, the uncertainty surrounding Jerusalem may have led to a different expression of the Bethel polemic.[44]

Gomes also highlights the reticence of exilic and postexilic texts to refer to Bethel as a sanctuary or as having any kind of ritual significance, though some form of existence of the city is clearly attested by its presence in city lists and tribal records.[45] He identifies numerous texts that suggest worship continued at Bethel during the Neo-Babylonian period and observes that, despite the silence of some texts, the final redaction of the Pentateuch presents Bethel in a positive light.[46] Middlemas observes a "veiled association of Bethel with matters of a religious

---

[39] See, e.g., Ezra 2:28, Neh 7:32, 11:31, Zech 7:2.

[40] Or any other functioning Yahwistic cultic site.

[41] Strine has argued for hidden or implicit polemic against other figures or groups during this period in Ezekiel, manifested through "ambiguities," "hidden identities," and "hidden transcripts" (*Sworn Enemies*, 193–211, 228–66). See also Yairah Amit's discussion of anti-Saulide traditions in "The Saul Polemic in the Persian Period," in Lipschits and Oeming, *Judah and the Judeans in the Persian Period*, 647–61; and see further Amit, *Hidden Polemics in Biblical Narrative*, trans. Jonathan Chipman, BibInt 25 (Leiden: Brill, 2000), esp. 93–249.

[42] Yairah Amit, "Epoch and Genre: The Sixth Century and the Growth of Hidden Polemics," in Lipschits and Blenkinsopp, *Judah and the Judeans in the Neo-Babylonian Period*, 135–53.

[43] Ibid., 139–41. See also Amit, "Bochim, Bethel and the Hidden Polemic (Judg 2:1–5)," in *Studies in Historical Geography and Biblical Historiography: Presented to Zechariah Kellai*, ed. Gershon Galil and Moshe Weinfeld, VTSup 81 (Leiden: Brill, 2000), 121–31, where she views the reference to Bochim as referring to Bethel.

[44] Amit, "Epoch and Genre," 142, 145.

[45] Gomes, *Sanctuary at Bethel*, 185–86.

[46] Ibid., 92–95.

nature in Zechariah 7:2" and argues in overall agreement with Blenkinsopp that Zech 7 hints at Bethel functioning as a religious center before the return.[47]

It seems, therefore, that the sixth-century texts sought to diminish the importance of Bethel, achieved via deliberate omission. Notably, the majority of these sixth-century texts also downplay the importance of Benjamin. Neither Ezekiel, Lamentations, nor Isa 40–55 mentions any of the Benjaminite sites, and Jeremiah mentions Mizpah only in chapters leading to the emptying of the land (Jer 40–41) and Bethel in a single debatable reference (Jer 48:13). As D. R. Jones says, "silence can be eloquent of contempt, but only if that which is ignored is common knowledge."[48] The sixth-century writers would have been well aware that Benjamin had replaced Jerusalem as the political and social center of Judah, so their silence is clearly deliberate. The lack of reference to Bethel in the sixth-century texts has been rightly accepted, but it should also be acknowledged that the sixth-century texts are largely silent about the Benjaminite region as a whole and have a tendency to omit reference to any other cult centers. In this context, the lack of explicit reference to Bethel or Benjamin in Isa 40–55 cannot be taken as proof that neither Bethel nor the Benjaminite sites existed during this time. Nor can it prove that the existence of the Benjaminite sites had no influence on the Isaianic author. Rather, the omission of explicit references to Bethel and Benjamin in Isa 40–55 is entirely in keeping with the rhetoric of the other sixth-century texts.

III. Jacob and Bethel in the Exilic Period

I turn now to an examination of the literary and theological traditions associated with Bethel, particularly with regard to Jacob. This section is a logical progression of the argument laid out in the preceding sections. If the author of Isa 40–55 can be located in Judah (section I) at a time when the Benjaminite region was prominent and Bethel (and thus its traditions) continued to function (section II), then this ought to have left some trace in the text. It is in this vein that we now focus on Jacob as the main patriarch of Bethel—and a surprisingly dominant character in Isa 40–48.

The literary and editorial history of the Jacob cycles is notoriously complex and cannot be explored here.[49] For present purposes the relevant issue is the

---

[47] Middlemas, *Templeless Judah*, 136; cf. Blenkinsopp, "Bethel in the Neo-Babylonian Period," 96–99.

[48] D. R. Jones, "The Cessation of Sacrifice after the Destruction of the Temple in 586," *JTS* 14 (1963): 12–31, here 13.

[49] See, e.g., Nadav Na'aman, "The Jacob Story and the Formation of Biblical Israel," *TA* 41 (2014): 95–125, here 96–100; Erhard Blum, "The Jacob Tradition," in *The Book of Genesis: Composition, Reception, and Interpretation*, ed. Craig A. Evans, Joel N. Lohr, and David L. Petersen, VTSup 152 (Leiden: Brill, 2012), 181–211; Jochen Nentel, *Die Jakobserzählungen: Ein literar- und*

association of Jacob with Bethel and the popularity of the patriarchal traditions in the exilic period. That there were traditions associating Jacob and Bethel in the preexilic period can be seen from Hos 12:2–6.[50] The majority of scholars accept that the Jacob traditions were likely northern in origin, due to the prominent position of Bethel in the narratives.[51] The tensions surrounding Bethel's legitimacy contributed to its complex portrayal in the biblical texts. On the one hand, Bethel was reportedly established as a deliberate anti-Jerusalem sanctuary (1 Kgs 12:26–30) and housed one of the much-maligned calf statues. On the other hand, Bethel was an ancient sanctuary associated with Samuel (1 Sam 7:16) that retained an important position in the Jacob and Abraham narratives and seemingly survived the fall of both Israel and Judah.[52] Additionally, through the setting of the patriarchal traditions in the premonarchic period, Bethel laid claim to traditions older than YHWH's election of Jerusalem, traditions that were independent of the fate of the monarchy. Indeed, if Bethel continued after 586, it is easy to see how it would have presented a challenge to Jerusalem, whose own legitimacy was tied to a fallen monarchy and a ruined temple.

Questions about the nature of the relationship between Bethel and Jerusalem and, more broadly, between Benjamin and Judah in the seventh–fifth centuries

---

redaktionskritischer Vergleich der Theorien zur Entstehung des Pentateuch (Munich: AVM, 2009); Albert de Pury, "The Jacob Story and the Beginning of the Formation of the Pentateuch," in *A Farewell to the Yahwist? The Composition of the Pentateuch in Recent European Scholarship*, ed. Thomas B. Dozeman and Konrad Schmid, SymS 34 (Atlanta: Society of Biblical Literature, 2006), 51–72; Israel Finkelstein and Thomas Römer, "Comments on the Historical Background of the Jacob Narrative in Genesis," *ZAW* 126 (2014): 317–38, here 321–32.

[50] Whether Hosea knew some form of the Genesis textual tradition or drew from oral tradition is still open to debate, but either way the majority of scholars date Hos 12 to the preexilic period (see Marvin A. Sweeney, *The Twelve Prophets*, 2 vols., Berit Olam [Collegeville, MN: Liturgical Press, 2000], 1:120; W. D. Whitt, "The Jacob Traditions in Hosea and Their Relation to Genesis," *ZAW* 103 [1993]: 18–43; for a Persian-period dating, see James M. Bos, *Reconsidering the Date and Provenance of the Book of Hosea: The Case for Persian-Period Yehud*, LHBOTS 580 [London: Bloomsbury T&T Clark, 2013]), although it seems more plausible to posit an early date for some form of the Jacob traditions, which developed over time and increased in popularity in the exilic period, probably as a result of Benjamin's preeminence.

[51] E.g., Blum, "Jacob Tradition," 209; K. P. Hong, "Once Again: The Emergence of 'Biblical Israel,'" *ZAW* 125 (2013): 278–88, here 285–86; Hong, "The Deceptive Pen of the Scribes: Judean Reworking of the Bethel Tradition as a Program for Assuming Israelite Identity," *Bib* 92 (2011): 427–41, here 429–32; James Luther Mays, *Hosea: A Commentary*, OTL (London: SCM, 1969), 170; E. M. Good, "Hosea and the Jacob Tradition," *VT* 16 (1966): 137–51.

[52] Grace I. Emmerson, *Hosea: An Israelite Prophet in Judean Perspective*, JSOTSup 28 (Sheffield: JSOT Press, 1984), 134–35; see also Stephen L. Cook, "The Lineage Roots of Hosea's Yahwism," *Semeia* 87 (1999): 145–61, here 146; Steven L. Mckenzie, "The Jacob Tradition in Hosea xii 4–5," *VT* 36 (1986): 311–22; W. J. Dumbrell, "The Role of Bethel in the Biblical Narratives," *AJBA* 2 (1974): 65–79.

have led to a series of conversations about the "Emergence of 'Biblical Israel.'"[53] For Philip R. Davies, the importance of the Benjaminite sites in the sixth–fifth centuries, at a time when Judah and Jerusalem were at their lowest ebb, is crucial to the emergence of biblical Israelite identity. Davies argues that the fall of Jerusalem meant that Mizpah, Bethel, and Gibeon became the primary cities. This impacted Judah's self-understanding of its own identity such that the term *Israel* (which stemmed from Bethel's connections with Jacob-Israel) came to be used for all Judah.[54] Nadav Na'aman agreed that Bethel was likely an important site in the sixth century but argued, contra Davies, that the use of the term *Israel* to refer to the peoples of the two kingdoms is preexilic rather than postexilic. He holds that the fall of the northern kingdom provided an opportunity for Judah to take over some of Israel's traditions and claim them as their own.[55] Yigal Levin notes that the postexilic prophets do not make a distinction between Judah and Benjamin. In his view, the redactional development of the story of Joseph in the Pentateuch suggests that a later hand has added the theme of a struggle between Judah and Joseph for control over Benjamin. This move implies that Benjamin was at the center of some tension.[56] Following Na'aman's earlier dating and arguments about Judah seeking to take over Israelite traditions, K. P. Hong has argued for Judahite appropriation of the Jacob traditions in the wake of 722 and contends that Abraham plays an important role in this regard.[57] He proposes that Judahite scribes reworked the Jacob traditions and placed Abraham ahead of Jacob in order to justify their claim to the land, in much the same way that Sennacherib's scribes placed Assur ahead of Marduk in an Assyrian revision of Enuma Elish.[58] Further, the Abraham narratives may also contain implicit polemic against Jacob, as seen in the appearance of Jacob's main site, Bethel, in the Abraham traditions (Gen 13:3 and 12:8), and Abraham's reception of a similar promise of land and descendants.[59]

Yet, although Hong argues for the possibility of Judahite scribes beginning to replace the Jacob traditions with Abraham as early as the seventh century, the

---

[53] Nadav Na'aman, "Saul, Benjamin and the Emergence of 'Biblical Israel,'" *ZAW* 121 (2009): 211–24; Na'aman, "Saul, Benjamin and the Emergence of 'Biblical Israel' (Continued, Part 2)," *ZAW* 121 (2009): 335–49; Israel Finkelstein, "Saul, Benjamin and the Emergence of 'Biblical Israel': An Alternative View," *ZAW* 123 (2011): 348–67; Hong, "Once Again."

[54] Davies, "Origin of Biblical Israel," 142–45; contra Finkelstein, "Saul, Benjamin," 365.

[55] Na'aman, "Saul, Benjamin (Continued, Part 2)," 340–42; cf. Na'aman, "The Israelite-Judahite Struggle for the Patrimony of Ancient Israel," *Bib* 91 (2010): 1–23.

[56] Yigal Levin, "Joseph, Judah and the Benjamin Conundrum," *ZAW* 116 (2004): 223–41, here 231, 232–36.

[57] Hong, "Once Again," 285–86; Hong, "Deceptive Pen of the Scribes," 427–41.

[58] Hong, "Deceptive Pen of the Scribes," 438–40, here 438 n. 43: "With a successful program of promoting Judah as the new Israel, Judah in fact could assume and take advantage of all the Jacob tradition as our tradition (because we = Israel)." See also Finkelstein and Römer, "Comments on the Historical Background," 319, 332–34.

[59] Knauf, "Bethel," 322–23; cf. Na'aman "Jacob Story," 118; Hong, "Deceptive Pen of the Scribes," 439.

importance of Abraham in exilic texts is much more commonly attested.⁶⁰ Recently Thomas Römer, Tiemeyer, Strine, and Dalit Rom-Shiloni have all commented on the importance of the reference to Abraham in Ezekiel 33, where Ezekiel refutes the Judahite community's use of the Abraham traditions to claim ownership of the land.⁶¹ Tiemeyer has emphasized the importance of the recurring theme of Abraham in a range of Judahite exilic texts, and Strine has argued for the existence of a combined Abraham-Jacob tradition. Römer, however, rightly notes that Ezek 33 refers to the Judahite community's use of Abraham as "one" with no mention of Jacob or of the stylized "Abraham, Isaac, and Jacob" triad.⁶² Tiemeyer argues that Isa 41:8 and 51:2 affirm that the Abraham traditions were associated with the community in Judah, but, in contrast to Ezekiel, the Isaiah references support the Judahite community's claims to the land.⁶³ If so, then this would serve as further support for a Judahite origin of Isa 40–55.

In Isa 40–55, however, the references to Jacob-Israel far outweigh those to Abraham; it is Jacob that must be approached as the central figure of Isa 40:1–49:6.⁶⁴ Meira Polliack has suggested that the author of Isa 40–55 uses Jacob predominantly because his story is marked by more struggle and transformation than that of Abraham, and thus she concludes that an exilic audience would have found more relevance in Jacob's story.⁶⁵ Jacob's story does, admittedly, have struggle as a central motif that may have been attractive to the author of Isa 40–55, but the better-attested tendency of other exilic groups to prefer Abraham somewhat detracts from Polliack's emphasis on Jacob's relevance as opposed to Abraham's.

The question then arises with regard to Isa 40–55: how to situate Jacob in an

---

⁶⁰ E.g., John Van Seters, "Confessional Reformulation in the Exilic Period," *VT* 22 (1972): 448–59; Na'aman, "Jacob Story," 95–125.

⁶¹ Thomas Römer, "Abraham Traditions in the Hebrew Bible outside the Book of Genesis," in Evans, Lohr, and Petersen, *Book of Genesis*, 159–81, here 162–63; Tiemeyer, "Abraham," 50–52; Strine, *Sworn Enemies*, 181–90. Dalit Rom-Shiloni presents the discussion in terms of in-group and out-group claims and configurations (*Exclusive Inclusivity: Identity Conflicts between the Exiles and the People Who Remained [6th–5th Centuries BCE]*, LHBOTS 543 [London: Bloomsbury T&T Clark, 2013], 144–56; see also Joseph Blenkinsopp, "Judeans, Jews, Children of Abraham," in Lipschits, Knoppers, and Oeming, *Judah and the Judeans in the Achaemenid Period*, 461–83, here 471–73).

⁶² Tiemeyer, "Abraham," 65; Strine, *Sworn Enemies*, 177–215; Römer, "Abraham Traditions," 162–63. Whether one views the patriarchal traditions as combined or competing during the Babylonian exile, it is clear that the traditions themselves and the books that used them were continually developing throughout the sixth century and later.

⁶³ Tiemeyer, "Abraham," 56–57.

⁶⁴ Römer has even questioned whether the Abraham references in Isa 41:8 and 51:2 are part of a later redactional layer seeking to unify themes across the book of Isaiah and are perhaps later than Isa 40–55. Abraham occurs elsewhere in Isa 29:22, 41:8, 51:2, and 63:16. See Römer, "Abraham Traditions," 169–71.

⁶⁵ Meira Polliack, "Deutero-Isaiah's Typological Use of Jacob in the Portrayal of Israel's National Renewal," in *Creation in Jewish and Christian Tradition*, ed. Henning Graf Reventlow and Yair Hoffman, JSOTSup 319 (London: Sheffield Academic, 2002), 72–110, here 79.

exilic context where Abraham was becoming a figurehead for the Judahite exilic community, while Jacob had been previously associated with northern Israel and Bethel? Perhaps the answer lies in Benjamin. The Benjaminite region survived the destruction of Jerusalem, and it is entirely probable that, in the wake of 586, Benjaminite traditions would have been strengthened by the legitimacy of survival. It seems possible that a community in Benjamin, perhaps around Bethel, may have claimed legitimacy via Jacob, much as others claimed legitimacy via Abraham. While Jacob was more closely linked to the regions north of Jerusalem, Abraham seems to have been more closely connected to Jerusalem and the area south of it, as a result of his connections with Hebron and the southern tribes. Given the disparity between the functioning cities north of Jerusalem and the destroyed and empty ones in the south, it seems entirely possible that there may have been multiple communities in Judah claiming ownership of the land via recourse to different Judahite traditions. We turn now to Isa 48:1–11.

IV. Isaiah 48:1–11 and the House of Jacob

A more detailed study would explore all the references to Jacob in Isa 40–55 in light of the preceding discussions in sections I–III of this article. Within the scope of the present discussion, it is possible to focus on only one section here.[66] Isaiah 48:1–11 has been selected for consideration because, first, verses 1–2 constitute the most specific identification of the house of Jacob in chapters 40–55, and, second, 48:1–11 has proven difficult for commentators. Despite the prevalence of the term *Jacob* and its common parallelism with *Israel* in Isa 40–55, the term *house of Jacob* occurs only once elsewhere (46:3).[67] Given that *Jacob-Israel* are such

---

[66] For an overview of the occurrences of Jacob in Isa 40–66, see H. G. M. Williamson, "Jacob in Isaiah 40–66," in *Continuity and Discontinuity: Chronological and Thematic Development in Isaiah 40–66*, ed. Lena-Sofia Tiemeyer and Hans M. Barstad, FRLANT 255 (Göttingen: Vandenhoeck & Ruprecht, 2014), 219–31. I am grateful to Professor Williamson for providing me with a copy of his article. See also Gary N. Knoppers, "Did Jacob Become Judah? The Configuration of Israel's Restoration in Deutero-Isaiah," in *Samaria, Samarians, Samaritans: Studies on Bible, History and Linguistics*, ed. József Zsengellér, SJ 66, StSam 6 (Berlin: de Gruyter, 2011), 39–68. In this article Knoppers argues that some of the references to Jacob-Israel in Isa 40–55 have a much broader audience in view than others (cf. 43:1–7, 45:22–25, 46:3–4, 49:1–6). Knoppers cautions against the tendency to view all the Jacob-Israel references as having a single narrow audience. Interestingly, he raises the possibility that the "tribes of Jacob" in 49:6 need not necessarily refer to the old ancestral traditions but, rather, could demonstrate acknowledgment of the complicated diaspora demographics (67). To be clear, in arguing that Isa 48:1–11 has a specific referent, I do not deny that the audience/group referred to as Jacob-Israel elsewhere may be far broader; I am merely arguing that the house of Jacob in Isa 48:1 may be one part of this greater whole.

[67] The term *house of Jacob* occurs elsewhere in Isaiah only in 2:3, 5, 6; 8:17; 10:20; 14:1; 29:22; 46:3; 58:1, while *house of Israel* occurs only in 5:7, 8:14, 14:2, 46:3, 63:7.

common terms in Isa 40–55, yet "house of Jacob" occurs only twice and "house of Israel" only once, when these houses do appear they likely have a more specific agenda than the broader Jacob-Israel references found numerously elsewhere.

Commentators who view the bulk of the passage as original to a sixth-century prophet have noted that in chapter 48 the tension between prophet and audience, previously only hinted at (40:18–20, 27; 43:22–28; 44:9–20; 45:9–11; 46:5–12), comes to the fore.[68] Not only does the prophet speak in a harsher tone than before, but the passage occurs at a turning point in the book. Chris Franke emphasizes the pivotal nature of chapter 47 and notes that in chapters 40–46 Jacob-Israel lives in fear and oppression, whereas in 47, "the theme of downtrodden Israel is replaced by the prophecy of downtrodden Babylon."[69] Elsewhere, H. G. M. Williamson has suggested that 49:1–6 is another pivotal point. Although in chapters 40–48 there were indications that the servant was Jacob-Israel (41:8–10; 44:1, 2, 21; 45:4; 48:20), Williamson argues that in 49:3 the statement "you are my servant" functions as a redesignation of the servanthood that did not come to fruition with Jacob-Israel and is now passed to an individual or group whom YHWH hopes will be more successful.[70] It seems significant that the harshest passage against the house of Jacob occurs between the vivid image of the fall of Babylon (ch. 47) and a potential redesignation of the servant (49:1–6). Notably, after 49:6 the figure of Jacob-Israel largely disappears from the text and is replaced by Zion-Jerusalem.

In 48:1–2 the members of the house of Jacob are identified in various ways. They are "called by the name of Israel," but "came forth from the loins (or waters) of Judah" (וממי יהודה יצאו); they "swear by the name of YHWH" and "invoke the God of Israel, but not in truth or righteousness."[71] They "call themselves after the holy city" and "lean on the God of Israel." These verses are the first time in Isa 40–55 that Jacob is explicitly associated with the community of Judah. The point here is that, although the group in question calls itself Israel, the members of the house of Jacob are inherently Judahite. It is interesting that the author emphasizes this point, as we would have expected the house of Jacob to be from Judah and thus not requiring emphasis.[72] Francis Nataf notes that the very fact that Jacob has two names—

---

[68] Joseph Blenkinsopp, *Isaiah 40–55: A New Translation with Introduction and Commentary*, AB 19A (New York: Doubleday, 2000), 287; K. Jeppesen, "From 'You, My Servant' to 'The Hand of the Lord Is with My Servants': A Discussion of Is. 40–66," *SJOT* 4 (1990): 113–29, here 115–16.

[69] Chris A. Franke, "The Function of the Satiric Lament over Babylon in Second Isaiah (xlvii)," *VT* 41 (1991): 408–18, here 410–11.

[70] Williamson, "Jacob in Isaiah 40–66," 224; see further Williamson, *Variations on a Theme: King, Messiah and Servant in the Book of Isaiah*, Didsbury Lectures 1997 (Carlisle: Paternoster, 1998), 147–55, here 148.

[71] Commentators are divided on whether to render ממי יהודה with the MT as "waters of Judah" or to emend with the suggestion in *BHS* of ממעי יהודה, "womb/loins of Judah." Either way the emphasis is on the group's close relationship with Judah.

[72] Although this could be seen as a comment aimed at the Babylonian exiles who sought to distance themselves from the Judahites—Ezekiel's use of the phrase "house of Israel" springs to

Jacob/Israel—is a deviation from the usual biblical type scene whereby things have one name and if a new name is given it usually replaces the old (e.g., Abram-Abraham).[73] Nataf argues that by retaining the old name (Jacob) alongside the new name (Israel), the Bible maintains a dual legacy of Jacob.[74] It seems that Isa 48:1 uses this dual legacy inherent in the character of Jacob to state that the house of Jacob is still caught up in Jacob's sin.[75] For the author, although the house of Jacob may have changed their name to Israel and claimed a new identity, they were still intertwined in the old heritage of Jacob, as shown by the illegitimacy of their cultic actions.

Reinhard G. Kratz observes that the author of Isa 40–55 is aware of a difference still existing between Israel and Judah, and he views 48:1 as the prophetic author saying that only the Judeans who come out of the waters of Judah are called by the name of Israel. Therefore, the author uses the title "house of Jacob" to address the nation as a whole in order to level out the geographical and political differences.[76] Although Kratz seems correct in his observation that the use of Jacob-Israel in Isa 40–55 may well entail an effort to level out geographical and political differences between Judahite groups, the reference to the house of Jacob in 48:1–11 seems more specific. The reference to the house of Jacob having come from the waters, or loins, of Judah makes it seem unlikely that the entire community is envisaged as the addressee, as do the statements of the following verses. In 48:1–2 the dismissal of the house of Jacob's swearing by YHWH and invocations of the God of Israel are dismissed as nonrighteous and without truth, which is at odds with the more positive portrayal of Jacob-Israel elsewhere in chapters 40–55. Even in 40:27 (the only time Jacob-Israel speaks), in which Jacob-Israel is critical of YHWH, he is not accused of invoking or addressing YHWH illegitimately.[77] This also seems to

---

mind—the reference to the group calling themselves after the "holy city" perhaps does not fit so well with the exiles, who had a tendency to portray Jerusalem and the cities of Judah as corrupt and sinful. R. N. Whybray argues that Jacob-Judah-Israel in 48:1 has the whole nation in view and not merely the Judeans, though the specificity of the identification of the group seems to work against this (*Isaiah 40–66*, NCB [London: Oliphants, 1975], 127). Differently, J. D. W. Watts contends that those called by the name of Israel in 48:1 are those who have participated in covenant ceremonies (*Isaiah 34–66*, WBC 25 [Nashville: Nelson, 2000], 722). Schoors emends the verse because of its uniqueness (*I Am God Your Saviour*, 286), but this seems unnecessary.

[73] Francis Nataf, "What's in a Name? Ya'akov and/or Yisrael," *JBQ* 40 (2012): 241–46.
[74] Ibid., 46.
[75] Contra Reinhard G. Kratz, who argues that Jacob in Isa 40–55 represents a new beginning ("Israel in the Book of Isaiah," *JSOT* 31 [2006]: 103–28, here 113). Steven L. McKenzie contends that the reference in 48:1–2 is an allusion to the changing of Jacob's name, as the reference to the waters or loins of Judah seems to refer to Jacob as the individual patriarch ("Jacob in the Prophets," in *Jacob: Commentaire à plusieurs voix de Gen. 25–36: Mélanges offerts à Albert de Pury*, ed. Jean-Daniel Macchi and Thomas Römer, MdB 44 [Geneva: Labor et Fides, 2001], 339–57, here 355).
[76] Kratz, "Israel in the Book of Isaiah," 123.
[77] There might be a similar tone in 43:22–28, wherein Jacob-Israel is criticized for having brought offerings and sacrifices to YHWH, but this is a much-debated passage. John Goldingay

suggest that the criticism of the house of Jacob in 48:1–11 is aimed at a more specific group than the usual audience addressed by the broader nomenclature Jacob-Israel.

It has long been noted that the imagery in 48:4 of a neck of iron sinew and the hard bronze forehead is part of common language signaling obstinacy that is found elsewhere (Exod 32:9; 33:3, 5; Jer 6:8; Deut 9:6, 13; 31:27; Ezek 3:7–8). But the references to "things you have never heard" (48:6, 7), the "unopened ear from of old" (48:8), and the statement "from birth you were called a rebel" (48:8), have posed something of a puzzle for commentators. Some have argued that the verses are interpolations, as it hardly makes sense to state that Israel's ear was not opened "from of old."[78] If, however, the house of Jacob in 48:1 refers to a specific group within the broader conception of Jacob-Israel, then there is no contradiction between the harsh statements of 48:1–11 and the message of comfort promised to Jacob-Israel elsewhere in chapters 40–55. Isaiah 48:6–8 can be understood as directed to a specific group who are singled out for a message of judgment, in much the same way as the author singled out those who were tempted by idols (40:19; 41:7, 28–29; 42:17; 44:9–20; 45:16; 46:5–7; 48:5).

That the house of Jacob claimed to know YHWH's plans (48:5–6; cf. 58:2) suggests some form of cultic activity, which fits well with the idea of these verses being directed to a group based around a sanctuary (perhaps also supported by the reference to the holy city in 48:2). The claim of 48:6–8 that the house of Jacob "never knew" the things YHWH was about to do and "from of old" their ear was not opened, suggests that the house of Jacob had a long history and was not an entirely new innovation. Furthermore, chapters 46 and 48 both associate the house of Jacob with rebellion (46:8, 48:8), and something similar can be seen in 58:1–2. Scholars usually note that other prophets have similar conceptions of Israel being a rebel from the beginning and some have even suggested links between this verse and Ezekiel or Jeremiah.[79] The theme of rebellion, however, is found also in 1 Kgs 12, where the establishment of Bethel and Dan in opposition to Jerusalem is narrated.

---

concludes that 43:22–28 addresses the present generation and is designed to make them aware of their shortcomings in preparation for YHWH's plan ("Isaiah 43, 22–28," *ZAW* 110 [1998]: 173–91), but Thijs Booij understood it as a reference to the preexilic cult ("Negation in Isaiah 43, 22–28," *ZAW* 94 [1982]: 390–400). In contrast, John L. McKenzie argues that Isa 43:22–28 includes both generations: when Israel was able to offer sacrifices in the preexilic period they did so without devotion, and now that they cannot offer them in the exilic period they fail to worship YHWH properly (*Second Isaiah: Introduction, Translation and Notes*, AB 20 [New York: Doubleday, 1968], 60).

[78] Walter Bruggemann, *Isaiah*, 2 vols., WeBC (Louisville: Westminster John Knox, 1998), 2:103; Claus Westermann, *Isaiah 40–66: A Commentary*, OTL (London: SCM, 1969), 196; Blenkinsopp, *Isaiah 40–55*, 289.

[79] E.g., Shalom M. Paul, *Isaiah 40–66: Translation and Commentary*, ECC (Grand Rapids: Eerdmans, 2012), 311–12; J. L. McKenzie notes that the theme of early rebellion is current in the exile, whereas previous prophets (Hos 2:17; Jer 2:2) contrasted early fidelity with current unfaithfulness (*Second Isaiah*, 96); John N. Oswalt notes that many commentators interpret this as a

Given that Bethel was established as a deliberate act of rebellion against Jerusalem, it is possible to read 48:8 as a reference to Bethel's origin.

It is perhaps also noteworthy that the Benjaminite cities that survived the Babylonian invasions—seemingly because they surrendered when Judah did not—may well have been viewed by those within the ruined Judahite cities as having rebelled against Judah. The history of the region may also have contributed to its having a rebellious reputation; Benjamin appears to have been closely linked to Judah in the early days of the monarchy, then it became part of the northern kingdom, then it became part of Judah again, and then it survived when Jerusalem did not. As a region, Benjamin seemingly had a habit of changing sides and outlasting the kingdom that controlled it.

Although the figure of Jacob-Israel is pervasive in Isa 40–48, he is not presented as a model of good behavior. He complains against YHWH (40:27), displays stubbornness (48:4) and rebellion (43:27, 46:8, 48:8), fails in cultic practice (43:22–28), and perhaps fails in servanthood.[80] YHWH has punished him (42:24–25, 43:27–28, 48:9–10), and the fact that the house of Jacob still existed was for YHWH's own sake (48:9–11) and not due to any inherent righteousness or holiness of the group in question. Tiemeyer argues that Jacob-Israel probably refers to a group in Judah, and in light of sections I–III of this article, I propose that the group referred to as the house of Jacob in 48:1–11 could be understood as a sixth-century community in the Benjaminite region, most likely in the vicinity of Bethel.[81]

V. Conclusions

For much of the sixth century, the Benjaminite region replaced Jerusalem as the social and political center of Judah, and it is highly likely that, as a consequence of this newfound importance, Benjaminite traditions would have increased in popularity during this time. I have argued that, if we are to posit a Judahite origin for the core material of Isa 40–55, then this background should be taken into consideration. Further, I have contended that the house of Jacob in Isa 48:1–11 refers to a specific group within the broader conception of Jacob-Israel in Isa 40–55. This solves some of the perceived inconsistency between Israel's relationship and communication with its God, and the statements of 48:1–11 that the house of Jacob calls on YHWH illegitimately and that they have never known YHWH's plans. In light of evidence demonstrating settlement continuity in the Benjaminite region and arguments that Bethel continued to function after 586, combined with the centrality of Bethel in the Jacob and Abraham traditions, I have proposed that the house

---

reference to the exodus (*The Book of Isaiah: Chapters 40–66*, NICOT [Grand Rapids: Eerdmans, 1998], 268); cf. also Blenkinsopp, *Isaiah 40–55*, 290; Westermann, *Isaiah 40–66*, 198.

[80] Cf. Williamson, "Jacob in Isaiah 40–66," 223–25.

[81] Tiemeyer, *For the Comfort of Zion*, 219–20, 225, 237, 239, 240–43.

of Jacob in Isa 48:1–2 be identified with a group in Benjamin, perhaps in the vicinity of Bethel. This may better explain the author's choice of Jacob as the central figure (rather than Abraham), the mistrust of the self-identification of the group in 48:1–2, and the accusation of their Yahwistic actions being illegitimate. Read this way, 48:9–11 serves as an explanation that the preservation of this group—and perhaps the city in which they were based—was due not to its holiness or righteousness but only to YHWH's choice not to profane his name. Although Bethel is not mentioned explicitly in 48:1–11, or elsewhere in chapters 40–55, this omission is in keeping with other sixth-century texts that omit references to any Yahwistic shrines and tend to avoid mentioning the Benjaminite cities altogether. The region of Benjamin may well have offered some hope to the Judahites in the early years of the exile, and perhaps the mounting frustration in Isa 40–48 that comes to a head in 48:1–11 speaks to this situation, expressing the failure of this Yahwistic community and thus looking forward to the hope of the new servant and the restored Zion.

NEW FROM IVP ACADEMIC

CHRISTIANITY AT THE CROSSROADS
How the Second Century Shaped the Future of the Church
Michael J. Kruger

Christianity in the twenty-first century is a global phenomenon. But in the second century, its future was not at all certain. Michael Kruger's introductory survey examines how Christianity took root in the second century, how it battled to stay true to the vision of the apostles, and how it developed in ways that would shape both the church and Western culture over the next two thousand years.

256 pages, paperback,
978-0-8308-5203-1, $30.00

ECHOES OF EXODUS
Tracing a Biblical Motif
Bryan D. Estelle

Israel's exodus from Egypt is the Bible's enduring emblem of deliverance. But more than just an epic moment, the exodus shapes the telling of Israel's and the church's gospel. In this guide for biblical theologians, preachers, and teachers, Bryan Estelle traces the exodus motif as it weaves through the canon of Scripture, wedding literary readings with biblical-theological insights.

384 pages, paperback,
978-0-8308-5168-3, $40.00

Visit IVPACADEMIC.COM to request an exam copy.

 800.843.9487 | ivpacademic.com

The Role of Performance and the Performance of Role: Cultural Memory in the Hodayot

SHEM MILLER
stmille1@olemiss.edu
University of Mississippi, University, MS 38677
University of the Free State, 9300 Bloemfontein, South Africa

In this article, I explore how the Hodayot—an anthology of thanksgiving hymns— were experienced through oral performance and used for identity formation in the sectarian communities associated with the Dead Sea Scrolls. In particular, I describe the impact of the Hodayot's oral performance for both community members and a community leader, the Maskil. I begin with a survey of internal evidence that establishes public praise as a plausible sociolinguistic setting for the Hodayot. On the basis of performance criticism, I focus on the impact of the Hodayot as spoken words (speech) that appear in oral performance (reading). The Hodayot embodied the sectarian movement's cultural memory, and the manner in which the Hodayot represent the "self" enables speakers to imagine, or "re-member," themselves through oral performance. On the one hand, the membership's oral performance of the Hodayot functioned to produce collective identity, transform personal identity, and socialize members through narration of shared stories. On the other hand, the leadership utilized oral performance to self-identify with the pedagogical leadership, special knowledge, and institutional authority of the Maskil. Through oral performance, ordinary members could reimagine their identity as model sectarians, and a qualified leader could appropriate the Maskil's office.

Following the initial publication of the Dead Sea Scrolls, a wide variety of methodologies were applied in sophisticated manners to the newly discovered writings. The hermeneutic at work in some prominent methodologies (e.g., textual criticism), however, approaches the scrolls almost exclusively as written documents.[1] After all, texts are what we have available for study. So written texts

[1] Concerning the so-called great divide between orality and literacy, see Susan Niditch, "Hebrew Bible and Oral Literature: Misconceptions and New Directions," in *The Interface of Orality and Writing: Speaking, Seeing, Writing in the Shaping of New Genres*, ed. Annette Weissenrieder and Robert B. Coote, WUNT 260 (Tübingen: Mohr Siebeck, 2010), 3–18.

naturally become the objects of investigation, and discussions about social context revolve around criticism of literary works. This textual orientation can obscure the role of orality in the ancient Jewish sectarian communities associated with the Dead Sea Scrolls.[2] Viewed in their sociolinguistic context, however, the Dead Sea Scrolls were dynamic discourses that represented spoken words (speech) heard in shifting contexts of oral performance (reading). To understand the scrolls' significance, we must consider them within this oral world. In addition to the context-dependent sense of literary texts, the Dead Sea Scrolls also have meaning as oral discourse—that is, meaning in the situation of speech.[3] For these reasons, a move toward a more functional view of texts that incorporates orality into the use and transmission of texts would be productive.[4] With this broad goal in mind, I turn to the topic of this article.

In this essay, I explore the pivotal role oral performance plays in the processes of identity formation for community members and for a community leader, the Maskil. In particular, I scrutinize how one specific text, an anthology of poetic thanksgiving hymns (the Hodayot), was experienced through oral performance

---

[2] In past scholarship, the Community Rule was often associated with a single, large Essene community living at Qumran, whereas the Damascus Document was associated with smaller, satellite camps outside Qumran. In my view, however, the scribes of the Community Rule also describe smaller, dispersed communities (see 1QS VI, 1b–4). See John J. Collins, *Beyond the Qumran Community: The Sectarian Movement of the Dead Sea Scrolls* (Grand Rapids: Eerdmans, 2010), 65–69. Moreover, differences between Rule texts (e.g., the Community Rule and the Damascus Document) and between copies of the same Rule text (e.g., Cave 1 and Cave 4 copies of the Community Rule) evidence the historical development of these communities within a broader sectarian movement. Concerning textual development, see Sarianna Metso, *The Serekh Texts*, LSTS 62, Companion to the Qumran Scrolls 9 (London: T&T Clark, 2007), 15–19, 63–70. Concerning historical development, see Charlotte Hempel, "Emerging Communal Life and Ideology in the S Tradition," in *Defining Identities: We, You, and the Other in the Dead Sea Scrolls: Proceedings of the Fifth Meeting of the IOQS in Groningen*, ed. Florentino García Martínez and Mladen Popović, STDJ 70 (Leiden: Brill, 2007), 43–61, esp. 44–47.

[3] We could also think of "meaning in the situation of speech" as the "illocutionary" or "perlocutionary" meanings of speech that are not completely inscribed in texts. For an explanation of these technical terms, see Paul Ricœur, "The Model of the Text: Meaningful Action Considered as a Text," *New Literary History* 5 (1973): 91–117, esp. 93–95; John R. Searle, *Speech Acts: An Essay in the Philosophy of Language* (Cambridge: Cambridge University Press, 1969), 22–28, 59–61; J. L. Austin, *How to Do Things with Words* (Cambridge: Harvard University Press, 1962), 116–39.

[4] Concerning a "more functional view of texts," see George J. Brooke, "The Qumran Scrolls and the Demise of the Distinction between Higher and Lower Criticism," in *Reading the Dead Sea Scrolls: Essays in Method*, EJL 39 (Atlanta: Society of Biblical Literature, 2013), 1–17, esp. 16–17. For other studies that integrate orality into Second Temple Judaism, see Richard A. Horsley, *Scribes, Visionaries, and the Politics of Second Temple Judea* (Louisville: Westminster John Knox, 2007), 89–108; David M. Carr, *Writing on the Tablet of the Heart: Origins of Scripture and Literature* (Oxford: Oxford University Press, 2005), 228–34; Martin S. Jaffee, *Torah in the Mouth: Writing and Oral Tradition in Palestinian Judaism 200 BCE–400 CE* (Oxford: Oxford University Press, 2001), 28–38.

and used for identity formation. Because the prevailing scholarly trend casts doubt on the Hodayot's liturgical performance, section I will establish communal oral performance as a plausible sociolinguistic setting through a survey of internal evidence (e.g., times of prayer, plural imperatives, first-person plural nouns and verbs, and descriptions of communal praise and worship). In this section, I will also take stock of form-critical objections to the Hodayot's liturgical use.

In section II, I utilize the concept of "cultural memory" from memory studies as an avenue to explore the effect of the Hodayot's performance. For both members and leaders, the Hodayot embodied the culturally determined memory of the sectarian communities. Oral performance of the Hodayot within the proper performance arena therefore produced collective identity, transformed personal identity, and socialized members through narration of shared stories.

In section III, I examine several passages in the so-called Community Hymns and Teacher Hymns (in the Hodayot) that could be used to co-opt the Maskil's performance role. In the proper social setting, any qualified leader could recite the Hodayot in order to self-identify with the Maskil's pedagogical leadership and special knowledge.[5]

Finally, I describe two oaths that were drawn from initiation ceremonies and incorporated into the Hodayot (1QH^a VII, 21–25 and 1QH^a VI, 28–32). Through oral performance of these oaths, a qualified leader could renew or appropriate the institutional authority of the Maskil's office.

I. The Sociolinguistic Context of the Hodayot

The Hodayot exhibit a literary affinity with thanksgiving psalms in the Hebrew Bible and were used for a similar purpose: public worship. During the initial phase of the Hodayot's publication, multiple theories emerged proposing various liturgical uses within the community: nightly study sessions,[6] initiation and covenant ceremonies,[7] and community meals.[8] But a significant number of scholars have

---

[5] By "proper social setting," I intend to convey (1) the appropriate, culturally defined social circumstances and (2) the proper "performance arena." Performance arena designates the literal or figurative place of oral performance—both a geographical site and a metaphorical arena where performers and audience go to experience a text (John Miles Foley, *Homer's Traditional Art* [University Park: Pennsylvania State University Press, 1999], 23; Foley, *The Singer of Tales in Performance*, Voices in Performance and Text [Bloomington: Indiana University Press, 1995], 47–48).

[6] M. Delcor, "Qumran: Les Hymnes," *DBSup* 51:861–904, esp. 897–900.

[7] Svend Holm-Nielsen, *Hodayot: Psalms from Qumran*, ATDan 2 (Aarhus: Universitetsforlaget, 1960), 344–45.

[8] B. Reicke, "Remarques sur l'histoire de la forme (Formgeschichte) des textes de Qumran," in *Les manuscrits de la Mer Morte: Colloque de Strasbourg 25–27 Mai 1955*, ed. J. Daniélou (Paris: Presses Universitaires de France, 1957), 37–44, esp. 41–44.

subsequently questioned a liturgical setting because of the Hodayot's incongruence with liturgical works. According to this view, the various collections of prayers in the Dead Sea Scrolls "all share certain features that point to a public and communal *Sitz im Leben*, that is, to liturgical usage."[9] These signposts of liturgical usage, such as prayer formulated in the first-person plural, are scant in the Hodayot. Moreover, according to some scholars, the literary style of the Hodayot is incompatible with liturgical usage. The Hodayot's overloaded poetic style in comparison to Psalms (e.g., irregular "meter" and collapse of psalmic forms), abundant "I" language, and concrete references to personal experiences are unsuitable for liturgical use.[10] In light of this trend, I will establish the plausibility of the Hodayot's public oral performance before I discuss its impact.

First and foremost, some form-critical arguments against the Hodayot's liturgical usage assume that public prayers must contain a balanced prosody and elementary style. For example, Bilhah Nitzan asserts "poetry recited by the public must have simple rhythm and be easily recited."[11] Ethnopoetic studies on oral poetry from around the world significantly problematize this assumption.[12]

---

[9] Eileen M. Schuller, "Some Reflections on the Function and Use of Poetical Texts among the Dead Sea Scrolls," in *Liturgical Perspectives: Prayer and Poetry in Light of the Dead Sea Scrolls: Proceedings of the Fifth International Symposium of the Orion Center for the Study of the Dead Sea Scrolls and Associated Literature, 19–23 January, 2000*, ed. Esther G. Chazon, with Ruth Clements and Avital Pinnick, STDJ 48 (Leiden: Brill, 2003), 173–89. According to Schuller, "scholars have come to general agreement on criteria for recognizing liturgical texts: the individual prayers are relatively short; they contain set formulae, particularly at the opening and conclusion; they employ rubrics or titles specifying when the prayers are to be recited, and sometimes by whom; they utilize a dialogical element implying two or more voices; they are formulated in the first person plural; their content is communal and/or cosmological (not individualistic and specific)" (174).

[10] Bilhah Nitzan, *Qumran Prayer and Religious Poetry*, trans. Jonathan Chipman, STDJ 12 (Leiden: Brill, 1994), 321–55; Hans Bardtke, "Considérations sur les cantiques de Qumrân," *RB* 63 (1956): 220–33, esp. 227–29. Bardtke considered the form of the Hodayot's poetry to be a mixture of different biblical psalm genres (223–26).

[11] Nitzan, *Qumran Prayer and Religious Poetry*, 348. The poetry of the Hodayot, according to Nitzan, is "clumsy" and "burdened with theoretical statements which weigh upon the flow of the poetry" (ibid., 345). As I have argued elsewhere, I do not agree with her (and others') pejorative assessments of the Hodayot's poetry (see Shem Miller, "Innovation and Convention: An Analysis of Parallelism in Stichographic, Hymnic and Sapiential Poetry in the Dead Sea Scrolls" [PhD diss., Florida State University, 2012], 181–83, 242–50, 399–401). On the contrary, the clear delimitation of poetic structure (i.e., cola, lines, and strophes) and the prevalence of certain poetic devices (e.g., lists, keywords, repetition, and formulaic language) reflect a literary style amenable to oral performance.

[12] Ruth Finnegan, *The Oral and Beyond: Doing Things with Words in Africa* (Chicago: University of Chicago Press, 2007), 77–95; Dell Hymes, *Now I Know Only So Far: Essays in Ethnopoetics* (Lincoln: University of Nebraska Press, 2003), 370–79; Paul Zumthor, *Oral Poetry: An Introduction*, trans. Kathryn Murphy-Judy, Theory and History of Literature 70 (Minneapolis: University of Minnesota Press, 1990), 97–113.

Moreover, these form-critical arguments pertain to a specific definition of liturgical usage, not to oral performance. According to Nitzan, for example, the Hodayot were not part of a service to God *with a fixed order or pattern*.[13] But even if the Hodayot were not performed according to an established pattern or a liturgical cycle, this does not preclude their oral performance in communal worship.[14] As Trine Hasselbalch correctly notes, a particular view of prayer's historical development underlies Nitzan's argument.[15] According to Trine B. Hasselbalch, Nitzan's argument "rests on the unjustified assumption that only prayers conducted in accordance with a recognizable, fixed pattern could be part of social life" in the sectarian communities associated with the scrolls.[16]

Other arguments against liturgical use of some hymns are founded on a form-critical bifurcation of the Hodayot. Past scholarship divided the Hodayot's anthology into two classes of hymns with divergent literary styles and social contexts.[17] The so-called Teacher Hymns comprise the middle of the Cave 1 Hodayot manuscript (1QH^a IX, 1–XIX, 5) and begin with אודכה אדוני ("I thank you, my Lord"). The founder of the community, the Teacher of Righteousness, authored these hymns, and they describe the Teacher's experiences of suffering and redemption. These hymns employ "I" language and fit best in a private, devotional context. The so-called Community Hymns comprise the beginning and end of the Cave 1 Hodayot manuscript (1QH^a I, 1–VIII, 41; XIX, 6–XXVIII) and begin with the incipit ברוך אתה ("Blessed are you"), among others.[18] They employ "we" language,

---

[13] Nitzan, *Qumran Prayer and Religious Poetry*, 321.

[14] Indeed, as Holm-Nielsen argued more than fifty years ago, the Hodayot "may have been used anywhere in the service, without there being an established order and without their being linked to special holy occasions" (*Psalms from Qumran*, 348).

[15] As Trine B. Hasselbalch correctly emphasizes, Nitzan's argument presupposes that prayer developed from "free, often individual usage evidenced in the Bible into fixed, institutionalized prayer reflected in the Scrolls" (*Meaning and Context in the Thanksgiving Hymns: Linguistic and Rhetorical Perspectives on a Collection of Prayers from Qumran*, EJL 42 [Atlanta: SBL Press, 2015], 19). For Nitzan's explanation of this development, see *Qumran Prayer and Religious Poetry*, 37–41.

[16] Hasselbalch, *Meaning and Context*, 18.

[17] For helpful overviews of early scholarship on the division of Teacher and Community Hymns, see ibid., 2–12; Angela Kim Harkins, *Reading with an "I" to the Heavens: Looking at the Qumran Hodayot through the Lens of Visionary Traditions*, Ekstasis 3 (Berlin: de Gruyter, 2012), 17–24; Eileen M. Schuller, "Recent Scholarship on the *Hodayot* 1993–2010," *CurBR* 10 (2011): 119–62, esp. 119–20, 133–46.

[18] For a description of the incipits, see Hartmut Stegemann, "The Number of Psalms in 1QHodayot^a and Some of Their Sections," in Chazon, *Liturgical Perspectives*, 191–234, esp. 220–22. I should note, however, that inconsistency complicates this form-critical basis of division. In fact, the formula ברוך אתה occurs only thrice in the entire composition (see 1QH^a VII, 21; XIII, 22; XVII, 38). Moreover, 1QH^a XIII, 22 actually contains both formulas: the initial scribe wrote אודכה אדוני, and a subsequent scribe replaced this incipit with ברוך אתה. Last, אודכה אדוני occurs only twice in the incipits of the so-called Community Hymns (cf. אוד[ך אדוני] in 1QH^a VI, 34 and אודכה אלי in 1QH^a XIX, 6).

are less personal, and deal with more general concerns such as "divine salvific action and the human condition."[19] They best suit a context of public worship. At least four of these hymns are prescribed "for the Maskil"—an authoritative teacher and liturgical master in the sectarian movement (1QH[a] V, 12 [*hodayah* V, 12–VI, 33], VII, 21 [*hodayah* VII, 21–VIII, 41], XX, 7 [*hodayah* XX, 7–XXII, 42], XXV, 34 [*hodayah* XXV, 34–XXVII, 3]).[20]

Although this theory has remained popular since it was proposed over fifty years ago, interdisciplinary studies during the past two decades have undermined its credence. For our purposes, three relevant counterarguments emerge. First, Hasselbalch's and Carol Newsom's work blurs the line between "I" and "we" language by demonstrating that both types of speaker (leader and member) occur in each supposed class of hymns.[21] Put bluntly, as Hasselbalch argues, the hybridity of several compositions undercuts a tidy dichotomy of social groups and settings.[22] Second, Angela Kim Harkins undercuts the form-critical basis of the so-called Teacher Hymns. In particular, she dismantles the spurious, modern assumptions about authorship used to establish the literary unity of these hymns.[23] Third, Harkins and Newsom have convincingly argued that the "I" of the so-called Teacher Hymns does not necessarily describe a single, historical person. Rather than autobiographical poetry of a founding figure, according to Newsom, the Hodayot are a "collection of models for oral performance."[24] Moreover, these models articulate (1) a leadership myth and (2) an ideal sectarian that could be appropriated for the purposes of identity formation. On account of these three counterarguments, I employ a reading strategy that leaves aside the prevailing scholarly theory about

---

[19] Eileen M. Schuller, "Prayer, Hymnic, and Liturgical Texts from Qumran," in *The Community of the Renewed Covenant: The Notre Dame Symposium on the Dead Sea Scrolls*, ed. Eugene Ulrich and James VanderKam, CJAn 10 (Notre Dame, IN: University of Notre Dame Press, 1994), 153–71, esp. 154.

[20] My division of individual psalms follows Stegemann, "Number of Psalms," 228–29.

[21] Hasselbalch, *Meaning and Context*, 26–34; Carol A. Newsom, *The Self as Symbolic Space: Constructing Identity and Community at Qumran*, STDJ 52 (Leiden: Brill, 2004), 6–12, 287–300, 325–27. Additionally, varying grammatical person blurs the line between supposed hymn types. For example, the discourse in one *hodayah* (1QH[a] XI, 20–37) changes person three times (cf. 1QH[a] XI, 20–24).

[22] Hybrid hymns, according to Hasselbalch, exhibit literary features of both hymn classes (*Meaning and Context*, 34–37). In her words, both classes often evoke "one and the same type of worshiper: someone seeing himself as belonging to the elite and taking some sort of leadership responsibility upon himself" (17).

[23] Angela Kim Harkins, "Who Is the Teacher of the Teacher Hymns? Re-Examining the Teacher Hymns Hypothesis Fifty Years Later," in *A Teacher for All Generations: Essays in Honor of James C. VanderKam*, ed. Eric F. Mason et al., 2 vols., JSJSup 153 (Leiden: Brill, 2012), 1:449–67.

[24] According to Newsom, "the *Hodayot* may not have been simply a textual corpus for reading and reciting, but perhaps a collection of models for oral performance" (*Self as Symbolic Space*, 203).

the form-critical bifurcation of the Hodayot, particularly as it differentiates between individual praise (Teacher Hymns) and communal worship (Community Hymns).

Public Praise and Worship

Whether the entire anthology was sung or recited on specific occasions as part of a liturgical service is difficult to determine. But the angelic liturgy offers strong evidence that, at the very least, some of the Hodayot's hymns were used in public praise and worship (for more on the "angelic liturgy," see below). Additionally, internal clues ensconce several hymns within a liturgical setting. One incipit explicitly indicates a liturgical context: "[For the Instruc]tor, [th]anksgiving and prayer for prostrating oneself and supplicating continually at all times" (1QH^a XX, 7 [*hodayah* XX, 7–XXII, 42]); moreover, introductory rubrics associate two hymns with daily times of prayer (see 1QH^a V, 12–14 [*hodayah* V, 12–VI, 33] and 1QH^a XX, 7–12 [*hodayah* XX, 7–XXII, 42]).[25] A list of plural imperatives in 1QH^a IX, 36–39 (*hodayah* [IX, ?]–X, 4) is also remarkably apposite to public oral performance.[26]

The references to singing, music, and worship associate the Hodayot with liturgical worship.[27] Although some descriptions of musical performance are metaphorical, most portrayals of singing depict vocal performance of praise.[28] For example, 1QH^a XIX, 6–29 (*hodayah* XIX, 6–XX, 6) portrays actual singing. Shortly after the beginning of this hymn, the speaker proclaims, "you have put thanksgiving into my mouth, pr[ai]se upon my tongue, and (made) the utterance of my lips as the foundation for jubilation, so that I might sing of your kindness and reflect

---

[25] Daniel K. Falk, *Daily, Sabbath, and Festival Prayers in the Dead Sea Scrolls*, STDJ 27 (Leiden: Brill, 1998), 100–103. Unless otherwise stated, all transcriptions and translations of the Hodayot are from Eileen M. Schuller and Carol A. Newsom, *The Hodayot (Thanksgiving Psalms): A Study Edition of 1QH^a*, EJL 36 (Atlanta: Society of Biblical Literature, 2012). In a few noted instances, I make minor changes to the translation.

[26] In this list, the speaker begins with a command to hear, indicating an aural context of instruction, and then offers exhortation to five varieties of people: those who are eager, straight, righteous, perfect, and afflicted. Concerning the use of imperative calls to praise, first-person plural, and possible temporal expressions indicating prayer times in Cave 4 copies of the Hodayot, see Schuller, "Function and Use of Poetical Texts," 179.

[27] For a discussion of the various possible settings of singing, see Daniel K. Falk, "The Contribution of the Qumran Scrolls to the Study of Ancient Jewish Liturgy," in *The Oxford Handbook of the Dead Sea Scrolls*, ed. Timothy H. Lim and John J. Collins (Oxford: Oxford University Press, 2010), 617–51, esp. 633–34.

[28] For a discussion of metaphorical descriptions of singing and music, see Schuller, "Function and Use of Poetical Texts," 180–83. In 1QH^a XIX, 6–29, for example, a metaphorical description reads: "I will sing upon the lyre of salvation, and the harp of jo[y, and the timbrel of rejoi]cing, and the flute of praise, without ceasing" (1QH^a XIX, 26–27). The use of standard biblical instruments combined with poetic phrasing (e.g., "sing upon the lyre," "harp of joy," and "flute of praise") promotes a metaphorical interpretation.

on your strength all the day" (1QH^a XIX, 7–9).²⁹ Nothing in this passage connotes a metaphorical reading; moreover, multiple parallelisms between "thanksgiving" and "mouth" connote literal singing.³⁰

More importantly, some portrayals of singing refer to common rejoicing, which conveys a context of communal praise and worship. For example, according to 1QH^a XIX, 28–29 (*hodayah* XIX, 6–XX, 6), members will "*proclaim together* with a joyous voice" (ישמיעו יחד בקול רנה)."³¹ Similarly, 1QH^a XI, 24 (*hodayah* XI, 20–37) states, "that he might praise your name in a *common rejoicing* (להלל שמכה ביחד רנה)."³² In other instances, the authors of the Hodayot use the first-person plural to express community praise. In *hodayah* VII, 12–20, for instance, the speaker contrasts the community and its opponents with insider/outsider rhetoric.³³ "They" are unable to recite, sing with a voice, or praise the wondrous acts of God because "they" do not have insight; but "we" are able to praise God though oral performance because "we" possess proper knowledge. Through the rhetorical use of grammatical person, the speaker underscores that singing, recitation, and praise are communal: we reply, we instruct, and we recount God's deeds.³⁴

A social setting of communal oral performance is suggested also by multiple passages in the Hodayot describing an "angelic liturgy"—liturgical worship in which members joined angels in one choir of praise.³⁵ At the very least, these passages offer strong evidence that the ancient sectarian communities associated with the scrolls sung or recited some of the Hodayot's hymns on specific occasions as part of a liturgical service. In this passage from the "self-glorification hymn," for

---

²⁹ Schuller and Newsom, *Hodayot (Thanksgiving Psalms)*, 59.

³⁰ The parallelism between "I thank you, God" (אודכה אלי) in the incipit and "you have put thanksgiving into my mouth, pr[ai]se upon my tongue" (ותתן בפי הודות ובלשוני ת[ה]לה) in the ensuing line is unmistakable; furthermore, this bicolon line forms an *inclusio* with "and you have put into the mouth of your servant hymns of pr[a]is[e]" ([ה]ל[ה] ותשם בפי עבדכה הודות ת[ה]ל[ה]; 1QH^a XIX, 6–7, 36).

³¹ Schuller and Newsom, *Hodayot (Thanksgiving Psalms)*, 61.

³² Ibid., 37. Cf. also "rejoice in common assembly" (השתחוו ביחד קהל) in 1QH^a XXVI, 13–14. For other examples of common rejoicing, see 1QH^a II, 14; VIII, 15; IX, 32–33.

³³ E.g., "gave us insight" (השכלתנו), "what shall we reply" (מה נשיב), "you show us" (גמלתנו), "and as for us" (ואנחנו), "we are inst[ruc]ted" (נ[ו]ס[רה]), "and we ex[ult] ([ו]נר[ננה]), and "we will recount (it) together" (נספרה יחד). Concerning the use of us/them rhetoric in the Hodayot, see Newsom, *Self as Symbolic Space*, 303–8.

³⁴ Cf. also "yo[u yourself have revealed] in our hearing" in 1QH^a VI, 13, which suggests a communal context.

³⁵ For a description of the angelic liturgy, see Esther Chazon, "Human and Angelic Prayer in Light of the Dead Sea Scrolls," in Chazon, *Liturgical Perspectives*, 35–47; Devorah Dimant, "Men as Angels: The Self-Image of the Qumran Community," in *Religion and Politics in the Ancient Near East*, ed. Adele Berlin, Studies and Texts in Jewish History and Culture 1 (Bethesda: University Press of Maryland, 1996), 93–103.

example, the Maskil calls the community to praise God together with the eternal host:³⁶

> [Sing praise, O beloved ones! Sing to the king of glory!] Rejoic[e in the congregation of God! Cry gladly in the tents of salvation! Give praise in the holy dwelling!] Exalt [together with the eternal host! Ascribe greatness to our God and glory to our king! Sanctify his] na[me with strong lips and a mighty tongue! Lift up your voices by themselves at all times!] Sound al[oud a joyful noise! Exult with eternal joy and without ceasing! Worship] in common [assembly!... Bless the one who wondrously does majestic deeds]. (1QHᵃ XXVI, 9–14 // 4QHᵃ 7 I, 12–18)

The series of imperative calls to praise and second-person plural addresses situates this hymn in a social setting of liturgical performance.³⁷ Moreover, this passage emphasizes the oral/aural features of performance. On the one hand, the speaker commands the audience to sanctify God's name with "strong lips" (בשפתי עוז) and with a "mighty tongue" (ולשון נצח). On the other hand, the speaker adjures the congregation to *lift up* their [in the text, 'your'] "voices" (קולכם) and *sound aloud* a "joyful noise" (הגי רנה). The *hiphil* verbs "lift up" (הרימו) and "sound aloud" (השמיעו) stress the audible aspect of this praise—the participants should *cause* their voices to be heard. Last, this hymn concludes with a sequence of first-person plural verbs, which draw attention to the communal nature of this performance (cf. 1QHᵃ XXVI, 32–39).³⁸

Although some of the liturgical signposts exhibited in the "self-glorification hymn" are exceptional, the even distribution of the angelic liturgy throughout the Hodayot indicates that this hymn is not idiosyncratic.³⁹ The paucity of imperative

---

³⁶ Schuller and Newsom, *Hodayot (Thanksgiving Hymns)*, 79. For the text of the Cave 4 copies of the Hodayot, which fills in the lacunae of this passage, see E. Chazon et al., eds., *Qumran Cave 4.XX: Poetical and Liturgical Texts, Part 2*, DJD XXIX (Oxford: Clarendon, 1999). Scholarly treatment of the "self-glorification hymn" is too voluminous to recapitulate here. For a concise bibliography of studies, see Harkins, *Reading with an "I,"* 12 n. 29.

³⁷ E.g., "sing" (זמרו) and "שירו"), "rejoice" (שמחו), "cry gladly" (הרנינו), "give praise" (הללו), "exalt" (רוממו), "ascribe greatness" (הבו גדול), "sanctify" (הקדישו), "lift up" (הרימו), "sound aloud" (השמיעו), "exult" (הביעו), "worship" (השתחוו), and "bless" (ברכו).

³⁸ E.g., "we know you" (ידענוכה), "we understand your truth" (והשכלנו באמתכה), "we see your zeal" (ראינו קנאתכה), "we recognize your judgments" (והכרנו משפטיכה), and "we speak to you" (דברנו לכה).

³⁹ Esther Chazon has demonstrated that the angelic liturgy is evenly distributed throughout 1QHᵃ ("Liturgical Function in the Cave 1 Hodayot Collection," in *Qumran Cave 1 Revisited: Texts from Cave 1 Sixty Years after Their Discovery; Proceedings of the Sixth Meeting of the IOQS in Ljubljana*, ed. Daniel K. Falk et al., STDJ 91 [Leiden: Brill, 2010], 135–49). Concerning the view that the self-glorification hymn "cannot be taken as a key to [the liturgical character of] the Hodayot" on account of its "exceptional nature" vis-à-vis the entire anthology, see John J. Collins, "Amazing Grace: The Transformation of the Thanksgiving Hymn at Qumran," in *Psalms in Community: Jewish and Christian Textual, Liturgical, and Artistic Traditions*, ed. Harold W. Attridge and Margot E. Fassler, SymS 25 (Atlanta: Society of Biblical Literature, 2003), 77–85, esp. 84–85.

calls to praise and second-person plural addresses notwithstanding, the hymns of the Hodayot are interspersed with descriptions of an "angelic liturgy" in which members join one another in public praise. For a more typical example of the "angelic liturgy," I turn to 1QHª XI, 20–24 (*hodayah* XI, 20–37):

> I thank you, Lord, that you have redeemed my life from the pit and that from Sheol-Abaddon you lifted me up to an eternal height, so that I walk about on a limitless plain. I know that there is hope for one whom you have formed from the dust for an eternal council. And a perverted spirit you have purified from great sin that it might take its place with the host of the holy ones and enter into community with the congregation of the children of heaven. And you cast for a person an eternal lot with the spirits of knowledge, that he might praise your name in a common rejoicing and recount your wonderful acts before all your works.[40] (1QHª XI, 20–24)

This passage portrays communal oral performance with an angelic choir: the speaker has been stationed "with the host of the holy ones" (עם צבא קדושים), who come together with the "congregation of the children of heaven" (עדת בני שמים) in order to praise God's name "in a common rejoicing" (להלל שמכה ביחד רנה). Overall, descriptions of the angelic liturgy distributed throughout the Hodayot foreground the integral role of communal praise and public worship. They highlight how performance in the form of "a priestly service before God with the angels" was a crucial component of each member's oral performance.[41]

II. The Cultural Memory of Community Members

Although performance criticism is an underutilized methodology in scrolls scholarship, it illuminates the dynamic interaction between author, performer, and audience.[42] Performance criticism focuses on the meaning of "text" as a form of oral discourse by treating texts as spoken words (speech) that appear in oral performance (reading). Oral performance is the reading, recitation, or enactment of a text before an audience, whether by reciting from memory or by reading from a

---

[40] Schuller and Newsom, *Hodayot (Thanksgiving Hymns)*, 37.

[41] Carol A. Newsom, *Songs of the Sabbath Sacrifice: A Critical Edition*, HSS 27 (Atlanta: Scholars Press, 1985), 64. Because the sect believed praising God was a primary task of angels (Dimant, "Men as Angels," 98–103), the "angelic liturgy" also calls attention to the presence of singing. As Schuller concludes, it is appropriate that "song and praise, particularly in poetic form, could be expected to play a crucial role in their worship" ("Function and Use of Poetical Texts," 189).

[42] Marvin Lloyd Miller's performance criticism of 4QMMT is one noteworthy exception: *Performances of Ancient Jewish Letters: From Elephantine to MMT*, JAJSup 20 (Göttingen: Vandenhoeck & Ruprecht, 2015), 221–66.

text.⁴³ Throughout this article, I focus on the third aspect of this definition: enactment. In the context of oral performance, enactment refers to the process of "acting out" performance roles or "recreating" experiences described in a text. More specifically, my performance criticism below elucidates the impact of the Hodayot's oral performance for both community members and a community leader, the Maskil. I argue that members created their identity as model sectarians, and a qualified leader appropriated the Maskil's leadership office *through oral performance*.

In this section, I focus on the significance of the Hodayot's oral performance for ordinary community members. In particular, I utilize the concept of "cultural memory" from memory studies in order to illuminate how oral performance could effectively produce collective identity, transform personal identity, and socialize members through narration of shared stories. Since memory studies have not yet been adequately incorporated into scrolls scholarship, I begin with a definition of cultural memory.⁴⁴

Jan Assmann and Aleida Assmann's research, which focuses on the constitutive role of memory in the process of identity formation, is particularly relevant to the Hodayot. Broadly speaking, their theory of "cultural memory" integrates culture into memory.⁴⁵ According to this theory, neurology provides the "hardware" of memory, but culture and society provide its "operating system" and "software." In Jan Assmann's words, memory's "contents and the use we make of it are determined by our intercourse with others, by language, actions, communication, and by our emotional ties to the configurations of our social existence."⁴⁶ In a nutshell, cultural memory is that part of an individual's memory that is "socially and culturally determined."⁴⁷ Three key ideas regarding the Assmanns' theory of cultural memory are particularly useful for unlocking the impact of the Hodayot's oral performance: (1) we are what we remember; (2) we are what we belong to; and (3) we remember what we are through cultural texts.

First, the Hodayot's oral performance could effectively produce collective

---

⁴³ Rafael Rodríguez, *Oral Tradition and the New Testament: A Guide for the Perplexed*, Guides for the Perplexed (London: Bloomsbury T&T Clark, 2014), 27.

⁴⁴ As far as I know, only two memory studies of the Dead Sea Scrolls have been done. See George J. Brooke, "Memory, Cultural Memory, and Rewriting Scripture," in *Reading the Dead Sea Scrolls*, 51–66; Benjamin G. Wold, "Memory in the Dead Sea Scrolls: Exodus, Creation and Cosmos," in *Memory in the Bible and Antiquity: The Fifth Durham-Tübingen Research Symposium (Durham, September 2004)*, ed. Stephen C. Barton, Loren T. Stuckenbruck, and Benjamin G. Wold, WUNT 212 (Tübingen: Mohr Siebeck, 2007), 47–74.

⁴⁵ Jan Assmann, "Form as a Mnemonic Device: Cultural Texts and Cultural Memory," in *Performing the Gospel: Orality, Memory, and Mark*, ed. Richard A. Horsley, Jonathan A. Draper, and John Miles Foley (Minneapolis: Fortress, 2006), 67–83, esp. 68.

⁴⁶ Jan Assmann, *Religion and Cultural Memory: Ten Studies*, trans. Rodney Livingstone, Cultural Memory in the Present (Stanford, CA: Stanford University Press, 2006), 2.

⁴⁷ Ibid., 8.

identity because all identities are imagined—that is, we are what we remember. In Assmann's words, "It is not 'blood' or 'descent' as such that keeps a group together but the shared consciousness of it, the idea of a common descent."[48] As an illustration, I turn to a brief analysis of one notable excerpt from the so-called Teacher Hymns:

> For I remember my guilty acts together with the unfaithfulness of my ancestors, when the wicked rose against your covenant and the vile against your word. And I said, "In my sin I have been abandoned, far from your covenant." But when I remembered the strength of your hand together with your abundant compassion, I stood strong and rose up, and my spirit held fast to (its) station in the face of affliction. For I am supported by your kindness, and according to your abundant compassion to me, you pardon my iniquity and thus clean[se] a person from guilt through your righteousness.[49] (1QH^a XII, 35–38)

This passage bears marked similarities to a confession of sins during the annual covenant renewal ceremony (CD XX, 27–30; 1QS I, 24–26).[50] According to the Damascus Document, this confession reads, "we have wickedly sinned, we and our ancestors by living contrary to the covenant laws; just and true are your judgments against us" (lines 28–29).[51] The annual confession of sins evokes a common ancestry and appeals to a historical recollection of God's judgment on Israel's sin. What catches my attention, however, is that the Hodayot's confession explicitly describes "remembering" this common descent twice: "For *I remember* my guilty acts together with the unfaithfulness of my ancestors," and "*I remembered* the strength of your hand together with your abundant compassion." In the proper arena, any ordinary member could recite this confession to reimagine their identity—"remember" themselves anew—by appropriating the sectarian movement's common descent.

Throughout the rest of the Hodayot, however, memory is symbolically portrayed in terms of oral performance. According to the rhetoric of the Hodayot, we are what we remember, and we remember who we are through oral performance. In other words, we "remember" our sectarian identity by "recounting" or by "reciting" God's wonderful acts, judgment, and glory.[52] In *hodayah* XI, 20–37, for example, the speaker "remembers" God's wonderful deeds by recounting:

---

[48] Assmann, "Form as a Mnemonic Device," 67.

[49] Schuller and Newsom, *Hodayot (Thanksgiving Psalms)*, 41.

[50] For discussion of this confession in the Community Rule and the Damascus Document, see Falk, *Daily, Sabbath, and Festival Prayers*, 217–30, esp. 220, 228.

[51] Unless otherwise stated, all translations of the Community Rule and the Damascus Document are from Michael O. Wise, Martin G. Abegg Jr., and Edward M. Cook, *The Dead Sea Scrolls: A New Translation* (New York: HarperOne, 2005).

[52] For passages that describe "recounting" God's past acts and wonders, see 1QH^a VII, 18; IX, 32–35; XI, 24; XVIII, 16, 22; XIX, 9, 27; XXI, 9; XXVI, 35. For passages that describe "reciting" God's past acts and wonders, see 1QH^a IV, 29; VII, 14; IX, 35; XIV, 14.

> And a perverted spirit you have purified from great sin that it might take its place with the host of the holy ones and enter into community with the congregation of the children of heaven. And you cast for a person an eternal lot with the spirits of knowledge, that he might praise your name in a common rejoicing and recount your wonderful acts before all your works. (1QHᵃ XI, 22–24)

In this passage, recounting God's deeds—remembering—is defined as an act of communal, oral performance (cf. also 1QHᵃ VII, 13–19). Overall, the portrayal of memory as oral performance indicates that members could imagine their collective identity by recounting or reciting God's acts in the Hodayot.

Second, the Hodayot's oral performance could effectively transform personal identity because memory and identity are inextricably intertwined. In the words of J. Assmann, the slogans "we are what we remember" and "we are what we belong to" are "two sides of the same coin."[53] Confessions and professions throughout the Hodayot utilize both of these closely related ideas to transform personal identity. The passage quoted earlier (1QHᵃ XII, 35–38), for instance, contains an oral confession of sins in the form of historical recollection. The speakers first remember their guilty acts together with the unfaithfulness of their ancestors (lines 35–36). But the purpose of remembering is to self-identify with the common descent of the community. In indirect speech, the speakers confess that their sin alienates them from God, just as their ancestors' sin separated them from God's covenant. The repeated use of the first person in the initial four words of the confession, "but as for me, I said, 'in my sin I have been abandoned' [ואני אמרתי בפשעי נעזבתי]," foregrounds the transformation of self-understanding that is triggered by "remembering" the sect's common descent (line 36).[54]

Other passages in the Hodayot contain professions in which speaker self-identification is explicitly indicated (e.g., VII, 22–25; VIII, 28–30). In the passage below from the so-called Community Hymns, the speakers acknowledge their sinful state before God, choose to cleanse themselves, and entreat God to cleanse their sins:

> Because I know that you have recorded a spirit of righteousness, *I myself have chosen* to cleanse my hands according to your wil[l]. The soul of your servant abhors every malicious deed. I know that no one can be righteous apart from you, and so I entreat you with the spirit that you have placed in me that you make your kindness of your servant complete [for]ever, cleansing me by your holy spirit and drawing me nearer by your good favor.[55] (1QHᵃ VIII, 28–30)

In the phrase "I myself have chosen" (ואני בחרתי), the grammatically superfluous pronoun "I" foregrounds speaker self-identification. In another noteworthy passage (1QHᵃ VII, 22–25), the speakers affirm that they have loved God with their

---

[53] Assmann, "Form as a Mnemonic Device," 68.
[54] This is my translation.
[55] Schuller and Newsom, *Hodayot (Thanksgiving Psalms)*, 29.

whole heart, swear to follow God's commandments, and declare that they will stand firm until the final judgment. In a manner similar to 1QHª VIII, 28–30, speaker self-identification is explicitly indicated in 1QHª VII, 22–25 by the phrase "and as for me."

The use of the independent personal pronoun "I" with the *vav* conjunction (ואני), translated as "and as for me" or "but as for me," is a vital aspect of the Hodayot's rhetoric of identity transformation.[56] In fact, the morphemic frequency of ואני is higher in the Hodayot than in any other nonbiblical scroll.[57] This literary characteristic reflects the speaker's stress on "self" that occurred during the Hodayot's oral performance. Overt subject pronouns usually signal emphasis.[58] Additionally, an overview of the semantic range of verbs used with ואני underscores its function to transform personal identity. The majority of occurrences come together with verbs of knowledge ("but as for me, I know …") or contain dramatic descriptions of the self vis-à-vis God ("but as for me, I am …").[59]

Third, the Hodayot's oral performance could effectively socialize members through narration of shared stories. For members in the sectarian movement, memory and identity were inextricably intertwined, and what they remembered was often constructed by cultural texts, such as the Hodayot. In the terminology of memory studies, the Hodayot are "formative cultural texts" for they "formulate the self-image of the group" and "transmit identity-confirming knowledge by narrating shared stories."[60] As expressed in the above passage (1QHª XII, 35–38),

---

[56] Interestingly, many subsections within individual hymns are demarcated by a small *vacat* before ואני (see Hartmut Stegemann, Eileen Schuller, and Carol Newsom, eds., *Qumran Cave 1.III: 1QHodayotª, with Incorporation of 1QHodayotᵇ and 4QHodayotᵃ⁻ᶠ*, DJD XL [Oxford: Clarendon, 2008], 243). These *vacats* could graphically represent a linguistic or paralinguistic feature of oral performance that coincides with the speaker's self-identification with the Maskil's mythos.

[57] The Hodayot contains over 64 percent of all occurrences of ואני in nonbiblical Dead Sea Scrolls. Concerning the morphemic frequency of personal pronouns in the Hodayot, see S. Miller, "Innovation and Convention," 243–47.

[58] This is especially true when paired with the conjunction *vav*. Concerning the emphatic use of independent pronouns in subject or object positions within finite verbal clauses, see Robert Holmstedt, "Pro-Drop," in *Encyclopedia of Hebrew Language and Linguistics*, ed. Geoffrey Khan et al., 4 vols. (Leiden: Brill, 2013), 3:265–67; Jacobus A. Naudé, "The Distribution of Independent Personal Pronouns in Qumran Hebrew," *JNSL* 27 (2001): 91–112; Naudé, "Qumran Hebrew as a Null Subject Language," *South African Journal of Linguistics* 9 (1991): 119–25.

[59] Cf. 1QHª V, 35; VI, 23, 28; VII, 25, 35, 38; IX, 23; X, 13; XI, 24; XII, 31; XIII, 24; XVI, 15; XVIII, 7; XIX, 6, 10; XX, 14; XXII, 8; XX, 27; XXI, 11; XXIII, 24. Other occurrences explicitly related to identity formation include: "but as for me, I choose …" (VI, 36; VIII, 28), "but as for me, I hold fast to …" (X, 30; XII, 23; XXII, 14), and "but as for me, I rely upon …" (XV, 21; XXII, 12).

[60] Assmann, "Form as a Mnemonic Device," 76. Clifford Geertz coined the term "cultural text" ("Deep Play: Notes on the Balinese Cockfight," *Deadalus* 134 [2005]: 56–86, esp. 83–86). For our purposes, a "cultural text" is an oral or written text that is "constantly taken up and reproduced"

socialization is enabled by a characteristic rhetorical device of formative cultural texts: instrumentalized past.[61]

The authors of the Hodayot fabricate a politicized and counterfactual memory; that is, what its readers remember has nothing to do with historical facts.[62] Instead, the readers of this hymn remember Israel's past in terms that validate sectarian interpretation and mythology: the covenant abandoned by their ancestors was maintained by a handful of faithful seers and visionaries. In addition, God's covenant continues to be followed by repentant members in the sect. Only in this "historical" context—God's righteous judgment on a wayward Israel and God's compassionate forgiveness of a faithful remnant—do the speakers remember their own guilt. Through oral performance of this shared story, this confession socializes members with regard to acceptable views of God (i.e., theodicy) and humanity (i.e., judgment for outsiders and salvation for insiders).

III. The Performance Role of the Maskil

In the first half of this section, I examine passages in the so-called Community Hymns and Teacher Hymns that could be used to transform the speaker's identity into the Maskil. In the proper social setting, any qualified leader could recite the Hodayot in order to self-identify with the pedagogical leadership and special knowledge of the Maskil's performance role. In the second half, I consider two oaths of the Maskil's office that were drawn from initiation ceremonies and incorporated into the Hodayot (1QH^a VII, 21–25 and VI, 28–32). Through oral performance of these oaths, any qualified leader could renew or appropriate the institutional authority of the Maskil's office. I begin with an explanation of "performance role" and two attributes of the Maskil's performance role—namely, liturgical master and authoritative teacher.

In Newsom's innovative study of the Hodayot, she proposes that "*Hodayot* of the leader," as she calls them, "articulate a leadership myth that was appropriated by the current leader."[63] For Newsom, the Maskil is an authoritative position

---

on account of its "special normative and formative authority" for a society (J. Assmann, "Form as a Mnemonic Device," 76; Assmann, *Religion and Cultural Memory*, 104).

[61] Assmann, *Religion and Cultural Memory*, 24.

[62] In other words, the "I" of the Hodayot is not a report of a person's specific experiences or of historical events in the communities. In the terminology of Harkins, the "I" of the Hodayot is "imaginal"—that is, "I" is "constructed from popular experiences of well-known visionaries" (Harkins, *Reading with an "I,"* 5, 45). Moreover, the Hodayot's rhetoric functions to transform the reader's self-understanding by inviting him or her to identify with the experiences of this imaginal "I" (ibid., 111–12).

[63] Newsom, *Self as Symbolic Space*, 288–89.

ascribed to multiple individuals rather than a unique, historical figure.[64] The rhetoric of the Hodayot presents the Maskil as a leadership office with special responsibilities—an office that could be appropriated through performance. Newsom's rhetorical criticism of the Hodayot resonates with performance criticism and memory studies. Memory studies stress how oral performance both reflects and creates social roles. More importantly, according to performance theory, each component of a performance (e.g., participants, performers, and audience) has a culturally defined performance role.[65] Seen from this perspective, the authors of the Hodayot portray the Maskil as a leadership office with a particular "performance role."

The "rules for the Maskil" in the Community Rule (1QS IX, 12–26a) indicate that oral performance is a key, requisite element of the Maskil's leadership office.[66] More importantly for my present topic, four hymns prescribed "for the Maskil" in the Hodayot highlight two crucial attributes of the Maskil's performance role.[67] First, the Maskil is a liturgical master who orchestrates public worship (XXVI, 9–14, 26, 41). His performance is infused with blessings (V, 15; VII, 21; VIII, 26; XXI, 18; XXII, 34–35; XXVI, 31a), thanksgivings (XX, 7), and psalms (VII, 21). He leads liturgical prayer at specific times, daily and annually (XX, 7–12). Second, the Maskil is an authoritative teacher who imparts his god-given knowledge to members through pedagogical praise (V, 13–14; VI, 19–20). The Maskil is blessed with special knowledge of God's word, commandments, and precepts (VIII, 23–25). Through the holy spirit placed in him (V, 36; VIII, 20, 24; XX, 14–15; XXI, 34), God endows the Maskil with (1) esoteric knowledge concerning the true meaning of God's acts (V, 19; XX, 14–16) and (2) insight into the spiritual qualities of people (VI, 19–22). He utilizes this knowledge to place people into their appropriate rank within the community hierarchy (VI, 29–30) and utter a proper "answer of the tongue" (VIII, 24).

The Maskil's Fictional Character

One of Newsom's most insightful contributions to Hodayot scholarship pertains to the rhetorical function of the independent personal pronoun "I." Newsom argues that "I" is a sort of "fictional character," as she aptly describes it, which

---

[64] Ibid., 291.

[65] Richard Bauman, *Verbal Art as Performance* (Prospect Heights, IL: Waveland, 1977), 16, 29–35.

[66] Concerning the textual division of the end of the Community Rule, including the "rules for the Maskil," see n. 93 below. Concerning the depiction of the Maskil's performance in the "rules for the Maskil," see below under "The Maskil's Oaths of Office."

[67] Cf. 1QH^a V, 12 (*hodayah* V, 12–VI, 33); VII, 21 (*hodayah* VII, 21–VIII, 41); XX, 7 (*hodayah* XX, 7–XXII, 42); XXV, 34 (*hodayah* XXV, 34–XXVII, 3).

"strategically obscure[s]" the identity of the speaking subject.[68] In the majority of cases, the rhetoric of the Hodayot camouflages any unique coloring of "I." Therefore, "I" can be construed as the implied author or as a leading character, or as the listening audience or reading speaker who sympathizes with a leading character. Through oral performance, a number of people could identify with the "I" of the Hodayot's hymns and imagine or "re-member" themselves as ideal sectarians. Identity, after all, "is a product of imagination and of mental representation."[69]

In some instances, however, the fictional character "I" undeniably presents the attributes of the Maskil's performance role. In both the so-called Community Hymns and Teacher Hymns, these sorts of passages also contain a rhetoric that could be enacted and co-opted by any current, qualified leader. The most obvious examples come from passages that directly identify the speaker with the Maskil:

> And I, the Maskil, I know you, my God, by the spirit that you have placed in me [ברוח אשר נתתה בי]. Faithfully I have heeded your wondrous secret counsel. By your holy spirit [ברוח קודשכה] you have [o]pened up my knowledge within me through the mystery of your wisdom and the fountainhead of [your] pow[er]. (1QHª XX, 14–16)

In the proper social setting, any leader who spoke these words could self-identify with the Maskil's performance role, particularly as an authoritative teacher endued with God's holy spirit and blessed with special, God-given knowledge.

Examples in which the fictional character "I" indirectly identifies with the Maskil by appropriating the attributes of his performance role, however, are more subtle. But if we consider the Hodayot as spoken words in oral performance, the speaker self-identifies with the Maskil's pedagogical leadership in several passages. Below I examine two examples from the so-called Teacher Hymns that illustrate this point. In this first instance, God himself has placed the speaker in a leadership position in order to provide holy council:

> And you, O my God, have given me to the weary for holy counsel. You have [strengthened m]e in your covenant, and my tongue has become like (the tongues of) those taught by you.[70] (1QHª XV, 13)

Recitation of this passage places the performer's speech in continuity with those who came before him: "my tongue has become like (the tongues of) those taught by you." Like previous teachers, the speaker is endowed with divinely instituted authority and God-given knowledge. Most importantly, the speaker of this *hodayah* subsequently self-identifies with the pedagogical leadership of the Maskil's office: "you have made me a father to the children of kindness and like a foster father to

---

[68] Newsom, *Self as Symbolic Space*, 197–200.
[69] Assmann, "Form as a Mnemonic Device," 67.
[70] Schuller and Newsom, *Hodayot (Thanksgiving Psalms)*, 49.

the people of good omen (XV, 23–24)."⁷¹ Similar to his predecessors, the speaker affirms that his teaching derives from a special relationship with God and his performance role entails oversight over God's people.

In the broader context of this second example, the speaker compares himself with someone silenced in Sheol (1QHᵃ XVI, 33–39):⁷²

> Though you have made the tongue strong in my mouth, unrestrained, yet it is not possible to lift up (my) voice or to make (my) disciples hear, in order to revive the spirit of those who stumble and to support the weary with a word. (lines 36–37)

Although the speaker longs to guide and support his disciples with his oral/aural instruction (i.e., "lift up [my] voice" [להרים קול] and "make [my] disciple hear" [ולהאזין למודים]), the crippling attacks on his tongue prevent him from doing so. These attacks are part of a long anatomical list that invokes twelve parts of the body culminating with the mouth, tongue, and heart.⁷³ An *inclusio* indicates that the heart is a central part of the speaker's body, and the denouement implies that muteness—namely, the inability to speak his heart—is the gravest calamity.⁷⁴ Overall, through recitation of this passage a speaker could self-identify with the Maskil's performance role, especially as an authoritative teacher who leads through oral instruction.

In addition to pedagogical leadership, the speaker sometimes self-identifies with the special knowledge of the Maskil's performance role. Below I will examine two illustrative examples from the so-called Teacher Hymns. In this first instance, the speaker utilizes one of the confessional statements scattered throughout the Hodayot to proclaim and co-opt the Maskil's knowledge:

> I will respond with an answer to those who would confound me and with a reproach to those who are despondent on account of me. And his judgment I will declare wrong, but your decision I will declare right. *For I know your truth*, and I choose my judgment and accept my afflictions, because I wait expectantly for your kindness. You put a prayer of supplication in the mouth of your servant. ⁷⁵ (1QHᵃ XVII, 8–11)

---

⁷¹ Ibid., 49.

⁷² Ibid., 53.

⁷³ The list contains heart, flesh, loins, arm, joint, hand, leg, knees, foot, arm, tongue, and mouth.

⁷⁴ An *inclusio* occurs between "my heart has been poured out like water" (XVI, 33) and "they have laid waste to the tablet of his heart" (XVI, 38). The ordering of listed items accentuates this *inclusio*, because anatomical lists in biblical poetry often catalogue the parts of the human downwards from the head to toe. Instead, this list culminates with anatomical parts related to speech: mouth, tongue, and heart. Concerning lists in biblical poetry, see Wilfred G. E. Watson, *Classical Hebrew Poetry: A Guide to Its Techniques*, JSOTSup 26 (Sheffield: JSOT Press, 1984), 353–55.

⁷⁵ Schuller and Newsom, *Hodayot (Thanksgiving Psalms)*, 55.

As Newsom points out, the expression "I know" (ידעתי) in the Hodayot frequently has "something of the quality of a confessional statement rather than a cognitive one."[76] In other words, "I know" often indicates the speaker's acknowledgment and acceptance rather than mere comprehension.[77] In the above passage, for example, the speaker acknowledges that he accepts God's truth rather than his opponents' judgments.[78] Moreover, similar to the Maskil's God-given ability to give a proper "response of the tongue" (מענה לשון), the speaker affirms he will "respond with an answer" to those that would try to confound him (ואשיבה דבר).[79] In confessional passages like this, the speaker comes to experience himself as one possessing the Maskil's knowledge by reciting it, and the audience comes to experience the speaker as one possessing the Maskil's knowledge by hearing him tell it.[80]

In this second example, the speaker affirms his authority to examine members at communal, liturgical gatherings (i.e., "gathered together for your covenant" and "council of the holy ones") and proclaims that his teaching is consonant with correct instruction (i.e., "the way of your heart"):

> You have not covered in shame the faces of all who have been examined by me, who have gathered together for your covenant. Those who walk in the way of your heart listen to me, and they marshal themselves before you in the council of the holy ones.... Through me you have illumined the faces of many, and you have increased them beyond number. For you have made me understand your wonderful mysteries, and in your wonderful council you have shown yourself strong to me.[81] (1QHᵃ XII, 24–26, 28–29)

By reciting the phrase "through me you have illumined the faces of many," any qualified leader could have self-identified with the pedagogical leadership of the Maskil. More importantly, the speaker affirms his possession of inspired, divinely revealed, esoteric knowledge: "for you have made me understand your wonderful mysteries" (הודעתני ברזי פלאכה). According to the "the rules for the Maskil" in the Community Rule (1QS IX, 12–26a), the "wonderful mysteries" (רזי פלא)—a designation for esoteric knowledge concerning the true meaning of God's acts—fall under the authority of the Maskil's office (IX, 18).[82] Thus, this type of knowledge

---

[76] Newsom, *Self as Symbolic Space*, 211.

[77] Ibid., 209.

[78] The speaker asserts that he will condemn the "judgment" (וארשיעה דינו) of those who attempt to confound him and declare right God's "decision" (ומשפטכה אצדיק).

[79] 1QHᵃ VIII, 24; see also X, 9; XV, 14, 16; XIX, 31, 37. Concerning the Maskil's ability to give a "response of the tongue," see Judith H. Newman, "The Thanksgiving Hymns of 1QHᵃ and the Construction of the Ideal Sage through Liturgical Performance," in *Sibyls, Scriptures, and Scrolls: John Collins at Seventy*, ed. Joel Baden, Hindy Najman, and Eibert Tigchelaar, 2 vols., JSJSup 175 (Leiden: Brill, 2016), 940–57, esp. 953–54.

[80] Newsom, *Self as Symbolic Space*, 211.

[81] Schuller and Newsom, *Hodayot (Thanksgiving Psalms)*, 41.

[82] For a description of "wonderful mysteries," see Samuel I. Thomas, *The "Mysteries" of*

pertains specifically to the Maskil's performance role, and the speaker of this passage would assert that he too is blessed with the Maskil's special knowledge. Through recitation of this passage, any qualified leader could redefine himself by appropriating the Maskil's God-given knowledge.[83]

The Maskil's Oaths of Office

Another way in which the Hodayot's discourse transforms leadership identity stems from the oral performance of speech acts. In two instances, oaths with emphatic speaker identification (i.e., "but as for me" [ואני]) are demarcated as independent units of speech by *vacats* (see VI, 28–31; VII, 21–25). Both of these oaths were likely drawn from initiation ceremonies and incorporated into the performance of the Hodayot. Moreover, both passages strongly resemble an oath of office, in which the speaker states the obligations of the Maskil's office and swears to uphold them. Through oral performance of these oaths, a leader could renew or appropriate the institutional authority of the Maskil's office.

The first oath is positioned at the beginning of a hymn prescribed "for the Maskil" (*hodayah* VII, 21–VIII, 41). This oath therefore directly identifies the speaker with the Maskil:

> *vacat* Bless[ed are you, God of compassion, with a] song, a psalm for the Tea[cher] […] glad cry [… th]ey love you forever. *But as for me*, […] tru[th …] and I love you freely. With all (my) heart and with all (my) soul I have purified (myself) from iniquity. [And upon] my [li]fe [I] have sw[orn no]t to turn aside from all that you have commanded. I will stand firm against the many appointed for the [day of slaughter, no]t abandoning any of your statutes *vacat*.[84] (1QH[a] VII, 21–25)

Through this oath, the speaker identifies with two responsibilities of the Maskil's office. On the one hand, the speaker proclaims that he has purified himself "with all (his) heart and with all (his) soul." This creedal statement was likely drawn from earlier, less-elaborate initiation rites, which required members to swear an oath to return to the law "with all one's heart and with all one's soul" (cf. 1QS V, 7c–9a; CD XV, 5b–10a).[85] According to the beginning of the Community Rule, this initiation oath encapsulates a central obligation of the Maskil's pedagogy: "He is to teach

---

Qumran: Mystery, Secrecy, and Esotericism in the Dead Sea Scrolls, EJL 25 (Atlanta: Society of Biblical Literature, 2009), 136–50.

[83] Assmann, "Form as a Mnemonic Device," 76.

[84] Schuller and Newsom, *Hodayot (Thanksgiving Psalms)*, 25.

[85] According to Charlotte Hempel, the early admission requirements reflected in 1QS V, 7c–9a; CD XV, 5b–10a centered on this oath ("Community Structures in the Dead Sea Scrolls: Admission, Organization, Disciplinary Procedures," in *The Dead Sea Scrolls after Fifty Years: A Comprehensive Assessment*, ed. Peter W. Flint and James C. VanderKam, 2 vols. [Leiden: Brill, 1999], 2:67–92, esp. 70–71).

them to seek God with all their heart and with all their soul" (1QS I, 1c–2a).[86] On the other hand, the speaker swears not to turn aside from all of God's commandments. This fundamental duty of membership (1QS I, 15) also constitutes a core responsibility of the Maskil, who is charged with teaching members "to do that which is good and upright before Him, just as He commanded through Moses and all His servants the prophets" (1QS I, 2b–3a).[87]

The second oath occurs at the conclusion of another hymn prescribed "for the Maskil" (*hodayah* V, 12–VI, 33). As I will detail below, this oath bears striking similarities with the "rules for the Maskil" in the Community Rule (1QS IX, 12–26a), especially the portrayal of the Maskil's role in the admission process (1QS IX, 15–16). The close verbal parallels with the Community Rule suggest that parts of this oath (1QH[a] VI, 29–30, 32) were drawn from an entrance ceremony:[88]

> *vacat* **But as for me**, I have knowledge by means of your abundant goodness and by the oath I pledged upon my life not to sin against you [and] not to do anything evil in your sight. And thus I was brought into the community [הוגשתי ביחד] with all the men of my counsel. According to his insight I will bring him near, and according to the amount of his inheritance I will love him [לפי שכלו אגישנו וכרוב נחלתו אהבנו]. But I will not regard evil, and a b[rib]e (given) in wi[cked]ness I will not acknowledge. [And] I will no[t] exchange your truth for wealth nor any of your judgments for a bribe. But according as [... a per]son, [I will l]ove him, and according as you place him far off, thus I will abhor him (לפי [... אי]ש [אה]בנו וכרחקך אותו כן אתעבנו). And I will not bring into the council of [your] tr[uth any] who turn away [from] your [cov]enant *vacat*.[89] (1QH[a] VI, 28–33)

As noted by Newsom, "one has the distinct impression that the speaker is implicitly addressing the members of the sect through prayer."[90] Comparable to the use of "I"

---

[86] Wise, Abegg, and Cook, *Dead Sea Scrolls*, 117.

[87] Ibid.

[88] For a comparison of the close verbal parallels with technical terminology in the Community Rule, see Newsom, *Self as Symbolic Space*, 278 n.117. According to Stegemann and Schuller, the phrase "I was brought into the community" (הוגשתי ביחד) refers to "the formal ceremony of entrance into the community (cf. 1QS IX 15–16)"; moreover, "the text from לפי to the end of line 33 could be a citation of the text of the entrance ceremony, perhaps the words spoken concerning those being received, a 'liturgy' in which the one responsible for the new candidate stated his obligations" (Stegemann, Schuller, and Newsom, *Qumran Cave 1.III*, 93). Additionally, Bonnie Pedrotti Kittel posits that similarities between "the central לפי clauses" and directions "for yearly examination of a member's religious insight [cf. 1QS 5:23–24] ... suggest that these lines are creedal statements, or are drawn from vows taken by the community" (*The Hymns of Qumran: Translation and Commentary*, SBLDS 50 [Chico, CA: Scholars Press, 1981], 153).

[89] Schuller and Newsom, *Hodayot (Thanksgiving Psalms)*, 23. See also Newsom, *Self as Symbolic Space*, 280. Concerning the placement of *vacats*, see Stegemann, Schuller, and Newsom, *Qumran Cave 1.III*, 88.

[90] Newsom, *Self as Symbolic Space*, 278.

in the oral performance of creeds and oaths, the speaker proclaims correct beliefs and avows proper comportment to the audience. More specifically, this oath explicitly associates the speaker with the three aspects of the Maskil's performance role described in the "rules for the Maskil" in the Community Rule (1QS IX, 12–26a). First, the Maskil is responsible for establishing and maintaining the hierarchy of the sectarian communities (IX, 14–16). Thus, this oath ends with the solemn promise, "I will not bring into the council of your truth any who turn away from your covenant." Note also that the speaker describes the community as "the men of *my* council."[91]

Second, according to the "rules for the Maskil" in the Community Rule, the Maskil establishes community hierarchy based on his God-given insight into the spiritual qualities of people and their foreordained inheritance (1QS IX, 14–16; cf. also IV, 16, 24):

> In each case he [i.e., the Maskil] decides one's judgment according to one's spiritual qualities, drawing close to each according to their purity and bringing each near [i.e., admitting them] according to their wisdom; and thus (shall be) his love and his hate [i.e., in this manner, he will determine each person's rank]. (1QS IX, 15–16; my translation)

In a similar vein, as pointed out by Newsom, the speaker of the oath in 1QH^a VI, 28–33 "acts through the knowledge that has been given to him by God."[92] The Maskil proclaims that he will bring near (i.e., admit) and "love" (אהבנו) members according to their insight and their inheritance (VI, 29–30): "according to his insight I will bring him near, and according to the amount of his inheritance I will love him" (לפי שכלו אגישנו וכרוב נחלתו אהבנו). But he will "abhor" (אתעבנו) members according to the measure by which God places them far off (i.e., ostracizes them; VI, 32): "as you place him far off, thus I will abhor him" (וכרחקך אותו כן אתעבנו).

Third, the speaker affirms that his hierarchical decisions will be based on God's truth and judgments (משפטיך) rather than upon wealth (בהון). Similarly, in "the rules of the Maskil," the Teacher proclaims he will disregard wealth (הון; 1QS IX, 22). Instead, he teaches his followers with wisdom in order that they may answer those who are only zealous for "wealth" (הון); "as for me," the Maskil sings in the final hymn, "my judgment lies with God" (כיא אני לאל משפטי) (1QS XI, 2).[93]

---

[91] In this instance, I take the use of "council" and "community" to be the same technical use as in the Community Rule (e.g., 1QS XI, 8).

[92] Newsom, *Self as Symbolic Space*, 279.

[93] The ending of the Community Rule is composed of several originally independent units that were probably "recycled from other contexts" (Newsom, *Self as Symbolic Space*, 167). Subsequent to the "rules for the Maskil," all copies of the Community Rule save 4QS^e (4Q259) contain a calendar of prayer times (1QS IX, 26b–X, 8a) and a first-person hymn (1QS X, 8b–XI, 22). Concerning the textual division of the Community Rule, see Sarianna Metso, *The Textual Development of the Qumran Community Rule*, STDJ 21 (Leiden: Brill, 1997), 119, 142. Concerning

Overall, the speaker of this oath (1) affirms God's agency in his future actions and (2) attributes to himself key aspects of the Maskil's performance role outlined by the "rules for the Maskil" in the Community Rule (1QS IX, 12–26a). During oral performance, these utterances would have had the effect of an inauguration oath, in which a leader swears to uphold the duties of his office. Through oral performance, a leader could renew or appropriate the God-given knowledge and institutional authority of the Maskil's office.

V. Conclusion

I have investigated how one specific text, an anthology of poetic thanksgiving hymns, was experienced through oral performance and used for sectarian identity formation in the communities associated with the Dead Sea Scrolls. My performance criticism focused on the impact of the Hodayot as oral discourse by treating its hymns as spoken words (speech) that appeared in oral performance (reading). In particular, I was concerned to explain how members and leaders could have identified with the experiences and roles constructed by the Hodayot. Through oral performance of the Hodayot, speakers could create their identity as ordinary members and qualified leaders could transform their identity into the Maskil.

I began by establishing the plausibility of the Hodayot's public oral performance in praise and worship. On the one hand, some form-critical objections to liturgical use are based on assessments of "liturgical signposts," a narrow definition of "liturgical," or a problematic form-critical bifurcation of the Hodayot. The hybridity of the Hodayot collection undermines a dichotomy into private and communal social settings, and the polyvalence of "I" blurs the line between supposed hymn classes. On the other hand, the angelic liturgy offers strong evidence that, at the very least, some of the Hodayot's hymns were used in public praise and worship. Additionally, internal clues (i.e., times of prayer, plural imperatives, grammatical person, singing, and communal worship) situate some hymns in a liturgical context.

In the heart of this article, I utilized the concept of "cultural memory" from memory studies to explore three ways oral performance could have an impact on ordinary members. In particular, I argued that the Hodayot's performance produced collective identity, transformed personal identity, and socialized members through narration of shared stories. The Hodayot's oral performance could produce collective identity because its rhetoric evokes a common descent of membership and symbolically portrays memory in terms of oral performance. Oral performance could transform personal identity because the Hodayot contains discourse in which the speaker (1) explicitly self-identifies with confessional statements and

---

the association of this hymn with the Maskil's responsibilities, see Falk, *Daily, Sabbath, and Festival Prayers*, 103–10.

(2) co-opts the common descent of the community. The manner in which the Hodayot's rhetoric represents the self encourages the speaker to imagine or "remember" oneself through oral performance. Oral performance could effectively socialize members because the Hodayot's hymns narrate shared stories and transmit identity-confirming knowledge. For members in the sectarian movement, what they remembered was partly constructed by cultural texts such as the Hodayot.

The authors of the Hodayot portray the Maskil as a leadership office with a particular "performance role" rather than as a historical person. I discussed how four hymns prescribed "for the Maskil" define the Maskil's performance role as a liturgical master and authoritative teacher, and I examined passages in the so-called Community Hymns and Teacher Hymns that could be used to identify with the Maskil's performance role and appropriate the Maskil's office. On account of the fictional character "I," any qualified leader could recite the Hodayot in order to self-identify with the pedagogical leadership and special knowledge of the Maskil's performance role. Finally, I considered two oaths of the Maskil's office that were drawn from initiation ceremonies and incorporated into the Hodayot. Through oral performance of these oaths, any qualified leader could renew or appropriate the institutional authority of the Maskil's office.

Can a Man Commit πορνεία with His Wife?

DAVID WHEELER-REED
dwheelerreed@albertus.edu
Albertus Magnus College,
New Haven, CT, 06511

JENNIFER W. KNUST
jknust@bu.edu
Boston University,
Boston MA 02215

DALE B. MARTIN
dale.martin@yale.edu
Yale University, New Haven, CT 06511

In Classical and Hellenistic Greek, apart from use by Jewish and Christian authors, πορνεία meant "prostitution." Different words from the same word group (built on πορν-) all had something to do with prostitution. Πόρνη denoted a female prostitute, while πόρνος referred to a male prostitute who might be paid for sex with a man or a woman. Τὸ πορνεῖον referred to a brothel, and some form of the verb πορνεύω referred to one prostituting oneself or someone else. Πορνο-τρόφος referred to a pimp. Somewhere along the way, a group of words that in Greek and Latin seem to have originally referred simply to prostitution became in English a word referring, in most people's usage, to any sexual intercourse outside the bonds of marriage. But is that all that Paul or other New Testament writers mean when they condemn or warn against πορνεία? In other words, does πορνεία when used by a New Testament writer refer only to "extramarital sex" between a man and a woman, or does it include other activities also? This article suggests that the answer varies depending on whom you ask.

Recent scholars have tended to understand the term πορνεία simply as "sex outside marriage."[1] This point of view, however, is mistaken, whether the subject is ancient Greece or the later writings of Jews and Christians, and misrepresents the

---

[1] See, e.g., Kyle Harper, *From Shame to Sin: The Christian Transformation of Sexual Morality in Late Antiquity* (Cambridge: Harvard University Press, 2013). Harper maintains that the Christian injunction against πορνεία is in "radical opposition to all same sex intercourse." Furthermore, he opines, "The significance of *porneia*, in historical terms, was precisely that it gave a single name to an array of extramarital sexual configurations not limited to but specifically including prostitution." But he also notes, "Asking what *porneia* means is like asking how a fumigation bomb is shaped" (11–12). Throughout the rest of *From Shame to Sin*, the reader is greeted with a highly ideological reading of Christian texts that use πορνεία disguised as straightforward history. For an alternative to Harper's work, see David Wheeler-Reed, *Regulating*

history and range of meanings of this term and its cognates. In Classical and Hellenistic Greek, apart from use by Jewish or Christian authors, πορνεία meant "prostitution." Different words from the same word group (built on πορν-) all had something to do with prostitution. Πόρνη denoted a female prostitute, while πόρνος referred to a male prostitute who might be paid for sex with a man or a woman. Τὸ πορνεῖον referred to a brothel, and some form of the verb πορνεύω referred to one prostituting oneself or someone else. Πορνοτρόφος referred to a pimp.

Yet πορνεία came to be translated into later Latin by using an older Latin word in a new way. The notion was that prostitutes would often stand under "archways" when attracting customers. The Latin for "arch" was *fornix*. Some form of that word began to refer to prostitutes or prostitution. *Fornicatio* became a term for visiting a prostitute. Among Christian writers, its meaning was further broadened to refer to all kinds of illicit sex. The King James Version of the New Testament uses "fornication" to translate πορνεία.

Somewhere along the way, a group of words that in Greek and Latin seem to have originally referred simply to prostitution became in English a word referring, in most people's usage, to any sexual intercourse outside the bonds of marriage. Most dictionaries will provide the meaning of fornication as something like "consensual sexual intercourse between two people not married to one another." Fornication may be differentiated from adultery in that fornication can take place between two people neither of whom is married to someone else, whereas adultery refers to sexual intercourse in which at least one of the persons is married to someone else. In any case, fornication is usually used to refer to extramarital sex.

But is that all that Paul and other New Testament writers mean when they condemn or warn against πορνεία? In other words, does πορνεία, when used by a New Testament writer, refer only to extramarital sex between a man and a woman, or does it include other activities also? Hence the question posed by this article: Can a man commit πορνεία with his wife? The answer: It depends on whom you ask.

I. Classical Greek Usage

The obvious meaning of words of the πορν- group in Classical and Hellenistic Greek has something to do with prostitution. The term πορνεία itself survives in only a handful of texts.[2] The Hippocratic text *Epidemics* 7.122 uses it, spelled πορνείη. Demosthenes charges an opponent with it, though it seems in this context

---

Sex in the Roman Empire: Ideology, the Bible, and the Early Christians, Synkrisis (New Haven: Yale University Press, 2017).

[2] Indeed, according to Harper, in only four texts ("*Porneia*: The Making of a Christian Sexual Norm," *JBL* 131 [2011]: 363–83, here 369, https://doi.org/10.2307/23488230). Jennifer A. Glancy, though disagreeing with other conclusions posed by Harper, agrees with his count ("The Sexual

to be not literal prostitution but an insult that the man has allowed himself to be "screwed" by many other men (*Fals. leg.* 200). Dionysius of Halicarnassus (*Ant. rom.* 4.24.4) mentions slaves selling themselves sexually to raise money with which to buy their own freedom. Here he seems to be including male slaves, who would probably be selling their sexual favors to men as well as to women.

The verb form also occurs but, again, always referring either literally or metaphorically to prostitution. Herodotus claims that the daughters of a certain region prostituted themselves to raise money for their own dowries (*Hist.* 1.93). Aeschines accuses his opponent Timarchus of prostituting himself to many men (*Tim.* 52). As in the above example from Demosthenes, this accusation is more an insult than a claim that Timarchus was literally a prostitute. Aeschines repeats the insult in *De falso legatione* 144, again using the verb form and accusing Timarchus. The translator of the Loeb version, Charles Darwin Adams, renders the Greek as referring to Timarchus's "lewdness," but the context clearly allows an accusation of (at least metaphorical) prostitution.[3] In addition, Demosthenes repeats his insult, this time with the verb form, to refer, probably, to an opponent's "passive" sexual availability to other men (*Fals. leg.* 233).

The feminine form πόρνη occurs more often and always as a reference to prostitutes, as a quick glance at LSJ will show. The lexicon, in fact, suggests that the word derives from the verb πέρνημι ("to sell"), "probably ... because Greek prostitutes were commonly *bought slaves*" (LSJ, s.v. "πορνεία").[4] Male prostitutes are referred to with the term πόρνος (e.g., Xenophon, *Mem.* 1.6.13; Polybius, *Hist.* 12.15.2). The use of the πορν- word group to refer to prostitution and prostitutes extends into later Greek. The reference to Dionysius of Halicarnassus above provides one example from the late first century BCE. Artemidorus's *Onirocritica* (*Dream Handbook*) provides an example from the second or third century CE. This work does not use the actual word πορνεία, but it refers to a brothel as τὸ πορνεῖον (*Onir.* 1.78).

That the πορν- word group in Greek texts continued to refer to prostitution— and not to "fornication" or forbidden sexual activity in general—is borne out by an examination of papyri from the first century and later. Very few surviving papyri employ terms in the πορν- group, and those that do presuppose the basic meaning "prostitute" or "prostitution." Prostitution was legal and taxed, though the common terms for the tax in the documentary evidence is τέλος ἑταιρικόν.[5] The few tax

---

Use of Slaves: A Response to Kyle Harper on Jewish and Christian *Porneia*," *JBL* 134 [2015]: 215–29, https://doi.org/10.15699/jbl.1341.2015.2838).

[3] Aeschines, *Speeches*, trans. Charles Darwin Adams, LCL (Cambridge: Harvard University Press, 1919).

[4] For agreement that πορνεία derived etymologically from πέρνημι ("to sell"), see Allison Glazebrook, "Prostitution," in *A Cultural History of Sexuality in the Classical World*, ed. Mark Golden and Peter Toohey, Cultural Histories (London: Bloomsbury, 2011), 145–68, here 147.

[5] Roger Bagnall, "A Trick a Day to Keep the Tax Man at Bay? The Prostitute Tax in Roman

receipts that do use one of the πορν- terms refer to the pimp (the πορνοβοσκός),⁶ who was apparently responsible for paying the tax due from the brothel, perhaps on a yearly basis.⁷ Still, there are a few instances of πόρνη to be found. In a private letter from a husband (Serenos) to his wife (Isidora) from Oxyrhynchus (second century CE), Serenos tries to answer her complaint that he "has sold her as a prostitute" (πόρνη), a statement she made through their shared acquaintance Kolobos. Did she mean that her husband actually prostituted her to other men, or was she suggesting that some other action of his led her to such a drastic action? The letter is poorly spelled and the drama behind the episode unclear, but Serenos's response suggests that he was desperate to make amends for whatever he had done.⁸ A fourth-century (359 CE) collection of juristic decisions from Hermopolis offers another example. In one legal case, the mother of a prostitute (πόρνη) requests that the magistrate require the murderer of her daughter to provide for her since, without the earnings from her daughter's prostitution, she has been left destitute.⁹ The extraordinary circumstances of this case, and indeed of the rest of the sexual crimes recounted in this small codex, may suggest that this papyrus is a rhetorical exercise rather than an actual juridical record.¹⁰ It is striking that the surviving tax documents refer to prostitutes as ἑταῖραι, not πόρναι, reserving the πορν- family of terms for lurid cases or as a title for pimps. As papyrologists Johannes Diethart and Ewald Kislinger conclude in their survey of later Byzantine papyri, πόρνη carried the implications of slur while also serving as a label for a profession.¹¹ Thus, though the word πορνεία is unusual in non-Christian Greek authors, it and other instances of the same word group are consistently used to refer not simply to sex or to "illicit"

Egypt," *BASP* 28 (1991): 5–12; C. A. Nelson, "Receipt for Tax on Prostitutes," *BASP* 32 (1995): 23–33.

⁶ See, e.g., PSI 9 1055 b (25 February 265 CE), which registers the payment of the tax from the pimps of the city brothel (… πορνοβοσκοὺς ὀφείλοντας ὡς ὄντας μισθωτὰς τῶν κοινείων τῆς πόλεως) and SB 20 14517 (500–599 CE), which also registers the tax received from a πορνοβοσκός.

⁷ This may have been a yearly sum. See J. R. Rea, "P. Lond. Inv. 1562 Verso: Market Taxes in Oxyrhynchus," *ZPE* 46 (1982): 191–209. The reference in this receipt is to a κοινεῖον (brothel).

⁸ P.Oxy. 3 528: "Serenus to his beloved Sister, Isidora, many greetings.… You sent me letters which would have shaken a stone, so much did your words move me.… Apart from your saying and writing 'Colobus has made me a prostitute, he [Colobus] said to me, "Your wife sent me a message saying, 'He himself [Serenus] has sold the chain and himself put me in the boat"'" (Bernard P. Grenfell and Arthur S. Hunt, *The Oxyrhynchus Papyri*, vol. 3 [London: Egypt Exploration Fund; Oxford: Oxford University Press, 1903]).

⁹ *BGU* 4 1024 = P.Aktenbuch Ms. pp. 3–8.

¹⁰ James G. Keenen, "Roman Criminal Law in a Berlin Papyrus Codex (BGU IV 1024–1027)," *APF* 35 (1989): 15–23; Joëlle Beaucamp, *Le statut de la femme à Byzance, 4e–7e siècle*, 2 vols., TMCB 5–6 (Paris: De Boccard, 1990–1992), 1:54.

¹¹ Johannes Diethart and Ewald Kislinger, "Papyrologisches zur Prostitution im Byzantinischen Ägypten," *JÖB* 41 (1991): 15–23, here 21. Compare Dominic Montserrat, *Sex and Society in Graeco-Roman Egypt* (London: Kegan Paul, 1996): "Thus *gynē*, *hetaira* and *pornē* are status designations rather than professional names. Eventually *hetaira* and *pornē* seem to lose their more precise meanings: in the Roman period they have become virtually synonymous" (109).

or "immoral" sex in general but to prostitution, prostitutes, or houses for prostitution.

Both Philo and Josephus follow this Classical Greek usage. Every occurrence of any of the words from the πορν- group in Philo can be taken to refer to prostitution of some sort, even though some English translations render it as "fornication."[12] This is not surprising since Philo was well educated in Classical Greek. He remained faithful to the Classical and Hellenistic Greek uses of the terms.

Josephus uses these words rarely. He seems never to use the actual word πορνεία. Twice, he uses πορνεῖον as a term for a brothel (B.J. 4.562; A.J. 19.357), and he calls the mother of Jehu (2 Kgs 9:22) a sorceress and prostitute (πόρνη; A.J. 9.118). Indeed, it seems that Josephus avoids the πορν- words for the most part. Even when he is retelling a story from the Bible that uses terms for prostitutes, Josephus uses other language. For example, when Josephus introduces the story of how the prostitute Rahab helped the Hebrew spies in Jericho (Josh 2), he makes Rahab an innkeeper and says nothing about prostitution (A.J. 5.5–15). It seems that he is intentionally "cleaning up" biblical stories to render Israel and its history more "respectable" for Greek and Roman consumption. At any rate, on the rare occasion Josephus uses these terms, they always refer to prostitution of some sort. Both Philo and Josephus, therefore, follow the consistent Greek practice of taking πορνεία to refer to prostitution.

II. Πορνεία in Second Temple Jewish Texts

The LXX follows the Classical and Koine practice of using πορνεία and its related words only for prostitution. Such words usually translate the Hebrew זנה, meaning "to be a prostitute or prostitute oneself" (Gen 34:31, 38:15, Judg 16:1, Jer 2:20, Amos 2:7, Mic 1:7, and many others). For example, זנות: prostitution or unfaithfulness likened to prostitution (Num 14:33, Jer 3:2, Hos 4:11); זנונים: prostitution (sometimes metaphorically used to refer to promiscuity more generally; Hos 1:2, Nah 3:4); תזנות: prostitution or lust (Ezek 16:15; 23:7, 11). Some of these occurrences admittedly refer more to idolatry than literal prostitution (Jer 2:20 and many other places in Jeremiah and Ezekiel; see esp. Ezek 23), but it is clear that idolatry is being condemned by metaphorical equation to prostitution.

In Sir 23:27, πόρνος is used for a husband who commits adultery, and a wife who commits adultery is accused of engaging ἐν πορνείᾳ (23:23; the Hebrew of Ben Sira is usually dated to before 180 BCE, and the Greek translation to sometime after

---

[12] See, e.g., Mos. 1.300: F. H. Colson renders the word as "fornication," but the context suggests that prostitution is more accurate. The king trying to defeat Israel is advised to turn the women of his own kingdom into prostitutes in order to lead the Israelite men to sin (see Num 25). Philo calls one of these women explicitly a πόρνη (1.302). Other instances in which Colson translates πόρνος as "fornicator" and πόρνοι as "fornicators" include Leg. 3.8. But the words could just as easily be references to prostitution.

132 BCE). In these cases, we must assume that the terms are not meant literally; rather, they mean that a spouse who commits adultery is by that action "playing the whore." The reference to prostitution is nonetheless not far afield.

In other Second Temple Jewish texts, πορνεία is broadened to include all sorts of actions or even desires that the particular writer considers forbidden. In several instances in the Testaments of the Twelve Patriarchs (which, apart from later Christian interpolations, may be dated to the second century BCE), the different forms of the πορν- word group refer to any kind of "sexual immorality." In the Testament of Benjamin, πορνεύω and πορνεία are linked to Sodom, though what precise sexual action the author has in mind is not made explicit (T. Ben. 9:1). General admonitions against πορνεία, with no more precise meaning than some kind of "sexual immorality," occur often in the Testaments (e.g, T. Reu. 3:3, 5:3, 6:1; T. Levi 9:9; T. Jud. 18:2). In Ascen. Isa. 2:5, πορνεία occurs in a list of various sins attributed to the advocacy of Manasseh, along with adultery, sorcery, magic, augury, divination, and "persecution of the righteous." (This part of the text, sometimes designated as the "Martyrdom" of Isaiah, may be dated to the second century BCE.) In these references, all from later forms of Judaism than that represented in the Hebrew Bible, πορνεία takes on a broader meaning, referring to whatever the writers take to be sexual immorality.

In some texts, however, the word group has more specific meanings. In Tobit, for example, the parents of Tobias admonish him, "Beware, my son, of every kind of πορνεία (ἀπο πάσης πορνείας). First of all, marry a woman from among the descendants of your ancestors; do not marry a foreign woman, who is not of your father's tribe" (4:12 NRSV; with substitution of πορνεία for "fornication"; Tobit could be from the third century BCE, though of course the Greek would be later). The translators of the NRSV use the English "fornication," but it is obvious that here πορνεία does not refer to "sex outside marriage." Rather, it refers to exogamy or miscegeny. It may even include marriage outside the very Israelite tribe of the parents. The word does not mean "fornication" in the common English sense but intermarriage with persons not of one's own tribe.

The Greek translation of 1 Enoch uses the word in a similar way. The offspring born of sexual intercourse between the "Watchers" and human women (expanding on the story of the mating of the "sons of God" and human women from Gen 6:1–4) are called "half-breeds," "bastards," and "sons of miscegenation," the last word a translation of πορνεία (1 En. 10:9–10). In his commentary on 1 Enoch, George W. E. Nickelsburg rightly argues that πορνεία here refers not to literal prostitution but to "intercourse to forbidden degrees."[13] The reference is clearly to the sexual mixing of human with nonhuman beings, but it is correct to point out that, by this time and in certain forms of Judaism, πορνεία was used to condemn all kinds of sexual

---

[13] George W. E. Nickelsburg, *1 Enoch 1: A Commentary on the Book of 1 Enoch, Chapters 1–36, 81–108*, Hermeneia (Minneapolis: Fortress, 2001), 223; translations are Nickelsburg's.

behaviors of which writers disapproved. Nickelsburg is also correct to point out that the word πορνεία was used by Jews of this period to "paradigmatically attack marriage with Gentiles."[14] For at least some Jews, πορνεία was the gentile sin par excellence, along with idolatry.

Although in some instances Jewish writers could combine references to adultery with those to πορνεία, sometimes πορνεία was used to include a reference to adultery more particularly. In the Testament of Reuben, Reuben's sexual intercourse with his father's concubine is called πορνεία (T. Reu. 1:6; see also T. Jud. 13:3). In the Testament of Joseph, Joseph says that Potiphar's wife was attempting to lure him "into πορνεία" (T. Jos. 3:8; an expansion on Gen 39). The Testament of Reuben uses the same terminology for Potiphar's wife's attempt on Joseph (4:8, 11). The word in these contexts is translated by Howard Clark Kee as "sexual promiscuity," which would probably be better worded with the even more open-ended "sexual immorality."[15] By this time, many Jews have taken a word that classically meant prostitution and used it to refer to any kind of sexual behavior they condemned.

Finally, we come to a couple of Jewish texts that clearly extend the meaning of πορνεία to include even sexual actions that a man may do with, or passions he could entertain for, his wife. In particular, some Jews considered it to be πορνεία for a man to have sex with his wife motivated purely by sexual passion and lust. In a curious scene in Tobit, Tobias instructs his bride on their marriage night that they should get out of bed and pray rather than consummate their marriage by sexual deeds that night. They refrain from sexual intercourse on their wedding night in order that Tobias can say he is "taking" his "kinswoman" "not because of lust [διὰ πορνείαν] but with sincerity [ἐπ'ἀληθείας]" (8:7 NRSV). After the prayer, they say "Amen" and immediately go to sleep. Whatever else we may take the scene to mean, it obviously assumes that even sex with one's wife can count as πορνεία if indulged for the wrong reason.

We recall that πορνεία in Classical Greek always refers in some way to prostitution. The word group is broadened by Second Temple Jews to include other meanings. It is thus significant that texts from the Dead Sea Scrolls do the same with a word commonly used by the Hebrew Bible for prostitution—some form of the Hebrew זנה. For example, 4QD^e (4Q270) 7 I, 13 says, "Whoever approaches to have illegal sex with his wife, not in accordance with the regulation, shall leave and never return."[16] The word translated as "illegal sex" is זנות, which, as we have seen above, normally refers in the Hebrew Bible to prostitution. The shift in meanings here, from prostitution to even sexual activities within the bonds of marriage, is taken, we think correctly, by Hannah Harrington to mean that a man who has

---

[14] Ibid., 46.

[15] Howard Clark Kee, "Testaments of the Twelve Patriarchs," *OTP* 1:775–828, here 784.

[16] Trans. Florentino García Martínez and Eibert J. C. Tigchelaar, *The Dead Sea Scrolls Study Edition*, 2 vols. (Leiden: Brill, 1997–1998), 1:616–17.

"sexual intercourse for pleasure" rather than procreation, even with his wife, thereby makes her, at least metaphorically, a prostitute.[17]

But the scrolls use some form of the same word for other activities, such as marriage between an uncle and his niece, a man taking two wives, and even divorce and remarriage.[18] Indeed, several scholars of the Dead Sea Scrolls agree that some form of the word זנה in the scrolls is regularly used for all kinds of sexual deeds condemned by their authors.[19] The Hebrew-language scrolls exhibit the same shift we discerned in Second Temple Jewish texts in Greek: a word group that referred to prostitution in "Classical" Hebrew or Greek, comes to be used by later Jews to include condemnation of any kind of sexual action of which the writers disapproved. At least for some Jewish texts from the Second Temple Period, the answer to our question is, "Yes! A man can commit πορνεία with his wife."

III. Jewish Notions of "Sexual Immorality" in the Hellenistic and Roman Periods

We may get some idea of what Jewish authors considered immoral sexual activities by noting what they condemn even when not explicitly using the term πορνεία. Jubilees 50:8, for example, condemns any man for "lying with his wife" on the Sabbath. Josephus insists that good Jews engage in marriage and sex "only for the procreation of children" (*C. Ap.* 2.199 [Thackeray, LCL]). In the same context, Josephus says that a Jewish man will not have sex with his wife if she is pregnant, implying once again that some Jews condemned sex apart from the possibility of pregnancy. Philo insists on the same. He has his character Joseph insist that, for Jews, the goal of marriage is not "pleasure" but procreation of "lawful children" (*Ios.* 43 [Colson, LCL]). Elsewhere he teaches that even sex "according to nature," and

---

[17] Hannah K. Harrington, *The Purity Texts*, Companion to the Qumran Scrolls 5 (London: T&T Clark, 2004), 47; see also 17 for CD forbidding people from having sex on the Sabbath.

[18] These actions are from CD IV, 20–V, 11. For the condemnation of a man taking more than one wife (in his lifetime), see the thorough discussion of different possible interpretations in Cecilia Wassen, *Women in the Damascus Document*, AcBib 21 (Atlanta: Society of Biblical Literature, 2005), 114–18. Wassen argues that, since remarriage of a widow was not condemned in the scrolls, what is probably meant is polygyny. On what is meant by "fornication with one's wife," Wassen surveys different possible meanings but settles on sex purely for pleasure without the goal of procreation (173–79). Yonder Moynihan Gillihan shows that זנות was used to condemn many different sexual actions, including intermarriage with outsiders. See his *Civic Ideology, Organization, and Law in the Rule Scrolls: A Comparative Study of the Covenanters' Sect and Contemporary Voluntary Associations in Political Context*, STDJ 97 (Leiden: Brill, 2012), 244, 256–57 n. 393, 267, 424, 472, 723, 723 n. 40. See 4QMMT^c (4Q396) IV, 4, 11.

[19] Besides the works of Wassen and Gillihan already cited, see also Gillihan, "Jewish Laws on Illicit Marriage, the Defilement of Offspring, and the Holiness of the Temple: A New Halakic Interpretation of 1 Corinthians 7:14," *JBL* 121 (2002): 711–44, https://doi.org/10.2307/3268578.

even within marriage, must be condemned if it is prompted by immoderate or insatiable desire. He also condemns sex while the woman is menstruating, because that would entail the "wasting of seed." It makes sense, then, that he also condemns sex with a barren woman or sex with a woman the man knows to be sterile because of a previous childless marriage (*Spec.* 3.9, 33, 34, 36).[20]

The Jewish author whom scholars call Pseudo-Phocylides also includes several different deeds and desires among condemned sexual sins, though he does not use the word πορνεία in this context. He advises men not to "outrage" their wives "by shameful ways of intercourse" (ἐπ᾽ αἰσχυντοῖς λεχέεσσιν, 189).[21] He warns against any "unlawful sex" (ἐς Κύπριν ἄθεσμον) that transgresses "the limits set by nature," including same-sex intercourse, women taking the "male" role in sex (λέχος ἀνδρῶν), and any sort of "unbridled sexuality" (ἔρωτα ... ἀκάθεκτον) even with one's wife (190–193). A few lines before, he had already ruled out sex with one's wife when she is pregnant (186). Pseudo-Phocylides does urge marriage and procreative sex (175–176). But just about anything outside that is condemned, even if done with one's spouse. For many Jews, the only "legitimate" sexual activity was procreative sex with one's lawful wife or husband—and apparently with the husband as the "penetrator" and the wife the "penetrated." Everything else was forbidden.

IV. "According to Nature" and "Contrary to Nature"

A number of different ancient authors address what they considered to be "natural" and "unnatural" sexual activity, including Jewish as well as non-Jewish writers. Artemidorus, the second-century CE Ephesian author of the *Onirocritica*, considered the topic by examining the possible meanings of dreams in which one has some kind of sex with some kind of person. He divides up sexual relations into three categories: natural and lawful, natural and unlawful, and unnatural or

---

[20] See the discussion in Mary Rose D'Angelo, "Gender and Geopolitics in the Work of Philo of Alexandria: Jewish Piety and Imperial Family Values," in *Mapping Gender in Ancient Religious Discourses*, ed. Todd Penner and Caroline Vander Stichele, BibInt 84 (Leiden: Brill, 2007), 63–88. D'Angelo mentions "gormandizing and wine-bibbing leading to bestiality," sex again with one's divorced wife if she has had sex with another man since her divorce, prostitution, and various other activities, many of which a man could commit with his wife. D'Angelo convincingly argues that Philo is throughout trying to outdo the piety of the strictest Romans in Augustan "family values."

[21] Trans. Pieter W. van der Horst, *OTP* 2:581. Note the footnote by van der Horst: "Though several explanations of this line are possible (intercourse during menstruation, Lev 18:19; 'variations'; violating; adultery), probably it forbids intercourse that is not for the sake of procreation, strongly condemned by both Jewish and (some) Gk. writers." For the Greek text, see Douglas Young, ed., *Theognis; Ps.-Pythagoras; Ps.-Phocylides; Chares; Anonymi Aulodia; Fragmentum Teliambicum*, 2nd ed., BSGRT (Leipzig: Teubner, 1971).

contrary to nature.[22] Artemidorus presumes that the subjects of almost all these actions are men, advising his (male) clients that natural and lawful includes sex with one's wife, with female prostitutes, with a woman one does not know, with one's male or female slave, with a woman one knows, either penetrating or being penetrated by another man, masturbation, and being masturbated by a slave. The category "natural and unlawful" includes mostly incest with a family member of different relations. Sex "contrary to nature" includes having sex with oneself, kissing one's own genitals, oral sex with oneself, a woman penetrating another woman, a woman being penetrated by another woman, sex with a god or goddess, sex with the moon, sex with a dead person either male or female, and sex with a wild beast either active or passive (sex with domesticated animals is strangely not mentioned).

This last category seems to include only those actions that at least Artemidorus considered impossible, seemingly because he could not imagine how they would be accomplished. It is interesting, though, that Artemidorus considered male–male penetration completely natural and lawful. He knew that it happened all the time. But he seems not to have been able to imagine how one woman could sexually penetrate another, so that counted as "contrary to nature."[23]

Jewish authors also supply quite different categories for natural and unnatural sex. As we have seen, Philo condemned having sex with a woman the man knew could not become pregnant, but he adds that doing so would make the man an "enemy of nature" (*Spec.* 3.34–36). Philo believed that the men of Sodom "threw off the law of nature" in being wealthy, enjoying excess of luxury, indulging in unbridled lust for their wives and the wives of their neighbors, and having sex with other men, which Philo abhors because it would necessarily overturn the hierarchy of "nature" (*Abr.* 133–136).[24]

Philo believes he is following Plato in condemning male–male or female–female sexual intercourse as contrary to nature. "Natural" intercourse occurs "when male unites with female for procreation" (*Spec.* 1.636a–c). That male–male sex is unnatural is demonstrated by the fact that "wild beasts" do not practice it. Moreover, that kind of sex springs from excess, luxury, and lack of self-control. Note that the *desire* itself is natural, the indulgence is not. What makes the sex "unnatural" is that one of the males would have to "play the woman's part." Condemnation of same-sex intercourse is therefore based in misogyny: a man must not be penetrated like a woman because men are superior to women—and to effeminate men also. Unlike Artemidorus, therefore, Philo considers many kinds

---

[22] The discussion is at *Onir.* 1.78.

[23] As Bernadette J. Brooten points out, "In Artemidoros's eyes, female penetration is not real penetration, and female homoeroticism is a pale and futile imitation of male sexual behavior" (see her *Love between Women: Early Christian Responses to Female Homoeroticism*, Chicago Series on Sexuality, History, and Society [Chicago: University of Chicago Press, 1996], 186).

[24] Whereas Artimedorus taught that a male being penetrated by another male was both "lawful" and "natural," Philo believes male–male intercourse "contrary to nature" no matter the position taken by any specific male.

of sexual behaviors to be "contrary to nature," and therefore condemned. The only "natural" sex is with one's wife for the purposes of procreation.

V. Πορνεῖα IN THE NEW TESTAMENT

In the Gospel of Matthew, Jesus forbids a man to divorce his wife "except on the basis of πορνεία" (παρεκτὸς λόγου πορνείας, 5:32; μὴ ἐπὶ πορνείᾳ, 19:9); if she is sent away for any other reason, her husband makes her into an adulteress (ποιεῖ αὐτὴν μοιχευθῆναι, 5:32).[25] A similar denunciation of divorce is preserved in the Gospels of Mark and Luke as well as in Paul's letters, but the πορνεία exception clause is unique to Matthew. Other examples of these sayings present Jesus forbidding divorce entirely (Mark 10:11-12, Luke 18:18, 1 Cor 7:10-11). Matthew never clarifies what is meant by this exception, but at the very least πορνεία seems to be something other than adultery (μοιχεία). If the writer had meant to indicate that divorce was permissible for *adultery*, why not employ the more specific term? The two terms are also employed in a vice list, when Jesus explains that evil intentions, murder, μοιχεία, πορνεία, theft, false witness, and blasphemy "come from the heart" (15:19). In the context of the divorce sayings, πορνεία is identified with the woman, μοιχεία with the man (he makes the woman an adulteress or becomes an adulterer himself, either by remarriage or by marriage to a divorced woman; 5:32, 19:9). On the face of it, then, the πορνεία of the wife and the μοιχεία of the husband distinguish two separate categories of behavior.

Seeking further clarity, modern New Testament scholars have proposed a variety of interpretive options for the woman's πορνεία, concluding that Matthew was referring to (1) her involvement in prostitution, either before or during her marriage;[26] (2) her status as an unbeliever (the man has therefore contracted an "exogamous marriage"); (3) the incestuous nature of the union (as a gentile and prior to adopting Christ, the man contracted a marriage forbidden by Leviticus);[27] or (4) her status as a concubine rather than a wife (the marriage was therefore never "legal").[28] Some scholars conflate the two categories, arguing that πορνεία

---

[25] For an overview, see Dale B. Martin, *Sex and the Single Savior: Gender and Sexuality in Biblical Interpretation* (Louisville: Westminster John Knox, 2006), 125–47.

[26] Jerome made this suggestion in the fifth century (*Comm. Matt.* 3.19.9). Abel Isaakson suggests that premarital sex was in view (*Marriage and Ministry in the New Temple: A Study with Special Reference to Mt. 19.3–12 and 1 Cor. 11.3–16*, trans. Neil Tomkinson and Jean Gray, ASNU 24 (Lund: Gleerup, 1965), 132–39. See also Dale C. Allison, "Divorce, Celibacy, and Joseph," *JSNT* 49 (1993): 3–10. But for a different interpretation, see William Loader, *Sexuality and the Jesus Tradition* (Grand Rapids: Eerdmans, 2005), 70–72.

[27] Joseph A. Fitzmyer, "The Matthean Divorce Texts and Some New Palestinian Evidence," *JTS* 37 (1996): 197–226; and James R. Mueller, "The Temple Scroll and the Gospel Divorce Texts," *RevQ* 10 (1980): 247–56, here 255–56.

[28] John L. McKenzie, *Commentary on the Gospel according to Matthew* (1981; repr., Eugene,

is a functional equivalent of μοιχεία,[29] though to us this seems the least persuasive point of view. Given the care with which Matthew differentiates between πορνεία and μοιχεία, it seems safe to conclude that πορνεία refers to something other than extramarital sexual intercourse on the part of a wife.[30] But exactly what it refers to remains a mystery.

According to Cecilia Wassen, only two documents from the Second Temple period, Tobit and 1 Thessalonians, use πορνεία in the context of marriage.[31] Rarely found in the gospels, πορνεύω occurs frequently in the Pauline letters.[32] For Paul, πορνεία may refer to any illicit sex. In 1 Cor 7:2, for example, marriage saves a man from πορνεία. But for the most part, πορν- words occur only in vice lists (1 Cor 5:11, 15:9, 2 Cor 12:21, Gal 5:19, Col 3:5, 1 Tim 1:10, Eph 5:3). A major exception is 1 Thess 4:3–6. Here Paul condemns all forms of nonmarital sex as sexual immorality, and he labels improper sexual relations within marriage as πορνεία—especially when such actions are based on desire:

> For this is God's will, your sanctification: that you abstain from πορνείας. Each one of you should know how to possess [κτᾶσθαι] your σκεῦος in holiness and honor, not in the passion of desire [πάθει ἐπιθυμίας], like the gentiles who do not know God. Let no one take advantage or cheat his brother in this matter.[33] (our translation)

Σκεῦος refers either to a man's body or to his wife. The scholarship on the subject is evenly divided.[34] Ernest Best, however, makes a convincing case that σκεῦος refers

---

OR: Wipf & Stock, 2015), 19–20; Alexander Sand, "Die Unzuchtsklausel in Mt 5,31.32 und 19,3–9," *MTZ* 20 (1969): 118–29.

[29] Most recently, William Loader, *The New Testament on Sexuality*, Attitudes towards Sexuality in Judaism and Christianity in the Hellenistic Greco-Roman Era (Grand Rapids: Eerdmans, 2012), 246–47.

[30] See Deut 24:1 (LXX), which allowed a man to divorce his wife for any "unseemly deed" (ἄσχημον πρᾶγμα). Kyle Harper has argued that πορνεία and μοιχεία refer to the same activity: Matthew employed πορνεία to evoke the shame of the woman's sexual activity outside marriage, but he intended to indicate her infidelity (Harper, "*Porneia*," 376). Origen also links Deut 24:1 to Matt 19:9, but, unlike Harper, he worries that the πορνεία exception could be interpreted too loosely. Origen points out that the focus of the Lord's saying is the husband and his conduct, which can all too easily seem to tolerate adultery on the part of the wife: if he sends her away falsely, he makes her an adulteress; if he fails to control her, allows her to befriend other men, or fails to satisfy her sexual desires, he may also make her an adulteress. The πορνεία exception therefore calls the man to a higher standard (*Comm. Matt.* 14.24). On the reception of the πορνεία exception in the writings of the church fathers, see Elizabeth A. Clark, *Reading Renunciation: Asceticism and Scripture in Early Christianity* (Princeton: Princeton University Press, 1999), 239–50.

[31] Wassen, *Women in the Damascus Document*, 176.

[32] Incest is called πορνεία in 1 Cor 5:1, and in 1 Cor 6:9 πορνεύω is used alongside μοιχεύω.

[33] First Thessalonians was likely written to a male audience. For more on this theory, see Lone Fatum, "Brotherhood in Christ: A Gender Hermeneutical Reading of 1 Thessalonians," in *Constructing Early Christian Families: Family as Social Reality and Metaphor*, ed. Halvor Moxnes (London: Routledge, 1997), 183–97.

[34] For an overview of the scholarship, see Abraham J. Malherbe, *The Letters to the*

to a "wife" rather than a "vessel." He bases his interpretation on a parallel passage in 1 Pet 3:7 and the use of כלי ("vessel") in Second Temple Jewish documents.[35] In 4QInstruction[b] (4Q416) 2 II, 21, for example, we find the expression כלי [ח]יקכה, "the wife of your [bo]som," which suggests that σκεῦος in 1 Thess 4:4 likely refers to a wife. Moreover, the word κτάομαι ("acquire"), which Paul also employs in v. 4, has sexual overtones. When used in the context of marriage, it typically means "to possess a woman sexually," or "to live with a woman."[36] In 1 Thess 4:3–6, Paul contrasts the attitude toward marital sex of Christ followers with that of the gentiles. As Wassen asserts, "Whereas Christians who are pure and holy (2 Thess 3:13; 4:7) can engage in marital relations with holiness and sanctity, the sinful gentiles, who do not know God, have sexual relations with lustful passion."[37] Thus, as we have already seen with Tobit, Paul uses πορνεία to refer to illicit sexual relations in marriage, especially sexual actions driven by passion and desire (πάθει ἐπιθυμίας).

It is significant that in 1 Thess 4:3 the word πορνείας is preceded by the definite article τῆς, which has a "generic quality."[38] Some manuscripts replace the definite article with πάσης ("all"; ℵ² Ψ 104 365) or add πάσης to the article (F G^c), which means that some copyists understood πορνεία in v. 4 as having the "general sense of immorality, including fornication."[39] If we were to ask Paul, then, if a man can commit πορνεία with his wife, he would say, "Yes!" especially if he has sex with her out of lustful desire. In our opinion, Matthew likely thinks the same thing.

VI. Πορνεία in the Church Fathers

Overall, the church fathers do not like marriage. John Chrysostom compares it to slavery (*Vid.* 40.1), while Basil of Ancyra is just as brash when he writes, "With her dowry, a woman buys herself a master" (*Virg.* [PG 30:718]). Gregory of Nyssa goes so far as to proclaim that the virginal life is how Christians stop death (*Virg.* 14.1), and Augustine claims that, though marriage brings forth children, "it is better not to marry, because it is better for human society itself not to need this

---

Thessalonians: A New Translation with Introduction and Commentary, AB 32B (New York: Doubleday, 2000), 226–28. See also John T. Noonan Jr., *Contraception: A History of Its Treatment by the Catholic Theologians and Canonists* (Cambridge: Belknap Press of Harvard University Press, 1965), 41.

[35] Ernest Best, *A Commentary on the First and Second Epistles to the Thessalonians*, HNTC (New York: Harper & Row, 1972), 166.

[36] John Strugnell, "More on Wives and Marriage in the Dead Sea Scrolls: (4Q416 2 ii 21[cf. 1 Thess. 4:4] and 4QMMT B," *RevQ* 17 (1996): 537–47; translations are Strugnell's. Best points out that κτάομαι can also mean, "to win someone for oneself" (*Epistles to the Thessalonians*, 166).

[37] Wassen, *Women in the Damascus Document*, 177.

[38] Ernst von Dobschütz, *Die Thessalonicherbriefe*, 7th ed., KEK (Göttingen: Vandenhoeck & Ruprecht, 1909), 163.

[39] Malherbe, *Letters to the Thessalonians*, 225. See also Best, *Epistles to the Thessalonians*, 160; and Béda Rigaux, *Saint Paul: Les Épîtres aux Thessaloniciens*, EBib (Paris: Gabalda, 1956), 502.

activity" (*Bon. conj.* 9).⁴⁰ But do any of the fathers ever suggest that γάμος ("marriage") is πορνεία or that a man can commit πορνεία with his wife?

In the mid-second century, Tatian baldly asserts that γάμος is πορνεία.⁴¹ We see this clearly in *On Perfection according to the Savior*, where Tatian insists that Paul links sexual activity to uncontrolled, satanic fornication in 1 Corinthians 7 (ἀκρασίᾳ καὶ πορνείᾳ καὶ διαβόλῳ; Clement, *Strom.* 3.12 = Tatian, *Fragments* 5). Additionally, he pronounces marriage a "bond between husband and wife … a physical union leading to corruption." Furthermore, he claims that marriage is "a partnership in corruption," which weakens prayer.⁴² Finally, in his *Oratio ad Graecos*, he declares, "I have no desire to rule, I do not wish to be rich; I do not seek command, I hate sexual immorality [πορνείαν μεμίσηκα]" (11.1). Since sex enslaves a person to the devil, the only solution is to renounce any and all sexual activity. Otherwise, every time a married couple sleeps with each other, they commit πορνεία.

Irenaeus condemns Tatian and charges him with "encratism" since, in his estimation, Tatian's rejection of marriage is at odds with Gen 1:27–28, which for many Christians and Second Temple Jews demands procreation (*Haer.* 1.28.1).⁴³ But others did not entirely agree with Irenaeus's outright assault on Tatian. Clement of Alexandria, for example, condemns Tatian's "encratism" while simultaneously finding some truth in his proclamation that γάμος is πορνεία. But instead of referring to marriage as πορνεία, he stops short, linking it instead with μοιχεία. Like Irenaeus, Clement points to Gen 1:28 and argues that it is incumbent on all Christians to be fruitful and multiply.⁴⁴ The best way to fulfill this goal is by having a large family

---

⁴⁰ For an overview of Augustine's complex views, see David G. Hunter, *Marriage, Celibacy, and Heresy in Ancient Christianity: The Jovinianist Controversy*, OECS (Oxford: Oxford University Press, 2007), 269–84.

⁴¹ Clark, *Reading Renunciation*, 32.

⁴² All English quotations from Tatian, with some modifications, come from Molly Whittaker, *Tatian: Oratio ad Graecos and Fragments*, OECS (Oxford: Clarendon, 1982).

⁴³ Though the Western church condemns Tatian from the start, the Syrian church will not pronounce any sort of judgment on him until the twelfth century. The reason for this is that well into the third century, Syriac-speaking Christians took a vow of celibacy at baptism or later after having one or two children. See Arthur Vööbus, who reasons that if Tatian had been born in the East instead of the West, he would have been claimed as a saint rather than condemned as a heretic (*Celibacy: A Requirement for Admission to Baptism in the Early Syrian Church*, PETSE 1 [Stockholm: Estonian Theological Society in Exile, 1951], 17). For a complete recounting of the charges against Tatian, see William L. Petersen, "Tatian the Assyrian," in *A Companion to Second-Century Christian "Heretics,"* ed. Antti Marjanen and Petri Luomanen (Leiden: Brill, 2008), 142–52. For a general overview of encratism, see Gilles Quispel, "The Study of Encratism: A Historical Survey," in *La tradizione dell'enkrateia: Motivazioni ontologiche e protologiche; Atti del Colloquio internazionale, Milano, 20–23 aprile 1982*, ed. Ugo Bianchi (Rome: Edizioni dell'Ateneo, 1985), 35–81.

⁴⁴ Clement's interpretation of Genesis follows Philo, who understood the LXX as endorsing procreation. For an overview, see David T. Runia, *Philo in Early Christian Literature: A Survey*, CRINT 3.3 (Minneapolis: Fortress, 1993), 132–56; and Annewies van den Hoek, *Clement of*

(*Paed.* 2.10.83). Even though Clement acknowledges that certain biblical texts command large families, he places severe limits on Christian sexual intercourse.

Reinterpreting Deut 14:7, "Do not eat the hare or the hyena," Clement maintains that God "does not want man to be contaminated by their traits nor even to taste of their wantonness, for these animals have an insatiable appetite for coition" (*Paed.* 2.10.83). Additionally, he notes that eating the hare is a condemnation of pederasty. Later he asserts, "The mysterious prohibition [of Moses] in reality is but counsel to restrain violent impulses, and intercourse in too frequent succession."[45] In this condemnation, Clement includes relations with a pregnant woman, pederasty, adultery, and lewdness (2.10.88). In fact, Clement goes far beyond some Second Temple writers, such as Philo, by noting that the two-word Tenth Commandment in the LXX, οὐκ ἐπιθυμήσεις (Exod 20:17 LXX; Deut 5:21 LXX), makes any instance of sex for pleasure rather than procreation apostasy (*Protr.* 108.5; *Strom.* 3.71.3, 3.76.1, and 3.57.1–2).[46]

In many respects, Clement imposes a much more restrictive rule on Christians than Paul or any other Second Temple author. Wives, for example, must never take the initiative in the sexual act. They belong on the bottom since they are subordinate to their husband (*Strom.* 3.94.5). And a husband must never ejaculate in a part of his wife's body other than her vagina, and then only for procreation.[47] This means, of course, that Clement forbids all forms of oral and anal sex.

Book 2 of Clement's *Paedagogus* contains an entire chapter devoted to the subjects of wedlock and sexual intercourse. Though Clement is not as forthright as Tatian, he does discuss γάμος and sex between a husband and wife under the heading of πορνεία. He begins chapter 10 by naming various impurities, which he terms ὀνόματα πορνικά. These include: coarse speech (ῥημάτων δὲ ἀκολάστων), disgraceful behavior (σχημάτων ἀσχημόνων), sensuous love affairs (φιλημάτων), and other unspecified acts of coition (τοιουτωνί τινων λαγνευμάτων). He urges Christians to follow what he believes are the words of Paul in Eph 5:3: "But all πορνεία and ἀκαθαρσία and πλεονεξία must not even be named among you, as is proper among the saints." Next he maintains that the only type of sexual intercourse (συνουσία) acceptable under the law (νόμος) is the kind that produces children (ἐπὶ παιδοποιίᾳ). He even adds that committing adultery with a prostitute is a death wish (τὴν μοιχείαν ἐπὶ πόρνῃ τηρουμένη). Furthermore, he deems same-sex acts among males

---

Alexandria and His Use of Philo in the Stromateis: An Early Christian Reshaping of a Jewish Model, VCSup 3 (Leiden: Brill, 1988).

[45] Translations of Clement are from Clement of Alexandria, *Christ the Educator*, trans. Simon P. Wood, FC 23 (Washington, DC: Catholic University of America Press, 1954; repr., 2008).

[46] For more on this, see Harry O. Maier, "Clement of Alexandria and the Care of the Self," *JAAR* 62 (1994): 725–28.

[47] See the important comments of Bernadette J. Brooten, *Love between Women: Early Christian Responses to Female Homoeroticism*, Chicago Series on Sexuality, History, and Society (Chicago: University of Chicago Press, 1996), 325–26.

παρὰ φύσιν. Thus, Clement not only defines πορνεία in its Classical Greek sense; he expands it to include racy speech, disgraceful behaviors, and any acts of coition that do not ultimately lead to the production of children.

But the most stunning thing Clement says is still to come. Though he does not directly link γάμος with πορνεία, he does argue that any man who has sex with his wife for the purpose of pleasure (ἡδονή) adulterates his marriage (μοιχεύει γὰρ τὸν ἑαυτοῦ γάμον ὁ ἑταιριζόμενος αὐτόν). For Clement, a man might not be able to commit πορνεία with his wife, but he can certainly commit μοιχεία with her. Having said that, we should keep in mind that everything Clement says falls under the heading of ὀνόματα πορνικά, so it is possible that he thinks sex for the sake of pleasure is not just μοιχεία but also πορνεία. As much as Clement seeks to distance himself from Tatian, "he nonetheless agrees with the encratites that innate sexual desire is fornicating servitude to Aphrodite and Eros."[48]

VII. Conclusion

The definition of πορνεία as "sex outside marriage" is predicated on the presumption that male–female sexual intercourse was the governing norm throughout antiquity and neglects to account for the much broader definitions we have detected here. Πορνεία, as ancient Christians and Jews employed it, cannot be limited to the definition "sex outside marriage" because it regularly included sexual activity both inside and outside marriage's confines. As we have argued, πορνεία in Second Temple Judaism and in the early church fathers often refers to exogamy or miscegeny and to sex between a husband and a wife based on lust and desire. Indeed, early Christians and Second Temple Jews expanded the "classical" definition of πορνεία to include activities well beyond visiting a prostitute and same-sex acts. This more expansive meaning from the Second Temple writers and the church fathers should likely be assumed as the meaning of πορνεία for New Testament writers as well. In particular, we should assume this broader meaning for Paul and the Gospel of Matthew.

Though it may seem difficult to pinpoint exactly what this word study means for modern readers of the New Testament, we believe the answer is quite simple. By the reckoning of early Christian authors, including those of the New Testament, anyone who has engaged in a sexual act and enjoyed it is guilty of πορνεία. This means, of course, that modern attempts to relegate πορνεία to same-sex acts and sex outside marriage need to be reevaluated. It is not just sex acts outside marriage that were deemed illicit and were condemned by Second Temple Jews and early Christians; certain acts within marriage also received the stigma of πορνεία. Thus we return to our original question, Can a man commit πορνεία with his wife? In certain circumstances, the answer of the New Testament writers was yes he can.

---

[48] Kathy L. Gaca, *The Making of Fornication: Eros, Ethics, and Political Reform in Greek Philosophy and Early Christianity*, HCS 40 (Berkeley: University of California Press, 2003), 270.

Castration for the Kingdom and Avoiding the αἰτία of Adultery (Matthew 19:10–12)

R. JARRETT VAN TINE
RJV3@st-andrews.ac.uk
University of St. Andrews, KY16 9AJ, United Kingdom

The difficulties raised by the form and content of Matthew's eunuch pericope (19:10–12) have provoked unfavorable evaluations. In this article, I offer a new reading of this passage that makes sense of some of its problems. My approach is rooted in the broader narrative and rhetoric of Matthew's Gospel in particular. In section I, I focus on the disciples' response (19:10) to Jesus's teaching on divorce and remarriage (19:3–9), arguing that ἡ αἰτία τοῦ ἀνθρώπου μετὰ τῆς γυναικός in 19:10a should be translated as "the charge against the man with his wife," referring to the charge of adultery in 19:9. In section II, I demonstrate that multiple elements in 19:3–12 inextricably link the eunuch passage to Jesus's call to self-dismemberment (5:29–30 and context). Matthew's eunuch metaphor is a rhetorical device exhorting would-be disciples who have illegitimately divorced their wives to "cut off" (figuratively) what causes them to stumble (i.e., their male organ), lest they commit adultery in remarriage (cf. 5:29–30). Thus, Matthew's "eunuchs" function literarily as exemplars of those who make extraordinary sacrifices in this age (i.e., a spouse and children) so that they might obtain immeasurably more in the kingdom of heaven. Section III provides corroborative support for this reading from the broader Second Temple Jewish and early Christian contexts. I conclude by showing how the Latin translation of this passage likely led to what I argue is the pervasive misreading of 19:10(–12) that we have today.

The difficulties raised by the form and content of Matthew's eunuch pericope (19:10–12) have provoked unfavorable evaluations. For example, Craig A. Evans

I wish to express my sincere gratitude to Jonathan Pennington for nurturing this project in its initial stages and to David Moffitt for his insightful critiques and suggestions up to its completion. I also want to thank Elizabeth Shively for her thoughtful engagement, along with Kai Akagi and Ernest Clark for their special support.

relegates the passage to an "appendix."¹ Douglas R. A. Hare concedes, "Verses 10–12, found only in Matthew, are among the most difficult to understand in the Gospel."² The perceived problems stem predominantly from the disciples' "rather misogynist"³ response to Jesus's teaching on divorce and remarriage (19:3–9), rendered to the effect of, "If such is the case of a man with his wife, it is better not to marry" (19:10). Ulrich Luz reflects the dissonance felt by many interpreters:

> After [Jesus] has just spoken so highly of marriage in vv. 3–9, [the disciples'] comment that it would be better to remain single seems rather inappropriate. It is not clear why they prefer not to marry. Is it because one must remain single if the first marriage fails? Or is it because Jesus's command is too severe for them? It is clear that the wife's perspective again is no more a factor here than it is in the entire pericope.⁴

To get around these issues, some commentators look behind the text to a proposed *Sitz im Leben,* suggesting that the disciples' response reflects not their own view but that of Matthew's community.⁵ Others postulate source-critical solutions, suggesting that 19:10–12 is a secondary addition only loosely tied to the original pericope of 19:3–9.⁶ However its content and function are explained, scholars agree that the passage is redirected rather awkwardly by Jesus's reply in verse 11 toward its instructional telos in verse 12: those who are able to become eunuchs for the kingdom should do so. Whether eunuchs, here, are those who embrace celibacy for increased ministry such as Jesus and Paul (the majority position)⁷ or divorced

---

¹Craig A. Evans, *Matthew,* NCBiC (Cambridge: Cambridge University Press, 2012), 341.

²Douglas R. A. Hare, *Matthew,* IBC (Louisville: Westminster John Knox, 2009), 222. According to Francis Beare (summarizing the stance of many commentators), the passage as it stands is "embarrassing," "suffers from inconsistency," and is "confusing" in relation to 19:3–9 (Francis Wright Beare, *The Gospel according to Matthew: A Commentary* [Oxford: Blackwell, 1981], 389–90).

³John Nolland, *The Gospel of Matthew: A Commentary on the Greek Text,* NIGTC (Grand Rapids: Eerdmans, 2005), 775.

⁴Ulrich Luz, *Matthew: A Commentary,* trans. James E. Crouch, Hermeneia (Minneapolis: Fortress, 2001), 2:499–500.

⁵Hare, for example, postulates that verse 10 was written to engage with Matthew's largely gentile church "for whom Jesus's rule on divorce seemed hopelessly out of touch with reality" (Hare, *Matthew,* 222). Cf. Beare, *Gospel according to Matthew,* 389–90; F. Thiele, "αἰτία," TBLNT 3:1093.

⁶W. D. Davies and Dale C. Allison observe, "Vv. 10–12 have to do with celibacy. But what is the connexion between celibacy and the teaching in vv. 4–9? Many commentators have not found one. Clearly we have here two separate traditions" (*A Critical and Exegetical Commentary on the Gospel according to Saint Matthew,* 3 vols., ICC [Edinburgh: T&T Clark, 1997], 3:5). See also David R. Catchpole, "The Synoptic Divorce Material as a Traditio-Historical Problem," *BJRL* 57 (1974): 92–127; Craig S. Keener, *A Commentary on the Gospel of Matthew* (Grand Rapids: Eerdmans, 1999), 470–71.

⁷The following are representative: Davies and Allison, *Critical and Exegetical Commentary,*

persons who refuse to remarry (the minority),[8] depends on the referent of "this word" (τὸν λόγον [τοῦτον]) in verse 11, which only the enabled can accept (19:3–9 suggests that the referent is remarriage; 19:10 suggests that it is celibacy). Recent studies of 19:10–12 assume much of this basic framework while exploring the social context of eunuchs in the ancient world and the implications that this context might have for Jesus's call to make oneself a eunuch (19:12).[9]

In this article, I argue that a fundamental error undergirds traditional exegesis: the mistranslation of ἡ αἰτία τοῦ ἀνθρώπου μετὰ τῆς γυναικός in 19:10a as "the *case/situation/relationship* of a man with his wife." I propose an alternative based on the inherently legal sense of αἰτία, "the *charge* against the man with his wife," referring to the charge of adultery in 19:9. In this way, the disciples' response as a whole is recast in light of adulterous remarriage and is shown to be a logical inference from Jesus's declaration in verse 9. My approach throughout is rooted within the broader narrative and rhetoric of Matthew's Gospel in particular.[10]

In section I, I focus on the disciples' response (19:10) to Jesus's teaching on divorce and remarriage (19:3–9). I then demonstrate in section II that multiple elements in 19:3–12 inextricably link the eunuch passage to Jesus's call to self-dismemberment (5:29–30 and context). Matthew's eunuch metaphor is shown to be a rhetorical device exhorting would-be disciples who have illegitimately divorced

---

3:22–27; Richard T. France, *The Gospel of Matthew*, NICNT (Grand Rapids: Eerdmans, 2007), 721–26; and Donald A. Hagner, *Matthew 14–28*, WBC 33B (Dallas: Word, 1995), 549.

[8] Few argue for a reading of 19:10–12 in terms of remarriage, e.g., Stephen C. Barton, *Discipleship and Family Ties in Mark and Matthew*, SNTSMS 80 (Cambridge: Cambridge University Press, 2005), 201; Raymond F. Collins, *Divorce in the New Testament*, GNS 38 (Collegeville, MN: Liturgical Press, 1992); Jacques Dupont, *Mariage et divorce dans l'évangile: Matthieu 19:3–12 et parallèles* (Bruges: Abbaye de Saint André, 1959).

[9] See, e.g., Jennifer Sylvan Alexander, "Self-Made Eunuchs as Model Disciples: Matthew 19:12 in Narrative and Historical Context," in *The Theologically Formed Heart: Essays in Honor of David J. Gouwens*, ed. Warner M. Bailey. Lee C. Barrett III, and James O. Duke (Eugene, OR: Wipf & Stock, 2014), 89–114, here 95–96 n. 14; Walter Stevenson, "Eunuchs and Early Christianity," in *Eunuchs in Antiquity and Beyond*, ed. Shaun Tougher (Oakville, CT: Duckworth, 2002), 123–42; and Gary Robert Brower, "Ambivalent Bodies: Making Christian Eunuchs" (PhD diss., Duke University, 1996). Although I am not aware of anyone in recent scholarship arguing for a literal reading of Jesus's call to self-castration, this interpretation was apparently a problem in the early church. According to Eusebius, Origen castrated himself early on in his ministry (*Eccl. hist.* 6.8.1–3). The practice was apparently such a problem that both the Apostolic Constitutions (8.47.21–24) and the Nicaean Canons (can. 1) included statutes against self-made eunuchs among the laity and clergy. See the full discussion in Daniel F. Caner, "The Practice and Prohibition of Self-Castration in Early Christianity," *VC* 51 (1997): 396–415.

[10] Wittingly or not, Matthew's eunuch passage has often been read through the lens of Paul's instructions to the Corinthians on celibacy (1 Corinthians 7), even though Paul himself acknowledged that, as far as he knew, Jesus did not mention the issue (7:12, 25). See Quesnell, "'Made Themselves Eunuchs for the Kingdom of Heaven' (Mt 19,12)," *CBQ* 30 (1968) 335–58, here 341.

their wives to "cut off" (figuratively) what causes them to stumble (i.e., their male organ), lest they commit adultery in remarriage (see 5:29–30). Matthew's "eunuchs"—that is, illegitimately divorced disciples who choose to remain spouseless so as not to incur the charge of adultery—function literarily as exemplars of those who make extraordinary sacrifices in this age (i.e., a spouse and children) so that they might obtain immeasurably more in the kingdom of heaven.[11] Section III provides corroborative support for this reading from the broader Second Temple Jewish and early Christian contexts. I conclude by showing how the Latin translation of this passage likely led to the prevalent misreading of 19:10(–12) that we have today.

I. The Disciples' Response (19:10) to Jesus's Teaching on Divorce and Remarriage (19:3–9)

Λέγουσιν αὐτῷ οἱ μαθηταὶ [αὐτοῦ]· εἰ οὕτως ἐστὶν ἡ αἰτία τοῦ ἀνθρώπου[12] μετὰ τῆς γυναικός, οὐ συμφέρει [τῷ ἀνθρώπῳ ἑτέραν][13] γαμῆσαι. (Matt 19:10)

His disciples said to him, "If such, as you say, is the charge against the man with respect to his wife, then it is not better for that man to marry another." (my translation)

Αἰτία in Matthew 19:10a

Against "Case" or "Situation/Relationship"

The significance of the disciples' response in 19:10 hangs on the word αἰτία in verse 10a. Modern commentaries and translations overwhelmingly render this term as "case" (in a noncausal sense), or "situation" (i.e., condition)/"relationship" (i.e., relation between friends/people).[14] Several lexicons cite the former as if it were included in the semantic domain of the lexeme but provide no additional examples outside of Matt 19:10.[15] BDAG suggests the latter, taking αἰτία to be a Latinism from

---

[11] Cf. the parables of hidden treasure (13:44) and the costly pearl (13:45).
[12] D (05) replaces with τοῦ ἀνδρός, probably assimilating to Mark 10:2, 12.
[13] My explanatory insertion, to be discussed below.
[14] In fact, I know of no modern translation or commentary that deviates from this decision. The following translations are representative: NASB, "relationship"; NKJV, ESV, (N)RSV, "case"; NIV, "situation"; CEB, "the way things are"; Schlachter 2000, "Pflichten"; NEG (Nouvelle Edition de Genève), "la condition." The commentaries follow suit. See, e.g., Davies and Allison, *Critical and Exegetical Commentary*, 3:19; Luz, *Matthew*, 2:500 ("the way it is"); Nolland, *Gospel of Matthew*, 776; and Grant R. Osborne, *Matthew*, Zondervan Exegetical Commentary Series, New Testament 1 (Grand Rapids: Zondervan, 2010), 706.
[15] Cf. LSJ and *TBLNT*. *TDNT* does not have an entry on αἰτία or its cognates. G. W. H. Lampe

causa, which can signify a "situation" or a "relationship."[16] While they provide one additional example in support, it is doubtful.[17] More likely, BDAG's example is an instance of the philosophical usage of αἰτία.[18] There is, therefore, very little support

---

(*PGL*, s.v. "αἰτία") and Johan Lust, Erik Eynikel, and Katrin Hauspie do not include "case" or the Latinism (LEH, s.v. "αἰτία"). The absence of causality in this gloss is key. "Case" is a fairly generic word in English and may be used to translate αἰτία in some instances if a causal notion is understood. No commentator, translation, or lexicon, however, intends "case" to imply causality in any sense in 19:10a; it simply does not make sense. The gloss is cited *as a semantically distinct category*, although without additional support. (See below for the notion of causality in the lexeme.) Robert H. Gundry opts for this usage with the rather hollow explanation, "'cause' [αἰτία] (vs. 3) easily shades into 'case' [αἰτία; vs. 10]" (*Matthew: A Commentary on His Literary and Theological Art* [Grand Rapids: Eerdmans, 1982], 382).

[16] See Charlton Thomas Lewis and Charles Short, *A Latin Dictionary: Founded on Andrews' Edition of Freund's Latin Dictionary*, rev. ed. (Oxford: Clarendon, 1975), 303–4, s.v., "*causa*." There is no causal notion present in this usage. W. Radl also lists "die Sache/das Verhältnis" for Matt 19:10 although without explanation or support (*EWNT* 1:104, s.v. "αἰτία").

[17] The text cited by BDAG reads: "Plato:—'What is [ἡ αἰτία of] these phenomena?' Peteesis:—'Listen: the Sun is the right eye, the Moon the left, the tongue, smell, and hearing belong to Mercury, the viscera to Jupiter, the chest to Mars, the spleen to Venus'" (P.Ryl. 63, "Astrological Dialogue"; third century; translation slightly modified from J. de M. Johnson, V. Martin, and A. S. Hunt, eds., *Documents of the Ptolemaic and Roman Periods*, vol. 2 of *Catalogue of the Greek Papyri in the John Rylands Library*[Manchester: University Press, 1911–1952], 2–3, here 3).

The meaning of αἰτία is difficult to determine since the text is fragmented with only the title and the conclusion remaining. Assuming for the sake of argument that the Latinism/case rendition is a legitimate option, there are three interpretative possibilities: (1) "situation/condition/case," (2) "cause," or (3) "explanation/[causal] connection." ("Relationship" as a Latinism from *causa*—as often proposed for Matt 19:10—is not a possibility because the Latin term indicates a relation of *friendship*, which is clearly not what Plato had in mind.) The second option is a common usage of αἰτία, and the third is a *philosophical* usage of the term (J. O. Urmson, *The Greek Philosophical Vocabulary* [London: Duckworth, 1990], 15; this usage is not listed in BDAG).

In the passage Plato questions an Egyptian prophet named Peteesis about ἡ αἰτία between parts of the body and astrological entities. Johnson, Martin, and Hunt comment that "the reply *connects* the various parts of the body with the sun, moon, [etc.]" ("Astrological Dialogue," 2; emphasis mine). Unfortunately, we do not have the broader context necessary to determine *how* exactly they are connected. Nevertheless, of the available options, the philosophical usage appears to provide the best fit. The astrological entities are somehow linked with the parts of the body, with one *generating* the other, not literally (it would seem), but the way a signifier generates a signified in a metaphorical or symbolic relationship. In this sense, the usage still retains its inherent notion of causality, *explaining* or *connecting* the phenomena with each other. The Latinism does not retain this notion of causality, nor is it entirely clear what Plato's question would mean if "situation/condition" (or "case") were the sense of αἰτία. Plato wants an *explanation* of how the phenomena are *connected*. Furthermore, the philosophical context certainly lends itself to a philosophical usage of αἰτία.

[18] Another example of the philosophical usage of αἰτία is found in Philo. In his argument for the imperishable nature of the world, Philo quotes Plato's *Timaeus*: "for [the framer] reflected that when hot things and cold and all such as have strong powers gather round a composite body from without and fall unseasonably upon it they annoy it and bringing upon it sickness and age

provided for any proposed rendition of αἰτία. Moreover, αἰτία is never used as a Latinism, or to signify a noncausal "case" anywhere else in the New Testament (20 times), the LXX (21 times), Philo (238 times), Josephus (336 times), or in the documentary papyri (approximately 172 [legible] times between 300 BCE and 300 CE)[19]—to name just a few significant corpora. The only scholar to acknowledge the problem is Luz, who states, "there is no real evidence for this Latinism.[20]

The Charge against the Man with His Wife

By contrast, αἰτία communicates a variety of meanings associated with moral culpability in legal contexts, such as "charge," "accusation," "guilt," "crime," "blame," or "pretext/ground."[21] Indeed, its wide range of legal nuances can be disconcerting

---

cause it to decay. With this motive and on such reasons God fashioned it as a whole, with each of its parts whole in itself so as to be perfect, and free from age and sickness."

On the basis of Plato's reasoning, Philo draws the following conclusion: "We may take this as Plato's testimony to the indestructibility of the world; that it is uncreated follows the natural law of consequences. Dissolution is consequential to the created, indestructibility to the uncreated. The author of the verse 'All that is born is due to death' seems to have hit the truth and to have understood the *causal connexion* between birth and destruction [τῶν αἰτιῶν τῆς γενέσεως καὶ τῆς φθορᾶς]" (Philo, *Aet.* 1.26–27 [Colson and Whitaker, LCL]; emphasis added).

Regardless of how one takes BDAG's example, the question remains whether there is a gloss for Matt 19:10 that better accords with its natural usage and with the context of 19:3–12 in particular. (BDAG also cites BDF §5,3b, which lists αἰτία among other Latinisms in Matthew's Gospel although without support.)

[19] In addition to BDAG's (dubious) example of the Latinism, MM cross-references P.Par. 49 l. 27 (= UPZ 1.62) presumably by virtue of its similarities in form to 19:10a: εἴπερ οὖν ἐστιν αὕτη ἡ αἰτία. But this is clearly an example of the *reason/cause* (with culpability implied) usage, not a Latinism/case. It is part of a letter from Dionysius to Ptolemaeus in which Dionysius is urging Ptolemaeus to help him meet with a disgruntled mutual acquaintance. In this particular section, Dionysius writes, "But he appeared on that day to be occupied or else he was ashamed to meet with me. If, therefore, this is the reason [εἴπερ οὖν ἐστιν αὕτη ἡ αἰτία], and because of this will not come to me, being ashamed, call and send him to me for he is to be turned about/have his mind changed" (my translation).

[20] Luz, *Matthew*, 2:500 n. 112. Ivars Avotins published a supplement to LSJ's lexicon that suggests four possible examples of αἰτία being used as a Latinism. Each of these examples is taken from the "Novellae" part of Justinian's *Corpus iuris civilis* (N. 101.4.pr; N. 103.2; and N. 131.12.pr [two examples]; see Ivars Avotins, *On the Greek of the Novels of Justinian: A Supplement to Liddell-Scott-Jones together with Observations on the Influence of Latin on Legal Greek*, AWTS 21 [New York: Olms-Weidmann, 1992], 9). Even these examples, however, are questionable and, in any case, are far removed from the time of Matthew's Gospel (545, 536, 539, and 539 CE). I know of no other examples where αἰτία means "case" in the noncausal manner as is assumed in 19:10.

[21] Radl places this usage under the category of Rechtssprache with the glosses: "Schuld," "Verbrechen," "Beschuldigung," and "Anklagepunkt" (*EWNT* 1:104). Thiele states, "Meist hat die Vokabel den Sinn von *Beschuldigung, Anklage,* oder *Vorwurf* ... indem der Hergang eines Geschehens samt der es auslösenden *Schuld* dargestellt wird" (*TBNT* 3:1093). According to Lionel Pearson, "[Αἰτία] has the active meaning of 'accusation' 'complaint' 'grievance' and the corresponding

for English translators: whereas we prefer to differentiate them, Greek may simply use αἰτία. Outside of 19:10, Matthew uses the αιτι* lexeme four times, always to denote guilt.[22] With respect to 19:10a, the law-oriented context is apparent. The debate with the Pharisees concerning divorce has just culminated in Jesus's powerful declaration, "But I say to you: Whoever divorces his wife, except for sexual immorality, and marries another, commits adultery" (v. 9).

The legal import of Jesus's statement is striking. First, Jesus has just declared himself and his words to be more authoritative than the great lawgiver himself, Moses ("Moses may have permitted you to divorce your wives, but *I* declare to you ..."). Second, Jesus has asserted that remarriage after divorce (except for sexual immorality [πορνεία])[23] constitutes adultery: it breaks the Decalogue. I propose,

---

passive meaning 'guilt' 'blame' 'responsibility'; and by logical development it also means 'that which is responsible'—the 'cause'" (Lionel Pearson, "Prophasis and Aitia," *TAPA* 83 [1952]: 205–23, here 206). Thus, outside of legal contexts, αἰτία often means "cause," "reason," or "occasion" (in the causal sense). In Greek philosophical vocabulary, αἰτία (n.) and αἴτιος (adj.) can mean "connection" or "explanation" (Urmson, *Greek Philosophical Vocabulary*, 15). It seems questionable whether "occasion" or "motive" should be considered separate categories from "cause/reason" as in LSJ, at least based on the two examples cited (Pindar, *Nem.* 7.11; Lucian, *Tyr.* 13). Respectively, these can simply be translated as "cause" and "caused."

[22] Αἰτία, the noun form, is used in Matt 19:3, 10 and 27:37 (discussed below). The adjectival form, ἀναίτιος, is used twice (12:5, 7) referring to those who break the Sabbath and yet remain "guiltless." Cf. Josephus, *A.J.* 17.174–177 (ἀναίτιος and αἰτία are antonyms), 17.295; 1 Sam 22:22; 2 Macc 13:4; Sus 1:53; Luke 23:4, 14, 22.

The majority of NT uses of αἰτία outside Matthew also denote legal culpability. Still the evidence is somewhat limited with nine of twelve of these instances coming from the legal proceedings surrounding Jesus and Paul. Of the nineteen additional occurrences (19:10 aside) in the New Testament, twelve denote *charge/accusation/guilt/ground* (Matt 19:3, 27:37; Mark 15:26; John 18:38; 19:4, 6; Acts 13:28; 23:28; 25:18, 27; 28:18, 20) and seven denote *reason/cause* (Luke 8:47; Acts 10:21; 22:24; 2 Tim 1:6, 12; Titus 1:13; Heb 2:11).

The evidence from the LXX is sparse. Of the twenty-one occurrences, seventeen denote *cause/reason*, though often with overtones of blame or guilt (1 Esd 2:17; 1 Macc 9:10; 2 Macc 4:28, 35, 42, 49; 8:26; 12:40; 3 Macc 1:13, 15; 3:4; 5:18; 4 Macc 1:16; Wis 14:27; 17:12; 18:18; Sus 1:14); the remaining four denote (real or perceived) guilt/culpability (Gen 3:14, Prov 28:17, 3 Macc 7:7, Job 18:14).

There are multiple instances of αἰτία indicating culpability/guilt in the documentary papyri, which is not surprising considering the legal nature of many of the documents. See, e.g., BGU 4.1061; P.Köln 7.313; P.Mich. 1.107, 5.312 (with a personal genitive); P.NYU 2.45; P.Polit.Jud. 1; P.Ryl. 2.114; P.Tebt. 1.5 (2x), 1.14; 1.72, 1.124; SB 4.7285, 8.9899a, 20.15036 (3x), et al. For usage in the context of marital disputes/divorce, see P.Oxy. 49.3500 and, although late, PSI 141 (301–400 CE) and P.Flor. 1.93dupl (569 CE).

[23] In light of the obvious practical concerns, the meaning of the exception clause has been the subject of impassioned debate. I have intentionally chosen to remain silent on the issue, as it seems to have become a sort of exegetical red herring. While much ink has been spilled deciphering the meaning of πορνεία, it is only parenthetical; all the while, the critical relationship of 19:10–12 to 19:3–9 has been missed entirely. Furthermore, even those scholars who have argued for a remarriage reading of 19:12 (critical mistranslations in 19:10 notwithstanding) have tended to let

therefore, that ἡ αἰτία τοῦ ἀνθρώπου be rendered, "*the charge against* the man," referring to the charge of adultery from verse 9.[24] The disciples' statement in verse 10, then, should be understood as a thoughtful response to Jesus's law on divorce and remarriage. To paraphrase: "If the man who has (illegitimately) divorced his wife is charged with adultery by marrying another," they reason, "it would be better for such a one not to marry another."

Αἰτία with a Personal Genitive

But what of the personal genitive construction as a whole in 19:10a (ἡ αἰτία τοῦ ἀνθρώπου)? The personal modifier can communicate the *source* or *agent* of the accusation or blame (a subjective genitive). Applied to the case in point, it would denote, "the charge/blame *from* the man," that is, the charge made by the man. The usage seems rare—I have found only three examples[25]—and it does not fit the context.

More frequently the personal modifier will function as the *object* or *recipient* of the guilt/blame/fault or charge/accusation notion in αἰτία—"the charge *against* the man" (an objective genitive).[26] Matthew himself employs the construction in this way with reference to the sign on the cross: "Over his [Jesus's] head they put the charge against him [τὴν αἰτίαν αὐτοῦ], which read, 'This is Jesus the King of the Jews'" (27:37 NRSV; cf. Mark 15:26).[27] Genesis 4:13b, the only other example of this construction in the LXX or the New Testament, indicates the same. In response to his punishment for murdering Abel, Cain cries out to God: "… *my crime/guilt* [or, *the charge against me*] is too great to be forgiven [μείζων ἡ αἰτία μου τοῦ ἀφεθῆναί

---

their interpretation of the exception clause dominate subsequent exegesis. For example, Quesnell, in support of Dupont, writes, "the saying on eunuchs is not a call to celibacy, but a challenging formulation of the state of a man whose wife has been put away (set loose) on account of *porneia*" (Quesnell, "Made Themselves Eunuchs," 346; cf. William A. Heth and Gordon J. Wenham, *Jesus and Divorce*, updated ed. [Carlisle: Paternoster, 2002]).

[24] Indeed, αἰτία refers to a charge in the context of adultery in Athanasius, *Ep. Cast.* 28.877.17; Dorotheus, *Doctr. diver. i–xviii* 1.6.5; Cassius Dio, *Hist. Rom.* 67.12.2; Gregory of Nazianzus, *Sanct. pasch.* [or. 45] 36.468.13–18; John Chrysostom, *Exp. Ps.* 55.437.46; and Philo, *Spec.* 3.58. For other examples of the term with reference to violations of the Decalogue, see Josephus, *A.J.* 11.141, 346–347; and 14.173. More specifically in the case of Matt 19:10, οὕτως links ἡ αἰτία with the charge of adultery *as expounded by Jesus* in verses 4–9. Hence the translation, "If such, *as you say*, is the charge…." Cf. the same construction (οὕτω + εἰμί + nominative noun with a genitive modifier) in 1:18.

[25] Sophocles, *Phil.* 1404; Plutarch, *Per.* 30.3; Thucydides, *Hist.* 1.23.6. There are no examples of this type of personal genitive construction with αἰτία in the New Testament, the LXX, Philo, or Josephus.

[26] There may be other options for this construction, such as in philosophical contexts where the meaning of αἰτία is unique ("connection, explanation"), or in medical contexts indicating the *source* of the personal genitive. These need not be considered for 19:10a.

[27] Mark 15:26a: καὶ ἦν ἡ ἐπιγραφὴ τῆς αἰτίας αὐτοῦ ἐπιγεγραμμένη.

με]!"[28] Josephus also provides one example of αἰτία with a personal genitive: the Sidonians appeal to King Antiochus to command their governor "not to molest us in any way by attaching to us the charges of which the Jews are guilty [τὰς τῶν Ἰουδαίων αἰτίας], since we are distinct from them both in race and in customs" (Josephus, *A.J.* 12.261 [Thackeray, LCL]). Finally, amid the litany of injustices committed by Maxentius, Eusebius reports that, by means of "fabricated charges against multitudes [πεπλασμέναις αἰτίαις μυρίων] (of Senators)" (Eusebius, *Hist. eccl.* 8.14.4), he had them executed and stole their wealth. These examples are representative of what appears to be the primary sense of this construction: the culpability (actual or contrived) of the personal modifier.[29] Quotations of 19:10 in the church fathers,[30] and the Syriac translations[31] support this sense as well. Reading ἡ αἰτία τοῦ ἀνθρώπου as "the charge against the man," therefore, is eminently suitable.

Reframing 19:10: Remarriage and the Charge of Adultery

Usage of αἰτία in 19:10 versus 19:3: Jesus Turns the Tables

I prefer to translate ἡ αἰτία as "the charge" in 19:10a over "the guilt" or "the crime" of the man because "charge" elucidates the rhetorical connection with the

---

[28] ἡ αἰτία μου translates the Hebrew, עֲוֹנִי ("my guilt/sin/punishment"). In discussing this verse, Philo uses the same construction but substitutes ἔγκλημα ("charge/accusation") for αἰτία: ἔγκλημα τοῦ Κάιν (Philo, *Sacr.* 1.72). Examples like this suggest that the semantic domain of lexemes denoting "charge/accusation" can naturally lend themselves to the notion of "against" when taking a personal genitive.

[29] Cf. P.Mich. 5.312 (34 CE; διὰ τὴν τῶν μεμισθωμένων ἐτίαν [= αἰτίαν as in P.Lond. 6.1914; P.Oxy. 38.2859; SB 18.13948; Stud.Pal. 22.40]); Justin, *Dial.* 140.4.8, 9; John Chrysostom, *Comm. Job* 102.3; John of Damascus, *Sacr. parall.* 95.1353.10; Origen, *Comm. Matt.* 13.26; and Pseudo-Lucian, *Cyn.* 1.5.

[30] John Chrysostom, for example, explicitly equates αἰτία with guilt in 19:10: "But what is, Εἰ οὕτως ἐστὶν ἡ αἰτία τοῦ ἀνθρώπου μετὰ τῆς γυναικός (19:10a)? That is, if to this end he is joined with her, that they should be one, or, on the other hand, if the man shall get to himself *blame* for these things [Εἰ αἰτίαν λήψεται ἐπὶ τούτοις ὁ ἀνήρ], and always transgresses by putting away ..." (*Hom. Matt.* 62 [PG 58.599; *NPNF*[1] 10:365; emphasis mine]. I have kept the Greek original of 19:10a since, remarkably, Schaff translates the first instance of αἰτία as "case" and the second (i.e., Chrysostom's interpretation of the term) as "blame"! Cf. Origen, *Comm. Matt.* 14.25.12.

[31] In Sinaiticus, Curetonianus, and Peshitta ᶜdlyᵓ ("blame," "fault," or "guilt") translates αἰτία. The Harklean version (an "extremely literal translation of the Greek text" [George Anton Kiraz, *Comparative Edition of the Syriac Gospels: Aligning the Sinaiticus, Curetonianus, Peshiṭtâ and Ḥarklean Versions*, ed. Bruce M. Metzger, 4 vols., NTTS 21 (Leiden: Brill, 1996), xxxiii]) has ᶜltᵓ (ibid., 1:280). This word, like *causa*, seems to have a broad range of meaning, including (1) opportunity, means; (2) cause, reason, motive; (3) pretense, pretext; (4) evidence, proof; (5) occasion; (6) *sin, crime, accusation*; (7) thing, object (Michael Sokoloff, *A Syriac Lexicon: A Translation from the Latin, Correction, Expansion, and Update of C. Brockelmann's "Lexicon Syriacum"* [Winona Lake, IN: Eisenbrauns; Piscataway, NJ: Gorgias, 2009], 1106–7). As was (initially) the case in the Latin translations, the "crime/accusation" gloss was understood.

term in 19:3. Indeed, the latter is critical for understanding the relationship between the eunuch (19:10–12) and divorce passages (19:3–9). It reads: "Pharisees came to him [Jesus] in order to test him, and said, 'Is it lawful for a man to divorce his wife for any charge whatsoever [κατὰ πᾶσαν αἰτίαν]?" (19:3).[32] Typically, αἰτίαν is translated here simply as "reason" or "cause." The context, however, clearly requires the legal sense of "ground" or "accusation/charge." Thiele includes it as an example where "erscheint αἰτία in Verbindung mit gerichtlichen Beschuldigungen und mit Klagen, die gegen jemanden vorgebracht werden."[33] Similarly, Radl states, "Mt 19,3 geht es um den—mitunter lächerlichen—*Anlaß* zur Ehescheidung."[34] In Jesus's day marriage and divorce were legal matters involving a marriage contract, divorce documents, and a financial settlement.[35] Divorce was often finalized in a rabbinic court to protect the rights of each party and to enforce their respective obligations, although this was not required.[36] Thus, a legal gloss, such as "charge," is fitting for 19:3.

Translating αἰτία as "charge" in 19:3 and in 19:10 clarifies the rhetorical polemic in play in the passage as a whole. In Matthew, Jesus makes a habit of taking

---

[32] From a historical standpoint, the Pharisees' question appears to refer to the rabbinic debate between Hillel and Shammai over what constitutes legitimate grounds for divorce. The Mishnah summarizes the competing views, centered on the interpretation of ערות דבר ("matter of indecency") in Deut 24:1: "The School of Shammai say: A man may not divorce his wife unless he has found unchastity in her, for it is written, *Because he hath found in her* indecency *in anything*. And the School of Hillel say: [He may divorce her] even if she spoiled a dish for him, for it is written, *Because he hath found in her* indecency *in* anything. R. Akiba says: Even if he found another fairer than she, for it is written, *And it shall be if she find no favour in his eyes* (m. Git. 9:10 [cf. Sifre Deut. 269; y. Sota 1.2, 16b; m. Ketub. 7:6; b. Git. 90b]"; trans. Herbert Danby, *The Mishnah: Translated from the Hebrew with Introduction and Brief Explanatory Notes* [Oxford: Oxford University Press, 1933; repr., 1983], 321). The degree to which first-century practices can be derived from classical rabbinic traditions is, of course, fraught with difficulties. Philo (*Spec.* 3.30) and Josephus (*A.J.* 4.253) mention the grounds of divorce in Hillelite terms as if there were no debate at all. For a discussion of divorce texts from Qumran, see David Instone-Brewer, "Nomological Exegesis in Qumran 'Divorce' Texts," *RevQ* 18 (1998): 561–79.

[33] Thiele, *TBLNT* 3:1093 (emphasis original).

[34] Radl, *EWNT* 1:104 (emphasis original).

[35] For a divorce to be valid, the husband (or a representative) had to write out and present the wife with the *get* (divorce certificate). Upon receipt of the required *ketubah* (inheritance monies) from the husband, the wife would present him with the *quittance* (receipt) to confirm that he had fulfilled his financial obligations. See citations and discussion in David Instone-Brewer, *Divorce and Remarriage in the Bible: The Social and Literary Context* (Grand Rapids: Eerdmans, 2002), 117.

[36] Instone-Brewer explains, "A divorce did not require a court unless there was a dispute about the *ketubah* inheritance or the grounds for the divorce. It was usually safer, however, to conduct a divorce through a court because of the large amount of money involved. Any misunderstanding could result in later legal action that could bankrupt the former husband. Also, a mistake in the divorce procedure could mean that the divorce was invalid and thus any subsequent marriage by the woman would be adulterous" (ibid., 116–17).

a question or comment from the religious leaders and turning it against them, exposing their hypocrisy and disqualification to lead God's people.[37] Matthew 19:3–12 is a poignant example. The Pharisees approach Jesus to tempt/test (πειράζω) him by asking him how heinous or insignificant the charges must be for a man to dismiss his wife and marry another. Although the question is posed theoretically ("Is it lawful for a man to divorce…," v. 3), Jesus quickly makes it personal: "He said to them, 'On account of *your* hardness of heart Moses permitted *you* to divorce *your* wives, but it has not been this way from the beginning'" (v. 8). Moreover, their question is not innocuous: each of the five other occurrences of πειράζω in Matthew indicates opposition to Jesus's messianic status and mission.[38] Regardless of how exactly their inquiry cloaks an attack, the Pharisees clearly do not get the answer for which they hope. On the contrary, Jesus again turns the tables, transferring the focus from *every* (possible) *charge* against *their wives*,[39] to *the charge of adultery* against *the husband* who divorces his wife (μὴ ἐπὶ πορνείᾳ) and marries another.[40]

The polemical movement of 19:3–12 becomes clearer when we compare the two verses.

Καὶ προσῆλθον αὐτῷ Φαρισαῖοι πειράζοντες αὐτὸν καὶ <u>λέγοντες</u>· εἰ ἔξεστιν <u>ἀνθρώπῳ</u> ἀπολῦσαι <u>τὴν γυναῖκα αὐτοῦ</u> κατὰ πᾶσαν <u>αἰτίαν</u>; (19:3)

<u>Λέγουσιν</u> αὐτῷ οἱ μαθηταί· εἰ οὕτως ἐστὶν <u>ἡ αἰτία</u> <u>τοῦ ἀνθρώπου</u> μετὰ <u>τῆς γυναικός</u>, οὐ συμφέρει γαμῆσαι. (19:10)

The structure and content of the two verses mirror each other, with both quotations concerning the man (<u>ἀνθρώπῳ</u>//<u>τοῦ ἀνθρώπου</u>) who divorces his wife (<u>τὴν γυναῖκα</u>//<u>τῆς γυναικός</u>) being introduced by a form of λέγω (<u>λέγοντες</u>//<u>λέγουσιν</u>). The equivalent aspects of the parallelism draw attention to and heighten the rhetorical effect of the dissimilarity: the object of the *charge* (<u>αἰτίαν</u>//<u>ἡ αἰτία</u>) has been transferred from the wife to the man/husband and, by implication, to the multitudes of guilty Jewish men, Pharisees included.

Thus, in 19:9 Matthew's Jesus reiterates—although in a new way—his response to their previous attempt to test/tempt (πειράζω) him when they demanded a sign from heaven (16:1–4): they are an "*adulterous* generation" (16:4). Moreover, by rooting his view in the pre-fall narrative of Gen 1:27 and 2:24 (Matt 19:4–5), over and against the Pharisees appeal to Deut 24:1–4 (Matt 19:7), Jesus again makes clear that the Pharisees do not understand that the prophesied times of renewal are now at hand; that is, they still "are not able to interpret the signs of the times" (16:3).

---

[37] Cf. Matt 12:1–8, 9–14; 15:1–20, et al.

[38] Matt 4:1, 3; 16:1; 22:18, 35. The first two instances refer to Satan's work, creating a literary resonance that carries across the other four usages: the Pharisees' tests/temptations are in accord with the purposes of Satan.

[39] So, πᾶσαν αἰτίαν (19:3).

[40] ἡ αἰτία in 19:10 refers to Jesus's declaration in verse 9, which is against the Pharisees ("But I say to you …").

The protasis in 19:10, therefore, summarizes Jesus's answer (19:4–9) to the Pharisees' initial question from 19:3. To paraphrase the disciples' response: "If it is not lawful to divorce one's wife for any and every charge (see 19:3), and the man who does so and then remarries is himself charged with adultery (see 19:9), then…." The majority of scholars have interpreted the apodosis, 19:10b, with reference to marriage in general, with the sense, "it is better for people not to marry at all." The nature of the disciples' logic in this reading is confusing and misogynistic.[41] My proposal for ἡ αἰτία τοῦ ἀνθρώπου, however, suggests that 19:10b be read with reference to *remarriage*. In this reading the disciples statement is logically sound and entirely appropriate to the context; it really is "better" for such a man who has illicitly divorced his wife "not to marry [another]" if, in so doing, he incurs the charge/guilt of adultery. That is to say, the context drives the reader to fill in the gap of 19:10b in light of 19:9 and 19:10a: εἰ οὕτως ἐστὶν ἡ αἰτία τοῦ ἀνθρώπου μετὰ τῆς γυναικός, οὐ συμφέρει [τῷ ἀνθρώπῳ ἑτέραν] γαμῆσαι.[42]

Remarriage and the Grammar of 19:10

While the overarching rationale compels a remarriage reading of 19:10, it is also suggested by the grammar of 19:10 in relation to 19:3 and 9:

λέγω δὲ ὑμῖν ὅτι ὃς ἂν [ref. ἀνθρώπῳ of 19:3] ἀπολύσῃ τὴν γυναῖκα αὐτοῦ μὴ ἐπὶ πορνείᾳ καὶ γαμήσῃ ἄλλην[43] μοιχᾶται.[44] (19:9)

Λέγουσιν αὐτῷ οἱ μαθηταί· εἰ οὕτως ἐστὶν ἡ αἰτία τοῦ ἀνθρώπου μετὰ τῆς γυναικός, οὐ συμφέρει γαμῆσαι. (19:10)

Modern commentaries overlook the function of the οὕτως in 19:10: not only does it predicate the disciples' response on Jesus's teaching in 19:3–9, but it also binds the lexemes of 19:10 semantically to their equivalents in 19:3 and 9.[45] That is to say, from a grammatical standpoint, οὕτως directs the reader to interpret the terms of

---

[41] See the introduction above.

[42] Cf. Clement of Alexandria, *Strom.* 3.6.50.1–3.

[43] The transmission of this verse has been complicated due to assimilation with Matt 5:32. Here the exception clause has been changed to παρεκτὸς λόγου πορνείας in D *f*[13] 33 *pc* it (sy[c]) sa mae; and, along with the predicate, to παρεκτὸς λόγου πορνείας ποιεῖ αὐτὴν μοιχευθῆναι in B *f*[1] ff[1] bo. The text is supported by ℵ C[3] L (W) Z Θ 078 𝔐 l vg sy[s.p.h]. See Bruce M. Metzger, *A Textual Commentary on the Greek New Testament*, 2nd ed. (Stuttgart: Deutsche Bibelgesellschaft, 1994), 38.

[44] Several witnesses also add καὶ ὁ ἀπολελυμένην γαμῶν (or γαμήσας [B Z 𝔐]) μοιχᾶται (B C* W Z Θ 078 *f*[1.13] 33 𝔐 lat sy[p.h] bo). The longer reading results from assimilation with 5:32. The text is supported by: ℵ C3 D L 1241 *pc* it sy[p.c] sa bo[ms]. See Metzger, *Textual Commentary*, 38–39.

[45] Indeed, I know of no modern commentary to make this point. Davies and Allison make only the general observation, "οὕτως* and συμφέρει* are characteristic" (*Critical and Exegetical Commentary*, 3:19 n. 88). Usually οὕτως is not mentioned at all.

19:10, where possible,[46] in light of their antecedent(s).[47] "The man" (τοῦ ἀνθρώπου) in 19:10, therefore, should not be read as a general referent to any man,[48] since verses 3 and 9 have specifically defined this ἄνθρωπος as the one who divorces his wife according to any and every charge.[49] The presence of the article, although often untranslated, makes this connection even stronger.[50] Likewise, τῆς γυναικός in 19:10 does not refer to just any wife but rather to the recipient of the divorce by "the man," as is the case with its antecedents in 19:3 and 9—also confirmed by the article.[51] Thus, the (not-so-hypothetical) ἄνθρωπος and γυνή of all three verses (19:3, 9, and 10) are the same characters in each verse. These observations converge in a critical interpretative point: γαμῆσαι (19:10) should also be read in accordance with its earlier usage, γαμήσῃ (19:9), as referring to the marriage of *another* (i.e., remarriage), because the same (implied) subject of the action is the man who has already (illicitly) divorced his wife.

Both the logic and the grammar of 19:10, therefore, compel the reader to fill in the gap of 19:10b with the same ἄνθρωπος of 19:10a (cf. 19:3) in the context of 19:9:

[19:9] ὃς ἂν ἀπολύσῃ τὴν γυναῖκα αὐτοῦ μὴ ἐπὶ πορνείᾳ καὶ <u>γαμήσῃ ἄλλην</u> μοιχᾶται.

[19:10] εἰ οὕτως ἐστὶν ἡ αἰτία <u>τοῦ ἀνθρώπου</u> μετὰ τῆς γυναικός, οὐ συμφέρει [<u>τῷ ἀνθρώπῳ ἑτέραν</u>] <u>γαμῆσαι</u>.[52]

The traditional reading has interpreted the terms and filled in the gaps of the verse in a manner that is contextually untenable—a problem this proposal seeks to rectify. As a final summary, these two readings can be compared as follows.

Traditional Reading:

If such is the *relationship/case of a man* [generally speaking] with his wife, then it is better [for men] not to marry [anyone at all].

---

[46] The exception of ἡ αἰτία actually assumes the point as Jesus turns the tables against the Pharisees (see above).

[47] Although οὕτως does not necessitate that 19:10 be read with reference to remarriage, I think the grammar recommends it. In concert with the proposed inner logic of verses 3–10 thus far, I think the context requires it.

[48] That is, "a man/husband"; see CEB, ESV, NIV, NRSV.

[49] The phrase ὃς ἄν (19:9) refers to ἀνθρώπῳ of verse 3. Cf. ἄνθρωπος in vv. 5 and 6, which also contributes to this sense.

[50] The article functions as an article of referent.

[51] Cf. uses in verses 5 and 8.

[52] Cf. Clement of Alexandria, *Strom.* 3.6.50.1–3 In its terseness, the discussion among the three parties of 19:3–12—the Pharisees, Jesus, and the disciples—resembles the extant records of rabbinic debates.

Proposed Reading:

εἰ οὕτως ἐστὶν ἡ αἰτία τοῦ ἀνθρώπου	"If such, as you say, is the charge [i.e., adultery] against the man (ref. to the man who illegitimately divorces and then marries another in 19:9 [cf. 19:3])
μετὰ τῆς γυναικός	with respect to his wife (ref. to the γυνή illegitimately divorced by the man in 19:9 [cf. 19:3]; μετά with the genitive signifying *in his dealings with* [LSJ])[60]
οὐ συμφέρει [τῷ ἀνθρώπῳ ἑτέραν][61] γαμῆσαι.	then it is not better for that man to marry another." (carrying the subject of 19:10a over and reading γαμέω with ref. to *remarriage* as in 19:9)

For translation purposes, the more implied details from verse 9 that are woven into verse 10, the clearer its meaning will become.

II. Interpreting 19:10–12: Self-Dismemberment (5:20, 27–32) to Avoid the αἰτία of Adultery

Matthew creates structural, verbal, and thematic links between texts and subtexts across the gospel thereby indicating that the connected passages are to be read in light of each other.[55] In this manner, the conclusions reached in section I

---

[53] The phrase μετὰ τῆς γυναικός emphasizes the injustice committed against the man's first wife if he illicitly divorces her and marries another, as in Mark 10:11b: he "commits adultery *against her*" (μοιχᾶται ἐπ' αὐτήν). For other uses of μετά signifying *in one's dealings with* (LSJ), see Judg 1:24, 15:3, Luke 1:72, Acts 14:27, 15:4.

[54] Clement of Alexandria, *Strom.* 3.6.50.1–3.

[55] Jesus's prayer in Gethsemane (26:36–46) is a notable example, interweaving elements from the Lord's Prayer and the parable of the ten bridesmaids. By virtue of these links, Jesus is presented as the faithful disciple par excellence who maintains readiness for the parousia and final judgment through prayer. See the full discussion in R. Jarrett Van Tine, "Does Peter's Faith Peter Out?" (review discussion of *Peter: False Disciple and Apostate according to Saint Matthew*, by Robert H. Gundry), *Histos* 11, 22 February 2017, 14–28, here 22–24.

The nature and mutually interpreting effect of such intertextuality within a single work are explained by Michael Riffaterre: "Any subtext, or, more broadly still, any unit of significance that can be identified as the narrative unfolds, any segment of that narrative that can be isolated without cognitive loss, may serve as an intertext to some further such unit, if the latter has features in common with the former. Such features make it possible or necessary for the reader to see the two units as different versions of the same episode or of the same description, or two variants of the same structure. Components of the second will thus acquire a meaning other than what they convey in context because they will be perceived as referring also or primarily to their homologues in the first. ("The Intertextual Unconscious," *Critical Inquiry* 13 [1987]: 371–85, here 380–81; cf.

reactivate dormant elements within 19:3–12, revealing Matthew's eunuch pericope to be a shocking yet masterful recasting of Jesus's exhortation to self-dismemberment from 5:29–30.[56] Both passages are structured, in part, by the religious leaders' understanding of the law of Moses versus Jesus's messianic readministration of it.[57] As such, the pericopes share the same adversary, the Pharisees (see 5:20 and 19:3). Verbally, the most significant correlations are the following:

OUTLINE 1
Verbal Links Uniting 19:3–12 and 5:27–32

1. Phrases
   a. Verbatim
      i. ὃς ἂν ἀπολύσῃ τὴν γυναῖκα αὐτοῦ (5:31//19:9)
      ii. λέγω δὲ ὑμῖν (5:28, 32//19:8)
   b. Semantically equivalent
      i. παρεκτὸς λόγου πορνείας (5:32)//μὴ ἐπὶ πορνείᾳ (19:9)
      ii. ἀποστάσιον (5:31)//βιβλίον ἀποστασίου (19:7)
2. Noun forms
   a. γυνή (γυναῖκα; 5:28, 31, 32//(γυναῖκα [19:3, 9]; γυναικί [19:5]; γυναῖκας [19:8], γυναικός [19:10])
3. Verb forms
   a. γαμέω (γαμήσῃ [5:32, 19:9])
   b. μοιχεύω (μοιχεύσεις [5:27]; ἐμοίχευσεν [5:28]; μοιχευθῆναι, μοιχᾶται [5:32]//μοιχᾶται [19:9])
   c. ἀπολύω (ἀπολύσῃ [5:31]; ἀπολύων, ἀπολελυμένην [5:32]//ἀπολῦσαι [19:3, 7, 8]; ἀπολύσῃ [19:9])
   d. συμφέρω (συμφέρει [5:29, 30]//συμφέρει [19:10])

The thematic parallels of adultery and divorce–remarriage are apparent.

Ziva Ben-Porat, "The Poetics of Literary Allusion," *PTL: A Journal for Descriptive Poetics and Theory of Literature* 1 [1976]: 105–28, here 114 n. 9.)

The proposed reading could also be classified as an example of intra-Matthean *metalepsis*—a classical term that goes back at least to Quintilian. For a brief overview of this type of allusion and how it has been reworked and applied to biblical studies, see G. Brooke Lester, "Inner-Biblical Interpretation," *Oxford Encyclopedia of Biblical Interpretation*, ed. Stephen L. McKenzie (Oxford: Oxford University Press, 2013), 448–49.

[56] Matthew 5:27–32 encompasses two of the six antitheses in verses 21–48 (murder [vv. 21–26], adultery [vv. 27–28], divorce [vv. 31–32], vows [vv. 33–37], vengeance/retribution [vv. 38–42], hatred of enemies [vv. 43–47]), introduced by 5:17–20. The setting of the Sermon on the Mount is one of messianic and eschatological fulfillment (see D. A. Carson, "Matthew," in *The Expositor's Bible Commentary with the New International Version*, ed. Frank E. Gaebelein et al., 12 vols. [Grand Rapids: Zondervan, 1995], 8:3–599, here 128). But to enter the kingdom, Jesus says, his followers must have a righteousness exceeding that of Israel's religious leaders (5:20). Obedience to the Christ's laws concerning adultery and divorce–remarriage, then, are two examples of this type of required kingdom righteousness.

[57] Ἐρρέθη ... ἐγὼ δὲ λέγω ὑμῖν [5:27–28, 31–32]//λέγει αὐτοῖς ὅτι Μωϋσῆς ... λέγω δὲ ὑμῖν [19:(7), 8, 9]. For the expectation of the law being readministered in the last days, see Deut 18:18, Isa 2:3, 42:4, 51:4; Mic 4:2 et al.

What is less apparent, at least initially, is the final shared theme of self-dismemberment to enter the kingdom as it is recast in the form of a metaphor. Yet therein lies the rhetorical punch. The allusion[58] begins to unfold with the initial links to 5:20, 27–32 woven throughout Jesus's response to the Pharisees (vv. 3–9). Together, they draw the former text and its context into the attentive reader's mental periphery. In verse 10, however, the subtext takes control as the disciples conclude that "it is not better [οὐ συμφέρει]" for the man who divorces his wife to marry another, lest he incur the charge of adultery (ἡ αἰτία τοῦ ἀνθρώπου). The verb συμφέρει occurs three additional times in the gospel: two in the initial call to dismemberment (noted above), both with reference to adultery (as in 19:9), and the third in 18:6, which is itself a recapitulation of the principle. The narrative stage has thus been set to reach its full rhetorical force in the eunuch metaphor (19:12), whereby Jesus calls these men to "cut off" (cf. 5:29–30) that which would cause them to stumble (that is, their male organ), by remaining spouseless (i.e., "eunuchs") so as not to commit adultery.[59] They do so, διὰ τὴν βασιλείαν τῶν οὐρανῶν, which, in light of 5:20, 27–32, must mean, "to enter the kingdom of heaven."[60] The eunuch

---

[58] I use the term as defined by Ben-Porat, "Poetics of Literary Allusion," 107–8: "The literary allusion is a device for the simultaneous activation of two texts. The activation is achieved through the manipulation of a special signal: a sign (simple or complex) in a given text characterized by an additional larger 'referent.' This referent is always an independent text. The simultaneous activation of the two texts thus connected results in the formation of intertextual patterns whose nature cannot be predetermined." This mechanism can function the same way across a single literary work (see Riffaterre, quoted above in n. 56).

[59] Indeed, if the "hand" of 5:30 refers to one's male organ (cf. Isa 56:5; 57:8, 10; Cant 5:4; 1QS VII, 13; T. Sol. 1:2, 4), then the image of self-castration is employed in *both* passages.

Ben-Porat refers to the culmination of identified linkages between texts as *intertextual patterning*. Although she discusses references in a text to one or more subtexts outside the work, her comments are equally pertinent for explaining the intertextual patterning observed between 19:3–12 (esp. 10–12) and 5:20, 27–32. I relate her description to the case in point: "In terms of the end product, the formation of intertextual patterns, the marker [συμφέρει and others in outline 1]—regardless of the form it takes—is used for the activation of independent elements from the evoked text [the call to self-dismemberment to avoid eternal punishment]. Those are never referred to directly. The signal used might be a most transparent marker, explicitly denoting the text alluded to; but immediate identification of the source-text does not substitute for the activation of elements which remain to be identified [again, the self-dismemberment principle]. These elements may be secondary (weaker) with regard to the element which can best represent a given text, *but they are primary in terms of the actualized allusion*. Thus, the alluding text and its specific requirements *cause a shift in the hierarchy of representational elements in the original system*" ("Poetics of Literary Allusion," 108–9; emphasis added).

[60] As stated in the subtext, the purpose of Jesus's call to dismemberment is to prevent one's whole body from being destroyed in "Gehenna" (5:29, 30). Moreover, as mentioned, the call itself is set in the broader context of obtaining a righteousness that exceeds that of the scribes and Pharisees, without which nobody will enter the kingdom of heaven (5:20). Cf. the parallel to 5:29–30 in 18:8–9, which includes εἰς τὴν ζωήν and εἰς τὴν ζωὴν εἰσελθεῖν. Traditionally, διὰ τὴν βασιλείαν τῶν οὐρανῶν is understood in a more benign sense, referring to the undistracted

metaphor, therefore, is another of Matthew's extreme illustrations by which he summons his readers toward wholehearted devotion to Jesus so that they might enter his kingdom.[61] In this case he emphasizes the willingness to sacrifice essential present-age concerns (i.e., a spouse and children; cf. 13:22) rather than break the law (i.e., commit adultery) as administered by Christ—all in the hope of a greater reward in the age to come.[62]

III. Second Temple Jewish and Early Church Support

Corroboration for this reading of 19:10–12 can be found in its Second Temple Jewish and early Christian contexts. In regard to the former, the proposed link to Jesus's call to self-dismemberment finds a strong parallel in Philo's *That the Worse Attacks the Better*. In discussing Cain's banishment, Philo emphasizes the need to resist temptations, particularly those sexual in nature:

> And so, to my thinking, those who are not utterly ignorant would *choose to be blinded* rather than see unfitting things, and *to be deprived of hearing* rather than listen to harmful words, and *to have their tongues cut out* to save them from uttering anything that should not be divulged.... *It is better to be made a eunuch than to be mad after illicit unions* [ἐξευνουχισθῆναί γε μὴν ἄμεινον ἢ πρὸς συνουσίας ἐκνόμους λυττᾶν]. All these things [i.e., sins], seeing that they plunge the soul in disasters for which there is no remedy, would properly *incur the most extreme vengeance and punishment*. (Philo, *Det.* 173–178 [Colson and Whitaker, LCL; emphasis added])

---

devotion to kingdom affairs that celibacy affords (cf. 1 Cor 7:32–34). This is one example of how Matt 19:10–12 has been taken over and muted by Paul's discussion on celibacy in 1 Cor 7. Space precludes any attempt to address the apparent tension between διὰ τὴν βασιλείαν τῶν οὐρανῶν and 12:31 ("every sin and blasphemy will be forgiven people").

[61] Matthew's extreme examples of discipleship—positive and negative—exhort the reader to Pharisee-surpassing righteousness on the basis of their implicit greater-to-lesser paraenesis. See, e.g., the pericopes of the Syrophoenician woman (15:21–28) and the rich young man (19:16–26). Cf. 8:5–13, 19–20, 21–22, et al.

[62] My proposal exposes a tighter relationship between 19:3–12, 13–15, and 16–26 than has previously been explored. Within the confines of this article, it is worth noting that the reading put forth here explains the enigmatic reference to leaving "children" in 19:29: it refers, that is, to illegitimately divorced disciples who relinquish the hope of additional children, since they could only be born through an *adulterous* remarriage. Likewise, the reference to leaving "houses" and/or "fields" looks back to the pericope of the rich young man. Moreover, the proposed relationship between making oneself a eunuch and refusing illicit remarriage also clarifies the parallels between Matt 19:3–12 and Mark 10:2–12. Rather than shifting to celibacy in Matthew, the insiders' discussion of both accounts maintains the focus on the guilt of adultery incurred through remarriage (Matt 19:10–12//Mark 10:10–12).

The same logic is applied in both passages: "it is better" (ἄμεινον//συμφέρει [19:10]) to cut off your body parts, even make yourself a eunuch (the same verb, εὐνουχίζω, used twice in Matt 19:12), than to sin through those members, thereby incurring punishment.[63] The proposed reading, therefore, fits comfortably into the rhetorical and ethical milieu of at least some forms of Judaism during the Second Temple period.

In addition, Matt 19:10–12 was read in concert with 5:27–32 in the early church. The variant textual interpolations from 5:32 into 19:9[64] are indicative of this fact. Further confirmation is provided by the earliest discussion we have of 19:10–12, which connects these two passages in a manner notably close to the one I propose here. In his *First Apology*, Justin Martyr writes:

> Concerning chastity [Jesus] said this: "Whosoever looks upon a woman to lust after her has already committed adultery with her in his heart before God." [5:28] And: "If your right eye offends you, cut it out; for it is better for you to enter into the Kingdom of Heaven with one eye, than with two eyes to be cast into eternal fire." [5:29] And: "Whosoever shall marry her that is divorced from another husband, commits adultery." [5:32b/19:9b] And: "There are some who have been made eunuchs by men, and some who were born eunuchs, and some who have made themselves eunuchs for the Kingdom of Heaven's sake; but not all can receive this saying." [19:12, 11] So that all who according to human law make second marriages are sinners in the sight of our Master, as are those who look on a woman to lust after her. For not only the man who in act commits adultery is condemned by Him, but also the man who desires to commit adultery; since not only our deeds but also our thoughts are open before God. (Justin, *1 Apol.* 1.15)[65]

Not only does Justin connect 5:28, 29, 5:32b/19:9b,[66] and 19:12, but, in so doing, he seems to interpret the eunuch metaphor in light of adulterous remarriage after divorce.[67] My proposal, therefore, is not without precedent.[68]

---

[63] Commentators who note Philo's text do so only in passing, as the parallels are obscured by the celibacy reading of 19:10–12. See, e.g., Davies and Allison, *Critical and Exegetical Commentary*, 3:23; and David L. Turner, *Matthew*, BECNT (Grand Rapids: Baker Academic, 2008), 463.

[64] Cf. discussion of variants in nn. 43 and 44 above.

[65] Leslie William Barnard, *St. Justin Martyr: The First and Second Apologies*, ACW 56 (New York: Paulist, 1997), 32.

[66] The variant textual tradition makes it unclear whether Justin, in quoting "Whosoever shall marry her that is divorced from another husband, committeth adultery," refers to 5:32b, 19:9b, or both.

[67] "Twice married" almost certainly refers to those who remarry after divorce; see Barnard, *St. Justin Martyr*, 32 n. 95.

[68] Justin does not quote 19:10 directly, so it is not clear how exactly he is reading ἡ αἰτία. The Syriac translations and the quotations of 19:10 in the Greek fathers, however, indicate that the term was read in accordance with its traditional sense of moral culpability (see nn. 30 and 31

IV. Conclusion Explaining the Misinterpretation of 19:10(-12): The Latinizing of the Tradition

How then shall we account for the now-pervasive mistranslation of 19:10, which has led to the proposed misinterpretation of 19:10-12? I suggest the convergence of three key factors: the appropriation of Matt 19:10-12 (1) apart from the context of 19:3-9 (2) to celibacy in support of Paul's instructions in 1 Cor 7 (3) in Latin using the semantically broad terms *causa* and *homo* (particularly in the Vulgate), with the definiteness or indefiniteness of the latter in question.[69]

In support, it is notable that of the three figures who cite 19:10 in Latin—Ambrose, Ambrosiaster, and Jerome—none actually provides an informative exegetical discussion of the verse in the context of 19:3-12 as a whole.[70] Rather, in each case the disciples' statement is removed, by and large, from its Matthean context and referred to in support of a broader notion of celibacy within an explicitly Pauline framework. Initially, it is likely that *causa* in 19:10a was still understood to signify moral culpability. Over time and interpreted apart from 19:3-9, however, the significance of both *causa* and *homo* and the indefiniteness (in Latin) of the latter were naturally assimilated to support Pauline concepts regarding the benefits of celibacy (see 1 Cor 7): "If such is the *case/situation/relationship* of *a man* with his wife," so it was read, "it is better for men not to marry at all."[71] One need only

---

above). The passage is also unclear regarding how Justin is reading the exception clause and its relationship to 19:10-12.

[69] The Vulgate translates 19:10: Dicunt ei discipuli eius si ita est causa homini cum uxore non expedit nubere. As a noun, *causa*, like αἰτία, can communicate a *reason* or a *pretext/ground*. Although both can carry legal denotations, in judicial proceedings *causa* can also indicate the actual judicial *process/lawsuit* rather than just the culpability of those involved (as communicated by αἰτία). Outside the sphere of judicial proceedings, *causa* can signify *an employment, a relation of friendship*, or a *condition/state/situation/position* (Lewis and Short, Latin Dictionary, 303-4, s.v. "*causa*"). The latter two possibilities provide the basis for the traditional renderings of αἰτία in Matt 19:10 as *situation* or *relationship*. Indeed, it is reasonable at this point to postulate that the other popular gloss, "case," also originates from the Latin translation of αἰτία in 19:10 as *causa*, although I have kept the translational terms separate throughout this study (see Osborne and Arnold, *Matthew*, 706; and LSJ, s.v. "αἰτία").

Homo can signify a *man* or *humanity/the human race* (Lewis and Short, Latin Dictionary, 859-61, s.v. "*homo*"). Sometimes the variant *vir* is substituted for *homo*, which is only slightly less ambiguous out of context, signifying a *man, husband*, or *humanity* in general (see ibid., 1994-95, s.v. "*vir*"). In Latin there are no articles; the definiteness or indefiniteness of a term must be determined by other factors, such as context.

[70] Ambrose (*Virg.* 1.6.29; *Exh. virginit.* 1.3.18), Ambrosiaster (*Ep. B. Paul. Cor. Prim.* 10.22), and Jerome (*Jov.* 1.12 [2x]; *Epist. Amand.* 55.3).

[71] Although early discussions (second century) of Matt 19:10-12 support a remarriage interpretation (Clement of Alexandria, *Strom.* 3.6.50; Justin, *1 Apol.* 1.15), the passage was used predominantly to support the ideals of asceticism. For an overview of the controversies

reflect on the widespread historical influence of Latin to see how such a reading of 19:10(–12) could have embedded itself immovably in the subsequent tradition. Through the initial Old Latin version(s) and then through Jerome's Vulgate, Latin became the basis of early Bible translations, study, and debate in the Western church.[72] Thus, the influence of Latin on exegesis and later English translations was substantial. As Benjamin Kedar states, "[The influence of Latin in the Western church was] not merely a matter of quantitative diffusion: Europe had risen to predominance in human history, a rank it would hold for centuries to come. Consequently, it was the world which the Scriptures in their Latin dress set out to conquer."[73]

---

surrounding marriage and celibacy in the first three centuries, see David G. Hunter, *Marriage, Celibacy, and Heresy in Ancient Christianity: The Jovinianist Controversy*, OECS (Oxford: Oxford University Press, 2009), 87–129.

[72] Benjamin Kedar, "The Latin Translations," in *Mikra: Text, Translation, Reading, and Interpretation of the Hebrew Bible in Ancient Judaism and Early Christianity*, ed. Martin Jan Mulder and Harry Sysling, CRINT 2.1 (Assen: Van Gorcum; Minneapolis: Fortress, 1990), 335.

[73] Ibid.

The Death of Judas in Matthew: Matthew 27:9 Reconsidered

CATHERINE SIDER HAMILTON
csiderhamilton@wycliffe.utoronto.ca
Wycliffe College, Toronto, ON M5S 1H7, Canada

The account of Judas's death in Matthew's Gospel yields opposite readings. In the traditional reading, Judas's death is damning: his suicide enacts his self-exclusion from the salvation promised in Jesus. More recently, scholars have sought to rehabilitate Judas. Far from cementing his condemnation, Judas's death is a sign of his repentance, even heroism, and points toward redemption. Matthew's use of Scripture is, I propose, illuminating for the debate. Matthew 27:9 applies to the episode a quotation from Zechariah attributed (famously) to Jeremiah. Scholarly attention has focused on the problem of (mis)attribution. I argue, rather, that the "mistake" is useful: in calling up both Zech 11 and Jeremiah, Matthew sets the death of Judas within a particular scriptural history. A close reading of Jer 19 together with Zech 11 reveals a dense interweaving of vocabulary and themes, an intertextuality that informs Matt 27. Themes of innocent blood and defilement emerge in all three, and Judas's problematic "repentance" finds in LXX Zechariah's use of μεταμέλομαι a precursor that opens up the debate. Against this scriptural background, Judas's death unfolds as a story not of one man only but of a people and a land, a story set within Israel's larger story in which both devastation and hope—indeed restoration—may, in the blood of Jesus, be true.

How is the death of Judas in Matthew's Gospel to be understood? Matthew 27:3–10 has given rise to diametrically opposed readings. By the traditional reading, Judas's death is damning; his suicide enacts his self-exclusion from the salvation promised in Jesus. Judas is a man, Calvin says, "entirely shut out from the grace of God."[1] Many contemporary commentators agree. Robert H. Gundry entitles this

---

I would like to thank my daughter, Dr. Caitlin Anne Timmerman, for her generous help and excellent editorial eye. I am grateful also to the *JBL* reviewers for their helpful responses.

[1] John Calvin, *In harmoniam euang.*, Matt 27:3: ut ... exemplum esset hominis a Dei gratia prorsus abdicati. In *Commentarii in quatuor euangelistas Matthaeum, Marcum, Lucam, et Joannem* (Amsterdam: J. J. Schipper, 1671), 308. Translation from Calvin, *Commentary on a Harmony of the Evangelists, Matthew, Mark, and Luke*, trans. and collated by William Pringle, 3 vols. (Grand Rapids: Eerdmans, 1949), 3:269. The standard descriptor for Judas in ancient commentary is

419

section of his commentary "The Dreadful End of Judas"; Judas the traitor gets his just deserts. In N. T. Wright's words, "the tragedy of Judas is real, horrible and lasting."[2] Others, however, have sought to rehabilitate Judas. Far from cementing his condemnation, Judas's death is a sign of his repentance, even heroism, and points toward redemption. W. D. Davies and Dale C. Allison are representative. Judas is not "an everlasting failure doomed to destruction." He confesses his sin and seeks to make atonement by his suicide.[3] Indeed, William Klassen says that Judas is Jesus's true friend.[4]

How are we to adjudicate these competing claims? Is Judas betrayer or friend? Is he lost or is he saved—even, perhaps, saving? Matthew's use of Scripture is, I propose, illuminating for the debate. Matthew 27:9 applies to the episode a quotation from Zechariah attributed (famously) to Jeremiah. Scholarly attention has focused on the problem of (mis)attribution.[5]

In this article, I take up Davies and Allison's suggestion that the reference to Jeremiah "prod[s] us to read Zech 11.13 in the light of" Jeremiah,[6] and argue

---

"traitor." See, e.g., Irenaeus, *Haer.* 2.20.2: *proditor*; Judas *traditor* (PG 7:777); Tertullian, *Marc.* 4.40.2: *opera traditoris* (CCSL 1:655–56); Augustine, *Cons.* 3.7.31 (CSEL 43:308); Chrysostom, *Hom. Jo.* 70.1 (PG 59:381).

[2] Robert H. Gundry, *Matthew: A Commentary on His Handbook for a Mixed Church under Persecution*, 2nd ed. (Grand Rapids: Eerdmans, 1994), 552; N. T. Wright, *Matthew for Everyone*, 2 vols. (London: SPCK, 2002), 2:175. Cf. Pierre Bonnard, *L'Évangile selon saint Matthieu*, CNT 1 (Geneva: Labor et Fides, 1982), 393; Douglas R. A. Hare, *Matthew*, IBC (Louisville: John Knox, 1993), 314; Daniel J. Harrington, *The Gospel of Matthew*, SP 1 (Collegeville, MN : Liturgical Press, 1991), 386–87; Craig S. Keener, *A Commentary on the Gospel of Matthew* (Grand Rapids: Eerdmans, 1999), 658–60; Donald P. Senior, *The Passion Narrative according to Matthew: A Redactional Study*, BETL 39 (Leuven: Leuven University Press, 1975), 347–52, 384. Donald A. Hagner writes, "We can pity Judas, but we cannot make a hero out of him, nor alas even a believer" (*Matthew 14–28*, WBC 33B [Dallas: Word, 1995], 815).

[3] W. D. Davies and Dale C. Allison Jr., *A Critical and Exegetical Commentary on the Gospel according to Saint Matthew*, 3 vols., ICC (London: T&T Clark, 1988–1997), 3:561–65; quotation from 561.

[4] William Klassen, *Judas: Betrayer or Friend of Jesus?* (Minneapolis: Fortress, 1996). See also John Nolland, *The Gospel of Matthew: A Commentary on the Greek Text*, NIGTC (Grand Rapids: Eerdmans, 2005), 1153: Judas is the true disciple, "the first disciple to 'lose his life for [Jesus'] sake' (16:25)." See also David Daube, "Judas," *California Law Review* 82 (1994): 95–108; and Daube, "Judas," *Journal for the History of Law* 13 (1994): 305–30; Hyam Maccoby, *Judas Iscariot and the Myth of Jewish Evil* (New York: Free Press, 1992); Kim Paffenroth, *Judas: Images of the Lost Disciple* (Louisville: Westminster John Knox, 2001), 115; Caroline F. Whelan, "Suicide in the Ancient World: A Re-examination of Matthew 27:3–10," *LTP* 49 (1993): 505–22.

[5] See the reviews of the debate in Davies and Allison, *Gospel according to Saint Matthew*, 3:568–69; and Michael Knowles, *Jeremiah in Matthew's Gospel: The Rejected Prophet Motif in Matthean Redaction*, JSNTSup 68 (Sheffield: JSOT Press, 1993), 60–67.

[6] Davies and Allison, *Gospel according to Saint Matthew*, 3:569. They follow Raymond E. Brown: Matt 27:9 is a conflated citation containing words from both Zechariah and Jeremiah, identified by one name rather than both (*The Death of the Messiah: From Gethsemane to the Grave*;

beyond Davies and Allison that the "mistake" is deliberate and useful. In naming Jeremiah and echoing Zechariah, Matthew gains a rich referential background for the narrative of Judas's death. Sjef van Tilborg suggested some time ago that Matt 27:9 works deliberately to create meaning: the quotation from Zechariah, "hidden" by the attribution to Jeremiah, allows the reader who "hears and understands" (cf. Matt 13:14–15, 18–23) to read Matt 27:3–10 against the background of co-texts from Jeremiah and Zechariah that illuminate Matthew's narrative.[7] I wish to carry van Tilborg's important observation further. It is not just that Matthew's story of Judas recalls, as commentators have shown, both Jeremiah (in particular, I will argue, Jer 19) and Zech 11, nor even (as van Tilborg notes) that the echoes of each text illuminate Matthew. It is also that Matthew finds in Jeremiah and Zechariah together a shared logic and a particular history, a logic that informs the story of Judas and a history within which Judas's story unfolds. The logic, I will argue, is that of innocent blood and the problem of pollution. The history is that of a city and people in which the blood of the innocent and the threat of defilement loom large. To trace Matthew's use of Jeremiah and Zechariah is to see that Matthew sets the story of Judas within this scriptural history. Against the background of Zechariah and Jeremiah together, Judas and his blood money raise the urgent question: what now of Israel's fate and future?

My argument proceeds in two stages. Assuming with Ulrich Luz that "intertexts ... are part of the rhetorical strategy of a text," I seek to read with the grain of the text.[8] In the first place, I trace the referential background in order to establish its logic: what are the interrelationships between Jeremiah and Matt 27:3–10; between Jeremiah and Zechariah; between Zechariah and Matthew? What is the history of people and land that begins to emerge in the weave of intertexts?[9] Second,

---

A Commentary on the Passion Narratives in the Four Gospels, 2 vols., ABRL [New York: Doubleday, 1994], 1:651). See the similar suggestions of Gundry (*Matthew*, 557) and Knowles (*Jeremiah in Matthew's Gospel*, 67–69).

[7] Sjef van Tilborg, "Matthew 27.3–10: An Intertextual Reading," in *Intertextuality in Biblical Writings: Essays in Honour of Bas van Iersel*, ed. Sipke Draisma (Kampen: Kok, 1989), 159–74, here 164–65. Van Tilborg (cf. Robert H. Gundry, *The Use of the Old Testament in St. Matthew's Gospel: With Special Reference to the Messianic Hope*, NovTSup 18 [Leiden: Brill, 1975], 122–27) reads with great sensitivity to Matthean echoes of Zech 11 and Jer 32 and 19. He does not draw the Old Testament texts together, however, or find in them a common theme.

[8] Ulrich Luz, "Intertexts in the Gospel of Matthew," *HTR* 97 (2004): 119–37, here 122 (cf. 121, 125).

[9] On method, see esp. Dale C. Allison Jr., *The New Moses: A Matthean Typology* (Minneapolis: Fortress, 1993), 19–23. Cf. Luz, "Intertexts," 130–31. The interrelationships between texts become apparent (as Allison notes, 21–23) through a conjunction of elements: shared vocabulary and shared themes, or verbal echoes and a similar narrative structure, or quotation and shared content. The possibilities are manifold and the presence of intertextuality must be determined afresh for each passage. In the case of Matthew and Jeremiah or Zechariah, we are working with demonstrated relationships between texts (see below and esp. Gundry, *Use of the Old Testament*, 122–27; and van Tilborg, "Matthew 27.3–10"). In the case of Jeremiah and Zechariah, the relationship I seek

I ask about the import of this referential background. What is the meaning of Judas's death in the context of Jeremiah's and Zechariah's shared concern with innocent blood and defilement? To read Matthew against this background is, I propose, to discover a reading of Judas that goes beyond his individual fate to encompass the fates of both Jesus and the people. I hope to demonstrate that Matthew's use of Scripture is not atomistic but foundational and rich. Far from inserting isolated prooftexts into a gospel to which they are essentially extraneous, Matthew finds in his scriptural interlocutors a history encompassing large questions of purity and pollution, a people and a land, against and within which the history of Jesus and Judas unfolds.[10]

I. Jeremiah and Matthew

Although he quotes Zechariah, Matthew sets the story of Judas under the sign of Jeremiah: "Then was fulfilled the word spoken through the prophet Jeremiah" (27:9).[11] Several elements of the scene find echoes in Jeremiah.[12] Gundry notes

---

to demonstrate is one of resonance: shared images and a shared logic, rather than textual borrowing. As Luz demonstrates ("Intertexts," 122–25), the term *intertextuality* includes both specific textual borrowing and looser concinnities or relationships of various kinds. The work of Michael Fishbane (esp. *Biblical Interpretation in Ancient Israel* [Oxford: Clarendon, 1985]) and James L. Kugel (*In Potiphar's House: The Interpretive Life of Biblical Texts* [San Francisco: HarperSanFrancisco, 1990]; and *Traditions of the Bible: A Guide to the Bible As It Was at the Start of the Common Era* [Cambridge: Harvard University Press, 1998]) demonstrates the fundamentally interpretive and therefore allusive character of the biblical texts and texts based on them. Scriptural authors (or editors) habitually work against a background, steeped in the traditions of Scripture, speaking to it, with it, against it (allowing Scripture its broad sense, that is, the texts and traditions that a community considered sacred and authoritative). Matthew stands (as his story of Judas will, I hope, demonstrate) in this kind of Scripture-soaked and referential tradition.

[10] I would disagree with Luz's conclusion, namely, that the "innumerable biblical background-texts" in Matthew's gospel serve to illuminate and give legitimacy to "the new Matthean foundational story" ("Intertexts," 137); to this new story of Jesus "the foundational history of Israel" is subordinated. Matthew's use of Scripture—and in particular the fulfillment quotations—evidences for Luz "the painful experience of the parting of the ways" with Judaism (ibid., 136). On the contrary, I suggest that Israel's history and its future in the land are the matrix within which Matthew's new story of Jesus unfolds and are, in a primary sense, its goal.

[11] Translations of biblical passages are taken from the NRSV. Where they differ from the NRSV they are my own.

[12] See the helpful summary of possible references in Davies and Allison, *Gospel according to Saint Matthew*, 3:568–69; cf. Brown, *Death of the Messiah*, 1:650–52; and van Tilborg, "Matthew 27.3–10," 169–73. There are resonances with Jer 18 (18:2–6, 18–23: the potter and the plot against Jeremiah) and 32 (the purchase of a field), as well as significant parallels, both verbal and thematic, with Jer 19.

parallels with Jer 19:1–13 in particular.[13] The parallels are verbal as well as thematic, and many of them have been noted before. In tracing them here I seek to show that these parallels describe a particular logic, the logic of innocent blood.[14] It is a logic that, for Matthew—as, indeed, for Jeremiah and Zechariah—underlies and illuminates Judas's story. Jeremiah 19 begins with a declaration of sin, with an emphasis on *innocent blood*.[15] "'Hear the word of the Lord, O kings of Judah and inhabitants of Jerusalem …: the people have forsaken me, and have profaned this place [with idol worship] … and … have filled this place with *the blood of the innocent'*" (דם נקים; αἱμάτων ἀθῴων, 19:3–4).[16] Jeremiah is commanded to make this declaration

---

[13] Gundry, *Use of the Old Testament*, 125: blood of the innocents (Jer 19:4)/innocent blood (Matt 27:4); potter (Jer 19:1, 11; Matt 27:7, 10); elders and (chief) priests (Jer 19: 1; Matt 27:1, 3); the similarity between the names "Valley of Slaughter" (Jer 19:6) and "Field of Blood" (Matt 27:8) and the similar phrases that introduce each: "Wherefore this place shall be called" (Jer 19:6); "wherefore that field was called" (Matt 27:8). Gundry suggests a parallel also "between the burial of the Judaeans in the Valley of Hinnom and the burial of Judas in the potter's field," but Matthew does not mention Judas's burial (as Senior also notes, *Passion Narrative*, 360 n. 46). See also Senior, *Passion Narrative*, 359–61; Knowles, *Jeremiah in Matthew's Gospel*, 69–70; and Davies and Allison, *Gospel according to Saint Matthew*, 3:569. In addition to these specific parallels, Matthew's account (I argue) follows a logic like that of Jer 19. In focusing on the parallels with Jer 19 I do not intend to exclude resonances with Jer 18 and 32. Jeremiah 19, however, yields a concentration of verbal echoes and thematic parallels with Matt 27:3–10 and resonances with Zech 11 that suggest it is central to Matthew's purpose.

[14] For this argument see also, more briefly, Catherine Sider Hamilton, *The Death of Jesus in Matthew: Innocent Blood and the End of Exile*, SNTSMS 167 (Cambridge: Cambridge University Press, 2017), esp. 188–89. A number of commentators note the shared reference to innocent blood (Jer 19:4; Matt 27:4, e.g., Gundry, *Use of the Old Testament*, 125; Senior, *Passion Narrative*, 360; Davies and Allison, *Gospel according to Saint Matthew*, 3:569; van Tilborg, "Matthew 27.3–10," 169). Van Tilborg goes on to note the importance of innocent blood in Matt 27:3–10 and its connection to the destruction of Jerusalem: "The readiness to shed Jesus' innocent blood is the real cause of the disaster" ("Matthew 27.3–10," 174). The question, however, is why—and whether the story ends here. This is a question, I submit, to which Matt 27:9, with its curious commingling of Zechariah and Jeremiah, provides an answer that challenges van Tilborg's reading, which holds that the problem described under the term "innocent blood" is the rejection of the prophet, and the destruction that follows is the "final conclusion" of the story of Israel, a conclusion foreshadowed in the death of Judas. On the contrary, I propose that tracing the intertextual echoes reveals a scriptural vision that finds in innocent blood a different problem, the specter of defilement. Such a scriptural vision finds in innocent blood not only an explanation for the tragedy that has come upon the people but also the possibility of hope, precisely for "the holy city" (Matt 27:53).

[15] Verbal parallels are indicated with italics; thematic parallels by underlining. Note that in both Jeremiah and Matthew, innocent blood is introduced in the context of a declaration of sin.

[16] Gundry has argued persuasively that Matthew knows the biblical texts in Hebrew and in Greek versions (*Use of the Old Testament*, esp. 172–78). In discussions of Matt 27:3–10, most commentators assume the evangelist's knowledge of the MT and LXX. For a contrary view, see Maarten J. J. Menken, who argues that Matthew's Bible was a revised LXX (*Matthew's Bible: The Old Testament Text of the Evangelist*, BETL 173 [Leuven: Leuven University Press, 2004], esp. 3–10, 179–99, 280). Luz (*Matthew: A Commentary*, trans. James E. Crouch, 3 vols., Hermeneia

in the presence of *the elders of the people* and the senior priests (מזקני העם ומזקני הכהנים; LXX οἱ πρεσβύτεροι τοῦ λαοῦ; οἱ πρεσβύτεροι τῶν ἱερέων, Jer 19:1). So, too, in Matt 27. Judas says to *the elders* of the people and the chief priests (οἱ ἀρχιερεῖς; οἱ πρεσβύτεροι, 27:3; cf. 27:1 οἱ ἀρχιερεῖς καὶ οἱ πρεσβύτεροι τοῦ λαοῦ): "I have sinned; I have delivered up *innocent blood*" (27:4).

In Matthew, the chief priests refuse to listen to Judas. Because they do not listen, Judas hangs himself. In Jeremiah, the priest Pashhur strikes Jeremiah for his prophecy of disaster (20:2); because the priest and his friends will not listen, Jeremiah says, "they shall fall by the sword" (20:4). In both cases, an accusation about sin and innocent blood is made and the priests reject it. In both cases destruction follows: in Matthew immediately, for Judas; in Jeremiah in the future, for Pashhur and the whole people.[17]

The parallel logic continues. In Matthew, Judas throws the *blood* money (τιμὴ αἵματος, 27:6)—the price of Jesus's *innocent blood* (αἷμα ἀθῷον, 27:4)—into the temple. In Jeremiah, *innocent blood* (αἷμα ἀθῷον, 19:4) is shed in "this place": Jerusalem, with its temple in it (Jer 19:4). Indeed, Jeremiah depicts the city as a temple. Her sins are all those that involve temple worship: the people "have profaned this place by making offerings in it to other gods"; they have built high places of Baal and burned their children as sacrifices; they have thereby "shed innocent blood in this place" (Jer 19:4). The term "this place" encompasses city and temple both. In Jeremiah as in Matthew the blood of the innocent lands at the center of the worship of God.[18] Therefore Jeremiah prophesies slaughter: the city will become a burial

---

[Minneapolis: Fortress, 2005], 467), who follows Menken, nevertheless notes that in Matt 27:9 "there are many agreements with the MT, few with the LXX." He concludes that the quotation is pre-Matthean. The more obvious conclusion, especially given the evidence of Matthean editing in 27:9, is that Matthew knows not only the LXX but also the Hebrew text.

[17] Van Tilborg notes a "parallel narrative structure": the leaders throughout the book of Jeremiah do not listen to the prophet, as in Matthew they do not listen to Jesus; the persecution of the prophet puts at risk the future of the city and the land ("Matthew 27:3–10," 170). (Oddly, van Tilborg does not note in relation to Jer 19 the priest's rejection of Jeremiah's message.) This is not quite the parallel that Matthew draws in 27:3–10, however. In Matt 27:3–10, it is *Judas* to whom the leaders do not listen: they fail to heed his warning about innocent blood. Similarly, it is Jeremiah's prophecy of destruction following upon idolatry and innocent blood that Pashhur the priest refuses to hear. The center of gravity in both Matt 27:3–10 and Jer 19 lies not in the "rejected prophet" theme but in the problem of innocent blood (and, in Jeremiah, idolatry) and the fate of the people in its wake.

[18] See Charlene McAfee Moss, *The Zechariah Tradition and the Gospel of Matthew*, BZNW 156 (Berlin: de Gruyter, 2008), 182: in Jeremiah as in Matthew, the "trail of blood" leads to the temple because it is in the temple that Jeremiah prophesies destruction against the leaders of the people. In fact, the "trail of blood" is more concrete than McAfee Moss imagines. Jeremiah 19:4, like Matt 27:4–6, locates actual bloodshed—in 19:4, from child sacrifice—at the heart of temple worship. The problem here is not simply (as McAfee Moss and others suggest) the persecution of the prophet. The problem is the pollution of the holy place. On innocent blood and pollution, see further below.

ground (Jer 19:11–12 MT). In Matthew, the priests take the blood money and buy with it a burial ground outside the city. "Wherefore," Matthew says, "*that field was called* 'Field of Blood'" (27:8). Therefore, Jeremiah says, "*this place shall* no more *be called* Topheth ... but the Valley of Slaughter" (Jer 19:6). Gundry points out the similarity. The reference to Jeremiah follows in Matthew immediately.[19]

By means of these resonances, Matthew assimilates the story of Judas's death and Jesus's innocent blood to the history of idolatry, innocent blood, and destruction told by the prophet Jeremiah. In Jer 19, it is the history of a city and a people: "Hear the word of the Lord, O kings of Judah and inhabitants of Jerusalem" (19:3). The people forsake God; they worship idols; they shed the blood of the innocent, and the priests are complicit in it. In the same way, Judas in Matthew does not stand alone. The blood money comes from and returns to the priests; the chief priests and the elders *of the people* have sentenced Jesus to death (27:1). In 27:25, in a passage linked by innocent blood to 27:3–10, the people themselves will concur (and the whole people said, "His blood be upon us and upon our children").[20] Matthew, like Jer 19, tells a story of a city and a people.

II. Innocent Blood and the Problem of Pollution

The story told in Matt 27 is a story framed in terms of defilement and its consequences. In Jeremiah, the city is profaned by idols and filled with innocent blood. Innocent blood is in fact the crowning image of the people's sin, the horror of child sacrifice serving to sum up the people's abandonment of God. "I have sinned," Judas says. "I have delivered up innocent blood." Judas's words place the death of Jesus within a complex of ideas deeply rooted in the Hebrew Scriptures, having to do with bloodguilt and purgation, purity and pollution, the defilement of the land.[21]

---

[19] Gundry, *Use of the Old Testament*, 125.

[20] For the several links between 27:4–5 and 27:24–25, see Timothy B. Cargal, "'His Blood Be upon Us and upon Our Children': A Matthean Double Entendre?," *NTS* 37 (1991): 101–12, esp. 106–8; Brown, *Death of the Messiah*, 1:833–36; Davies and Allison, *Gospel according to Saint Matthew*, 3:590–91; Gundry, *Matthew*, 564–65. For πᾶς ὁ λαός as a phrase indicating the whole people, Israel, see my detailed argument in *Death of Jesus in Matthew*, esp. 10–11, 43–44, 185–87. See also, e.g., Brown, *Death of the Messiah*, 1:836–37; Senior, *Passion Narrative*, 258–61; Joseph A. Fitzmyer, "Anti-Semitism and the Cry of 'All the People,'" *TS* 26 (1965): 667–71, esp. 669. Compare, e.g., Davies and Allison, *Gospel according to Saint Matthew*, 3:592, following Anthony J. Saldarini, *Matthew's Christian-Jewish Community*, CSHJ (Chicago: University of Chicago Press, 1994), 32–33. That the phrase by my reading refers to Israel as a people does not, however, condone its use against Israel for anti-Jewish purposes, nor does the phrase imply that the gospel is anti-Jewish. Rather, as we will see, Matthew places this moment and the larger gospel narrative in conversation with the whole history of Israel. In this gospel and in its good news "the whole people" is intimately involved.

[21] This section is based in part on material published earlier in my article "'His Blood Be

The problem with the blood of the innocent, according to Numbers, is that "blood pollutes the land": "you shall not pollute the land in which you live; for blood pollutes the land, and no expiation can be made for the land, for the blood that is shed in it, except by the blood of the one who shed it. You shall not defile the land in which you live; in which I also dwell" (Num 35:33–34). Blood unjustly shed, by murder, child sacrifice, or judicial execution, is a danger to the land. Indeed, as Jacob Milgrom notes, in the land defiled by blood neither God nor Israel can dwell; the land itself will eventually vomit out its inhabitants.[22]

This is the logic of Jer 19, which draws a straight line from innocent blood to disaster precisely for the land. The consequence of idol worship and the blood of the innocent, Jeremiah says, is slaughter, the siege of Jerusalem (19:6–9). It is a slaughter to "make void the plans of Judah and Jerusalem" (19:7). The city's abandonment of God, evidenced by its idol worship and the shedding of innocent blood, leads to exile. All Judah will be carried captive to Babylon (20:4). Indeed, in the slaughter that follows upon idol worship and innocent blood, the city's defilement is enacted. "I will make this city a horror: ... I will make them eat the flesh of their sons and the flesh of their daughters" (19:8–9). They shall eat unclean food; even the land will become unclean: the city, Jeremiah says, will become a burial ground (19:11 MT).[23] "And the houses of Jerusalem," the prophet concludes, "and the

---

upon Us': Innocent Blood and the Death of Jesus in Matthew," *CBQ* 70 (2008): 82–100, esp. 91–93. See also now my discussion of bloodguilt and pollution in *Death of Jesus in Matthew*, 59–62. On bloodguilt and pollution in the Hebrew Scriptures, see further Tikva Frymer-Kensky, "Pollution, Purification, and Purgation in Biblical Israel," in *The Word of the Lord Shall Go Forth: Essays in Honor of David Noel Freedman in Celebration of His Sixtieth Birthday*, ed. Carol L. Meyers and M. O'Connor, ASOR Special Volume Series 1 (Winona Lake, IN: Eisenbrauns, 1983), 398–414; Hieronymus Christ, *Blutvergiessen im Alten Testament: Der gewaltsame Tod des Menschen untersucht am hebräischen Wort dām*, Theologische Dissertationen 12 (Basel: Friedrich Reinhardt, 1977). See also Jeffrey H. Tigay, *Deuteronomy* דברים: *The Traditional Hebrew Text with the New JPS Translation*, JPSTC (Philadelphia: Jewish Publication Society, 1996); and Jacob Milgrom, *Numbers* במדבר: *The Traditional Hebrew Text with the New JPS Translation*, JPSTC (Philadelphia: Jewish Publication Society, 1990). On purity, see Jonathan Klawans, *Purity, Sacrifice, and the Temple: Symbolism and Supersessionism in the Study of Ancient Judaism* (Oxford: Oxford University Press, 2006); Carl S. Ehrlich, Anders Runesson, and Eileen Schuller, eds., *Purity, Holiness, and Identity in Judaism and Christianity: Essays in Memory of Susan Haber*, WUNT 305 (Tübingen: Mohr Siebeck, 2013), and n. 24 below.

[22] See Milgrom, *Numbers*, 295. Cf. Lev 18:25–28.

[23] Unclean food and tombs, on the one hand, and innocent blood (murder), on the other, represent two different kinds of pollution in the Hebrew Scriptures: ritual and moral. As Jonathan Klawans observes, ritual impurity with which there is no wrongdoing associated is to be distinguished in the priestly purity paradigm from moral impurity, or sin (*Impurity and Sin in Ancient Judaism* [Oxford: Oxford University Press, 2000], 22–31). Yet the distinction permits an interrelation. Ritual impurity comes to serve in the Hebrew Scriptures as an image of moral corruption (see, e.g., Lam 4:13–15 with Lev 13:45–46). Adele Berlin comments: In its allusion to the leper, Lam 4:15 "metaphorically represents moral impurity as ritual impurity" (*Lamentations:*

houses of the kings of Judah shall be defiled like the place of Topheth.... And I will give all Judah into the hand of the king of Babylon" (19:13; 20:4). The history that begins in idolatry and innocent blood ends in a burial ground and exile.

Read in light of Jeremiah, Judas's story begins to look rather different. Now the center of gravity lies not in Judas's hanging but in the inexorable progression from sin and innocent blood to a burial ground. Matthew's narrative tracks Jeremiah, beginning in innocent blood and describing a history of defilement. Judas first confesses that he has delivered up innocent blood ("for blood pollutes the land," Num 35:33); next he throws blood money into the temple ("you shall not defile the land in which you live, in which I also dwell," Num 35:34), and then he hangs himself. Judas's hanging is itself an act of defilement. "Anyone hanged on a tree is under God's curse," Deut 21:23 asserts (cf. Gal 3:13). The hanged man defiles the land (Deut 21:23). The priests too are complicit in defilement. It is their money that is the "price of blood"—money, they themselves grant, that cannot stay in the temple. With it they buy a burial ground for foreigners.[24] Like Jer 19, the story of Judas moves from innocent blood to land that has become a burial ground. Judas's death is in a primary sense not just about Judas but about a defilement in which Judas and the priests alike are caught up, a defilement that haunts the land. When Judas seeks to return the blood money to the priests, Deut 27:25 sounds: "Cursed be anyone who takes a bribe to shed innocent blood."[25] This is the last in the series of blessings and curses that speak to the future of the Israelites in the promised land. In both Deut 27–28 and Jeremiah, innocent blood leads to exile, the loss of the land.[26]

A Commentary, OTL [Louisville: Westminster John Knox, 2002], 110). In the Holiness source ritual and moral impurity are already intertwined. According to Martha Himmelfarb, whereas the legacy of P (Priestly source) is a "radical separation between the realms of purity and morality," for H (Holiness source) "moral sins have ritual consequences: they render the sinner impure and the land as well" ("Impurity and Sin in 4QD, 1QS, and 4Q512," *DSD* 8 [2001]: 9–37, here 13). Milgrom goes further: even in the Priestly source "the ethical is bound up with and inseparable from the ritual, and the Pentateuchal codes make no distinction between them" in terms of training a people toward holiness (*Leviticus 1–16: A New Translation with Introduction and Commentary*, AB 3 [New York: Doubleday, 1991], 731; on purity in the ritual and ethical realms and their interrelation, see esp. 723–36, 1002–7). See also Hamilton, *Death of Jesus in Matthew*, 34–35 n. 6. For Jeremiah, as for Matthew, the burial ground in which both passages culminate witnesses to the corruption that now marks the land. This corruption, arising from idolatry, child sacrifice, and the blood of the innocent is moral, not merely ritual. Indeed, in Jeremiah (as in Zech 11:9; see below), ritual and moral defilement merge in the image of eating flesh—food that is ritually unclean and the hint of murder come together in a powerful image of pollution.

[24] On the (ritual) uncleanness of the dead (and so of the burial ground), see, e.g., Num 19:16; cf. Num 9:6; 19:11, 18; Lev 21:1, 11; Matt 23:27; Gerhard von Rad, *Old Testament Theology*, trans. D. M. G. Stalker, 2 vols. (New York: Harper & Row, 1962), 1:276; Klawans, *Purity, Sacrifice, and the Temple*, 56–58.

[25] NA[28] (on Matt 27:4) notes the allusion.

[26] Cf. Deut 28:36–37 with Deut 27:15–26 and Jer 19:9, 20:4. For the prophets, innocent blood

III. Jeremiah and Zechariah

Matthew names Jeremiah but quotes Zechariah. Like Jer 19, Zech 11 is the story of a people and their leaders—the shepherds and the flock—and the land.[27] It too raises the specter of defilement and the land's destruction, using words and images that appear also in Jer 19.[28] Zechariah 11 begins with an image of bloodshed. "Be a shepherd," God says to the prophet in verse 4, "of the flock doomed to slaughter" (ההרגה; LXX τὰ πρόβατα τῆς σφαγῆς). The word σφαγή is found elsewhere in the LXX only in Jeremiah: "The days are surely coming," says the Lord, "when this place shall ... be called ... the Valley of Slaughter" (ההרגה; LXX τῆς σφαγῆς, Jer 19:6; cf. 7:32).[29]

In Zechariah as in Jeremiah, the slaughter that is to come follows upon the slaughter that Judah itself practices. "Those who buy them [the flock] kill them," Zechariah says; and "their own shepherds have no pity on them" (11:5). The term "innocent blood" is not used, but the image is the same: the innocent—children, sheep—die at the hands of those who ought to be their shepherds. With regard to Zechariah, Carol L. Meyers and Eric M. Meyers comment, "This bespeaks a kind of internal corruption akin to what Ezekiel condemns in pre-exilic Jerusalem: Jerusalem is to be 'held guilty' for the blood it has shed (22:4)."[30]

---

is one of three grave sins, along with idolatry and unchastity, that defile and bring devastation upon the land. See, e.g., Isa 1:15; 59:7; Jer 2:30, 34–36; 7:4–15; 22:17, 26; Ezek 8:17–18; 22:13–15; 24:6–9; Hos 6:8–10, 12:15 MT (Eng. 12:14: "his crimes" translates דמיו, "bloodguilt"). See further Frymer-Kensky, "Pollution, Purification," esp. 404, 409–12; and Hamilton, "Innocent Blood," 93–95.

[27] "For I will no longer have pity on the inhabitants of the land [ישבי הארץ], says the Lord" (Zech 11:6). On ארץ as "land" here (contrast NRSV: "earth"), see Paul L. Redditt, *Haggai, Zechariah, Malachi*, NCB (Grand Rapids: Eerdmans, 1995), 124: "*NRSV* translates the word ʾereṣ by the word 'earth,' but there is no reason to assume a broad meaning for the word here. The land in question was Palestine or just Judah." So also Kenneth L. Barker, "Zechariah," in *The Expositor's Bible Commentary*, ed. Tremper Longman III and David E. Garland, rev. ed., 13 vols. (Grand Rapids: Zondervan, 2005–2012), 8:723–833, here 809. Cf. Carol L. Meyers and Eric M. Meyers, *Zechariah 9–14: A New Translation with Introduction and Commentary*, AB 25C (New York: Doubleday, 1993), 258–59: the phrase "inhabitants of the land" is "very common" (258); for its own sins, "Israel will lose the right to dwell in its land" (259).

[28] For the argument that Zech 11 is influenced by Jeremiah, see, e.g., Raymond F. Person, *Second Zechariah and the Deuteronomic School*, JSOTSup 167 (Sheffield: JSOT Press, 1993), esp. 125. In describing the parallels between Zech 11 and Jer 19 I am not claiming textual dependency; rather, I am pointing to a shared world of thought expressed in a common logic (from greed or idolatry and innocent blood to defilement and devastation) and even in specific images.

[29] Person, *Second Zechariah*, 125.

[30] Meyers and Meyers, *Zechariah 9–14*, 254. The Meyerses, however, immediately render this bloodshed metaphorical: "the blood it has shed" means "the abuse of office by 'the princes of Israel in you [Jerusalem]' ... (22:6, *NRSV*)" at the expense of the poor and powerless.

The result is devastation. "I will cause them, every one," says the Lord in Zechariah, "to fall each into the hand of a neighbor, and each into the hand of the king; and they shall devastate the land" (11:6). So too in Jeremiah, as we have seen. I will make them fall, the Lord says, "by the sword before their enemies, and by the hand of those who seek their life.... And I will make this city a horror" (19:7-8). From the blood of the innocent to the city's destruction: Zechariah and Jeremiah share a logic. The devastation in Zechariah is total. It falls upon "the inhabitants of the land" (ישבי הארץ; οἱ κατοικοῦντες τῆν γῆν, 11:6). The Meyerses note the parallel with Jeremiah's theme of the desolation of ישבי הארץ, the inhabitants of the land.[31]

Further, in both Jeremiah and Zechariah it is a desolation that not only derives from defilement but is described in terms of defilement. "What is to be destroyed, let it be destroyed; and let those that are left devour the flesh of one another!" (Zech 11:9; cf. 11:16)—a "vivid and horrible metaphor ... of internal corruption and consequent doom."[32] It is, as we have seen, Jeremiah's image too. "And I will make them eat the flesh of their sons ... and all shall eat the flesh of their neighbors in the siege," Jeremiah says (19:9).[33] With that, Zechariah breaks the staff Favor and the staff Unity (Zech 11:10; 11:14), and Jeremiah breaks the potter's jar (Jer 19:10).

IV. Zechariah and Matthew

The connection Matthew finds between Zechariah and Jeremiah thus need not hang on the word "potter" alone, as the Meyerses' reading of Zechariah at several points demonstrates.[34]

Zechariah paints a picture consonant with Jeremiah's of corrupt leaders and a city corrupted, of a progression from greed and bloodshed (or, in Jeremiah, idol worship and bloodshed) to devastation. It is not surprising that Matthew locates Zech 11:13 within the prophecy of Jeremiah. In the evangelist's view, both prophets tell the history of Israel, its leaders, its people, and its corruption, summed up in slaughter and innocent blood defiling the land and leading to its devastation. It is

---

[31] Ibid., 259; see Jer 1:14, 6:12, 10:18, 13:13; cf. 25:29 (references theirs). The Meyerses do not, however, connect the theme to the problem of innocent blood and defilement.

[32] Ibid., 267–68. They note the parallel with Jer 19:9 (cf. Person, *Second Zechariah*, 126).

[33] Meyers and Meyers (*Zechariah 9–14*, 40) note in Jeremiah one similar instance of "devouring flesh (in curses)" (Zech 11:9, 16), though they do not identify it.

[34] This is, nevertheless, still the primary explanation for the connection Matthew finds between Jeremiah and Zech 11. See, e.g., Senior, *Passion Narrative*, 356–57, 360; van Tilborg, "Matthew 27.3-10," 163; Audrey Conrad, "The Fate of Judas: Matthew 27:3–10," *TJT* 7 (1991): 158–68, esp. 162; Davies and Allison, *Gospel according to Saint Matthew*, 3:558–59, 569 n. 49; R. T. France, *The Gospel of Matthew*, NICNT (Grand Rapids: Eerdmans, 2007), 1042; Luz, *Matthew 12–28*, 468. McAfee Moss notes that the texts are linked also by "house of the Lord" (Zech 11:13, Jer 19:14–15) (*Zechariah Traditions*, 182–83).

a story that comes to a boil for Matthew in Judas and the chief priests and Jesus's innocent blood.

Zechariah 11, however, offers Matthew something that Jer 19 does not: a link to the particular story of Judas. "Then the Lord said to me, 'Throw it into the treasury [or: to the potter]'—this lordly price at which I was valued by them. So I took the thirty shekels of silver and threw them into the treasury [or: to the potter] in the house of the Lord" (Zech 11:13).[35] Recent commentary suggests that the traditionally negative reading of this act is a misreading influenced by Judas's act in Matthew.[36] Matthew, however, would seem to have read Zechariah correctly. For the money is payment, in Zech 11, from the sheep merchants who buy and kill the sheep (Zech 11:5, 7, 11–13).[37] This is tainted money, the price of innocent blood. When Judas throws the thirty silver pieces, the price of Jesus's blood, into the temple and when the priests buy with the blood money the potter's field, Zechariah's prophecy sounds. The chief priests buy Jesus's blood and Judas sells and grows rich.[38] The corruption of the leaders of Israel lived out on the backs of their people and at the price of their blood, a corruption described by Zechariah long ago, reaches now (as then) even into the holy place, and the temple is defiled. Matthew's quotation of Zechariah hammers home the gospel's indictment of the chief priests: these are the sheep merchants who deal in blood and bring destruction upon the land, even as they grant the truth of the verdict against them.[39]

Thus far, Matthew writes in concert with Jer 19 and Zech 11. The leaders deal in the blood of the innocent; the people and the land are corrupted. Judas's death and the Field of Blood are the signs and inevitable outworking of a defilement that

---

[35] For the textual problem, see the discussion of this verse in Meyers and Meyers, *Zechariah 9–14*, 276–77. The MT reads "to the potter" (אל־היוצר). The Syriac and Targum and Kennicott MS 530, however, emend "potter" to "treasury" (אוצר). Meyers and Meyers conclude: "Because four of the five letters of 'potter' and 'treasury' are the same"—and because the confusion of the initial *yod* of potter with the initial *aleph* of treasury is possible by scribal error—"the reading of the more appropriate 'treasury' is compelling" (277). In either case, the link with Matt 27:5 is clear: Judas *throws* the *thirty silver* pieces (price at which Jesus was valued by the leaders) into the *house of the Lord*. In fact, as commentators note, Matthew seems to be aware of both readings: when Judas throws the silver into the temple the priests say, "it is not lawful to 'cast' [βάλλω—cf. ἐμβάλλω Zech 11:13 LXX] this into the *treasury* since it is the price of blood"; hence they buy with it a *potter's* field.

[36] See the discussion in Meyers and Meyers, *Zechariah 9–14*, 278.

[37] See ibid., 262 (cf. 271): in Zech 11:7 and 11 the term *merchants* "represents the 'buyers' and 'sellers,' who are probably any Israelite leaders in positions of power or control over others."

[38] Cf. Zech 11:4: "Those who buy [the flock] kill them and go unpunished; and those who sell them say, 'Blessed be the Lord, for I have become rich.'"

[39] According to Meyers and Meyers, *Zechariah 9–14*, 273, the sheep merchants in Zechariah pay the shepherd who has uttered an oracle of condemnation against the city for its corruption. The payment recognizes the authority of the prophecy. In the same way, the chief priests in Matthew grant the truth of Judas's words even as they reject his appeal. The money is, they say, "the price of blood"; it cannot stay in the temple.

haunts the land. Against the background of Zechariah and Jeremiah, the problem of innocent blood and Judas's part in it comes into focus. Judas is no hero. Like the priests, he plays a role in the shedding of innocent blood and the destruction that comes upon the land. His hanging, indeed, far from being expiatory, intimates that destruction.[40] Like "innocent blood," the hanged man defiles the land. The blood money tracks its ominous way through the narrative after the death of Judas as before it. Donald Senior notes the omnipresence of the betrayal money: reference to the silver occurs in 27:3, 5, 6, 7, 9, 10; the blood money helps to unify the narrative.[41] The problem that the blood money presents, this defilement of the land, is not resolved with the death of Judas. Quite the contrary, corruption is all around, and both Judas's death and the blood money are the signs of it.

At the same time, however, Judas does not stand alone. The narrative of defilement traced by the blood money comes to a conclusion not in Judas's death but in the purchase of a field called, Matthew concludes, "'Field of Blood,' to this day" (27:8). If Judas is not a hero in his dying (still less friend to Jesus), neither is Judas the villain of the piece. The priests take up the blood money where Judas throws it down, and the narrative of defilement continues. Judas is caught up in a history of innocent blood in which he himself and the priests and the people all play a part. The consequences of that history, adumbrated in Judas's suicide, embrace finally the whole land.[42]

V. Μεταμέλεται: Matthew and the Destabilization of the Prophetic Narrative

If the narrative describes a spiral of defilement in which all the players are involved, it describes also, however, a difference between Judas and the chief priests. Judas "repents," μεταμέλεται (Matt 27:3). Scholarly judgments about Judas depend in part on the semantics of this word. Does it indicate "true repentance" or simply (and inadequately) regret? What is the nature of the regret here indicated? According to Davies and Allison, the word in the New Testament "is often distinguished

---

[40] See van Tilborg, "Matthew 27.3–10," 174: "Judas draws the final conclusion from his action. He hangs himself: a lugubrious example of what is waiting for the city and the land." This is correct, as far as it goes. In the paradigm of innocent blood, however, there is more to be said. Judas's death, like the destruction of Jerusalem, is not the final word.

[41] Senior, *Passion Narrative*, 378 and n. 110.

[42] For a positive reading of Judas's suicide and of suicide in the Greco-Roman and early Jewish contexts, see esp. Whelan, "Suicide in the Ancient World," 505–22. See also the discussion in Davies and Allison, *Gospel according to Saint Matthew*, 3:561–62 and the works listed in n. 5 above. The positive reading founders, in my view, on the problem of defilement, which is central to the passage as a whole and is associated in the Hebrew Scriptures with hanging.

from μετανοέω," the latter indicating "true repentance."[43] In Matthew, however, the word is used in a context that indicates repentance (21:29–32). In the LXX, Luz notes, both words are used to translate the *niphal* of Hebrew נחם; both words, he concludes, mean "to repent."[44] The debate is inconclusive; the word's semantic field, including as it does both senses, does not in itself decide the issue.[45] Precisely here, Matthew's use of Scripture is illuminating. It is, in fact, against the background of Zech 11 that the word μεταμέλομαι in Matt 27 comes into focus.

Μεταμέλομαι occurs also in Zech 11:5.[46] Blithely buying and killing their own people, the shepherds are not held guilty (לא יאשמו: NRSV "they go unpunished," Zech 11:5). Milgrom argues that the verb אשם here is an example of the "consequential *ʾāšām*," indicating retribution for wrong done.[47] In its consequential use, Milgrom goes on to say, the verb has an extended sense. It may indicate not only external punishment but the internal consequence of wrongdoing—feelings of guilt; the pangs of conscience: "*ʾāšām* without an object … denotes the suffering brought on by guilt, expressed now by words such as qualms, pangs, remorse, and contrition."[48] Though Milgrom does not note it, in Zech 11:5 אשם has no object. Οὐ μετεμέλοντο, the LXX renders the phrase: the sheep merchants have no regret, no pangs of conscience. They do not see their offense. The LXX, that is, reads the verb as Milgrom's "consequential *ʾāšām*" in the extended sense. For the LXX, Zech 11:5 depicts not just a failure of justice (the shepherds go unpunished) but a failure of conscience. The shepherds fail to hold themselves guilty for the slaughter of their people. In this they are like the chief priests in Matthew, who say to Judas's confession of guilt for delivering up innocent blood, "What is that to us?" (Matt 27:4).

In Matthew, however, the chief priests' refusal of repentance is not the whole story. Matthew, reading Zech 11, introduces (in contrast to Zechariah) the conscience of Judas: the recognition of sin in the face of innocent blood. "I have sinned in delivering up innocent blood," Judas says when he sees that Jesus is condemned to death. Against the background of Zech 11:5, Judas's statement can be understood

---

[43] Davies and Allison, *Gospel according to Saint Matthew*, 3:561. See, e.g., 2 Cor 7:8–9.

[44] Luz, *Matthew 21–28*, 470 n. 30. In Zech 11:5, of course, the MT has אשם.

[45] So, for instance, Hagner (*Matthew 14–28*, 812) and Davies and Allison (*Gospel according to Saint Matthew*, 3:561), both of whom note a distinction between μεταμέλομαι and μετανοέω, come to different conclusions about the meaning of μεταμέλομαι in Matt 27:3. Hagner finds in the word an indication of remorse but "not technically repentance." Davies and Allison argue that its occurrence in Matt 21:29 and 32 allows it to indicate repentance here. In fact, the focus on the question of repentance alone misses the point, as we shall see.

[46] Cf. van Tilborg, "Matthew 27.3–10," 166: "Judas' 'repentance' is the new allusion to Zech 11." Judas's "repentance" is, of course, the very point that needs to be established.

[47] Milgrom, *Leviticus 1–16*, 339–40. The verb, like other biblical terms for good and bad behavior, connotes both the wrong done and its retribution; either sense may be emphasized. I am grateful to Leslie Chisholm Demson for drawing my attention to Milgrom's discussion of this word.

[48] Milgrom, *Leviticus 1–16*, 343.

as a rendering of the consequential אשם: "consequential guilt," a man suffering the pangs of conscience. If, in keeping with Zechariah, there is no regret among the priests, nevertheless Judas μεταμεληθεὶς ἔστρεψεν τὰ τριάκοντα ἀργύρια, "he repented and brought back the thirty pieces of silver" (NRSV). Judas knows remorse, and returns the money, and confesses his offense. These three things— "feeling guilt" (אשם), confessing the wrong, and making reparation—constitute in Numbers (5:6b-7) the required reparation for wrongdoing.[49]

The word μεταμέλομαι is thus significant in Matthew not in isolation, with respect only to the breadth of its semantic field, but against the background of Zech 11. Judas feels the pangs of conscience and tries to make reparation. This says something about Judas. In Matthew's telling (and according to Numbers), he is a repentant sinner, but his repentance does not stop the chain of destruction he has set in motion. His confession falls on deaf ears; the blood money—and the plot— continues on its inexorable way toward a burial ground. Judas is not able to redeem the time. Indeed, his actions lead in Matt 27:3-10 only further into death and defilement. Yet Judas's remorse is critical—for, against the background of Zechariah, Matthew's use of μεταμέλομαι raises a question mark over the narrative. Is this, after all, quite the same story as that told by the prophet Zechariah? There is no exception, no softening, in the corruption and its consequences that assail Jerusalem in Zechariah's vision. No one repents, and the disaster is complete. "I took my staff Favor and broke it, annulling the covenant that I had made with all the peoples" (Zech 11:10). But Matthew, quoting Zechariah, nevertheless departs from Zechariah. Τότε Ἰούδας μεταμεληθείς: Judas's crisis of conscience opens a chink in the grim armor of Zechariah's prophecy. Οὐ μεταμέλομαι has become, in the case of one man, μεταμέλομαι. Judas's recognition of sin, contrasting with Zech 11 in a narrative that deliberately recalls Zech 11, destabilizes and opens up the prophetic narrative. Zechariah's prophecy of the corruption of the land and God's rejection of the covenant people sounds again in Judas and the chief priests and the blood money that lands in the temple. But Matthew signals precisely in the echo of Zechariah a difference.

Another verbal echo adds to this destabilization. Immediately after he "repents" (Matt 27:3), Judas returns the blood money to the priests, saying "I have sinned in delivering up innocent blood" (Matt 27:4). The word παραδίδωμι ("to deliver up") occurs also in Zech 11:6, immediately after the sheep merchants do *not* repent: ἰδοὺ ἐγὼ παραδίδωμι τοὺς ἀνθρώπους. In Zechariah it describes God's delivering up of the people to destruction. As the Meyerses note, Zechariah's use of אחמול/ παραδίδωμι is ironic, for in the Hebrew Scriptures "a significant portion of this form

---

[49] Milgrom, *Leviticus 1-16*, 345. The precise reparation required in Num 5:6-8 is full restitution + one-fifth and, when the money is given to the priest, a ram of atonement. Judas returns only the thirty silver pieces—thus preserving the parallel with Zech 11.

is used to indicate God's deliverance of Israel from bondage."⁵⁰ In Zechariah it describes exactly the opposite; the deliverance once promised is reversed.

In Matthew, it is Jesus who is handed over. Jesus faces at the hands of Judas and the chief priests precisely the fate of Jerusalem in Zechariah. He is delivered up to destruction. Thus far, Matthew's narrative recalls Zechariah, but, unlike Jerusalem in Zechariah, Jesus is innocent. He resembles the sheep who are slaughtered rather than the sheep merchants. Here again, Matthew is different. In Matthew's presentation, two opposite parts come together. Jesus is the innocent lamb, his blood bought and sold, portending as in Zechariah the city's destruction. Yet at the same time he is the one who is delivered up like the people in Zechariah, suffering ahead of time the destruction decreed in Zechariah against the corrupted city. The anomaly, like Judas's repentance, places a question mark against the narrative. What happens when the one delivered up to the destruction God has decreed is God's innocent one? It is a question Matthew answers in his account of Jesus's death.

VI. *And the Graves Were Opened:* Innocent Blood and the Death of Jesus

Matthew turns for an answer to the problem of innocent blood beyond the story of Judas, to the death of Jesus. The gospel draws a straight line from Judas's blood money to Jesus's crucifixion. "What is that to us?" the priests retort, when Judas confesses to delivering up Jesus's innocent blood. "See to it yourself" (Matt 27:4). "I am innocent of this man's blood," Pilate declares when he sentences Jesus to death. "See to it yourselves" (27:24). Commentators note the verbal echo.⁵¹ In both cases, the leaders—Pilate and the priests—refuse responsibility for Jesus's blood; in both cases, the text declares it to be innocent blood, the wrongful condemnation of an innocent man.⁵² And in both cases, they seek to place the consequences of innocent blood on the shoulders of others. Pilate washes his hands—ὑμεῖς ὄψεσθε—and the people say, "His blood be upon us" (Matt 27:25). Judas says, "I have sinned in delivering up innocent blood," and the priests say, "That is your

---

⁵⁰ Meyers and Meyers, *Zechariah 9–14*, 259.

⁵¹ See, e.g., Davies and Allison, *Gospel according to Saint Matthew*, 3:590–91; Brown, *Death of the Messiah*, 1:634, 835–36; Gundry, *Matthew*, 554; Frederick Dale Bruner, *Matthew: A Commentary*, rev. and exp. ed., 2 vols. (Grand Rapids: Eerdmans, 1990), 2:721–22; John T. Carroll and Joel B. Green, *The Death of Jesus in Early Christianity* (Peabody, MA: Hendrickson, 1995), 47; David E. Garland, *Reading Matthew: A Literary and Theological Commentary on the First Gospel*, Reading the New Testament (New York: Crossroad, 1993), 257. See also Hamilton, "Innocent Blood," 85, and in more detail Hamilton, *Death of Jesus in Matthew*, 33–35.

⁵² Though it is his own innocence Pilate declares, this is to indicate also the innocence of Jesus. Pilate seeks to avoid responsibility for unjust execution—judicial murder, or "innocent blood."

problem" (σὺ ὄψῃ). In the first place, innocent blood spells doom, in Matthew as in Zechariah, for both Judas and the city. Judas hangs himself; the whole people say, ominously, "His blood be upon us" (27:25). But for Matthew this is not the whole story.

Matthew has added Judas's regret to Zechariah's account of corruption; in Jesus handed over to death, the evangelist has conflated the fate of the sheep merchants and that of the innocent sheep. At the moment of Jesus's death, Matthew, alone among the evangelists, adds to the Markan account this striking scene: "and the earth was shaken and the rocks were split, and the tombs were opened and many bodies of the holy ones who had fallen asleep were raised, and they came out of the tombs after his resurrection and went into the holy city and appeared to many" (Matt 27:51-53). There is a great deal that can be said about the effect of these verses at this crucial point in Matthew's Gospel, not least with regard to their rich echoes of the prophets.[53] In the context of innocent blood, however, one thing in particular stands out.

At the moment of Jesus's death, the tombs are opened and the dead bodies are raised.[54] This is the moment of God's action, as the string of passive verbs and theophanic images indicate.[55] Ezekiel sounds in the background.[56] "Behold, I am going to *open your graves, and bring you up from your graves*, O my people; and *I will bring you back to the land of Israel*" (Ezek 37:12). Ezekiel's three-part action finds a counterpart in Matt 27:52-53: And *the graves were opened*, and the *bodies were raised*, and *they came out ... and went into the holy city*. Here, Matthew declares,

---

[53] Ezekiel 37, Zech 14:4-5, Dan 12:2, and, to a lesser degree, Isa 26:19 all have resonance in varying degrees in the passage. See the discussion in Warren Carter, *Matthew and the Margins: A Sociopolitical and Religious Reading*, Bible and Liberation (Maryknoll, NY: Orbis, 2000), 536; Davies and Allison, *Gospel according to Saint Matthew*, 3:628-29 (they find Zech 14:5 to be the primary reference); Dale C. Allison, "The Scriptural Background of a Matthean Legend: Ezekiel 37, Zechariah 14, and Matthew 27," in *Life beyond Death in Matthew's Gospel: Religious Metaphor or Bodily Reality?*, ed. Wim Weren, Huub van de Sandt and Joseph Verheyden, BTS 13 (Leuven: Peeters, 2011), 153-88.

[54] For this analysis and a more detailed discussion of Ezekiel 37 in relation to Matt 27:50-53, see Hamilton, *Death of Jesus in Matthew*, 208-12; cf. Hamilton, "Innocent Blood," 99.

[55] For rocks splitting and earth shaking when God goes out (especially in judgment), see, e.g., Judg 5:4, 5; 1 Kgs 19:11-12; Pss 18:7-9; 77:18; Isa 24:18-23; 29:6; Ezek 38:19-20; Joel 2:10-11; Nah 1:5-6. See also later parallels in 1 En. 1:6-7; 102:2; 4 Ezra 5:8; 2 Bar. 27:7; LAB 3:9; etc. For parallels, see Davies and Allison, *Gospel according to Saint Matthew*, 3:340-41 and n. 86, 632; cf. Senior, *Passion Narrative*, 313.

[56] For Ezekiel as the primary influence on 27:52-53, see, e.g., Gundry, *Matthew*, 576; Senior, *Passion Narrative*, 320 (possibly also Daniel); France, *Gospel of Matthew*, 1081-82 (with Dan 12:2 and Isa 26:19); Hagner, *Matthew 14-28*, 849; Harrington, *Gospel of Matthew*, 403. I take these verses to contain a primary reference to Ezek 37; however, this is not to deny the relevance of Zech 14:5, Dan 12:2, and Isa 26:19 but to suggest that Ezekiel's theme of exile and the restoration of the defiled land is particularly pertinent to Matthew's treatment of Jesus's death in terms of innocent blood and its consequences.

is the ancient promise to Israel of Israel's restoration, realized now in the death of Jesus. This is, surely, a striking conclusion to the history of innocent blood that the gospel has been at pains to trace in the death of Jesus. Innocent blood pollutes the land, and pollution drives God out of God's house.[57] Matthew has seen in the aftermath of innocent blood a land defiled—a Field of Blood—and the armies at the gate. "Jerusalem, Jerusalem, city that kills the prophets and stones those sent to her, how often have I desired to gather your children … and you would not. See, your house is left to you, desolate" (Matt 23:37–38; cf. 23:35–36). In the story of Judas, Matthew has described the death of Jesus deliberately as a matter of innocent blood. Yet at the moment of Jesus's death, it is Ezekiel's vision of hope that sounds: "I am going to open your graves, and I will bring you up from your graves, O my people, and I will bring you back to the land of Israel."

This is a picture of defilement overturned. The graves are opened. The burial ground yields now life and not death, at the death of Jesus. From the defiled land against all expectation the holy ones rise. "Son of Man, can these bones live?" YHWH asks the prophet in the time of Israel's exile (Ezek 37:3). Now at the death of Jesus, Matthew announces new life, precisely in the place of bones.

VII. Conclusion

If Matthew draws a straight line from Judas's blood money to the death of Jesus, if the story of betrayal and innocent blood leads to a burial ground for Judas and for Jesus, the story nevertheless does not end there. The Field of Blood points forward to the blood of Jesus, and another burial ground, and there it finds its answer. The graves were opened at the death of Jesus, and the holy ones were raised, and they went into the holy city. It is the life of the city that is announced, at the end of the story. As in Jeremiah and Zechariah, Matthew's saga of innocent blood is, in the end as in the beginning, the history of a city and a people.

To ask, as the debate about Judas does, is Judas villain or hero? is therefore to frame the problem in a way that runs against the grain of the text. What, now, of Jerusalem, in the wake of Judas's suicide and the Field of Blood? What of the land and the people? This is the question that emerges from Judas's story read through the lens of Jeremiah and Zechariah together. It is the question that drives the action. What of Judas *and* Jerusalem in the wake of Jesus's innocent blood? In Zech 11, the people are doomed to slaughter, and in Jer 19 the city becomes a burial ground. In Matthew, too, Judas's words—I have sinned; I have handed over innocent blood—lead to a burial ground. But in Matthew the action does not stop here. For this burial ground, this innocent blood, points forward, beyond Judas's repentance and his

---

[57] Cf. Hannah K. Harrington, *The Impurity Systems of Qumran and the Rabbis: Biblical Foundations*, SBLDS 143 (Atlanta: Scholars Press, 1993), esp. 36.

death, beyond the field of blood, toward another burial ground where, in the death of Jesus, death yields unexpectedly to life. In this history, Judas is intimately involved. His own death is intertwined with Jerusalem's defeat. His repentance signals at the same time a disturbance in the narrative of doom. Insofar as Judas's story points deliberately forward, linked in the image of innocent blood to the death of Jesus and the opening of the graves, it speaks not only doom but also hope.

Matthew gives us, in the episode of Judas, Jeremiah's story and Zechariah's, a history of corruption and bloodshed and a city's doom. But it is Zechariah "tweaked"—for Judas repents and *Jesus* is delivered up, and in this Matthew sees a mystery. Judas's death is not the end of the story, any more than the Field of Blood is the end of the story of Jerusalem. Death and life stand back to back, in the story of Judas and the blood of Jesus, as in the prophet Jeremiah. Both are true. A voice is heard in Ramah, lamentation and bitter weeping, the exile of the people (Jer 31:15; cf. Matt 2:18). Thus says the Lord. And thus, also, in Jesus's death: "Keep your voice from weeping and your eyes from tears.... There is hope for your future, says the Lord" (Jer 31:16–17).

New and Recent Titles

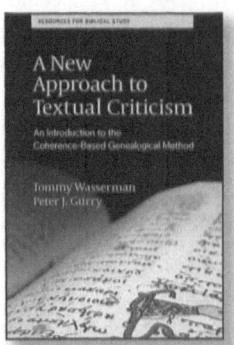

A NEW APPROACH TO TEXTUAL CRITICISM
An Introduction to the Coherence-Based Genealogical Method
Tommy Wasserman and Peter J. Gurry
Paperback $19.95, 978-1-62837-199-4   162 pages, 2017   Code: 060399
Hardcover $34.95, 978-0-88414-267-6 E-book $19.95, 978-0-88414-266-9
Resources for Biblical Study 80

WHEN TEXTS ARE CANONIZED
Timothy H. Lim, editor
Paperback $29.95, 978-1-946527-00-4   188 pages, 2017   Code 140359
Hardcover $44.95, 978-1-930675-95-7 E-book $29.95, 978-1-930675-99-5
Brown Judaic Studies 359

TOWARD A LATINO/A BIBLICAL INTERPRETATION
Francisco Lozada Jr.
Paperback $36.95, 978-1-62837-200-7   148 pages, 2017   Code: 060385
Hardcover $51.95, 978-0-88414-270-6 E-book $36.95, 978-0-88414-269-0
Resources for Biblical Study 91

SEA OF READINGS
The Bible in the South Pacific
Jione Havea, editor
Paperback $32.95, 978-1-62837-202-1   250 pages, 2018   Code 060695
Hardcover $47.95, 978-0-88414-278-2 E-book $32.95, 978-0-88414-277-5
Semeia Studies 90

GOSPEL JESUSES AND OTHER NONHUMANS
Biblical Criticism Post-poststructuralism
Stephen D. Moore
Paperback $24.95, 978-1-62837-190-1   164 pages, 2017   Code 060691
Hardcover $39.95, 978-0-88414-252-2 E-book $24.95, 978-0-88414-251-5
Semeia Studies 89

MIXED FEELINGS AND VEXED PASSIONS
Exploring Emotions in Biblical Literature
F. Scott Spencer, editor
Paperback $49.95, 978-1-62837-194-9   418 pages, 2017   Code: 060396
Hardcover $64.95, 978-0-88414-257-7 E-book $49.95, 978-0-88414-256-0
Resources for Biblical Study 90

SBL Press • P.O. Box 2243 • Williston, VT 05495-2243
Phone: 877-725-3334 (toll-free) or 802-864-6185 • Fax: 802-864-7626
Order online at www.sbl-site.org/publications

Bringing Sisters Back Together: Another Look at Luke 10:41–42

TOMMY WASSERMAN
tommy.wasserman@altutbildning.se
Ansgar Teologiske Høgskole, N-4635 Kristiansand, Norway

Luke's account of Martha and Mary of Bethany is present in the textual tradition in two versions. The majority of scholars and editors prefer the shorter reading, "only one thing is necessary." This view is also taken up by the influential UBS Committee, which regards the long reading as a conflation. This preference for the shorter reading is mistaken on several grounds. First, it builds on a factual error presupposing a reading that does not exist in the extant Greek textual tradition. Second, it neglects the history of interpretation and specifically its significance for the textual problem. Third, it is motivated at least in part by positing a dichotomy between the two sisters. In this article, I argue that the long reading in the passage in Luke 10:41–42, where Jesus replies to Martha that "few things are necessary, or indeed only one" is the initial text and the *lectio difficilior*, as well as the text that is best suited to its narrative context in Luke's Gospel.

In a Festschrift for Bruce M. Metzger from 1981, Gordon D. Fee presented an extensive discussion of the textual problem in the passage in Luke 10:41–42. In this passage, Martha complains to Jesus that she has to do all the work while Mary just sits at Jesus's feet listening.[1] The text-critical problem concerns Jesus's reply to Martha. Fee prefers the longer reading, as reflected in the NIV (the translation with which Fee was involved):

"Martha, Martha," the Lord answered, "you are worried and upset about many things, but few things are needed—or indeed only one [ὀλίγων δέ ἐστιν χρεία ἢ ἑνός]. Mary has chosen what is better, and it will not be taken away from her."[2]

---

[1] Gordon Fee, "'One Thing Is Needful'? Luke 10:42," in *New Testament Textual Criticism: Its Significance for Exegesis; Essays in Honour of Bruce M. Metzger*, ed. Eldon Jay Epp and Gordon D. Fee (Oxford: Clarendon, 1981), 61–75.

[2] Edwin H. Palmer et al., *The Holy Bible: New International Version; The New Testament* (Grand Rapids: Zondervan, 1973; rev. 1978, 1984). Fee was a member of the Committee on Bible Translation that translated the NIV and its revision, the TNIV (Today's New International Version).

Fee pointed out that this reading, ὀλίγων δέ ἐστιν χρεία ἢ ἑνός, had been adopted by editors like Westcott and Hort, Bernhard Weiss, Marie-Joseph Lagrange, and Augustinus Merk, as well as by a number of commentaries and a few translations.³ Nevertheless, the reading lacked a full-scale defense, which Fee now sought to provide. In spite of his arguments, however, the reading has not been adopted by scholars or translations since that time, with a few exceptions: Michael D. Goulder's commentary on Luke (1989); J. Lionel North in a journal article (1997); and Michael W. Holmes's SBL Greek New Testament edition, which appeared in 2010.⁴ Although the longer reading is supported by important manuscripts such as the fourth-century uncials Codex Sinaiticus (ℵ 01) and Codex Vaticanus (B 03), scholars largely came to prefer the shorter reading to the longer reading due to the discovery of the Beatty and Bodmer papyri P45 and P75, the earliest extant manuscript witnesses to the text.⁵ Both papyri support the shorter reading, ἑνός δέ ἐστιν χρεία, which can be translated:

---

³ B. F. Westcott and F. J. A. Hort, *The New Testament in the Original Greek*, 2 vols. (Cambridge: Macmillan, 1881); Bernhard Weiss, *Die Evangelien des Markus und Lukas*, 9th ed., KEK 1 (Göttingen: Vandenhoeck & Ruprecht, 1901); Marie-Joseph Lagrange, *Évangile selon saint Luc*, 2nd ed., EBib (Paris: Gabalda, 1921); Augustinus Merk, *Novum Testamentum: Graece et Latine*, 8th ed. (Rome: Pontifical Biblical Institute, 1957). Supporting translations include Phillips (1947), NASB (1963), JB (1966, 1973, 1985, 1998). For supporting commentaries up to 1981, see Fee, "'One Thing Is Needful,'" 65 nn. 19–20.

⁴ Michael D. Goulder, *Luke: A New Paradigm*, JSNTSup 20 (Sheffield: JSOT Press, 1989); J. Lionel North, "ὀλίγων δέ ἐστιν χρεία ἢ ἑνός (Luke 10.42): Text, Subtext and Context," *JSNT* 66 (1997): 3–13; Michael W. Holmes, ed., *The Greek New Testament: SBL Edition* (Atlanta: Society of Biblical Literature; Bellingham, WA: Logos Bible Software, 2010). Significant commentators who discuss the problem include Joseph A. Fitzmyer, *The Gospel according to Luke: Introduction, Translation, and Notes*, 2 vols., AB 28, 28A (Garden City, NY: Doubleday, 1981–1985); Léopold Sabourin, *L'Évangile de Luc: Introduction et commentaire*, 2nd ed. (Rome: Pontificia Università Gregoriana; 1992); John Nolland, *Luke 9:21–18:34*, WBC 35B (Waco, TX: Word, 1993); Joel B. Green, *The Gospel of Luke*, NICNT (Grand Rapids: Eerdmans, 1997); Luke Timothy Johnson, *The Gospel of Luke*, SP (Collegeville, MN: Liturgical Press, 2006); François Bovon, *Luke 2: A Commentary on the Gospel of Luke 9:51–19:27*, Hermeneia (Minneapolis: Fortress, 2013). A few commentators are undecided: Darrell L. Bock, *Luke*, 2 vols., BECNT 3 (Grand Rapids: Baker, 1996), 2:1043; Frederick W. Danker, *Jesus and the New Age: A Commentary on St. Luke's Gospel*, rev. ed. (Philadelphia: Fortress, 1998), 225; Wolfgang Wiefel, *Das Evangelium nach Lukas*, THKNT 3 (Berlin: Evangelische Verlagsanstalt, 1988), 211–12.

⁵ Fee, "'One Thing Is Needful,'" 73: "Since the influences behind the UBSGNT text are very clear, it is most probable that 𝔓75 as much as anything else led to the choice of ἑνός δέ ἐστιν χρεία with a (C) rating." Cf. Fitzmyer, *Gospel according to Luke*, 1:894: "The best reading is now *henos de estin chreia*, 'but of one (thing) there is need.'... The recent discovery of P⁷⁵, the oldest text of Luke, more or less decides the issue in favor of the reading in the lemma." The two papyri are assigned to the third century in the current Nestle-Aland edition. In a recent study by Pasquale Orsini and Willy Clarysse, "Early New Testament Manuscripts and Their Dates: A Critique of Theological Paleography," *ETL* 88 (2012): 433–74, both are dated to the first half of the third century. Cf. Brent Nongbri, "Reconsidering the Place of Papyrus Bodmer XIV–XV (𝔓75) in the

But the Lord answered and said to her, "Martha, Martha, you are worried and bothered about so many things; but *only* one thing is necessary [ἑνὸς δέ ἐστιν χρεία], for Mary has chosen the good part, which shall not be taken away from her." (NASB 1995; emphasis added)

Soon after the publication of P75 in 1960, the short reading was adopted in the critical editions of the United Bible Societies' *Greek New Testament*, the first of which appeared in 1966, as well as the Nestle-Aland editions, from the 26th edition in 1979 to the present. These editions represented a new approach, where the text was established on the basis of external and internal evidence, as evaluated by a redaction committee. Bruce M. Metzger, secretary of the UBS Committee, explained the decision to adopt the short reading in Luke 10:42:

> Most of the other variations seem to have arisen from understanding ἑνός to refer merely to the provisions which Martha was then preparing for the meal; the absoluteness of ἑνός was softened by replacing it with ὀλίγων (preserved today only in 38 and several versions); and finally in some witnesses (including p³ ℵ B L ƒ¹ 33) the two were combined, though with disastrous results as to sense.[6]

In my opinion, Fee's contribution was important for two reasons: First, he exposed a particular weakness in this explanation, which had become, and still is, the majority position—the preferred shorter reading can hardly explain the presence of the other readings, because the scenario described by Metzger of an original ἑνός regarded as the *lectio difficilior*, replaced with ὀλίγων (a softer reading) and, eventually, conflated to ὀλίγων ... ἢ ἑνός is, as we will see, unlikely.[7] Second, Fee presented the textual evidence in a comprehensive and unparalleled way, in particular the patristic evidence, which had only been partially accounted for, or even misrepresented.[8]

Textual Criticism of the New Testament," *JBL* 135 (2016): 405–37, https://doi.org/10.15699/jbl.1352.2016.2803, who assigns it to the fourth century.

[6] Bruce M. Metzger, *A Textual Commentary on the Greek New Testament: A Companion Volume to the United Bible Societies' Greek New Testament (3d ed.)*, 1st ed. (London: United Bible Societies, 1971), 153–54.

[7] For the foundational principle of textual criticism, to prefer the reading that explains all other readings, see Tommy Wasserman, "Criteria for Evaluating Readings in New Testament Textual Criticism," in *The Text of the New Testament in Contemporary Research: Essays on the Status Questionis*, ed. Bart D. Ehrman and Michael W. Holmes, 2nd ed., NTTSD 42 (Leiden: Brill, 2013), 582–83.

[8] For example, Monika Augsten ("Lukanische Miszelle," *NTS* 14 [1967–1968]: 581–83) and Aelred Baker ("One Thing Necessary," *CBQ* 27 [1965]: 127–37) discuss Origen's text without attention to the context, which results in incorrect conclusions about the text he was using. Fee's analysis shows that the patristic data of UBS³ was erroneous in six places (Basil [2x], Clement [2x], Origen, and Augustine) and incomplete in a number of other cases (Fee, "'One Thing Is Needful,'" 61–63). Jutta Brutscheck is aware of Fee's study but does not engage with it and misrepresents all these fathers (*Die Maria-Marta-Erzählung: Eine redaktionskritische Untersuchung zu Lk 10, 38–42*, BBB 64 [Frankfurt am Main: Hanstein, 1986], 4–29).

Nevertheless, a survey of a number of subsequently published commentaries on Luke shows that the insufficient explanation of the UBS Committee has prevailed.[9] And the patristic evidence continues to be largely neglected or misunderstood, even by editors of the standard critical editions.[10] The UBS Committee regarded the long reading as a conflation of two readings "with disastrous results as to sense."[11] Unfortunately, Fee's proposed interpretation of the long reading, influenced by Frédéric Godet, has not persuaded many to think otherwise, and it has therefore not been accepted as the initial reading of Luke 10:42 in the dominant critical editions. In this article, I will consider the textual evidence again and discuss ancient and modern interpretations of the passage, arguing that ὀλίγων δέ ἐστιν χρεία ἢ ἑνός is the initial text that gave rise to the other readings. Further, in regard to methodology, I will argue that we must understand the significance of the competing readings in the history of interpretation and, conversely, to use this understanding in the aid of textual criticism. Textual criticism must not become an isolated first step of exegesis. All textual variants stand in a hermeneutical relationship to each other and belong to the history of reception from the moment they arise.

I. The Variant Readings and Their Attestation

There are four basic text forms in the variation unit relating to Jesus's reply to Martha. I list them here with provisional translations and a textual apparatus:[12]

---

[9] Fitzmyer, *Gospel according to Luke*, 1:894: "The best reading is now *henos de estin chreia*.... One ms. (38) reads *oligōn* instead of *henos*.... However, a number of mss. ... have combined the two readings: *oligōn de estin chreia ē henos*"; Green, *Gospel of Luke*, 433 n. 133: "This [shorter] reading is probably original, but the starkness of ἑνός has given rise to several alternative readings—especially (1) substituting ὀλίγων for ἑνός ..., and (2) conflating these two readings"; Johnson, *Gospel of Luke*, 174: "Some copyists replaced 'one' with 'a few,' and still others combined the two phrases to accomplish total confusion"; Bovon, *Luke 2*, 74: "The third textual variant [the long reading] appears to be an awkward conflation, for the 'few things' suggests the idea of material possessions, while the '(only) one thing' refers to spiritual commitment to God.... The transformation of 'only one thing' into 'few things' in the course of the transmission of the textual tradition may be explained as a misunderstanding. Some scribes believed that Jesus was still talking about Martha's preparations."

[10] See Gordon Fee and Roderic L. Mullen, "The Use of the Greek Fathers for New Testament Textual Criticism," in Ehrman and Holmes, *Text of the New Testament* (2nd ed.), 351–73, here 355.

[11] Metzger, *Textual Commentary* (1st ed.), 154; cf. Baker, "One Thing Necessary," 135; Augsten, "Lukanische Miszelle," 581.

[12] NA[28] does not list the third reading because of its slim support, and the fourth reading is simply represented by Codex Bezae (D05), which reads Μάρθα, Μάρθα, θορυβάζῃ· Μαρία. UBS[5] lists these readings but splits the fourth reading in two (the Greek and Latin reading of Codex Bezae is presented separately). I will not treat the minor variation between θορυβάζῃ/τυρβάζῃ.

1. Μάρθα Μάρθα, μεριμνᾷς καὶ (θορυβάζῃ) περὶ πολλά, ἑνὸς δέ ἐστιν χρεία· Μαριὰ(μ) δέ/γάρ P45 P75 A C* W Θ Σ Ψ f¹³ 𝔐 aur f q vg sa sy^{c.p.h} Chr Nil Aug

   Martha, Martha, you are worried and upset about many things, but only one thing is necessary. Mary . . .

2. Μάρθα Μάρθα, μεριμνᾷς καὶ θορυβάζῃ περὶ πολλά, ὀλίγων δέ ἐστιν χρεία ἢ ἑνός· Μαριὰ(μ) γάρ P3 ℵ² [ℵ* om. χρεια] B [χρεια εστιν] C² L 070^{vid} f¹ 33 (579) sy^{hmg} (sy^{pal}) bo eth^{pp} Sinaiticus Arabicus Or Bas Cyr Hier Cn

   Martha, Martha, you are worried and upset about many things, but few things are necessary—or indeed only one. Mary . . .

3. Μάρθα, Μάρθα, μεριμνᾷς καὶ τυρβάζῃ περὶ πολλά, ὀλίγων δέ ἐστιν χρεία· Μαρία δέ (formerly 38 and Origen ½) bo^{ms} geo arm eth^{TH}

   Martha, Martha, you are worried and upset about many things, but few things are necessary. Mary . . .[13]

4. Μάρθα, Μάρθα· Μαρία D (+ θορυβαζη) a b (d) e ff² i l r¹ [c] Amb Poss

   Martha, Martha. Mary . . .

The shortest reading (4) is supported only by some Western witnesses; it could have resulted from a haplography due to homoioarcton (Μαρ-) or it could have been a deliberate omission. The Western text is otherwise divided between this reading and the first reading from which it probably originated. Codex Bezae D (05) attests to a middle form with θορυβάζῃ ("Martha, Martha, you are upset. Mary . . ."), so it is possible that the larger omission developed in two steps. Fee lists a few scholars who have argued for this reading from Friedrich Blass and onward.[14] John Martin Creed's explanation of the longer readings as "variants of an early gloss" is characteristic.[15] Blass, however, regarded the longer readings in this passage as

---

[13] This reading is now a subvariant of reading 2 in UBS⁵.

[14] Fee ("'One Thing Is Needful,'" 63) lists the following scholars in support of the shortest reading: Friedrich Blass, *Euangelium secundum Lucam* (Leipzig: Teubner, 1897); Julius Wellhausen, *Das Evangelium Lucae* (Berlin: Reimer, 1904), 54; J. Moffatt, *The New Testament: A New Translation*, 2nd ed. (New York: Hodder & Stoughton, 1913); Erich Klostermann, *Das Lukasevangelium*, HNT 5 (Tübingen: Mohr, 1919), 485; and William Manson, *The Gospel of Luke*, MNTC (New York: Harper, 1930), 132–33; John Martin Creed, *The Gospel according to St. Luke: The Greek Text with Introduction, Notes, and Indices* (London: Macmillan, 1930), 154; G. B. Caird, *The Gospel of St. Luke*, PNTC (Baltimore: Penguin, 1963), 149–50; repr. as *Saint Luke*, Westminster Pelican Commentaries (Philadelphia: Westminster, 1977). To Fee's list we may add Adalbert Merx, *Die Evangelien des Markus und Lukas*, vol. 2.2 of *Die vier kanonischen Evangelien nach ihrem ältesten bekannten Texte: Übersetzung und Erläuterungen der syrischen im Sinaikloster gefundenen Palimpsesthandschrift* (Berlin: Reimer, 1905), 280–82.

[15] Creed, *Gospel according to St. Luke*, 154. Cf. Weiss, *Die Evangelien des Markus und Lukas*, 8th ed., KEK 1 (Göttingen: Vandenhoeck & Ruprecht, 1892), 463: "Dazu kommt das auch durch

evidence not for a scribal omission but for a second "authentic form of the Gospel" of Luke.[16]

The main choice in light of external evidence is rather between the first and second readings. A crucial question in the debate to this date has been whether the third reading originated from the first or the second reading. As we have noted, the UBS Committee opted for the first scenario: they thought that scribes had substituted ὀλίγων (reading 3) for ἑνός (reading 1) to soften the text. In a second stage, the two readings were conflated, resulting in the long reading (reading 2). One of the earliest textual witnesses, Origen, was incorrectly cited in support of the third reading (ὀλίγων δέ ἐστιν χρεία) in the apparatuses UBS[1–3] ("Origen ½"), which then seemed to give significant support from a textual and chronological point of view to this proposed scenario.[17]

As Fee demonstrated, however, Origen knew only the longer reading (reading 2), so "the evidence for an early existence of this variant [reading 3] is so slight as to be nearly worthless."[18] Apparently Fee did not take time to verify this reading in the remaining Greek witness, Greg.-Aland 38, which otherwise has a Byzantine text in Luke.[19] My examination shows that it attests to the Majority text as expected. It is both remarkable and telling that this erroneous citation, which first appeared in Wettstein's 1751 edition, has continued to influence the discussion of the passage for over 250 years—I hope that the tide will now turn.[20] From UBS[4] (1993), the

---

AC it 3 … vertretene blosse ἑνός δέ ἐστιν χρεία, um die Frage nahe zu legen, ob nicht der durch B etc. vertretene Satz eine Combination zweier, vielleicht schon uralter Glossen (ὀλίγων δέ ἐστιν χρεία und ἑνός δέ ἐστιν χρεία) ist, von denen wieder die eine eine Correctur der andern sein mag" (Weiss later changed his position due to better "knowledge of documents," as reflected in the 9th ed. of 1901, "Die Lesart von ℵBL cop. aeth. Orig … ist unzweifelhaft ächt.… Dass letzere Lesart [of D05] ursprünglich und die der ältesten Maj. eine Kombination zweier verschiedener Glossen sein sollte, ist nach dem Charakter dieser Cod. [ℵBL] einfach unmöglich (gegen Aufl. 8)" (*Die Evangelien* [9th ed., 1901], 457–58).

[16] "[N]or is it, on the other hand, in any way easy to account for the omission of the words, if they are genuine, except by the theory of two original texts, one longer and another more abridged" (Friedrich Blass, *Philology of the Gospels* [London: Macmillan, 1898], 143, 148–49).

[17] Cf. Jacques Dupont, "De quoi est-il besoin (Lc x.42)?," in *Text and Interpretation: Studies in the New Testament Presented to Matthew Black*, ed. Ernest Best and R. McL. Wilson (Cambridge: Cambridge University Press, 1979), 115–20, here 116: "On se contente parfoise de ce critère pour écarter la seconde leçon contrastée, ὀλιγων; la prudence s'impose cependant, car elle semble ancienne (Origène), et la leçon longue pourrait en dériver et donc en attester indirectement la diffusion." Augsten regarded the third reading as the initial reading, since she thought it had the support from Origen ("Lukanische Miszelle," 582).

[18] Fee, "'One Thing Is Needful,'" 66.

[19] Frederik Wisse, *The Profile Method for the Classification and Evaluation of Manuscript Evidence, as Applied to the Continuous Greek Text of the Gospel of Luke*, SD 44 (Grand Rapids: Eerdmans, 1982), 53 (38 is classified as K[x]).

[20] J. J. Wettstein is the first scholar to cite minuscule 38 as reading ὀλίγων in Luke 10:42 (*Novum Testamentum Graecum* [2 vols.; Amsterdam: Dommerian, 1751-1752]), followed by J.

variant was cited as a subvariant of the long reading.²¹ The faulty explanation in the second edition of the *Textual Commentary* (1994), however, remained unchanged and continues to influence New Testament scholarship, in spite of the fact that the proposed scenario is built on air.²²

Thus, we are left with two readings, one of which gave rise to the other. The first reading has early and widespread support in two early papyri P45 and P75 and the majority of witnesses representing all the three major textual clusters (traditionally labeled the Alexandrian, "Western," and Byzantine text types).²³ The second reading also has strong textual support by the uncials ℵ, B and L. The fifth-century Codex Ephraemi Rescriptus was corrected to the second reading sometime in the sixth century, probably from the first reading.²⁴ The single-leaf P3 (Luke 7:36–45 and 10:38–42), edited by Karl Wessely, dates to the sixth–seventh centuries and is either an early lectionary or a private copy with a selection of gospel material.²⁵ According to Wessely, the text is closely related to ℵ and L.²⁶ The second reading is supported also by Family 1, minuscule 33 and a few other Greek manuscripts.

The versional evidence is divided but slightly favors the first reading with support from the Old Latin and Vulgate versions, the Sahidic Coptic, and the Old Syriac (Curetonian), Peshitta, and Harklensis versions. The second reading is

---

Martin Augustin Scholtz (1830) and Constantin von Tischendorf (from the 4th ed. of 1849, under siglum "al1"). The error was probably due to a misreading of John Mill's apparatus (1707), which lists ὀλίγων as the reading of "Colb. 8" (= Greg.-Aland 33), but Mill does not record the second part (with ἢ ἑνός). If this is the case, an incompletely recorded reading in Mill's edition through yet another error on the part of Wettstein became a ghost attestation that continues to haunt the discipline to this day. I want to thank Jan Krans, who assisted me in tracing the history of this error in conjunction with my presentation of this material at the SBL Annual Meeting in San Antonio, Texas, in 2016.

²¹ *The Greek New Testament*, ed. Barbara Aland et al., 4th rev. ed. (Stuttgart: Deutsche Bibelgesellschaft/United Bible Societies, 2001 [1st printing 1993]). Minuscule 38 is no longer cited explicitly.

²² Metzger, *Textual Commentary* (2nd ed.), 129.

²³ For a discussion of the current status of text types (or textual clusters), see Eldon Jay Epp, "Textual Clusters: Their Past and Future in New Testament Textual Criticism," in Ehrman and Holmes, *Text of the New Testament* (2nd ed.), 519–78.

²⁴ Constantin von Tischendorf says in his edition of C: "*ΟΛΙΓΩΝ ΔΕ ΕΣΤΙΝ ΧΡΕΙΑ Η ΕΝΟΣ* haud dubie a B scripta sunt; id quod ipso spatio probatur quod accurat expressimus. Inde satis probabile est scripsisse primam manum *ΕΝΟΣ ΔΕ ΕΣΤΙΝ ΧΡΕΙΑ· ΜΑΡΙ*. Eadem vero denique super alterius manus correctionem restituit manus tertia" (*Codex Ephraemi Syri Rescriptus sive fragmenta Novi Testamenti e codice graeco parisiensi celeberrimo quinti ut videtur post Christum seculi* [Leipzig: Tauchnitz, 1843], 326).

²⁵ Karl Wessely, "Evangelien-Fragmente auf Papyrus," *WSt* 4 (1882): 198–214. See also J. Neville Birdsall, "A Further Decipherment of Papyrus G 2323 of the Papyrussammlung of the Österr. Nationalbibliothek," *WSt* 76 (1963): 163–64.

²⁶ Wessely, "Evangelien-Fragmente," 205.

attested by the Bohairic and Ethiopic versions, and it is found in the margin of Harklensis reflecting a Greek manuscript(s) with the reading available to Thomas of Harkel in 616 CE.[27] To the information in NA[28], we may add that the Palestinian Syriac lectionary and the Armenian and Georgian versions, as well as the significant Codex Sinaiticus Arabicus (Sinai Ar. N.F. Parchment 8 + 28), most likely translated from a Greek *Vorlage*, all support the second reading with ὀλίγων.[28]

In regard to patristic evidence up to the fifth century, the second reading has the earliest support, attested by Origen (d. 254), Basil of Caesarea (d. 379), Jerome (d. 420), John Cassian (d. ca. 435), and Cyril of Alexandria (d. 444). The first reading is attested by John Chrysostom (d. 407), Nilus Ancyranus (d. ca. 430), and Augustine (d. 430). As Robert M. Grant has reminded us, "patristic citations are not citations unless they have been adequately analyzed."[29] Hence, in the following section I will analyze the patristic evidence and the history of interpretation in greater detail.[30] For reasons of space I have restricted myself to Greek and Latin authors up to the fifth century who attest to one of the two main readings (1 or 2).[31]

II. Patristic Evidence and the History of Interpretation (Second to Fifth Centuries)

Origen (d. 254)

Although neglected or misunderstood, Origen's citation and use of the passage are particularly significant for textual criticism and the history of interpretation.

---

[27] See Peter A. L. Hill, "The Harklean Version of St. Luke 1–11: A Critical Introduction and Edition" (PhD diss., University of Melbourne, 2002), 54. Thomas of Harkel, monk and bishop of Mabbug, undertook a thorough revision of the Philoxenian version based on collations of several Greek manuscripts, which he prepared at the Enaton monastery near Alexandria in 616. In the margin of his revised translation, the Harklean version, he supplied textual variants found in the Greek manuscripts (using three manuscripts for the Gospels).

[28] *The Gospel according to St. Luke: Chapters 1–12*, vol. 3.1 of *The New Testament in Greek*, International Greek New Testament Project (Oxford: Oxford University Press, 1984); Hikmat Kachouh, "Sinai Ar. N.F. Parchment 8 and 28: Its Contribution to Textual Criticism of the Gospel of Luke," *NovT* 50 (2008): 28–57, here 46 (variant 109).

[29] Robert M. Grant, "The Citation of Patristic Evidence in an Apparatus Criticus," in *New Testament Manuscript Studies: The Materials and the Making of a Critical Apparatus*, ed. Merrill M. Parvis and Allen P. Wikgren (Chicago: University of Chicago Press, 1950), 117–24.

[30] For solid treatments of the use of patristic evidence in New Testament textual criticism, see Gordon Fee, "The Text of John in Origen and Cyril of Alexandria: A Contribution to Methodology in the Recovery and Analysis of Patristic Citations," *Bib* 52 (1971): 357–94; Fee, "The Use of Greek Patristic Citations," *ANRW* 26.1:246–65; Fee, "The Use of the Greek Fathers for New Testament Textual Criticism," in *The Text of the New Testament in Contemporary Research: Essays on the Status Quaestionis*, ed. Bart D. Ehrman and Michael W. Holmes, SD 46 (Grand Rapids: Eerdmans, 1995), 191–207.

[31] Ambrose (*Exp. Luc* 1.9; CCSL 14:11) and Possidius (*Vit. Aug.* 24; PL 32:34) cite Luke 10:40–42 in the shortest version (reading 4) attested by some Western witnesses.

First, in a catena fragment attributed to Origen,[32] he refers to the passage loosely in a form that does not correspond to any known reading.[33] In this case Origen's citation may have been abbreviated and, therefore, cannot be used as an attestation of the third reading, since the words ἢ ἑνός would have occurred after what is cited.[34]

On the other hand, the citation is positive evidence of Origen's knowledge of a reading that at least included ὀλίγων δέ ἐστι χρεία. Significantly, he cites the passage in fuller form in another catena fragment, where the exegesis follows the same lines. He interprets this paradoxical wording by referring to the Ten Commandments (a few), which could ultimately be summarized in *one single* commandment, to love:

> Martha can also be the synagogue of circumcision, which received Jesus in his own territory, because it was engaged in worship according to the letter of the Law. But Mary is the Church of the Gentiles, which has chosen the good part, the "spiritual law," which is not to be taken from her and cannot be destroyed, like the glory upon the face of Moses. From the Law she takes the few beneficial things—or rather, she sums all of them up in one commandment: "You shall love." And, corresponding to the expression "one thing is necessary," you will understand, "you shall love your neighbor as yourself." And, to the expression, "there is need of few things," "you understand the commandments: You shall not commit adultery. You shall not murder," and what follows.[35]

---

[32] For a general discussion of the authenticity of the catena fragments, see Ronald E. Heine, "Can the Catena Fragments of Origen's Commentary on John Be Trusted," *VC* 40 (1986): 118–34.

[33] Origen, *Fr. Jo.* 78 (GCS 4:545): καὶ οὐκ ἀπιθάνως διὰ τὴν ἐν τῷ Μωϋσέως νόμῳ πολιτείαν φήσει εἰρῆσθαι τῇ Μάρθα. "Μάρθα Μάρθα, περὶ πολλὰ θορυβῇ καὶ περισπᾶσαι, ὀλίγων δέ ἐστι χρεία"· εἰς σωτηρίαν γὰρ οὐ τῶν πολλῶν κατὰ τὸ γράμμα τοῦ νόμου ἐντολῶν χρεία, ἀλλ' ὀλίγων, ἐν οἷς κρέμαται ὅλος ὁ νόμος καὶ οἱ προφῆται, τῶν περὶ ἀγάπης νενομοθετημένων, "And not unpersuasively do they say, because of the conduct in the law of Moses, that it is said to Martha: 'Martha, Martha, you are bothered about many things and distracted, but few things are necessary.' For not many commandments according to the letter of the law are necessary for salvation, but few, on which all the Law and the Prophets hang—those are legislated about love" (my translation).

[34] Fee, "'One Thing Is Needful,'" 67 (contra Augsten, "Lukanische Miszelle," 582). For this same reason, the citation of Luke 10:42 by Clement of Alexandria in *Quis div.* 10.6 (GCS 3:166) cannot be used to support reading 4.

[35] Origen, *Homilies on Luke; Fragments on Luke*, trans. Joseph T. Lienhard, FC 94 (Washington, DC: Catholic University of America Press, 1996), 192–93 = Origen, *Fr. Luc.* 39 (GCS 9:298): δύναται δὲ Μάρθα μὲν εἶναι καὶ ἡ ἐκ περιτομῆς συναγωγὴ εἰς τὰ ἴδια ὅρια δεξαμένη τὸν Ἰησοῦν, περισπωμένη περὶ τὴν ἐκ τοῦ γράμματος τοῦ νόμου πολλὴν λατρείαν, Μαρία δὲ ἡ ἐξ ἐθνῶν ἐκκλησία "τὴν ἀγαθὴν" τοῦ "πνευματικοῦ νόμου" "μερίδα" ἐκλεξαμένη ἀναφαίρετον καὶ μὴ "καταργουμένην" ὡς ἡ ἐπὶ τοῦ προσώπου Μωυσέως δόξα, ὀλίγα τὰ χρήσιμα ἐκ τοῦ νόμου ἐπιλέξασα ἢ πάντα ἀναφέρουσα εἰς ἓν τὸ "ἀγαπήσεις." καὶ εἰς μὲν τό· "ἑνός ἐστι χρεία" χρήσῃ τό· "ἀγαπήσεις τὸν πλησίον σου ὡς σεαυτόν," εἰς δὲ τό· "ὀλίγων ἐστὶν" "τὰς ἐντολὰς οἶδας· οὐ μοιχεύσεις· οὐ φονεύσεις" καὶ τὰ ἑξῆς. The authenticity of the Greek catena fragments (whether they are Origenian) has been discussed, but to my knowledge these two particular fragments, *Fr. Jo.* 78 and *Fr. Luc.* 39, have not been assigned to any other author. Although they may reflect summaries of Origen's teaching, it

In other words, Origen's explanation of this passage, in both fragments, presupposes the second reading with ὀλίγων δέ ἐστιν χρεία ἢ ἑνός.[36] Hence, from the UBS[4] (published 1993), Origen is correctly cited exclusively in support of the longer reading, albeit in a parenthesis. On the other hand, NA[28] does not cite Origen at all.

The interpretation reflected in the two passages partly depends on the exegesis of Origen's predecessor, Clement of Alexandria, who refers to the passage in a sermon on the rich man (Mark 10:17–31) and his salvation, *Quis div.* (ca. 190–210 CE).[37] Clement juxtaposes Martha's service with Mary's sitting at the feet of Jesus. Just like Martha, the rich man had been busy with many things; he "had fulfilled every demand of the law" but could not accomplish "the one thing, the work that brings life":[38]

> And just as the Saviour said to Martha when she was busy about many things, distracted and troubled by serving, and chiding her sister because she had left the household work and was seated at His feet spending her time in learning: "Thou are troubled about many things, but Mary hath chosen the good part, and it shall not be taken away from her,"—so also He bade this man cease from his manifold activities and cling to and sit beside one thing, the grace of Him who adds eternal life.[39]

---

is significant that the exegesis follows along the same lines in both of the fragments. In my opinion, we can safely conclude that Origen referred to the longer reading.

[36] Baker's suggestion that Origen is discussing two different text variants in his *Commentary on Luke*: one with ὀλίγων from Alexandria (reading 2), another from Caesarea omitting it (reading 1)—without being explicit about it, I should add—is farfetched ("One Thing Necessary," 132). Fee, on the other hand, ascribes the highest degree of certainty to Origen's (and Basil's) attestation of reading 2 ("The Use of Greek Patristic Citations in New Testament Textual Criticism," in Eldon Jay Epp and Gordon D. Fee, *Studies in the Theory and Method of New Testament Textual Criticism*, SD 45 [Grand Rapids: Eerdmans, 1993], 344–59, here 356).

[37] See Daniel A. Csányi, "Optima pars: Die Auslegungsgeschichte von Lk 10, 38–42 bei den Kirchenvätern der ersten vier Jahrhunderte," *StudMon* 2 (1960): 5–78, here 10: "Abschliessend muss noch bemerkt werden, dass wir bei Origenes eine sehr *ähnliche* Deutung finden werden (Martha = Synagoge / Maria = Kirche).... Freilich muss man annehmen, dass Origenes für die Idee ... von Klemens abhängig ist." In addition, Origen cites the first two commandments, which Jesus cites in Mark 10:19 (and in the same order as Clement has them, μὴ μοιχεύσῃς μὴ φονεύσῃς).

[38] Clement of Alexandria, *Quis div.* 10 (GCS 3:165–66). Eng. trans.: G. W. Butterworth, *The Exhortation to the Greeks; The Rich Man's Salvation; To the Newly Baptized*, LCL 92 (Cambridge: Harvard University Press, 1919), 291.

[39] Ibid.; Greek text (GCS 3:166.14–21): ὁποῖόν τι καὶ πρὸς τὴν Μάρθαν εἶπεν ὁ σωτὴρ ἀσχολουμένην "περὶ" πολλὰ καὶ περιελκομένην καὶ ταρασσομένην διακονικῶς, τὴν δὲ ἀδελφὴν αἰτιωμένην, ὅτι τὸ ὑπηρετεῖν ἀπολιποῦσα τοῖς ποσὶν αὐτοῦ παρακάθηται μαθητικὴν ἄγουσα σχολήν· "σὺ περὶ πολλὰ ταράσσῃ· Μαρία δὲ τὴν ἀγαθὴν μερίδα ἐξελέξατο, καὶ οὐκ ἀφαιρεθήσεται αὐτῆς." οὕτως καὶ τοῦτον ἐκέλευε τῆς πολυπραγμοσύνης ἀφέμενον ἑνὶ προστετηκέναι καὶ προσκαθέζεσθαι, τῇ χάριτι τοῦ ζωὴν αἰώνιον προστιθέντος.

Clement further emphasized:

> Now the works of the law are good ... but only to the extent of being a kind of training accompanied by fear and preparatory instruction, leading on to the supreme law-giving and grace of Jesus. (*Quis div.* 9.2; GCS 3:165; Butterworth, LCL)

For some reason, Clement was cited in support of μεριμνᾷς καὶ τυρβάζῃ περὶ πολλά, ἑνὸς δέ ἐστιν χρεία (reading 1) in UBS³. This loose citation, however, cannot be used for text-critical purposes, and the attestation was removed in UBS⁴. Origen certainly developed Clement's interpretation further and played a key role in the history of interpretation of this passage.⁴⁰

In the first part of the passage of *Fr. Luc.* 39 (which Fee did not cite), Origen offers a different interpretation, where Mary represents θεωρία (contemplation) and Martha πρᾶξις (action, i.e., the practical life) (*Fr. Luc.* 39; GCS 9:298). Here Martha, corresponding to fledgling Christians, is said to have received the Word in her house (her soul) in a more fleshly manner (σωματικώτερον), and Mary, corresponding to mature Christians, listened in a spiritual way (πνευματικῶς).⁴¹ Origen clearly preferred contemplation to action, but he did not separate the two, regarding action as a means to contemplation:

> The mystery of love is lost to the active life [τῷ πρακτικῷ] unless one directs his teaching, and his exhortation to action, toward contemplation: Action [πρᾶξις] and contemplation [θεωρία] do not exist one without the other.⁴²

As François Bovon explains, this interpretation in particular "seems to have gained favor among monastic theologians, all the way from Basil of Caesarea to John Cassian by way of Evagrius Ponticus."⁴³ It is remarkable that Bovon, in his preceding text-critical treatment, rejects the second reading as an "awkward conflation"

---

⁴⁰This has been thoroughly demonstrated by Csányi, who preferred the second reading ("Optima pars," 5–78).

⁴¹The same interpretation is reflected in *Fr. Jo.* 80 (GCS 10:457): σύμβολόν ἐστι Μαρία μὲν τοῦ θεωρητικοῦ βίου, Μάρθα δὲ τοῦ πρακτικοῦ, "Mary is a symbol of the contemplative life, whereas Martha [is a symbol] of the active" (my translation). A third interpretation of the passage in Luke 10:38–42 is reflected in Origen's commentary on the Song of Songs, where Martha represents the Jewish Christians and Mary the gentile Christians (GCS 8:121). See Csány, "Optima pars," 24–27.

⁴²Eng. trans. by Lienhard, *Homilies on Luke*, 192. Origen, *Fr. Luc.* 39 (GCS 9:298): συμπεριαιρεῖται γὰρ τῷ πρακτικῷ τὸ τῆς ἀγάπης μυστήριον, εἰ μὴ πρὸς τὸ θεωρεῖν ἕληταί τις τὸ διδάσκειν καὶ προτρέπειν ἐπὶ πρᾶξιν· οὔτε γὰρ πρᾶξις οὔτε θεωρία ἄνευ θατέρου. On this point, see David Grumett, "Action and/or Contemplation? Allegory and Liturgy in the Reception of Luke 10:38–42," *SJT* 59 (2006): 125–39, here 128. I disagree with Grumett that this is "the earliest interpretative tradition" of the passage and "the first view of its theological significance," but he is correct in asserting that it "has been the majority view through subsequent Christian theological history of the relation between action and contemplation" (127–28). Cf. Csányi, "Optima pars," 75.

⁴³Bovon, *Luke 2*, 76.

where "the 'few things' suggests the idea of material possessions, while the '(only) one (thing)' refers to spiritual commitment to God," without realizing that this is the very text that Origen read. Origen's interpretation apparently became widespread and, as Bovon himself concludes, "was to have a large and lasting success."[44]

This illustrates the danger of isolating the task of textual criticism only to establish an initial text as a first step in the exegesis. Eldon Epp has described this danger well and instead promotes a "variant-conscious" approach to exegesis:

> When that goal is defined as restoring the original text of the various authors, variants tend to have a binary character—they are either in or out, that is, accepted or rejected.... At the opposite end of the spectrum, when the goal of textual criticism is to explore the wealth of information about the history and thought of the early churches that is disclosed by variant readings, then all meaningful variants are held in much higher esteem.[45]

Conversely, for scholars who examine patristic interpretations, a variant-conscious approach promotes attentiveness to which form of the text a certain interpretation presupposes, as far as it can be determined. Such an approach does not have to exclude a quest for the initial text but rather can facilitate it.[46]

Greek Authors (Fourth–Fifth Centuries)

Basil of Caesarea (d. 379) cites the passage twice in the longer form. First, in *Regulae fusius tractatae* 20.3 (*interrogatio* xx) he appeals to the passage in order to recommend minimum diet.[47] Here the "few things" refer to the food and drink that is prepared, and the "one thing" is the sole necessity to fill the need of the body (and nothing more).[48] Jesus did not praise Martha, who was distracted by many duties, preparing several dishes instead of the few needed. In *Regulae morales* 38.1 Basil

---

[44] Ibid., 74–75.

[45] Eldon Jay Epp, "It's All about Variants: A Variant-Conscious Approach to New Testament Textual Criticism," *HTR* 100 (2007): 275–308, here 275.

[46] Contra Allie M. Ernst, *Martha from the Margins: The Authority of Martha in Early Christian Tradition*, VCSup 98 (Leiden: Brill, 2009), 191–92.

[47] Basil of Caesarea, *Reg. fus. tract.* 20.3 (PG 31:973): Οὐκ ἐπήνεσε τὴν Μάρθαν εἰς πολλὴν διακονίαν περισπωμένην ὁ Κύριος· ἀλλά, Μεριμνᾷς, καὶ τυρβάζῃ, φησί, περὶ πολλά· ὀλίγων δέ ἐστι χρεία, ἢ ἑνός· ὀλίγων μέν, δηλονότι τῶν πρὸς παρασκευήν, ἑνὸς δὲ τοῦ σκοποῦ, ὥστε τὴν χρείαν ἐκπληρωθῆναι. Αὐτὸς δὲ ὁ Κύριος ὁποίαν παρέθηκε τοῖς πεντακισχιλίοις τροφὴν οὐκ ἀγνοεῖς, "The Lord did not praise Martha for being anxious about much serving, but He said, 'Thou art careful and art troubled about many things; few things—nay, one thing only is necessary': 'few things'— that is, the purpose, namely, to satisfy the need. You are well aware, also, of what sort of food the Lord Himself placed before the five thousand" (Basil of Caesarea, *Ascetical Works*, trans. Sister M. Monica Wagner, C.S.C., FC 9 [Washington, DC: Catholic University of America Press, 1950], 279).

[48] It is unclear how Basil understood the good part that Mary has chosen since he does not cite verse 42.

refers to the passage in Luke to demonstrate that the willingness to serve in the smallest things is favorable to God (PG 31:760; FC 9:117).

Evagrius Ponticus (345–399) cites the passage in a short treatise on monastic life *Rerum monachialum* 3. Evagrius seems to use the shorter form (reading 1), and the attestation is listed in parentheses in UBS[5] (not cited in NA[28]). In my opinion, however, the loose citation with a modified word order may be abbreviated, and I have therefore excluded it from my apparatus.[49] Evagrius's interpretation of this passage is otherwise similar to that of Basil, with whom he had much contact. The most important thing, says Evagrius, is to hear the divine word. Even if you have a guest, you must avoid excess. The Widow at Zarephath is a good example; she had a minimum of bread and drink to offer the prophet, and even if you cannot offer these things, you can give him a good word and gain his recognition.

John Chrysostom (d. 407) cites our passage in his *Homily on John* 44.1 in a context where he battles a heretical group, possibly the Messalians, who caused trouble for the church in Syria and Asia Minor in the fourth and fifth centuries. One group of Messalians were ascetics who emphasized the inner life to the extreme and despised manual labor and almsgiving.[50] Apparently, they justified their living in idleness by appealing to this and other passages such as Matt 6:25, 34 and John 6:27.[51] Chrysostom objects that not a few had misused these passages to live a life of leisure, as if Christ were rejecting manual labor here. He cites Luke 10:41–42 in the short form (reading 1) together with Matt 6:34, and then proceeds to clarify their meaning.[52] Jesus's words cannot be taken literally, or they would conflict with Paul, who stressed the necessity of manual labor (1 Thess 4:10–11, Eph 4:28, Acts 20:34). Jesus's reply to Martha, he concludes, does not concern work or manner of

---

[49] Evagrius of Pontus, *Rer. mon.* 3 (PG 40:1253): "Ἔχεις τὸν Κύριον Ἰησοῦν μεμφόμενόν πως τὴν τὰ τοιαῦτα σπουδάζουσαν ψυχὴν Μάρθαν, καὶ λέγοντα· Τί "περὶ πολλὰ" εἶ, καὶ "θορυβάζῃ; ἑνός ἐστι χρεία," τοῦ τὸν θεῖον, φησί, λόγον ἀκούειν, καὶ μετὰ τοῦτο ἀκμητὶ παντὸς τοῦ εὑρισκομένου, "You know how the Lord Jesus blames the soul that bruises itself with such things, namely, Martha: 'Why are you concerned and troubled about many things? There is need for one thing,' namely, he says, to listen to the divine word, and after that everything follows along easily" (trans. Robert E. Sinkewicz, *Evagrius of Pontus: The Greek Ascetic Corpus*, OECS [Oxford: Oxford University Press, 2003], 5). Fee does not examine the citation but accepts it in support of the first reading ("'One Thing Is Needful,'" 62). In a later study, however, he assigns this citation (and that of Nilus) the least degree of certainty ("Use of Greek Patristic Citations," 356).

[50] Daniel Caner, *Wandering, Begging Monks: Spiritual Authority and the Promotion of Monasticism in Late Antiquity*, Transformation of the Classical Heritage 33 (Berkeley: University of California Press, 2002), 90–92. The term *Messalians* is derived from Syriac, meaning "people of prayer."

[51] Csányi, "Optima pars," 34–47; Caner, *Wandering, Begging Monks*, 176.

[52] Chrysostom, *Hom. Jo.* 44.1 (PG 9:249): Πῶς οὖν τῇ Μάρθᾳ ὁ Ἰησοῦς εἶπεν· Μεριμνᾷς καὶ τυρβάζῃ περὶ πολλὰ, ἑνὸς δέ ἐστι χρεία· Μαρία δὲ τὴν ἀγαθὴν μερίδα ἐξελέξατο· καὶ πάλιν, Μὴ μεριμνήσητε εἰς τὴν αὔριον, "How is it then that Jesus said to Martha, 'You are anxious and troubled by many things, but there is need of only one thing. Mary has chosen the better part'; and again, 'Do not worry about tomorrow'" (my translation).

activity but rather the necessity to understand the right time, to set aside time for hearing instead of wasting it on fleshly things.⁵³

Baker points out that the chief literary exponent of the Messalians, Pseudo-Macarius (ca. 385–430) "criticizes certain extremists in the movement who refuse to do any work on the plea that 'one thing is necessary,' namely prayer," which shows that the Messalians used the shorter reading, which is obviously more attractive in this context.⁵⁴ The short reading is further attested in a Messalian tract (Pseudo-Basil, *Const. asc.* 1.1 [PG 31:1325c]), and Baker goes so far as to suggest that Chrysostom may have cited the text that his opponents used "to defeat them on their own ground."⁵⁵

There is an intriguing parallel in *Apophthegmata Patrum* (fourth–fifth centuries), Silvanus 4, where an ascetic monk criticizes manual labor by citing John 6:27 and Luke 10:42 ("Mary has chosen the good portion"). Abba Silvanus, however, cleverly uses his own words against the monk, setting him up in a cell with just a book to read all day. When the monk is not called to the evening meal, he complains to Silvanus, who explains why no one called him for supper:

> "Because you are a spiritual man and do not need that kind of food. We being carnal, want to eat, and that is why we work. But you have chosen the good portion and read the whole day long and you do not want to eat carnal food." When he heard these words the brother made a prostration, saying, "Forgive me, abba." The old man [Silvanus] said to him, "Mary needs Martha. It is really thanks to Martha that Mary is praised."⁵⁶

Chrysostom's disciple Nilus of Ancyra (d. ca. 430) wrote a treatise *On the Excellency of Monks*, in which he cites the shorter text (reading 1) and interprets it in a way similar to that of his teacher.⁵⁷ Martha was distracted by the service of the body (περὶ τὴν σωματικὴν λειτουργίαν περισπωμένης). She was blamed not because of her willingness to serve but because she neglected to sit by the Word, as Mary did, and to care about what is good for the soul.

In his *Commentary on John* 7.9.6 (John 11:6), Cyril of Alexandria (d. 444) paraphrases Origen's allegorical interpretation of the same passage where Mary is

---

⁵³ Ibid.

⁵⁴ Baker, "One Thing Necessary," 133. For the Greek text, see Werner Jaeger, *Two Rediscovered Works of Ancient Christian Literature: Gregory of Nyssa and Macarius* (Leiden: Brill, 1954), 288.

⁵⁵ Ibid.

⁵⁶ *Apophthegmata Patrum*: Silvanus 4 (PG 65:409; Eng. trans. by Benedicta Ward, *The Sayings of the Desert Fathers: The Alphabetical Collection*, rev. ed., CistS 59 [Kalamazoo: Cistercian Publications, 1984], 233). I agree with Douglas Burton-Christie, who reads the story as if the monk misunderstood the scriptural texts and Silvanus showed him the correct interpretation in a practical and ironical way (*The Word in the Desert: Scripture and the Quest for Holiness in Early Christian Monasticism* [New York: Oxford University Press, 1993], 163).

⁵⁷ Nilus, *De mon. praest.* 16 (PG 79:1079b): Μάρθα, Μάρθα, μεριμνᾷς καὶ τυρβάζῃ περὶ πολλά, ἑνὸς δέ ἐστι χρεία· Μαρία δέ....

the symbol for gentiles and Martha stands for the Jews. Martha is distracted by many things when only one thing or a few things are necessary for salvation—the few commandments of the law summarized in the law of love (Matt 22:4).[58] In a second passage in the commentary, Cyril follows Origen's second interpretation in the Lukan fragment of Martha as performing the practical virtue (τὴν πρακτικὴν ἀρετήν), whereas Mary is occupied with spiritual contemplation (τὴν πνευματικὴν θεωρίαν).[59]

Cyril cites Luke 10:38–42 twice in his sixty-ninth *Homily on Luke*, attesting to the long reading in v. 42.[60] Here he interprets the passage in a more literal sense: Martha is to be blamed not for her careful service but "for labouring in vain, by wishing to procure more than was necessary."[61] Then he concludes that the better part is earnestly to desire the divine doctrine. A similar literal interpretation is reflected in his thirty-ninth homily, where Christ, by his answer to Martha (the long reading), "is seen preventing excess, and reducing us to a bare sufficiency."[62]

Latin Authors (Fourth–Fifth Centuries)

Jerome (d. 420) cites Luke 10:41–42 in the long version (*pauca autem necessaria sunt aut unum*) in his *Epistle to Eustochium*, written in Rome in 384 (*Ep.* 22 [CSEL 54:178]). In the context, he exhorts his spiritual daughter, the virgin Eustochium, to be like Mary, who chose the good part (*bonam partem elegit*) in that she preferred the teaching as her food, which in this context implies the choice of monastic living. In a different epistle Jerome praises Martha for preparing a meal for Jesus and Mary for bathing his feet with tears and drying them with her hair (Luke 7:37–50; *Ep.* 71.2 [CSEL 55:3]). Curiously, in Jerome's Vulgate we find the

---

[58] Cyril of Alexandria, *Comm. Jo.* 7.9.6 (PG 74:40): "Μάρθα, Μάρθα, μεριμνᾷς καὶ τυρβάζῃ περὶ πολλά. Ἑνὸς δέ ἐστι χρεία," ἤτοι ὀλίγων· εἰς σωτηρίαν γὰρ, οὐ τῶν πολλῶν ἐντολῶν χρεία κατὰ τὸ τοῦ νόμου πρόσταγμα ἀλλ᾿ ὀλίγων τῶν περὶ ἀγάπης νενομοθετημένων, ἐν οἷς κρέμαται ὅλος ὁ νόμος καὶ οἱ προφῆται, "'Martha, Martha, you are anxious and troubled by many things. There is need of only one thing,' or a few things: For there is not need for many commandments according to the directive of the law for salvation, but of those few [commandments] that are legislated about love, on which all the Law and the Prophets hang" (my translation). Cf. Origen, *Fr. Jo.* 78 (GCS 4:545).

[59] Cyril of Alexandria, *Comm. Jo.* 12.2 (PG 74:73).

[60] Cyril of Alexandria, *Hom. in Luc.* 69 (CSCO 70:188). The homilies on Luke are mainly preserved in a literal Syriac translation.

[61] Eng. trans. by Robert Payne Smith, *A Commentary upon the Gospel according to St. Luke by St. Cyril*, 2 vols. (Oxford: Oxford University Press, 1859), 1:318.

[62] Cyril of Alexandria, *Hom. in Luc.* 39 (CSCO 70:77; PG 72:621): ἀνακόπτων ὁρᾶται Χριστὸς τὸ πέρα μέτρου, καὶ καταρρυθμίζων ἡμᾶς εἰς αὐτάρκειαν· ἔφη γάρ· "Μεριμνᾷς καὶ τυρβάζῃ περὶ πολλά" ὀλίγων δέ ἐστι χρεία, ἢ ἑνός, "Christ is seen preventing excess, and reducing us to a bare sufficiency. For He said, 'Martha, Martha: thou art careful, and hurried about many things: but few things are required, or one'" (Smith, *Commentary upon the Gospel*, 1:152).

shorter reading (*porro unum est necessarium*), and here Mary chooses "the best part" (*Maria optimam partem elegit*).⁶³ The Vulgate form of the passage soon came to dominate in the West with very few exceptions.

John Cassian (d. ca. 435) treats our passage at length in his major spiritual work *Conlatio* 1.8 and cites it a second time in 23.3. He uses the long version (reading 2), probably due to his long sojourn in Egypt.⁶⁴ Cassian explains the few things and the one thing in terms of *theoria* —contemplation of holy persons and of God alone:

> For when the Lord said: "You are concerned and troubled about many things, but few things are necessary, or even one," he placed the highest good not in carrying out some work, however praiseworthy, but in the truly simple and unified contemplation of him, declaring that "few things" are necessary for perfect blessedness—namely, that theoria which is first established by reflecting on a few holy persons. Ascending from the contemplation of these persons, someone who is still advancing will arrive with his help at that which is also called "one"—namely, the vision of God alone.⁶⁵

Apparently, Cassian made the same distinction as Origen between the active life (Martha) and the contemplative life characterized by *theoria* (Mary).⁶⁶ On the other hand, he clearly rejected the radical dichotomy between the two.⁶⁷

Augustine (d. ca. 430) cites the passage in *Speculum, Quaestiones Evangeliorum,* and several sermons, most often with the Vulgate wording and always reflecting reading 1.⁶⁸ Augustine downplayed the historical-literal meaning of the passage

---

⁶³ Baker notes that this discrepancy is odd, "not only because of the preference for the longer reading [in the letter], but also for the rendering of the Greek *de* by *autem*, whereas the Vulgate *porro* is seen as a typical characteristic of the new version as against the Old Latin" ("One Thing Necessary," 134).

⁶⁴ Fee, "'One Thing Is Needful,'" 74 n. 41. Cassian's Latin text form in turn influenced Irish monasticism, as reflected in the eighth-century Book of Mulling, *paucis vero opus est vel etiam uno.*

⁶⁵ John Cassian, *Conlatio* 1.8 (CSEL 13:14): Dicens enim Dominus: solicita es et turbaris erga multa, paucis vero opus est aut etiam uno, summum bonum non in actuali quamvis laudabili opere et multis fructibus abundanti, sed in sua contemplatione, quae vere simplex et una est collocavit, paucis opus esse pronuntias ad perfectam beatitudinem, id est illa theoria quae prius in paucorum servabatur consideratione sanctorum, a quorum consideratione conscendens is qui adhuc in profetu positus est ad illud quoque quod unum dicitur id est Dei solius intuitum … perveniet. Eng. trans. by Boniface Ramsey, *John Cassian, The Conferences,* ACW 57 (New York: Paulist, 1997), 47.

⁶⁶ Csányi ("Optima pars," 61–62) notes that Cassian is dependent on Evagrius of Pontus in his teaching on contemplative prayer and suggests that the phrasing in *Conlatio* 1.8 depends on Evagrius. It does not follow that Evagrius himself found his theory of contemplation implied in Luke's "few things … one thing" (and we cannot be sure that he had this text).

⁶⁷ See Giles Constable, *Three Studies in Medieval Religious and Social Thought* (Cambridge: Cambridge University Press, 1995), 17.

⁶⁸ Augustine cites the passage in *Spec.* 27 (CSEL 12:185); *Serm.* 103.2 (PL 38:614); 104.1 (PL

related to the preparation of a meal and emphasized the spiritual-theological meaning: he saw in Martha the earthly way of life —*vita laboriosa*—representing the life of the church in the present age, where works of compassion are necessary but will come to an end. Mary, on the other hand, represented the heavenly *vita otiosa*—the contemplative life, which starts already in this age and will last in eternity. Thus, like Origen and others, Augustine did not reject action in the present life—both sisters were acceptable to the Lord—although he favored Mary's contemplative way of life.[69] With Augustine we are far removed from the literal sense of the passage—advice about the preparation of a meal.[70]

Conclusion: Patristic Evidence and History of Interpretation

We have observed several lines of patristic interpretation of the passage extending from the literal sense—advice about the preparation of a meal and the need for the disciple to set aside time for listening to Jesus—to the allegorical and spiritual-theological interpretation where Martha and Mary are symbols for distinct groups (Jews vs. Christians or fleshly/beginning vs. spiritual/mature Christians) representing two ways of living (action/contemplation) or even two ages.

In a wider study of the interpretation of the story with a focus on the Middle Ages, Giles Constable draws a similar conclusion:

> These examples, of which others will be cited later, show that Mary and Martha were interpreted in many ways and that they were not always seen in contrast to each other or as alternatives. In addition to standing for two different types of activity, they sometimes stood for two aspects of the church, two periods of history, or two types of prayer.... Every word and detail of the story was interpreted in different and sometimes contradictory ways.[71]

Constable points out that the main lines of interpretation were established already in the age of the church fathers.[72] The earliest history of interpretation of this passage is clearly complex, but, in my opinion, the development reflects an increasing dichotomy between the two sisters and between the needs of the body and soul, respectively. This dichotomy corresponds to a dualistic worldview where spiritual concerns take precedence over mundane matters. It is therefore not surprising that the passage, in a dualistic interpretation, became popular and was even used as a plea in ascetical and monastic contexts. In relation to the textual variants, the distance between the two sisters is greater with the shorter text.[73]

38:616); 104.2 (PL 38:617); 170.14 (PL 38:925); 179.3 (PL 38:967); 256.6 (PL 38:1189); *Quaest. ev.* 11 (Luke) (PL 33:1341).

[69] See Csányi, "Optima pars," 71.
[70] Cf. Grumett, "Action and/or Contemplation," 128.
[71] Constable, *Three Studies*, 11.
[72] Ibid., 14.
[73] In the Latin tradition, the dichotomy is further reflected in the choice to translate τὴν

III. Internal Evidence

The discussion of patristic interpretations in the previous section is relevant to internal evidence and may inform both our understanding of what Luke may have meant and how other ancient readers, the scribes, may have interpreted and copied the text.

Many modern interpreters, however, have attempted to make sense of the longer reading without reference to ancient interpretations, and several have repeated the sentiment of the UBS Committee that it must be a combination of two readings "with disastrous results as to sense."[74] Fee, however, referred to Godet's interpretation of the long reading: "*There needs but little* (for the body), *or even but one thing* (for the soul)."[75] Thus, Fee argued that the "few things" refers to a meal to satisfy the body, and the "only thing" refers to what the soul needs, a reading that makes perfect sense, although it is subtle.[76] Therefore he identified it as the *lectio difficilior*, which led a scribe to clarify by omitting the perplexing reference to a "few things," because, ultimately, only one thing is necessary and that is what Mary chose.[77] If the long reading is original, Fee concluded, "the text is not so much a 'put down' of Martha, as it is a gentle rebuke for her anxiety. For a meal, Jesus says, there is no cause to fret over πολλά, when only ὀλίγα are necessary."[78]

This argument has been turned around, as is apparent in Metzger's commentary; he suggests that the absoluteness of ἑνός was softened by replacing it with

---

ἀγαθὴν μερίδα as the good part, *bonam partem* (d e) or the best part, *optimam partem* (a b c f i l q r; Vg), rather than the better part, *meliorem partem* (Ambrose, *Exp. Lc* 1.9; 7.86; and Augustine, *Serm.* 103.2 and 104.1–2; otherwise he follows the Vulg.). See Constable, *Three Studies*, 18: "The use of *melior* rather than *optima pars* suggested that Martha's part was good even if Mary's was better and tended to reduce the distance between the sisters." According to Constable, "the better part" is found in Ambrose, Rufinus, Aponius, Augustine, the Historia monachorum and others (ibid. 5–6).

[74] Metzger, *Textual Commentary* (1st ed.), 154 (repeated in the 2nd ed., 129).

[75] Fee, "'One Thing Is Needful,'" 71 (italics original). Frédéric Godet, *A Commentary on the Gospel of St. Luke*, trans. E. W. Shalders and M. D. Cush; 3rd ed.; 2 vols. (New York: Funk & Wagnalls, 1890), 2:45. As we have seen, similar interpretations are reflected among the church fathers.

[76] Nolland (*Luke 9:21–18:34*, 600), objects that Fee's explanation requires that "necessary" (χρεία) function in two quite different senses referring to Godet's translation. Cf. Green, *Gospel of Luke*, 433 n. 133. However, this would certainly not be the only example of an ambiguity on the part of Luke.

[77] Fee, "'One Thing Is Needful,'" 71–72. Wilhelm Meyer, on the other hand, suggested that ὀλίγων δέ ἐστιν χρεία ἢ ἑνός originated because of "the explanation which takes the passage as meaning one dish" (*Critical and Exegetical Hand-book to the Gospels of Mark and Luke*, ed. William P. Dickson, trans. Robert E. Wallis, suppl. notes Matthew B. Riddle, Meyer's Commentary on the New Testament 2 [New York: Funk & Wagnalls, 1884], 381).

[78] Fee, "'One Thing Is Needful,'" 75.

ὀλίγων and that finally in some witnesses the two were combined. As we have seen, this scenario must now be abandoned. Further, the explanation that scribes wanted to soften Jesus's radical words is, in my opinion, less plausible when the middle reading disappears.[79] My survey of the early history of interpretation suggests that the dichotomy between the two sisters increased over time. It is easy to see why scribes would remove the difficult reference to a few things and make the text straightforward, making a clear distinction between the two sisters and their distinct choices.

Mary Rose D'Angelo has called attention to another important piece of evidence that supports my argument.[80] There is a textual variant in verse 39, where P45 P75 ℵ* B² L Ξ 579 omit the relative pronoun ἥ, the presence of which may suggest that Martha too sat at the feet of Jesus at first (before she became distracted), implying that both sisters were disciples (cf. ASV, "And she had a sister called Mary, who also sat at the Lord's feet, and heard his word"). The pronoun is included in square brackets in NA[28], but most modern translations omit it. It is clearly the *lectio difficilior*, however. D'Angelo points out that, when the expression "sat at the feet" came to be understood less as a Lukan reference to discipleship and was viewed as "a literal description of the scene, the story made no sense [for scribes] if Martha also was sitting down."[81] Here we may observe again how the omission separates the two sisters and implicitly confines Martha to the kitchen.[82]

Turid Karlsen Seim's discussion of the passage is also illuminating in this regard, as it brings out Luke's positive portrayal of women disciples who serve. Thus, she objects to the proposal that Luke's aim was "to contest Martha's role of diaconal leadership."[83] Seim points out that the use of διακον- terminology in 10:40

---

[79] Brutscheck argues that the middle reading ὀλίγων δέ ἐστιν χρεία (which she thinks Origen and 38 attest) is the *lectio facilior*, "da sie die radikal-fordernde Aussage mildernd in eine banal-materielle umwandelt" (*Maria-Martha-Erzählung*, 9). She regards the long reading in Vaticanus as a combination of the reading in its presumed ancestor P75 and another existing reading resulting in a secondary reading that is milder than reading 1 (10).

[80] Mary Rose D'Angelo, "Women Partners in the New Testament," *JFSR* 6 (1990): 65–86, here 78–79.

[81] Ibid., 79. D'Angelo further argues that the long reading, presenting both sisters as disciples, supports her larger theory that "behind the stories [of Martha and Mary] in Luke and John lies a tradition about a famous missionary couple, Martha the *diakonos*, and Mary, the *adelphē*" (80). Regardless of the plausibility of her theory, Ernst rightly notes that "Martha is also described as ἀδελφή (Jn 11:1, 3)" (*Martha from the Margins*, 195).

[82] Recently, Jennifer S. Wyant has argued for the originality of the long reading in Luke 10:38b; that is, Martha welcomed Jesus "into her house" (εἰς τὴν οἰκίαν αὐτῆς) ("Giving Martha Back Her House: Analyzing the Textual Variant in Luke 10:38b" [paper presented at the Annual Meeting of the Society of Biblical Literature, Boston, 2017]. The prepositional phrase is omitted by P45, P75, and B. Wyant regards the long reading as the *lectio difficilior* and proposes several theological and cultural reasons why scribes might hesitate to describe Martha as the owner of her home, reasons that could lead to the omission of the phrase.

[83] Turid Karlsen Seim, *The Double Message: Patterns of Gender in Luke-Acts*, SNTW

is consistent with Lukan style and that "Martha is representative of the typical female figure in Luke-Acts" (Peter's mother-in-law in Luke 4:38–39; the women who follow Jesus in Luke 8:1–3; Tabitha in Acts 9:36–42; Mary the mother of John in Acts 12:12; Lydia, who shows hospitality to Paul in Acts 16:15, 40).[84] Significantly, Seim therefore realizes that the conflict between Martha and Mary in our passage where the two sisters' activities are contrasted "sheds a critical light on the whole of this presentation of women."[85] In her subsequent discussion of the text-critical problems, she rightly notes that the textual choice will influence how Martha's activity is regarded:

> For those who cannot bring themselves to sweep Martha aside completely, the variants with ὀλίγον are the most comfortable. They imply that something is said in Martha's favour; her mistake is simply that she bothers with much *more* than is necessary (cf. also πολλήν in 10.40 and περὶ πολλά in 10.41).[86]

Unfortunately, Seim's presentation of external evidence is deficient and she does not clearly argue in favor of any reading, acknowledging that there is a wide variety of opinion among other scholars about which reading is the *lectio difficilior*. Nevertheless, she suggests that any of the variants (except the short Western reading) could be interpreted without necessarily identifying "the one thing necessary" (10:42a) with "the good part" that Mary has chosen (10:42b).[87]

I regard Seim's observations as intrinsic evidence in favor of the long reading, here as well as in v. 39, which places the sisters closer together. Martha's mistake, as Seim suggests, is arguably that she bothers with more than necessary when preparing a meal and becomes upset at her sister: "Jesus' reply to Martha does not concern her serving [διακονεῖν], but the way it is done … the fundamental antithesis is not between hearing and serving, but between hearing and agitated toil."[88] In addition, a too-negative emphasis on "serving/doing," on the part of Luke, would

---

(Edinburgh: T&T Clark, 1994), 100. The proposal was put forth by Elisabeth Schüssler Fiorenza, "Biblische Grundlegung," in *Feministische Theologie: Perspektiven zur Orientierung*, ed. Maria Kassel (Stuttgart: Kreuz, 1988), 13–44, here 36. See also Pamela Thimmes, "The Language of Community: A Cautionary Tale (Luke 10.38–42)," in *A Feminist Companion to Luke*, ed. Amy-Jill Levine with Marianne Blickenstaff, FCNTECW 3 (London: Sheffield Academic, 2002), 232–45, esp. 241.

[84] Seim, *Double Message*, 100–101. Note in particular the διακον- terms in Luke 4:39, "Immediately she got up and began to serve [διηκόνει] them"; Luke 8:3, "and Joanna, the wife of Herod's steward Chuza, and Susanna, and many others, who provided [διηκόνουν] for them out of their resources"; and our passage in Luke 10:40, "Lord, do you not care that my sister has left me to do all the work [διακονεῖν] by myself?"

[85] Seim, *Double Message*, 101.

[86] Ibid., 104.

[87] Ibid.

[88] Ibid., 105. For a similar interpretation, see Warren Carter, "Getting Martha Out of the Kitchen," in Levine, *Feminist Companion to Luke*, 214–31.

in fact contradict the importance of "doing" in the previous pericope (the parable of the good Samaritan, 10:25–37).[89]

Subsequently, North has attempted to clarify what Luke could have meant with the longer reading, assuming it is original.[90] North agrees with many other scholars that a "food story" would suit Luke's interest and points to several details in this direction in the passage, but then adds: "the meal element is only the background of the picture that Luke wants to paint. In the foreground stand pedagogy and discipleship."[91] On the one hand, πόλλα, ὀλίγων, and ἑνός all refer to the meal, but, at the same time, North suggests, ὀλίγων and ἑνός, are references to discipleship.[92]

The question which of the two readings best suits Luke in terms of vocabulary and style is rather inconclusive in my opinion.[93] Weiss, however, has made an important argument concerning the choice of conjunction: "Dazu kommt, dass dieselben Cod., die das blosse ενος vetreten, durch Verwandlung des schwierigen γάρ in δε, das nur Trg txt. aufnimmt, sich als emendirt erweisen, und D it es ganz weglassen müssen."[94] His point is that it is difficult to understand why Luke would write γάρ with the shorter reading, and the same codices that have the shorter reading, he says, have changed γάρ to δέ. Similarly, Lagrange, who prefers the long reading, noted that the reading γάρ is the *lectio difficilior* in Luke 10:42b.[95]

---

[89] As Raj Nadella notes, "It is somewhat puzzling to Luke's readers that the same Jesus who repeatedly stressed the importance of 'doing' in the previous pericope [10:25–37] not only praises Mary for choosing not to 'do,' but also chides Martha's choice to 'do'" (*Dialogue Not Dogma: Many Voices in the Gospel of Luke*, LNTS 431 [London: Bloomsbury T&T Clark, 2011], 81–82). Then Nadella refers to Seim's solution and concludes, "Jesus' affirmation of Mary's choice and his critique of Martha's choice do not negate Martha's choice as much as they question Martha's negation of Mary's choice. Jesus chides Martha for disregarding Mary's choice and for implying that serving/doing takes precedence over hearing" (82).

[90] North, "ὀλίγων δέ ἐστιν χρεία," 3–13. For an overview of possible interpretations of the *Sitz im Leben*, Luke's intentions with the story, and the specific meaning of διακονία/διακονέω (v. 40), see Ernst, *Martha from the Margins*, 190–223.

[91] North, "ὀλίγων δέ ἐστιν χρεία," 4. Cf. Ernst, who points out that in "its current literary setting the story is embedded within the Lukan travel narrative whose major concern is discipleship, linked to this wider setting by its opening ('as they were on the way …'), as well as by the parallels between 10:38 and 10:1–9" (*Martha from the Margins*, 192).

[92] North seeks to demonstrate that not only ἑνός but also ὀλίγων δέ ἐστιν χρεία has a double meaning connected to a meal and discipleship; he proposes that it is a variation of a common classical idiom found in pedagogic contexts, for example, ὀλίγων δεῖται πρὸς τὴν μάθησιν ("he/she has almost learned"), so that Luke 10:42 suggests that Mary is close—better, very close to the kingdom of God—a Lukan adaptation of Mark 12:34 ("ὀλίγων δέ ἐστιν χρεία," 5–11).

[93] See Brutscheck, *Maria-Martha-Erzählung*, 10; and Dupont, "De quoi est-il besoin," 117.

[94] Weiss, *Die Evangelien* (9th ed., 1901), 458; cf. Alfred Plummer, *A Critical and Exegetical Commentary on the Gospel according to St. Luke*, 4th ed., ICC (Edinburgh: T&T Clark, 1901), 292: "The γάρ (ℵ B L Λ) would easily be smoothed into δέ (A C P), or omitted as difficult (D)."

[95] Lagrange, *Évanglie selon saint Luc*, 319.

The editors of NA²⁸ accept γάρ as the initial text, but most of the textual witnesses with the shorter reading read δέ or its equivalent (A C K P W Γ Δ Θ *f*¹³ 565ˢ 579 700 𝔐 f q vg^mss sy^c.p.h bo^pt Chr Nil Aug). In fact, p⁷⁵ is the only important textual witness that combines the short reading with γάρ, and it was of course unknown to Weiss (p⁴⁵ is lacunose).⁹⁶ All critical editions choose γάρ in this passage. Fee, who was unaware of earlier discussions, made an argument adding that, when Luke uses γάρ in direct discourse (there are thirty-five examples up to Luke 10:42), it clearly expresses cause or reason and is invariably translated "for" in the RSV.⁹⁷ Fee rightly argues that this force of γάρ in Luke 10:42 would require the long reading.⁹⁸

IV. Conclusion

I have argued in favor of the long reading in Luke 10:41–42: Μάρθα Μάρθα, μεριμνᾷς καὶ θορυβάζῃ περὶ πολλά, ὀλίγων δέ ἐστιν χρεία ἢ ἑνός· Μαριά(μ) γάρ ... as the *lectio difficilior*, where ὀλίγων, the "few things" may refer to the meal, and ἑνός, the "one thing" to discipleship. Both themes suit the context in Luke. The main alternative reading, Μάρθα Μάρθα, μεριμνᾷς καὶ θορυβάζῃ περὶ πολλά, ἑνὸς δέ ἐστιν χρεία· Μαριὰμ γάρ ... (NA²⁸) is less subtle and increases the distance between the two sisters Martha and Mary (as does the omission of the pronoun ἢ in v. 39).

Further, the long reading is more consistent with Luke's positive emphasis on "doing" in general (including the previous pericope) and with his portrayal of women's service in particular in Luke-Acts. In addition, most of the same codices that have the shorter reading in vv. 41–42 seem to have changed γάρ to δέ in v. 42, but γάρ, which fits better with the long reading, is retained in P75 (the reverse change, from δέ to γάρ, is difficult to explain if the shorter reading is the earlier). Hence, these data also speak in favor of the proposed scenario that the long reading has priority.

Origen, the earliest father who cites the text and whose interpretation has had great influence, attests to the long reading and should be cited accordingly in future critical editions. Unfortunately, Origen was erroneously cited in support of a different reading (reading 3) along with minuscule 38 in earlier editions of UBS/NA. The UBS Committee proposed a scenario where scribes softened Jesus's reply by

---

⁹⁶ A small number of manuscripts combine the shorter reading with γάρ: P75 Λ Ψ 69 157 1071 1424.

⁹⁷ Fee, "'One Thing Is Needful,'" 72.

⁹⁸ John J. Kilgallen has suggested, referring to BDF §452 (1), that γάρ in Luke 10:42 may refer not to Jesus's preceding words but to the dialogical situation to signal that a reason is being given for something unexpressed but real in the dialogue between Martha and Jesus ("A Suggestion Regarding *gar* in Luke 10,42," *Bib* 73 [1992]: 255–58).

replacing ἑνός with ὀλίγων and then two readings were conflated into the long reading. This explanation, which has influenced scholars and translations for decades, is untenable once the middle reading disappears. Why would scribes turn a straightforward reading into one that requires more explanation?

I argue, rather, that a development from the longer to the shorter reading corresponds best to the history of interpretation from the second to fifth centuries, which posits a growing dichotomy between the two sisters in the Greek East as well as the Latin West. This evidence suggests that a dualistic interpretation of the passage was facilitated by a scribal omission of the reference to "a few things," ὀλίγων/ *pauca*. In my opinion, the long reading in Luke 10:41–42 is the initial text.

A groundbreaking new portrait of the apostle Paul, from one of today's leading historians of antiquity

Paul
The Pagans' Apostle
Paula Fredriksen

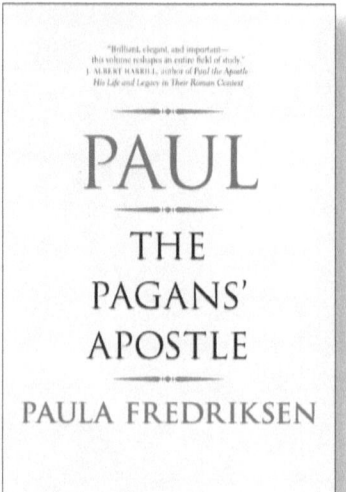

This original and provocative book offers a dramatically new perspective on one of history's seminal figures.

"Wide-ranging, deeply learned, but accessible. . . . A good source for historical context, a keen stimulus for rereading Paul's letters, and a great book to argue with."
— Sarah Ruden, *Commonweal*

"Brilliant, elegant, and important—this volume reshapes an entire field of study. Here stands the finest history of the Apostle Paul to appear in generations." — J. Albert Harrill, author of *Paul the Apostle: His Life and Legacy in Their Roman Context*

WINNER – THE ASSOCIATION OF AMERICAN PUBLISHERS' 2018 PROSE AWARD IN THEOLOGY AND RELIGIOUS STUDIES

Yale UNIVERSITY PRESS
www.YaleBooks.com

Double-Edged: The Meaning of the Two Swords in Luke 22:35–38

DAVID LERTIS MATSON
dlmatson@hiu.edu
Hope International University, Fullerton, CA 92831

Luke 22:38 often functions in a symbiotic relationship with Luke 22:51 to reinforce the picture of Jesus as a principled pacifist. If Jesus is countenancing some sort of violent action, his rebuke at his arrest makes it clear that he rejects the way of violence altogether. Some interpreters go so far as to suggest that Jesus commands the use of swords earlier precisely to rebuke their use later. Both verses, however, contain ambiguous Greek expressions, neither of which supports the contention that Jesus is rejecting violence per se. As with Luke 22:51, it is misguided to push Luke 22:38 in a pacifistic direction. The ambiguous ἱκανόν ἐστιν ("It is enough") is not a rhetorical ploy to cut the conversation short, nor does it mark out violence-prone disciples as the "lawless ones" of Isa 53. Rather, once released from the neutralizing effects of Luke 22:51 as an interpretive control, Luke 22:38 offers an altogether different picture of Jesus's stance toward violence.

Jesus's command to "buy a sword" in Luke 22:35–38 has proven problematic for readers of Luke, particularly for interpreters committed to the view that Jesus was a pacifist.[1] How can Jesus, the staunch proponent of nonviolent enemy love, encourage, much less command, his disciples to take up arms and then express satisfaction at their doing so?

To take the edge off this sharp Lukan pericope, commentators typically appeal to Jesus's rebuke of the sword-wielding disciple at Jesus's arrest: "No more of this!"

I wish to thank the two anonymous reviewers of this article for their helpful and insightful suggestions, as well as Joe Grana, Mark Huddleston, Robert Hull, and K. C. Richardson, who critiqued prior recensions of my work.

[1] The sword saying of Jesus has proven so defying for interpreters that Oscar Cullmann could remark over a generation ago: "The explanations suggested in the course of centuries are so numerous and diverse that it would be worthwhile to write a history of the exegesis of this saying" (*Jesus and the Revolutionaries*, trans. Gareth Putnam [New York: Harper & Row, 1970], 47 n. 21). For a useful taxonomy of recent interpretations, see Christopher R. Hutson, "Enough for What? Playacting Isaiah 53 in Luke 22:35–38," *ResQ* 55 (2013): 36–43. I am using the term *pacifist* to denote a principled stand against any and all forms of violence, including defensive measures.

(ἐᾶτε ἕως τούτου, Luke 22:51).² Jesus's stance toward violence here seems so unequivocal that his earlier command to purchase swords must surely admit of some other explanation. S. G. F. Brandon goes so far as to deem ἐᾶτε ἕως τούτου in Luke 22:51 a Lukan invention designed "to abate the implication of Jesus' arming of his disciples."³ Thus, Luke 22:38 and Luke 22:51 function in a symbiotic relationship to ensure Jesus's pacifist credentials.⁴

Rendering ἐᾶτε ἕως τούτου as a rebuke, however, is problematic at best, tendentious at worst, despite the prevalence of this translation since the publication of the RSV.⁵ The phrase literally reads, "Permit as far as this," and likely refers to Jesus's granting permission for his arrest. Jesus is not prohibiting the use of the sword per se but is telling his disciples to allow the arrest to go forward so that he may fulfill his twin destinies as Suffering Servant and Son of Man. This more natural reading of an enigmatic Lukan phrase removes a key plank in the argument that Jesus must not have meant the command to procure swords literally because he later condemns the wielding of the sword.

As in the case of Luke 22:51, Luke 22:38 contains its own enigmatic Greek expression. In response to the disciples' procurement of two swords, Jesus replies, "It is enough" (ἱκανόν ἐστιν). The ambiguity of this expression raises the same question as in 22:51: Is Jesus rebuking the disciples? If so, Jesus ends the conversation with an abrupt dismissal; if not, Jesus is literally remarking on the sufficiency of the swords. Only around the turn of the twentieth century do translations begin to treat the expression as a rebuke.⁶

I. Is Jesus Expressing a Rebuke?

The rather preposterous idea that the disciples could engage in violent anti-imperial activity with two measly swords leads some scholars to interpret Jesus's

---

²Unless otherwise indicated, all scriptural citations come from the NRSV.

³S. G. F. Brandon, *Jesus and the Zealots: A Study of the Political Factor in Primitive Christianity* (New York: Scribner's Sons, 1967), 317 n. 4.

⁴For example, Robert C. Tannehill thinks that Jesus "corrects the use of the sword and mends its damage in Luke 22:51" (*The Narrative Unity of Luke-Acts: A Literary Interpretation*, 2 vols. [Philadelphia: Fortress, 1986–1990], 1:268).

⁵See David Lertis Matson, "Pacifist Jesus? The (Mis)Translation of ἐᾶτε ἕως τούτου in Luke 22:51," *JBL* 134 (2015): 157–76, https://doi.org/10.15699/jbl.1341.2015.2848. The present essay assumes the reader's acquaintance with this earlier article throughout.

⁶Among the earliest was James Moffatt ("Enough! Enough!," 1913), who seems to have played a formative role in the history of English translation of *both* Luke 22:38 and 22:51. With regard to the latter, Moffatt's 1935 revision of ἐᾶτε ἕως τούτου, from "Let me do this at least," to "No more of that!" occurred while there was a lull in the Standard Bible Committee's work on the RSV, for which Moffatt was serving as general secretary. The RSV would eventually adopt a nearly identical translation. Adding a layer of intrigue, one wonders to what extent Moffatt's own evolution on the issue was impacting the work of the committee members, particularly Henry J. Cadbury and Edgar J. Goodspeed. See Matson, "Pacifist Jesus?," 169–76.

words in Luke 22:38 as a rebuke.[7] The disciples take Jesus's command literally when he is really speaking metaphorically. So Jesus cuts off the disciples' entire line of reasoning with an exasperated ἱκανόν ἐστιν ("it is enough!" or "enough of this!"), which is thought to reflect Semitic style for abruptly halting a conversation.[8]

This interpretation is popular but linguistically doubtful. The only real evidence for it comes from Deuteronomy, where the Lord summarily dismisses Moses's appeal to allow him entry into the promised land:

> "O Lord GOD, you have only begun to show your servant your greatness and your might; what god in heaven or on earth can perform deeds and mighty acts like yours! Let me cross over to see the good land beyond the Jordan, that good hill country and the Lebanon." But the LORD was angry with me on your account and would not heed me. The LORD said to me, "Enough from you! Never speak to me of this matter again!" (Deut 3:23–26)

The LXX translators render YHWH's rebuke of Moses in verse 26 with ἱκανούσθω σοι ("let it be enough to you"). The expression approaches a stylized formula in the LXX, occurring in the third-person singular imperative, followed almost always by a dative and an infinitive.[9] Given Luke's fondness for the LXX, he certainly was familiar with this expression and could have employed it in Luke 22:38. In fact, Luke never even uses the verb ἱκανόω in his two-volume work, a rather curious omission if Luke meant to convey this meaning.

By contrast, the adjective ἱκανός never occurs in connection with cutting off a conversation in the New Testament, the LXX, the Apostolic Fathers, Philo, or Josephus.[10] Luke shows a decided preference for the term, using it in twenty-seven of the thirty-nine instances in the New Testament but never with the meaning of

---

[7] Typical are Robert H. Stein, *Luke*, NAC (Nashville: Broadman, 1992), 556; R. Alan Culpepper, "The Gospel of Luke," *NIB* 9:3–490, here 430.

[8] See, e.g., Alfred Plummer, *A Critical and Exegetical Commentary on the Gospel according to S. Luke*, 5th ed. ICC (Edinburgh: T&T Clark, 1922), 507; I. Howard Marshall, *The Gospel of Luke: A Commentary on the Greek Text*, NIGTC (Grand Rapids: Eerdmans, 1978), 827; most recently, François Bovon, *Luke 3: A Commentary on the Gospel of Luke 19:28–24:53*, trans. James Crouch, Hermeneia (Minneapolis: Fortress, 2012), 183.

[9] See Num 16:7, Deut 1:6, 2:3, 3:26, 3 Kgdms 12:28, 19:4, 21:11, 1 Chr 21:15, Ezek 44:6, 45:9. Nowhere in these passages is the expression used to cut off a conversation except in the Deuteronomy example cited above.

[10] Nor does the term appear to have this meaning in the classical literature; see the standard entries in BDAG and LSJ. The closest one comes is in Philo, who occasionally uses ἱκανός (actually ἱκανῶς) as a literary segue (*Det.* 57; *Post.* 124; *Deus* 33; *Ebr.* 206; *Prov.* 2:42; see also Josephus *A.J.* 20.251; *C. Ap.* 2.288). But the term in these instances has no negative overtones and does not abruptly terminate a discussion. This usage could possibly make sense in Luke 22:38b if ἱκανόν ἐστιν is transitioning out of the entire discourse beginning at verse 14 (see John Nolland, *Luke*, 3 vols., WBC 35 [Dallas: Word, 1989–1993], 3:1077, who mentions it as a remote possibility). But this possibility is almost certainly ruled out by ὁ δὲ εἶπεν αὐτοῖς, which makes ἱκανόν ἐστιν a direct response to the disciples' statement. Taking Jesus's reply as a conclusion to the entire upper-room discourse would leave the disciples' statement hanging in midair.

exasperation or rebuke.¹¹ If Luke intends a rebuke in 22:38, the usage would certainly represent a significant linguistic departure from his usual practice.¹² It is not without warrant, therefore, that some scholars have questioned the presence of a rebuke in this verse.¹³ Confirming this judgment is the little-noticed fact that Codex Bezae substitutes the less ambiguous verb ἀρκέω, whose meaning denoting sufficiency or adequacy in the active voice is not in doubt.¹⁴ If the scribal tendency of the Western text to change words or phrases to provide greater clarity is operable here, it provides strong evidence of how Jesus's statement was understood in at least one prominent scribal tradition.¹⁵

In addition to these lexical and text-critical considerations, if Jesus were in fact rebuking his disciples in Luke 22:38, one wonders why Jesus expresses disgust at something that he commands his disciples to do. A more recent interpretation argues that the disciples misunderstand Jesus's intentions because of their sinfulness and hardness of heart. Robert C. Tannehill, for instance, following the lead of Paul S. Minear, thinks that the "lawless" (ἄνομος) among whom Jesus must be counted is none other than the disciples themselves, who are reacting out of blindness and fear.¹⁶

The fatal flaw in this creative interpretation is its importation of a distinctly *Markan* perspective into the Lukan text. Luke does *not* portray the disciples in a particularly negative light, certainly not to the extent of identifying the disciples as the lawless. Since space does not permit an extended discussion of Luke's

---

¹¹ The term in Luke always means "much" or "considerable" in relation to both time and numbers (W. von Meding, "ἱκανός," *NIDNTT* 3:728–30, here 729). Luke's usage lacks the theological significance sometimes attached to the term and its cognates by Paul (1 Cor 15:9, 2 Cor 2:16, 3:5–6; cf. Col 1:12). Given Luke's proclivity for ἱκανός, the absence of ἱκανόω in his writings is all the more striking.

¹² I am certainly mindful of the word-count fallacy here but do think that something is to be said for weighing an author's semantic preference, especially when that preference is so one-sided.

¹³ Joseph A. Fitzmyer, while still holding that Jesus is rebuking his disciples in Luke 22:38, nevertheless questions whether ἱκανόν ἐστιν is truly a Semitism somehow related to רַב־לָךְ (LXX ἱκανούσθω σοι) of Deut 3:26 (*The Gospel according to Luke: Introduction, Translation, and Notes*, 2 vols., AB 28, 28A [Garden City, NY: Doubleday, 1981–1985], 2:1434). So, too, Karl H. Rengstorf says that "we lack the necessary linguistic support for this view" ("ἱκανός, ἱκανότης, ἱκανόω," *TDNT* 3:293–96, here 295).

¹⁴ BDAG, s.v. "ἀρκέω" (see Matt 25:9, John 6:7, 14:8, 2 Cor 12:9). In the passive voice the word means to be satisfied or content with something (Luke 3:14, 1 Tim 6:8, Heb 13:5, 3 John 10).

¹⁵ G. W. H. Lampe notes that the Western text testifies to a literal interpretation of Luke 22:38 in antiquity ("The Two Swords [Luke 22:35–38]," in *Jesus and the Politics of His Day*, ed. Ernest Bammel and C. F. D Moule [Cambridge: Cambridge University Press, 1984], 335–51, here 349).

¹⁶ Tannehill, *Narrative Unity of Luke-Acts*, 1:267. See Paul S. Minear, "A Note on Luke xxii 36," *NovT* 7 (1964–1965): 128–34. So, too, Lampe thinks that the lawless ones are the disciples, anticipating their role in Luke 22:51 ("Two Swords," 346). Fitzmyer appropriately calls this line of interpretation "strange" (*Gospel according to Luke*, 2:1433).

redactional use of Mark, a few examples should suffice to cast sufficient doubt on Minear's proposal.[17]

First, Luke retains the three passion predictions inherited from his Markan source (Luke 9:21–22 [17:25]; 9:44; 18:31–33), but, unlike Mark, who underscores the disciples' failure to perceive or understand these predictions, Luke attributes the disciples' failure to divine purpose rather than spiritual obstinacy. After the first passion prediction, Luke omits Jesus's rebuke of Peter as the pawn of Satan and says nothing regarding the disciples' failure to understand Jesus's prophecy. After the second and third predictions, the disciples fail to understand, but divine passive constructions (ἦν παρακεκαλυμμένον ἀπ' αὐτῶν, "[its meaning] was concealed from them," Luke 9:45; ἦν . . . κεκρυμμένον ἀπ' αὐτῶν, "[what he said] was hidden from them," Luke 18:34) stress that their ignorance is not willful.[18] Under normal conditions the disciples are privy to eschatological secrets of old: "Blessed are the eyes that see *what you see*! For I tell you that many prophets and kings desired to see it, and to hear *what you hear*, but did not hear it" (Luke 10:23b–24). Such keen perception is simply untenable in Mark, who consistently portrays the disciples as failing to see and failing to hear.[19] In contrast, the disciples in Luke are far from blind or obtuse and thus worthy recipients of Jesus's pointed macarism.[20]

Second, and in even closer proximity to the swords passage, Luke brings his generally favorable treatment of the disciples into his Last Supper discourse. Most striking is Luke's omission of the prediction of the disciples' desertion (Mark 14:27) and the desertion itself (Mark 14:50); instead, the disciples stand by Jesus in his hour of need (Luke 22:28) and become rightful heirs of the kingdom over which

---

[17] Redaction criticism is at times a helpful aid in narrative analysis to help us see the distinctive elements in the Lukan text. For precedent, see Tannehill, *Narrative Unity of Luke-Acts*, 1:6, who employs a judicious use of redaction analysis in combination with narrative-critical analysis. I am obviously assuming Markan priority.

[18] A similar phenomenon occurs with the disciples on the road to Emmaus. Despite their slowness to perceive the prophetic writings (Luke 24:25), they have their eyes closed (οἱ δὲ ὀφθαλμοὶ αὐτῶν ἐκρατοῦντο, Luke 24:16) and then opened (αὐτῶν δὲ διηνοίχθησαν οἱ ὀφθαλμοί, Luke 24:31) by God so as to recognize Jesus in their midst. Later the disciples report that Jesus "had been made known" (ἐγνώσθη αὐτοῖς) in the breaking of the bread (Luke 24:35), again featuring a divine passive.

[19] Luke omits altogether Mark's severe denunciation of the disciples' hardness (Mark 8:16–21). For a study of characterization in Mark, see David Rhoads, Joanna Dewey, and Donald Michie, *Mark as Story: An Introduction to the Narrative of a Gospel*, 3rd ed. (Minneapolis: Fortress, 1999), 123–28. While admitting to some complexity in Mark's presentation, the authors nevertheless recognize that "the failures of the disciples constitute the primary literary device by which the narrator reveals Jesus' standards for discipleship" (125).

[20] In the immediate context of Luke 10:23b–24, Jesus is speaking to the seventy-two messengers who have returned from their Satan-defying mission to the nations (Luke 10:1, 17). That these seventy-two "others" include the Twelve is likely, though not certain; in 10:23a Luke calls the emissaries τοὺς μαθητάς, suggesting that he is not carefully distinguishing between the two groups.

they will rule (Luke 22:29–30).[21] True to form in Luke, the disciples remain faithful to Jesus to the end, when they reappear at the cross alongside certain women followers from Galilee (Luke 23:49).[22]

Third, Luke continues his sympathetic treatment of the disciples into his passion narrative. He reduces the Markan Jesus's threefold rebuke of the disciples to a single instance, omitting Peter's failure to stay awake (Mark 14:37; Luke 22:45–46). Furthermore, what little failure the disciples do display is attributable to a noble motive: excessive sorrow (ἀπὸ τῆς λύπης, Luke 22:45b). Thus, Luke minimizes the culpability of the disciples, if he does not exonerate them altogether.[23]

This highly perceptible Lukan *tendenz* makes it unlikely that Luke implicates the disciples as lawbreakers. Despite the growing popularity of Minear's view in recent years, his proposal remains unconvincing. Luke does not paint a perfect band of disciples, but neither does he sketch them in exceedingly negative terms.[24] Rather, a more natural reading of Luke suggests that Jesus was "counted among the lawless" (καὶ μετὰ ἀνόμων ἐλογίσθη) when he was crucified between two criminals (Luke 23:32–33). R. Alan Culpepper points to this passage as the "graphic fulfillment" of Isa 53:12.[25] Shortly after citing this prophecy, Jesus will be arrested as a common bandit (λῃστής) and thus reckoned among the lawless (Luke 22:52).[26]

---

[21] The perfect tense (διαμεμενηκότες) in Luke 22:28 should not be missed; the disciples have stood by Jesus during his entire ministry and will continue to stand with him to the end.

[22] However, the male disciples do not go to the tomb along with the women (Luke 23:55, 24:1), who report their findings to the apostles (Luke 24:9–10). On the likelihood of male disciples in Luke 23:49, Joel B. Green thinks that the οἱ γνωστοί "is a probable reference to the disciples and likely includes the apostles themselves, whose whereabouts have been unknown since the arrest (22:47–53)" (*The Gospel of Luke*, NICNT [Grand Rapids: Eerdmans, 1997], 828); so, too, Fitzmyer notes that, since the disciples never flee in Luke, some of them at least must be included in this group (*Gospel according to Luke*, 2:1520; see also his telling comments on Luke 22:28 [2:1418]). Thus, the disciples are imperfect but not failed disciples, since both the apostles and the women followers stand equally ἀπὸ μακρόθεν ("at a distance"), and Luke shows little interest in deprecating the women disciples.

[23] Marshall, *Gospel of Luke*, 833.

[24] For a somewhat different view of the disciples in Luke, see Joel B. Green, *The Theology of the Gospel of Luke*, NTT (Cambridge: Cambridge University Press, 1995), 103–4, who neglects or dismisses the positive elements in Luke's portrayal and fails to observe many of the Lukan redactions noted above. For Green, the disciples are passive recipients of Jesus's training until their commissioning, a training that they often fail to heed. For a treatment more in line with the view presented here, see W. R. Telford, *The Theology of the Gospel of Mark*, NTT (Cambridge: Cambridge University Press, 1999), 127–37.

[25] Culpepper, "Gospel of Luke," 430. An implied multiple reader like Theophilus is especially in position to make the connection.

[26] That Luke employs κακοῦργος in Luke 23:32, 33, 39 rather than ἄνομος does not spoil the parallel. Luke's only other usage of ἄνομος occurs in Acts 2:23, where it refers to gentiles (see also 1 Cor 9:21 and the related ἀνόμως in Rom 2:12), and Luke may have wanted to avoid confusion regarding the Jewish identity of the two criminals, who appear to hold zealot views (Luke

Unlike the new wine of Minear's proposal, this identification is not of recent vintage. A textual variant included by Erasmus in the Textus Receptus and appearing in Mark 15:28 in the dominant history of the English Bible (Tyndale, GNV [Geneva Bible], Bishops' Bible, KJV) provides a valuable window into the way at least some ancient readers interpreted Luke. First, the Markan wording of Isa 53:12 matches that of Luke exactly (καὶ μετὰ ἀνόμων ἐλογίσθη), strongly suggesting that the variant originated as a marginal gloss added by a copyist under the influence of Luke 22:37.[27] Second, the placement of the prophecy immediately following Mark's reference to the two robbers (Mark 15:27) makes it certain that the copyist saw the Isaianic prophecy in Luke 22:37 as applying to Jesus's crucifixion between two lawbreakers. This specific application is in full accord with Luke's own literary aims.[28] While Luke can point to the general fulfillment of prophecy (Luke 18:31; 21:22; 24:27, 44), at times he shows interest in the specific details (Luke 4:21, Acts 1:16).[29] Jesus's crucifixion between two criminals is one of those details.

II. Is Jesus Expressing Sufficiency for the Swords?

If Jesus is not expressing exasperation or rebuke, why does he think that swords are necessary?[30] And how many swords do the disciples actually have? Luke

---

23:39-41; so Marshall, *Gospel of Luke*, 871). Luke may also have simply found κακοῦργος in his source. At any rate, the term is sufficiently broad to cover any actions of an ἄνομος.

[27] Bruce M. Metzger, *A Textual Commentary on the Greek New Testament*, 2nd ed. (New York: United Bible Societies, 1994), 99. The variant is attested in some late uncials (L, Δ, Θ) and minuscules (f^1, f^{13}) but is missing from the earliest and best witnesses of both the Alexandrian and Western text-types (ℵ, B, C, D). Luke's language (καὶ μετὰ ἀνόμων ἐλογίσθη) does not correspond exactly to the LXX (καὶ ἐν τοῖς ἀνόμοις ἐλογίσθη). Luke's substitution of μετὰ for ἐν and omission of τοῖς may reflect more the influence of the MT (so Darrell L. Bock, *Luke*, 2 vols., BECNT 3 [Grand Rapids: Baker, 1994-1996], 2:1747; Fitzmyer, *Gospel according to Luke*, 2:1432). Contra Luke Timothy Johnson, who thinks that Luke is still writing under the influence of the LXX (*The Gospel of Luke*, SP 3 [Collegeville, MN: Liturgical Press, 1991], 347). At any rate, the precise correspondence between Luke and Mark is striking.

[28] Fitzmyer is typical of many commentators who see only a generalized fulfillment, such as when he says that "the real meaning of introducing the quotation from Isaiah is to make clear that if Jesus is to be so treated, so will his followers" (*Gospel according to Luke*, 2:1433). Nolland rejects the allusion to the two criminals altogether, opting for a general picture of a violent fate, though he later contradicts himself when he remarks that Luke 23:32 recalls the language of 22:37, putting Jesus in company with "lawless people" (*Luke*, 3:1138). While Luke can speak in the plural of "the things" (τὰ περί) fulfilled by Jesus (24:19, 27), in 22:37 it is a singular "thing" (τὸ περὶ ἐμοῦ) that Jesus must fulfill.

[29] Commenting on Judas's abdication and replacement in Acts 1:16, for example, Leon Morris writes, "Notice that the fulfillment here concerns not simply the general idea, not even the main event, but the *detail* of Judas' part in the betrayal. The whole thing was minutely planned by God" (*The Cross in the New Testament* [Grand Rapids: Eerdmans, 1965], 123; emphasis added).

[30] Chrysostom (*Hom. Matt.* 84.1) believed that the swords were really butcher knives used for carving the paschal lamb, a possible meaning of μάχαιρα (LSJ, s.v. μάχαιρα), a view defended

seems to indicate that they possess only two (22:38a), but further reading reveals that the arresting party led by Judas anticipates conflict on a much grander scale (22:52).[31] Since Judas was a member of the Twelve, Judas would certainly know the level of threat, if any, posed by Jesus and his disciples.[32] A "pacifist" Jesus of popular cultural imagination and in some strains of liberal Protestant theology has difficulty accounting for the degree of armed resistance expected by Judas and the arresting party.[33]

Yet, if the number of swords possessed by the disciples is only two, as Luke's wording seems to indicate, what purpose could they possibly serve? Recently, Dale B. Martin has argued that the historical Jesus expected his disciples to join in an apocalyptic battle with the heavenly angels against Rome and their clients, the Jewish temple authorities.[34] In this construal, the number of swords is immaterial,

---

by Frederick Field, citing Dionysius of Halicarnassus (*Ant. Rom.* 11.37; *Notes on the Translation of the New Testament* [Cambridge: Cambridge University Press, 1899; repr., Eugene, OR: Wipf & Stock, 2005], 76–77). Luke does not mention a sheath as do Matthew (26:52) and John (18:11), an omission that could support Chrysostom's interpretation. The μάχαιρα was typically the short sword or dagger, approximately sixteen inches or less (cf. Judg 3:16), used by ancient cavalry, to be distinguished from the ῥομφαία, a longer sword used for cutting and piercing and thus an apt spiritual metaphor in Luke 2:35, the only place where Luke uses it. Like the Hebrew חרב, however, μάχαιρα seems to cover several different types of implements: "What distinguishes a butcher knife from a soldier's dagger is the context in which the implement is used" (Mark J. Fretz, "Weapons and Implements of Warfare," *ABD* 6:893–95, here 893). R. C. H. Lenski surmises that the swords were already in the upper room, hanging on the wall (*The Interpretation of St. Luke's Gospel* [Minneapolis: Augsburg, 1946], 1070–71).

[31] I am assuming that the arresting party led by Judas (22:47) comprised chief priests, temple officials, and elders (22:52). Lampe points out that ὁ μὴ ἔχων in 22:36 implies that some of the disciples *do* possess swords ("Two Swords," 347). How many, of course, is the question. Robert Eisler postulates that the disciples possess two swords each (in Brandon, *Jesus and the Zealots*, 341 n. 1). See Robert Eisler, *The Messiah Jesus and John the Baptist according to Flavius Josephus' Recently Discovered "Capture of Jerusalem" and the Other Jewish and Christian Sources*, trans. Alexander Haggerty Krappe (New York: Dial, 1931), 369.

[32] Brandon surmises that "Judas had given warning that the disciples were well armed and that armed resistance was to be expected" (*Jesus and the Zealots*, 341). (I will qualify this conjecture later [see n. 40].) One might chalk this militaristic expectation up to the disciples' preresurrection understanding of Jesus (cf. Luke 24:21), but Acts 1:6 indicates that even after the resurrection (and after forty days of instruction by Jesus!) the disciples were still expecting some kind of armed response, perhaps in connection with the eschatological promise of Luke 22:28–30. How else would the kingdom to Israel be restored? Strikingly, Jesus does not rebuke the disciples but recasts their question in terms of worldwide gospel witness (Acts 1:7–8). The "preresurrection" question concerning the use of the sword in Luke 22:49 finds its natural counterpart in the "postresurrection" question concerning the time of kingdom restoration in Acts 1:6. In both, the disciples address Jesus as "Lord."

[33] Mark (14:43, 48), Matthew (26:47, 55), and John (18:3) all present the arresting party as armed to the hilt.

[34] Dale B. Martin, "Jesus in Jerusalem: Armed and Not Dangerous," *JSNT* 37 (2014): 3–24,

since Jesus and his disciples expected the imminent appearance of a heavenly army who will fight for and alongside them. A similar expectation expressed in a prayer preserved at Qumran reads:

> For Thou will fight with them from heaven.... For the multitude of the Holy Ones [is with Thee] in heaven, and the host of the Angels is in Thy holy abode, praising Thy name. And Thou hast established in [a community] for Thyself the elect of Thy holy people. Thou wilt muster the [hosts of] Thine [el]ect, in their Thousands and Myriads, with Thy Holy Ones [and with all] Thine Angels, that they may be mighty in battle, [and may smite] the rebels of the earth by Thy great judgments, and that [they may triumph] together with the elect of heaven. For Thou art [terrible], O God, in the glory of Thy kingdom, and the congregation of Thy Holy Ones is among us for everlasting succor. We will despise kings, we will mock and scorn the mighty; for our Lord is holy, and the King of Glory is with us together with the Holy Ones. Valiant [warriors] of the angelic host are among our numbered men. (1QM XII, 1–8)[35]

Here the hosts of heaven assist the elect in their fight against the Kittim (most likely Rome) in "the war of the heavenly warriors" (1QH XI, 35). In like manner, at the outbreak of the Jewish War instigated by the Zealots, Josephus reports that "chariots were seen high in the air all around the country and armed battalions rushing through the clouds encircling the cities" (B.J. 6.297–99).[36] In this intense apocalyptic situation, two swords may well be "enough," at least initially.[37]

---

esp. 6–7, 17–18. In some respects, Martin is reviving the older interpretation of Jesus as a political revolutionary seen, most notably, in Brandon, *Jesus and the Zealots*. Another recent argument in this direction is Reza Aslan, *Zealot: The Life and Times of Jesus of Nazareth* (New York: Random House, 2013). In contrast to these studies, I am arguing on the level of the Lukan narrative, not the historical Jesus. Where historical arguments intersect with the Lukan presentation, they are relevant to our discussion.

[35] Trans. Geza Vermes, ed., *The Complete Dead Sea Scrolls in English*, 4th ed. (London: Penguin Books, 1997), 175. The War Scroll is not a realistic military guide but relies "on divine and angelic aid rather than on military power" (John J. Collins, "Dead Sea Scrolls," *ABD* 2:85–101, here 96). Martin does not actually cite any passage from the War Scroll, but I assume that he has in mind passages like the one quoted above. For biblical examples of synergistic warfare, see Judg 5:20, 23; 2 Chr 14:11–12; 32:21.

[36] Cited in Richard A. Horsley and John S. Hanson, *Bandits, Prophets, and Messiahs: Popular Movements in the Time of Jesus* (San Francisco: Harper & Row, 1985), 182–83. They comment, "Here are the collective fantasies of God and the heavenly armies rushing through the clouds in anticipated relief of the oppressed—and about to be embattled—chosen people."

[37] Martin thinks that most, if not all, of Jesus's disciples were armed based on evidence from Mark's text considered in isolation. He further thinks that Luke limits the swords to two to counter the perception of Jesus as a political revolutionary ("Jesus in Jerusalem," 5–6). In biblical portrayals, angels are superior in strength (Ps 103:20, 2 Pet 2:11), sometimes wield swords (Num 22:23; Josh 5:13; 1 Chr 21:16, 30; 2 Macc 5:3; 3 En. 22:6), and fight on behalf of the people of God (Exod 23:20, 33:2, 2 Kgs 6:17, 2 Macc 3:22–30, 5:2–3, 10:29–31, 11:6–12, 15:22–27, 3 Macc 6:18–19, 4 Macc 4:10–11, T. Levi 3:3; 1 QM VII, 6; XIII, 10; XIX, 1; Matt 25:31, 26:53, 2 Thess 1:7–8, Jude 14–15).

While Luke is certainly aware of the military might of angels, who constitute the heavenly "army" (στρατιά, Luke 2:13, Acts 7:42), such a fantastic scenario is absent from Luke's account. Martin admits that his historical reconstruction conflicts with the literary presentation in Luke, who downplays any notion that Jesus was a political revolutionary.[38]

A similar interpretation posits that Luke wants Jesus to *appear* in the guise of a political revolutionary, enough to get himself arrested and "counted among the lawless" (22:37), thus fulfilling his role as Isaiah's Suffering Servant (Isa 53:12). On this interpretation, two swords would be sufficient.[39] This interpretation has more to commend it, but a couple of problems remain. On a macro level, the generally *pro imperio* perspective of Luke-Acts argues against the notion that Luke desires to present Jesus as a political revolutionary. On a micro level, the chief priests had *already determined* to do away with Jesus in the story line of Luke (19:47, 20:19, 22:2). The arresting party comes predetermined to seize Jesus without necessarily any knowledge about Jesus's private communication in the upper room with his disciples about swords.[40] Moreover, the possession of two swords would not necessarily carry revolutionary overtones since swords were often an essential accoutrement for travelers in first-century Israel. This point is underscored by the fact that armament plays no role in Jesus's trial before Pilate.[41] One must also keep in mind

---

During the Assyrian assault on Judah, a single angel was capable of wiping out 185,000 men (2 Kgs 19:35, Isa 37:36), a feat that left an indelible mark in the memory of Second Temple Judaism (2 Macc 15:22, 2 Bar. 63:7).

[38] According to Martin, Luke surpasses his Synoptic counterparts in explaining away "any rebellious or political significance of the idea that Jesus' disciples may indeed have been armed at his arrest" ("Jesus in Jerusalem," 6). C. Kavin Rowe's more recent attempt at a via media between pro- and anti-imperial perspectives recognizes Luke's fundamental presentation of the Christian way as innocent of the charge of στάσις (*World Upside Down: Reading Acts in the Graeco-Roman Age* [Oxford: Oxford University Press, 2010], 53–89). His view of the Way as a force for cultural destabilization, however, runs up against the hard fact of the Christian centurion, who successfully negotiates between his Christian and Roman identities. Would that Rowe had engaged Philip F. Esler on the question of legitimation in Luke-Acts (*Community and Gospel in Luke-Acts: The Social and Political Motivations of Lucan Theology*, SNTSMS 57 [Cambridge: Cambridge University Press, 1987], 205–19).

[39] See, most recently, Craig S. Keener, *The IVP Bible Background Commentary*, 2nd ed. (Downers Grove, IL: InterVarsity Press, 2014), 237.

[40] This narrative feature also presents a serious obstacle for Hutson's view that the two swords "function as props so that the whole group can appear to the authorities like a band of miscreants skulking around on the Mount of Olives in the middle of the night" ("Enough for What?," 50). Luke is silent as to when Judas departed from the upper room. Whether or not Judas was present to hear Jesus's specific sword instructions, as a member of the Twelve, he could already assess the potential for violence.

[41] This point must be carefully weighed, since two seemingly contradictory assertions sometimes appear in the scholarly literature, namely, that swords were expensive and difficult to obtain and that they belonged to the standard equipment of the Jewish traveler (for the latter, see Martin

the context of the Passover: given the large number of Passover lambs that had to be prepared at that time and the stipulation that the Passover had to be eaten inside Jerusalem's walls, the city would seemingly be teeming with knives.[42]

III. Is Jesus Establishing a Rear Guard?

What, then, is the key for understanding Jesus's directive to procure swords? The enigmatic character of the saying forces one to look for clues, however subtle. A decisive clue often overlooked is Jesus's own expressed *reason* or *rationale* for the procurement of swords:

> He said to them, "But now, the one who has a purse must take it, and likewise a bag. And the one who has no sword must sell his cloak and buy one. For [γάρ] I tell you, this scripture must be fulfilled in me, 'And he was counted among the lawless'; and [γάρ] indeed what is written about me is being fulfilled." (Luke 22:36-37)

In this text, the conjunction γάρ (unfortunately left untranslated in the NIV and CEB) functions as a connective to a previous assertion.[43] Modern linguistic analysis confirms the older grammatical view that the primary function of γάρ is to

---

Hengel, *Was Jesus a Revolutionist?*, trans. William Klassen, FBBS 28 [Philadelphia: Fortress, 1971], 21–22). Josephus speaks about workers on Nehemiah's temple having ready access to swords (*A.J.* 11.177) and how Essenes often armed themselves (ἔνοπλοι) for protection against bandits when they traveled (*B.J.* 2.125). Martin claims that carrying swords inside Rome and other Greco-Roman cities was illegal and would have attracted the attention of the authorities ("Jesus in Jerusalem," 7–9), but whether those strictures pertained to a city like Jerusalem is doubtful, particularly when Israelite heads of households were slitting the throats of sacrificial victims in the temple precincts (cf. Luke 13:1; Josephus, *A.J.* 17.216; see Alfred Edersheim, *The Life and Times of Jesus the Messiah* [1883; repr., Peabody, MA: Hendrickson, 1993], 810). Martin overlooks Vespasian's ending the practice of searching imperial visitors, which would assume the presence of knives in Rome (Suetonious, *Vesp.* 12.; cf. *Claud.* 13, 36; I thank K. C. Richardson for pointing out these references). That Peter and John were charged by Jesus with preparing the Passover (Luke 22:7-13) presumes that they had ready access to implements of some sort.

[42] How many knives were deposited in the temple in a room known as the בית החליפות ("chamber of knives") is uncertain. (I here rely on a personal observation of Joshua Garroway.) In my opinion, the number must have been considerable. Even if Josephus's estimate of 255,600 Passover lambs slaughtered in the temple precincts is an exaggeration (*B.J.* 6.424; cf. *A.J.* 17.213), one must still reckon with an extraordinary number of sacrificial victims. Martin's argument that no lamb was present at the Last Supper is unconvincing in light of the clear linguistic connection in Luke 22:7-8 ("Jesus in Jerusalem," 16–17; so rightly Lenski, *Interpretation of St. Luke's Gospel*, 1036–37).

[43] BDAG (s.v. γάρ) assigns an explanatory function to the use of the term in Luke 22:37. The conjunction can sometimes function simply as a narrative marker, but its explanatory function is readily observable here.

explain or provide rationale for a previous assertion; the conjunction does not advance the discussion but strengthens or supports what precedes.[44]

The relationship between the two γάρ clauses is not entirely clear. The first clause relates back to the main clause of verse 36b and establishes the reason why the disciples must sell their cloaks and buy a sword—to ensure fulfillment of the Isaianic prophecy.[45] If the second clause is grammatically coordinate with the first, it restates the rationale in slightly different form but with essentially the same meaning (taking ἔχει as a futuristic present).[46] However, if the object of ἔχει has the "end" (τέλος) of Jesus's life in view, the second γάρ could be subordinate to the first, explaining how Jesus's fulfilling the Isaianic prophecy will eventuate in his death.[47] Despite this ambiguity, less uncertain is the role of the first clause in providing the reason why swords must be procured.

Determining the extent to which Luke sees Jesus fulfilling Isa 53 with its theme of vicarious suffering lies beyond the scope of this article.[48] Relevant here is the simple but important insight that Jesus instructs the disciples to procure swords expressly to ensure that he will be counted among lawbreakers. The strong adversative ἀλλὰ νῦν ("but now"), which prefaces Jesus's command to buy swords (22:36a),

---

[44] Steven E. Runge, *Discourse Grammar of the Greek New Testament: A Practical Introduction for Teaching and Exegesis*, Lexham Bible Reference Series (Peabody, MA: Hendrickson, 2010), 52. Thus, verse 37 should not be dismissed simply as an intrusion into the text, interrupting the flow of discourse between verses 36 and 38. Even if Luke is working with sources, one must still reckon with the function of verse 37 in its present location.

[45] Does γάρ in verse 37a ground *all* of verse 36 (both ὁ ἔχων and ὁ μὴ ἔχων clauses) or verse 36b only? If the former, one wonders how purse and bag help fulfill the prophecy; if the latter, only the swords relate to the scriptural fulfillment. That the disciples respond only to the sword directive (v. 38a) points strongly to the latter. In this case, purse and bag may enjoy a wider application than the swords, looking beyond the immediate situation.

[46] See the futuristic present renderings in the CEB, HCSB, NAB, NIV, and NLT. Contra Green, *Gospel of Luke*, 776, whose interpretation is overly dependent on ἔχει construed as a continuous present.

[47] Morris subscribes to this second view, arguing that καὶ γὰρ τὸ περὶ ἐμοῦ τέλος ἔχει means something like "Indeed for me the course is run" (Morris, *Cross in New Testament*, 76, relying on the translation of E. V. Rieu, *The Four Gospels: A New Translation from the Greek* [Baltimore: Penguin, 1953]). I prefer to take the two γάρ clauses as parallel, despite Nolland's concern about repetitiveness (*Luke*, 3:1077). Nolland thinks the τέλος of 22:37 should be linked to the τελειοῦμαι of 13:32 (ibid).

[48] See the more recent essays in William H. Bellinger Jr. and William R. Farmer, eds., *Jesus and the Suffering Servant: Isaiah 53 and Christian Origins* (Harrisburg, PA: Trinity Press International, 1998), especially the contrasting essays by Otto Betz ("Jesus and Isaiah 53") and Morna D. Hooker ("Did the Use of Isaiah 53 to Interpret His Mission Begin with Jesus?"). For Hooker's landmark study denying an essential link between Jesus and Isa 53, see her *Jesus the Servant: The Influence of the Servant Concept of Deutero-Isaiah in the New Testament* (London: SPCK, 1959). For a recent maximalist approach to Isa 53, see the essays in Darrell L. Bock and Mitch Glaser, eds., *The Gospel according to Isaiah 53: Encountering the Suffering Servant in Jewish and Christian Theology* (Grand Rapids: Kregel, 2012).

introduces a decisive temporal break with what has gone before. Previously the disciples labored under the idyllic reign of God during the one year of Jesus's ministry when Satan was absent (4:13); now that Satan has returned and entered into the heart of Judas (22:3), they can no longer expect the same protective conditions. The time has come when swords may be necessary.[49]

Necessary for what? While it is true that the disciples do not wield swords in the course of their mission in Acts, this point can be overstated; in Acts disciples do not carry purses or bags either.[50] Since the disciples are responding directly to Jesus's sword directive (Luke 22:38a), one should not look ahead to the future mission in Luke's second volume but rather stay within the immediate context of Luke's narrative. This methodological procedure allows a more pedestrian explanation to emerge, yet one imbued with deeper significance.

Ever since Jesus first entered Jerusalem and commandeered the temple precincts for his teaching activity, the chief priests and the scribes were looking for a way to kill him, but Jesus's popularity with the people frustrates their attempts (Luke 19:47–48). At one point Luke even says that they desired to lay their hands on Jesus "at that very hour" but feared the people's reaction (20:19), a detail found only in Luke. Nevertheless, the chief priests and the scribes keep a close eye on Jesus, sending spies to trap him in something that he might say so as to have grounds for sending him to the Roman governor (20:20), another detail unique to Luke. As Passover drew near, Luke says that the chief priests and the scribes were looking for a way to put Jesus to death (22:1–2), omitting Mark's comment that the priestly authorities sought him by stealth (Mark 14:2). The Lukan passages show that the chief priests and scribes posed a clear and present danger to Jesus *throughout his entire tenure in Jerusalem*, perhaps explaining why Jesus refused to stay in the city overnight (21:37; 22:10, 39).[51] The imminent threat to Jesus's life explains why Jesus acted so secretively to secure a venue within the city for eating the Passover (22:7–13). Jesus will be arrested on his terms, not theirs.

Here, then, is an important clue to the function of the swords. Rather than acting as transgressors, the disciples are prepared to take defensive measures to ensure Jesus's safe arrival at the Mount of Olives, Jesus's destination of choice and

---

[49] I am following Hans Conzelmann's threefold Lukan temporal schema without subscribing to all of the particulars (*The Theology of St. Luke*, trans. Geoffrey Buswell [Philadelphia: Fortress, 1982]).

[50] One can only presume that Acts' missionaries traveled with bag (βαλλάντιον) and purse (πήρα) since Luke nowhere mentions them. Are we to assume from this omission that Luke intends the same negative attitude toward bags and purses as he supposedly intends toward swords?

[51] Noted by Brandon, *Jesus and the Zealots*, 339–40, 342. John 11:57 is illuminating here: "Now the chief priests and the Pharisees had given orders that anyone who knew where Jesus was should let them know, so that they might arrest him." Luke assumes a similar if not more precarious situation.

customary place of prayer.⁵² That the disciples later instinctively ask Jesus if they should employ their swords (22:49) is telling; by giving his disciples prior instruction about swords, Jesus has prepared his disciples for just such a possibility.⁵³ At this point it is helpful to recall the meaning of ἐᾶτε ἕως τούτου in Luke 22:51 ("permit as far as this," that is, "let the arrest proceed"). God's plan must go forward, and the disciples have a role to play.

Luke narrates Jesus's journey to the Mount of Olives immediately after the instructions about the swords (22:39). A subtle note of divine determinacy is detectable in Luke's description.⁵⁴ Once there, Jesus will pray and undergo arrest, setting in motion the events leading to his crucifixion between two criminals in fulfillment of Isa 53. Jesus will "go" the way of the Son of Man as it has been determined (22:22), and being attacked by the priestly authorities or their henchmen on his way out of the city is not part of that plan.⁵⁵ Not just the occurrence but the mode of Jesus's death is ordained by God (Acts 2:23; cf. 20:28).⁵⁶ Thus, when Jesus encounters the arresting party led by Judas (Luke 22:47), the betrayer is simply acting out his divinely assigned role (22:21–22). God, not the chief priests, is in control of Jesus's destiny.

---

⁵²Lenski mentions safe escort out of the city as a possible explanation for the swords but rejects this interpretation, supposing that the city was peaceful and quiet. Passover, of course, was anything but a tranquil time politically. Lenski further fails to consider the plotting of the priestly authorities, who have been targeting Jesus ever since he made his first appearance in Jerusalem (*Interpretation of St. Luke's Gospel*, 1071). Plummer suggests that the disciples had already armed themselves with swords to guard against bandits on their journey from Galilee. Thus, the swords could well have performed a similar defensive function, protecting Jesus lest he be subject to attack on his way out of the city (*Gospel according to* St. *Luke*, 506).

⁵³Only in Luke do the disciples pose this question to Jesus, as only in Luke does Jesus give them prior instructions about swords. Thus, Hutson is off-base when he writes, "The disciples' readiness to use swords in 22:49–50 is a misunderstanding of Jesus' intention in 22:35–38" ("Enough for What?," 37). The disciples' question in Acts 1:6 implies a similar readiness to use swords, albeit on a much grander scale.

⁵⁴The verb πορεύω often carries implications of divine direction in Luke (Fitzmyer, *Gospel according to Luke*, 1:166–69; Bock, *Luke*, 1:420).

⁵⁵Though Luke indicates at one point that the authorities are willing to give Jesus up to the Romans (20:20), Luke also indicates the willingness of the chief priests to put Jesus to death directly (19:47, 22:2). The verbs used in these passages (ἀπόλλυμι, ἀναιρέω) suggest killing Jesus directly (cf. they "were seeking to assassinate him" [19:47, NET]). The verb ἀναιρέω typically denotes killing via battle, execution, murder, or assassination (BDAG, s.v. "ἀναιρέω"). Whether or not the Jerusalem leaders had the right to inflict the death penalty in cases related to the temple, in Luke's narrative the priestly authorities are willing to take matters into their own hands, as they were later against the apostles (Acts 5:33) and against Paul (Acts 23:12–15, 27; 25:3). In a similar manner, the Damascene Jews and Hellenistic Jews of Jerusalem seek to kill Saul without recourse to legal proceedings (Acts 9:23–24, 29). Luke, of course, will go on to narrate an illegal execution in the death of Stephen (Acts 8:54–60), who dies at the hands of a mob.

⁵⁶The word προσπήξαντες ("having fixed/fastened," i.e., "nailed") in Acts 2:23 is likely a participle of means. Crucifixion as a mode of death is thus part of the ὅσα ("what things") predestined by God (Acts 4:28).

This interpretation, of course, presupposes that the swords are literal. While some degree of hyperbole is discernible in Jesus's instructions, such as the willingness to sell one's "cloak" (ἱμάτιον), an inalienable possession under Jewish law (Exod 22:26-27), such hyperbole serves in this instance to underscore the urgency of Jesus's sword directive.[57] Hyperbolic language does not necessarily preclude a practical and immediate application of Jesus's words.[58]

A modern bas-relief at the Church of Saint Peter in Gallicantu in Jerusalem depicts Jesus and the disciples en route to the Mount of Olives. Note the presence of two staffs (Luke's "swords"?), one at the front and the other at the back, presumably for defensive measures. Photo by Staci Nakamura Matson (2017).

Several factors point to the literalness of Jesus's command. First, the disciples' response, "Lord, look, here are two swords" (22:38a), clearly assumes that the disciples understand Jesus literally. Little justification exists in Luke for thinking that the disciples misunderstand Jesus due to blindness or obstinacy; in calling Jesus "Lord," the disciples are expressing their obedience, not their disobedience. Second, Jesus's response, "it is enough" (ἱκανόν ἐστιν), is further evidence that Jesus understands the disciples literally. As indicated earlier, no linguistic evidence supports interpreting these words as a dismissive rebuke; rather, Jesus's words should be accorded their natural meaning of sufficiency, especially in a context where numerical quantity is the immediate point at hand.[59] Third, Jesus prefaces his

---

[57] That the disciples already possess swords suggests that Jesus is simply underscoring the urgency of the situation in the hyperbolic language of selling and buying. Peter and John certainly possessed implements with which they slaughtered and (presumably) carved the Paschal lamb (Luke 22:7-8).

[58] Contra Johnson, *Gospel of Luke*, 347.

[59] The use of the singular ἐστιν suggests that Jesus sees the two swords as a single entity and treats them as such—hence "That is enough"/"That's enough" (1984 NIV, TNIV, NCV [New Century Version], Scholars Version, NLT) or "That will do" (Fenton). Codex Bezae retains the third-person singular (ἀρκεῖ), even when the choice of verb indicates that Jesus is commenting

instructions to the disciples by pointing back to an earlier time when he sent them out without purse, bag, or sandals (22:35; see 10:4).[60] If these words had a literal application on their first occasion, why not on their second? Why would Jesus establish a literal interpretive framework in the minds of the disciples (and the reader) only to castigate them for responding with a literal answer? Tannehill admits: "If the instructions about purse and bag are literal instructions for the church's mission, it is not clear why the instruction about the sword should be interpreted metaphorically."[61]

The upshot of all these exegetical observations is that the swords function literally to get Jesus safely to the Mount of Olives, advancing the plot of the story and setting in motion the particulars of the divine plan. But why is it necessary for Jesus to reach the Mount of Olives? Could not Jesus merely have been apprehended on his way out of the city, leading to the same inevitable result?

IV. Jesus on the Mount of Olives

At least part of the answer involves recognizing the special role that the Mount of Olives plays in the ministry and passion of the Lukan Jesus. Recall here that even the geographical movements of Jesus are subject to divine control in Luke (22:22).[62] As the location of Judas's predicted betrayal, the Mount of Olives assumes its own predetermined role in the divine drama. Luke always directs the reader's attention to this mount (19:29, 37; 21:37; 22:39; Acts 1:12)—never to Gethsemane (à la Mark and Matthew) or a garden (à la John)—often calling attention to its name (τὸ καλούμενον, Luke 19:29, 21:37, Acts 1:12). That Luke thinks of this mount as "a sabbath day's journey" from Jerusalem (Acts 1:12b), referring to the maximum distance that could be traveled on the Sabbath, provides realism to Jesus's command since two swords would seemingly be enough to ward off any would-be attackers.[63]

The Mount of Olives occupies a special place in Lukan topography. Only Luke

---

literally on the quantity of the swords. W. Western thinks that the impersonal force of ἱκανόν ἐστιν is best explained as Jesus assessing the length of the disciples' fishing knives to see if they "are large enough for the all the fighting you need to do" ("The Enigma of the Swords, St. Luke 22:38," *ExpTim* 52 [1940–1941]: 357). Even more improbable is that ἐστιν refers not to the swords but to the point that Jesus is making: "it is enough that you recognize this."

[60] Curiously, the reference is to the sending out of the seventy-two, not to the Twelve (Luke 9:3).

[61] Tannehill, *Narrative Unity of Luke-Acts*, 1:267. Noting Paul's encounters with robbers and brigands (2 Cor 11:26), Lenski thinks that literal swords were necessary for protection in the course of missionary travel: "The language is not figurative. Purse, wallet, sword are not to be allegorized into something spiritual as the ancient fathers thought they must be" (*Interpretation of St. Luke's Gospel*, 1068).

[62] On the importance of πορεύω, see n. 54 above.

[63] A Sabbath day's journey of approximately two thousand cubits was calculated based on the conflation of Exod 16:29 and Num 35:5, measured from the walls of Jerusalem. In his estimate

recounts that Jesus regularly spent the night outside the city on this mount (21:37) and that it was his "custom" or habit (ἔθος) to go there often (22:39).[64] Judas later leads the arresting party there, suggesting that the location was familiar and prearranged, for Judas knew the place (Luke 22:47, Acts 1:16).[65] This unique emphasis attaches greater importance to the Mount of Olives than the limited references in Luke might indicate.

Why does Luke accord the Mount of Olives such importance, so much that he has Jesus enlist the use of swords to ensure his safe arrival there? The prayer scene on the Mount of Olives (22:39–46) provides a clue. Immediately upon leaving the upper room, Jesus goes out to the Mount of Olives (22:39), leading his disciples to "the place" (ὁ τόπος) where he desired that he and his disciples should pray (22:40). Luke's wording intimates that Jesus had a specific locale in mind. That it was customary for Jesus to go to this place suggests that Jesus has prayed there before.[66] Only in Luke does Jesus proceed to command his disciples to pray; in Mark, Jesus initially commands his disciples only to sit and watch while Jesus himself prays (Mark 14:32, 34).[67] After walking a short distance, Jesus kneels and prays, asking his Father to remove the cup from him while at the same time expressing his desire to obey his Father's will (Luke 22:41–42). Luke adds poignancy to the scene by depicting Jesus's rising from prayer, a detail absent in Mark and Matthew. Jesus finds the disciples sleeping due to their grief and exhorts them once again to pray (22:45–46). In this way the Mount of Olives functions for Luke as a mountain of prayer.[68] Offering prayer and solitude as well as a place of communion for Jesus and his disciples, the Mount of Olives becomes the strategic launch pad for Jesus's twin destinies as Suffering Servant and Son of Man.[69]

---

of the distance from Jerusalem to the Mount of Olives, Josephus is slightly inconsistent, mentioning six στάδια in the *War* (*B.J.* 5.70) and five στάδια in *Antiquities* (*A.J.* 20.169).

[64] The imperfect ηὐλίζετο in Luke 21:37 is likely customary: "he used to go to the Mount of Olives," that is, as a matter of course or habit. Whereas Mark (11:11) and Matthew (21:17) indicate that Jesus spent his evenings in Bethany, Luke seems to put a degree of separation (πρός) between Bethany and Olivet (Luke 19:29; cf. 24:50).

[65] Brandon thinks that Jesus had made prior arrangements to meet at that location "since Judas Iscariot knew of it and was able to inform the Jewish leaders in time to allow their organization of an arresting force" (*Jesus and the Zealots*, 340). Peter later refers to Judas's strategic role in guiding the arresting party to this location (Acts 1:16).

[66] Mikeal C. Parsons, *Acts*, Paideia (Grand Rapids: Baker Academic, 2008), 30. Parsons observes, "Important here is the narrator's effort to inform the audience that the Mount of Olives was a familiar place to Jesus."

[67] Mark only later has Jesus command his disciples to pray, but in the context of their continual watching (14:39). Of course, in typical Markan fashion, the disciples fail, succumbing to sleep (14:40–41).

[68] Paul Borgman, *The Way according to Luke: Hearing the Whole Story of Luke-Acts* (Grand Rapids: Eerdmans, 2006), 240.

[69] Jesus ascends to heaven from the Mount of Olives, to which he will also return as the cosmic Son of Man (Luke 12:40; 17:22, 24, 26, 30; 21:27, 36; cf. Acts 1:11–12; 2:33–36; Zech 14:4–5). Historically, the Mount of Olives served as a launch pad for invasions of Jerusalem,

V. Conclusion

Lukan scholars often seek to neutralize the militaristic implications of Luke 22:38 by appealing to Jesus's supposed rebuke in 22:51. They assume that, since Jesus rebukes the use of the sword in the latter, he *must* be doing the same in the former. David L. Tiede, for example, recognizes a limited role for the swords up to verse 51 but then says that Jesus intervenes to "remedy the violence with healing."[70] Justo González asserts that the swords should be understood symbolically since Jesus later rebukes one of his disciples for literally wielding the sword.[71] Luke Timothy Johnson is even more explicit in wedding the two passages, remarking on Luke 22:38: "Jesus' exasperated termination of this discussion ('enough,' *hikanon estin*) here is matched by his chagrin when the sword is actually used (*eate eōs* [sic] *toutou*, 'enough of that')!"[72] But it is highly doubtful that ἐᾶτε ἕως τούτου means anything of the sort.[73] So, the intriguing question that has undergirded this essay throughout is: what does Luke 22:38 look like if freed from the neutralizing effects of Luke 22:51 as commonly interpreted?

The two passages do in fact inform each other but not for the reasons most scholars think. Both Lukan texts make the same important point: nothing must deter God's salvific plan. In Luke 22:38, taking up the sword ensures Jesus's safe transit to the Mount of Olives in prayerful preparation for his ensuing arrest; in Luke 22:51, putting away the sword ensures that the arrest will proceed.[74] This interlocking interpretation commends itself when one recognizes that the explanatory γάρ accords ἱκανόν ἐστιν its most natural meaning and gives coherence to both Luke 22:38 and 22:51 in the overall context of the Lukan drama, including the deterministic character of Jesus's passion and death. Such is the thrust of Luke's double-edged sword.

---

including that of the Egyptian false prophet (Josephus, *A.J.* 20.169; *B.J.* 2.262) and Titus (*B.J.* 5.70, 135, 157).

[70] David L. Tiede, *Luke*, ACNT (Minneapolis: Augsburg, 1988), 388–89. Tiede remarks that the two swords are enough "for Jesus to proceed with the drama that follows" but unfortunately does not indicate the precise nature of their role.

[71] Justo L. González, *Luke*, Belief: A Theological Commentary on the Bible (Louisville: Westminster John Knox, 2010), 250.

[72] Johnson, *Gospel of Luke*, 347.

[73] To his credit, Tiede retains the translation "as far as this" in his analysis of the passage (*Luke*, 389).

[74] Cf. Chrysostom: "Wherefore then did He suffer them to have them [the swords]? To assure them that He was to be betrayed" (*Hom. Matt.* 84.1; trans. Prevost, *NPNF¹*). Thus, what Aslan posits of the historical Jesus I think holds true for the Lukan Jesus, namely, "his views on the use of violence were far more complex than it is often assumed" (*Zealot*, 79).

A Meal in the Background of John 6:51–58?

JAN HEILMANN
jan.heilmann@rub.de
Technische Universität Dresden, 01062 Dresden, Germany

The new paradigm presented by the Society of Biblical Literature Meals in the Greco-Roman World Seminar challenges, among other things, the exegesis of John. Both the "eucharistic overtones" of selected passages in the Gospel of John and the assumption of a cultic meal on the level of the community have been called into question. The Bread of Life discourse (John 6:22–59) can be analyzed as a textual phenomenon that makes use of the imagery of eating and drinking but does not refer to a specific meal practice of early Christians. In this article, I argue that the complex metaphorical network in the Bread of Life discourse rests on conceptual imagery that we might refer to as EATING/DRINKING IS ADOPTING TEACHING. The intensification of the concept of adopting teaching into the language of eating the flesh has several parallels in antiquity. Moreover, this vivid imagery in John 6:53–58 is a conscious provocation of the recipients at the level of the narrated world and part of a typical Johannine misunderstanding scene. In the narrative strategy of John 6, these strong metaphors narratively enact the separation of the believing from the unbelieving disciples. The metaphors do not, however, point directly to specific practices of the believers. The argument will focus on the motif of drinking the blood of Jesus in John 6:53–58. An analysis of the ancient reception of this motif shows that it entered the discourse on meals prior to its influence on the ritual semantics itself. This observation suggests that it was the textual reception of the Gospel of John that influenced the development of a ritual and not the ritual that gave rise to the text.

The Johannine Jesus commands his hearers to eat his flesh and drink his blood in order to have eternal life (John 6:51–58). Many Johannine scholars interpret these comments as references or allusions to a sacramental/eucharistic meal practice in early Christianity.[1] In this article, I will argue that there is *no* specific meal

My thanks to the three anonymous reviewers for *JBL* for their helpful comments and to Sara Parks and Bradley Rice for language correction.

[1] See, e.g., Charles H. Cosgrove, "The Place Where Jesus Is: Allusions to Baptism and the Eucharist in the Fourth Gospel," *NTS* 35 (1989): 522–39; C. K. Barrett, *The Gospel according to St. John: An Introduction with Commentary and Notes on the Greek Text* (London: SPCK, 1962), 246–48; John M. Perry, "The Evolution of the Johannine Eucharist," *NTS* 39 (1993): 22–35;

in the background of John 6:51–58 but rather that the passage refers in more general terms to the universal human practice of eating and drinking. This universal human practice, in turn, can be identified as the source domain of the metaphor on which the imagery of John 6 is based.

My argument is structured in five parts. I will begin with some preliminary remarks on a new paradigm of analysis for the origins and development of the Christian Eucharist that challenges the traditional interpretation of the Gospel of John as having eucharistic allusions or overtones. This will be followed by observations about the network of metaphors in John 6 in the context of which, I argue, verses 51–58 should be interpreted. I will then, in two steps, propose a new way of understanding Jesus's request to drink his blood and eat his flesh. Finally, I will comment on the influence of John 6 on the development of eucharistic meals in later church history.

I. A New Perspective on Early Christian Meals

The new perspective on early Christian meals began with the studies of Matthias Klinghardt and Dennis E. Smith and continued, for example, in the work of the Society of Biblical Literature Meals in the Greco-Roman World Seminar and in the work of Andrew McGowan, Hal Taussig, Clemens Leonard, and others.[2] The

---

Carsten Claussen, "The Eucharist in the Gospel of John and in the *Didache*," in *Trajectories through the New Testament and the Apostolic Fathers*, ed. Andrew F. Gregory and Christopher Tuckett (Oxford: Oxford University Press, 2007), 135–63; Udo Schnelle, *Das Evangelium nach Johannes*, 5th ed., THKNT 4 (Leipzig: Evangelische Verlagsanstalt, 2016), 176–82; Jean Zumstein, *Das Johannesevangelium*, KEK 2 (Göttingen: Vandenhoeck & Ruprecht, 2016), 270–75. See also the references in the discussion of this article in section III.

[2] See Matthias Klinghardt, *Gemeinschaftsmahl und Mahlgemeinschaft: Soziologie und Liturgie frühchristlicher Mahlfeiern*, TANZ 13 (Tübingen: Francke, 1996); Dennis E. Smith, *From Symposium to Eucharist: The Banquet in the Early Christian World* (Minneapolis: Fortress, 2003); Dennis E. Smith and Hal Taussig, eds., *Meals in the Early Christian World: Social Formation, Experimentation, and Conflict at the Table* (New York: Palgrave Macmillan, 2012); Matthias Klinghardt and Hal Taussig, eds., *Mahl und religiöse Identität im frühen Christentum / Meals and Religious Identity in Early Christianity*, TANZ 56 (Tübingen: Francke, 2012); Susan Marks and Hal Taussig, eds., *Meals in Early Judaism: Social Formation at the Table* (New York: Palgrave Macmillan, 2014); Andrew B. McGowan, *Ascetic Eucharists: Food and Drink in Early Christian Ritual Meals* (Oxford: Oxford University Press, 1999); McGowan, "Rethinking Agape and Eucharist in Early North African Christianity," *StLi* 34 (2004): 165–76; McGowan, "Rethinking Eucharistic Origins," *Pacifica* 23 (2010): 173–91; Hal Taussig, *In the Beginning Was the Meal: Social Experimentation and Early Christian Identity* (Minneapolis: Fortress, 2009); Clemens Leonhard, *The Jewish Pesach and the Origins of the Christian Easter: Open Questions in Current Research*, SJ 35 (Berlin: de Gruyter, 2006); Clemens Leonhard and Benedikt Eckhardt, "Art. Mahl V (Kultmahl)," *RAC* 23:1012–1105; Soham Al-Suadi, *Essen als Christusgläubige: Ritualtheoretische Exegese paulinischer Texte*, TANZ 55 (Tübingen: Francke, 2011); R. Alan Streett, *Subversive Meals: An Analysis of the*

basic principle of this approach is the distinction between practice or form on the one hand, and discourse on the other hand, when it comes to meal rituals. The use of ritual theory in this approach has revealed a methodological problem in earlier and even recent studies on the Eucharist.[3] All knowledge about meal rituals is based on texts, but the primary objective of these texts is not to represent or describe the rituals themselves. The cited studies thus reject the theories of meal typologies of early Christian meals proposed by Hans Lietzmann and others who share this methodological flaw.[4] The starting point of this new paradigm is the meal practices common to gentile, Jewish, and Christian meals of the Greco-Roman era, as they are known from both archaeological and textual sources.[5]

The evening meal gathering had a three-part structure: (1) the *deipnon*, the eating of foodstuff in the narrow sense; (2) the libation ceremony; and (3) the subsequent *symposion* that included food, wine, conversation, discussion, entertainment, banquet music, and so on. Those gathered for the meal generally reclined on *triclinia* or the *sigma*. This reconstruction is based on numerous sociohistorical references in ancient sources.[6] The New Testament evidence suggests that early

---

Lord's Supper under Roman Domination during the First Century (Eugene, OR: Pickwick, 2013), 7–51.

[3] For a critical evaluation of the Pauline term *Lord's Supper* (1 Cor 11:20), see Andrew B. McGowan, "The Myth of the 'Lord's Supper': Paul's Eucharistic Meal Terminology and Its Ancient Reception," *CBQ* 77 (2015): 503–21. In my view, McGowan is right to interpret the term as "an occasional rhetorical construction dependent on immediate context" (503).

[4] See, e.g., Hans Lietzmann, *Messe und Herrenmahl: Eine Studie zur Geschichte der Liturgie*, AKG 8 (Bonn: Marcus & Weber, 1926); Ernst Lohmeyer, "Vom urchristlichen Abendmahl," *TRu* 9 (1937): 168–227; Oscar Cullmann, "Die Bedeutung des Abendmahls im Urchristentum (1936)," in Cullmann, *Vorträge und Aufsätze 1925–1962*, ed. Karlfried Frölich (Tübingen: Mohr Siebeck, 1966), 505–23; Bernd Kollmann, *Ursprung und Gestalten der frühchristlichen Mahlfeier*, GTA 43 (Göttingen: Vandenhoeck & Ruprecht, 1990); Gerd Theissen, "Sakralmahl und sakramentales Geschehen: Abstufungen in der Ritualdynamik des Abendmahls," in *Herrenmahl und Gruppenidentität*, ed. Martin Ebner, QD 221 (Freiburg im Breisgau: Herder, 2007), 166–86.

[5] Taussig, "Introduction," in Smith and Taussig, *Meals in the Early Christian World*, 1.

[6] It is not possible to list here all of the geographically and chronologically widespread references in literature, inscriptions, and papyri (e.g., invitations) or all of the archaeological evidence from Italy to Jordan. See the discussions of evidence in Klinghardt, *Gemeinschaftsmahl und Mahlgemeinschaft*; Smith, *From Symposium to Eucharist*; Smith and Taussig, *Meals in the Early Christian World*; Klinghardt and Taussig, *Mahl und religiöse Identität im frühen Christentum*; for the Greco-Roman meal in general, see, e.g., Nicholas R. E. Fisher, "Greek Associations, Symposia, and Clubs" and "Roman Associations, Dinner Parties, and Clubs," in *Civilization of the Ancient Mediterranean: Greece and Rome*, ed. Michael Grant and Rachel Kitzinger (New York: Scribner's Sons, 1988), 1167–97 and 1199–225; Oswyn Murray, ed., *Sympotica: A Symposium on the Symposion* (Oxford: Clarendon, 1994); Inge Nielsen and Hanne S. Nielsen, eds., *Meals in a Social Context: Aspects of the Communal Meal in the Hellenistic and Roman World*, ASMA 1 (Aarhus: Aarhus University Press; Oxford: Alden Press, 2001); Katherine M. D. Dunbabin, *The Roman Banquet: Images of Conviviality* (Cambridge: Cambridge University Press, 2003); Konrad Vössing, *Mensa regia: Das Bankett beim hellenistischen König und beim römischen Kaiser*, Beiträge

Christian meals should be understood along these same lines.[7] Nonetheless, within this cultural framework, the practice of meals shows great diversity and heterogeneity, for example, regarding the food, the décor, and the ritual acts.

Christian meals were substantial evening repasts with staple foods (not exclusively bread and wine). The liturgical forms and prayers were not fixed until the third century CE. There is no evidence that the so-called words of institution (Jesus's words at the Last Supper as narrated by Matt 26:26–28, Mark 14:22–24, Luke 22:19–20, and by Paul in 1 Cor 11:24–26)[8] were part of the meal prayers. The overtly liturgical use of the words of institution is first documented in the eucharistic prayer of the newly ordained bishop in the Apostolic Tradition, which apparently dates to the fourth century.[9]

---

zur Altertumskunde 193 (Munich: Saur, 2004); Vössing, ed., *Das römische Bankett im Spiegel der Altertumswissenschaften* (Stuttgart: Steiner, 2008); for the Jewish meal as part of Greco-Roman meal practice, see esp. the articles in Marks and Taussig, *Meals in Early Judaism*; Leonhard and Eckhardt, "Art. Mahl V (Kultmahl)," 1054–74; Clemens Leonhard, "Brotbrechen als Ritualelement formeller Mähler bei den Rabbinen und in der Alten Kirche," in *"Let the Wise Listen and Add to Their Learning" (Prov. 1:5): Festschrift for Günter Stemberger on the Occasion of His 75th Birthday*, ed. Constanza Cordoni de Gmeinbauer and Gerhard J. Langer, SJ 90 (Berlin: de Gruyter, 2016), 501–19.

[7] For instance, the following elements are typical of the Greco-Roman *deipnon/symposion*: The use of verbs like κατάκειμαι (Mark 2:15; Matt 14:3; Luke 5:29; 7:37; 1 Cor 8:10), ἀνάκειμαι (Mark 6:20; 14:18; 16:14; Matt 9:10; 26:7, 20; Luke 22:27; John 6:11; 12:2; 13:23, 28), συνανάκειμαι (Mark 2:15; 6:22; Matt 9:10; 14:9; Luke 7:49; 14:10, 15), κατακλίνω (Luke 7:36; 9:14–15; 14:18; 24:30), ἀνακλίνω (Mark 6:39; Matt 8:11; 14:9; Luke 7:36 [A W Θ Ψ f^{13} Byz]; 12:37; 13:29), and ἀναπίπτω (Mark 6:40; 8:6; Matt 15:35; Luke 11:37; 14:10; 17:7; 22:14; John 6:10; 13:12) refers to reclining; note also the use of the verb στρωννύω in Mark 14:15 and Luke 22:12—related to στόρνυμι, which is used to describe the preparation of dining couches (see, e.g., Herodotus, *Hist.* 6.139.3; Athenaeus, *Deipn.* 4.138b; 6.239b [= Diodorus of Sinope]); 1 Cor 11–12, Luke 14:7, 22:24–30, and John 13–15 refer to the typical content of sympotic table talk or social conflicts and values connected with meals (see Klinghardt, *Gemeinschaftsmahl und Mahlgemeinschaft*, 75–97, 153–74, 286–96; for John, see George L. Parsenios, *Departure and Consolation: The Johannine Farewell Discourses in Light of Greco-Roman Literature*, NovTSup 117 [Leiden: Brill, 2005]); singing at the symposium (see Mark 14:26 par.) is typical of Greco-Roman meal practice (cf. Klinghardt, *Gemeinschaftsmahl und Mahlgemeinschaft*, 99–129); note also the typical Greco-Roman meal terminology δεῖπνον (Mark 6:21; 12:39 par.; Luke 14:12, 16, 17, 24; John 12:2, 4) and δειπνέω (Luke 17:8; Rev 3:20); the phrase μετὰ τὸ δειπνῆσαι (1 Cor 11:25; Luke 22:20) separates the *deipnon* (full meal) from the following symposium, whereas the ritual actions of Jesus narrated in 1 Cor 11:25, Luke 22:20, and Mark 14:23–25 par. mark the transition betweeen those two parts (see below).

[8] The term "words of institution" is used here to refer to these words due to the lack of accurate alternatives. However, the term is problematic because it was originally associated with "monocausally-historicizing" (Klinghardt) hypotheses concerning the development of the Eucharist. See Klinghardt, *Gemeinschaftsmahl und Mahlgemeinschaft*, 2–3.

[9] Cf. Paul Bradshaw, *Reconstructing Early Christian Worship* (Collegeville, MN: Pueblo, 2010), 50–51. In the beginning of the third century, Tertullian knows of a distribution of eucharistic food in the morning (Tertullian, *Cor.* 3.3; *Or.* 19), but this cannot serve as evidence for a celebration

II. The Anachronism of "Eucharistic" Interpretations of John 6

Consequently, at the time when the Gospel of John was written there is no evidence to suggest that there existed a "cultic" Christian ritual in the sense of the later Eucharist in which bread and wine were consumed and symbolically interpreted as the body and blood of Christ. To presuppose such a ritual requires a circular argument.[10] The crucial point concerning the words of institution is that when the narrated Jesus speaks about the bread and cup, he is not interpreting the so-called elements, bread and wine, but his complete ritual action. Moreover, Jesus's words in the four Gospels show great differences in syntax and meaning and, in my view, have to be understood in the context of the narrated world of the biblical texts. For example, the words over the cup in Mark 14:24 and Matt 26:28 refer to a *proposis* ritual whereas Luke 22:20 clearly refers to a libation ritual.[11] From this it follows

---

of the Eucharist in the morning and an independent, noneucharistic *agapē* meal in the evening. On the contrary, Tertullian understands "eucharistic" meals to be common meals in the evening (see *Apol.* 39; *Ux.* 2.4.2; 2.8.8; *Jejun.* 17.2-3). About fifty years later, however, the writings of Cyprian include the earliest proof of a celebration of the Eucharist in the morning that is independent of the *deipnon/symposion* in the evening (Cyprian, *Ep.* 63.16). This does not mean that before Cyprian there was no worship in the morning. Morning liturgies, however, were noneucharistic in the beginning. Only when the communities grew too big for celebrating a *symposion/convivium* in the evening did the celebration of the Eucharist shift to the morning. The development of the ritual form of the Eucharist that one can observe in the writings of Tertullian and Cyprian in the late second and early third centuries is regionally related to North Africa (Carthage). All in all, we have to assume a complex and inconsistent evolution from the *deipnon/symposion* to the eucharistic Mass in the third and fourth centuries. In a short period of time, the community meal became an act "der individuellen Heilsvergewisserung und Heilsaneignung" (Martin Wallraff, "Christliche Liturgie als religiöse Innovation in der Spätantike," in *Liturgie und Ritual in der alten Kirche: Patristische Beiträge zum Studium der gottesdienstlichen Quellen der alten Kirche*, ed. W. Kinzig, U. Volp, and J. Schmidt, Studien der Patristischen Arbeitsgemeinschaft 11 [Leuven: Peeters, 2011], 69-97, here 89). See also Clemens Leonhard, "Morning *salutationes* and the Decline of Sympotic Eucharists in the Third Century," *ZAC* 18 (2014): 420-42.

[10] For a detailed explanation of this view in scholarship, see Jan Heilmann, *Wein und Blut: Das Ende der Eucharistie im Johannesevangelium und dessen Konsequenzen*, BWANT 204 (Stuttgart: Kohlhammer, 2014), 9-20.

[11] In the context of a meal, the *libation* is a ritual pouring of liquid which, together with a sung prayer, marks the transition from the *deipnon* to the symposium (see, e.g., Xenophon, *Symp.* 2.1; *Anab.* 6.1.5-6; Plutarch, *Quaest. conv.* 1.1 (*Mor.* 615b); Athenaeus, *Deipn.* 4.149c; P.Lond. 7.2193; IG 2.2:1338). The term *proposis* refers to the well-documented practice of drinking a sip of the still unmixed wine at the beginning of the symposium (see, e.g., Athenaeus, *Deipn.* 15.693c/d [= Theophrastus]), which could be done from one cup to emphasize table fellowship (see, e.g., Athenaeus, *Deipn.* 10.504a [= Menander]; Pollux, *Onom.* 6.31; Philostratus, *Vit. Apoll.* 8.12). For further reading on the interpretation of the words of institution, see Matthias Klinghardt, "Bund und Sündenvergebung: Ritual und literarischer Kontext in Mt 26," in *Mahl und religiöse Identität*,

that an early eucharistic ritual in which the participants consumed bread and wine as if they were flesh and blood of Christ cannot be deduced from the words of institution.

These points suggest that the eucharistic interpretation of John 6:51–58 stems from an anachronistic understanding of early Christian eucharistic rituals. The common notion of "eucharistic overtones" in Johannine scholarship has been challenged by the work of the SBL Meals seminar.[12] According to the results of the SBL seminar, this approach seems inadequate for the analysis of, on the one hand, the relationship between John 6:51–58 and the ritual life of early Christianity and, on the other, of the relationship between John 6:51–58 and the *differing* accounts of the words of institution in the Synoptics. The results of the work of the SBL seminar remind us to determine carefully the relationship between text and ritual in each account of the Last Supper. Thus, for heuristic reasons, distinguishing among the following elements is essential for interpreting "meal texts" in the New Testament:

1. Early Christian meals that were actually performed
2. The (literary) discourse on meals that is represented in texts "which follow their own discursive … logic respectively"[13]
3. The narrative enactment of the meal practice of Jesus
4. Textual phenomena that make use of imagery related to eating and drinking but do not refer to a specific practice of meals that were actually performed.

I will return to these differentiations after analyzing John 6:51–58 in the context of the metaphoric network in John 6.

III. The Metaphoric Network in John 6

I leave aside the literary-critical debate about verses 51–58, as recent research has decided in favor of the literary unity of John 6.[14] Instead, I will focus on the

---

159–90; Klinghardt, "Der vergossene Becher: Ritual und Gemeinschaft im lukanischen Mahlbericht," *Early Christianity* 4 (2012): 33–58; summarized in Heilmann, *Wein und Blut*, 85–104.

[12] For an overview of the issue of "eucharistic overtones" in the exegesis of the Gospel of John, see Heilmann, *Wein und Blut*, 2–8. The SBL seminar also challenges the question of a supposed replacement of "the Eucharist" in John 13. If the words of institution do not prove a "cultic" ritual in which the early Christians consumed bread and wine as the body and blood of Christ, the foot washing should be seen merely as another variant caused by the different narrative concept of the Fourth Gospel. It is a phenomenon that should be compared to other differences between the Fourth Gospel and the Synoptics, for example, the table talk in Luke 22:24–37 and that in the Johannine Farewell Discourse.

[13] Klinghardt, "Bund," 162 (my translation).

[14] See, e.g., Hartwig Thyen, *Das Johannesevangelium*, HNT 6 (Tübingen: Mohr Siebeck,

metaphoric network of John 6. Ulrich Busse, Ruben Zimmermann, and Jan G. van der Watt have described the numerous, interrelated metaphors in John 6. They argue that verse 27 introduces the metaphorical level of the Bread of Life discourse and that the center of this network is the "I am" saying in verse 35.[15]

The source domain of the metaphors is formed by the practice of eating rather than by the materiality of food.[16] This view is supported by the use of the lexeme βρῶσις in verse 27. Unlike the lexeme βρῶμα ("food"), βρῶσις refers to the practice of eating, as numerous passages in the New Testament and other ancient sources show.[17] The imagery that forms the basis for the metaphoric network of John 6 is made explicit in verse 51: whoever *eats* of the living bread that came down from heaven will live forever. In other words, in the thought world of the Gospel of John, whoever receives the incarnated word and believes in it will live forever. For heuristic purposes only, this idea may be conceptualized by the following metalinguistic definition: According to the *conceptual metaphor theory* of George Lakoff and Mark Johnson, the basic conceptual metaphor EATING/DRINKING IS ADOPTING TEACHING is the conceptual basis on which the complex metaphor network in the Bread of Life discourse is formed. The term "basic conceptual metaphor" refers to cognitive concepts that shape communication and perception. Lakoff and Johnson's basic example ARGUMENT IS WAR, for example, suggests that most descriptions of "fighting with words" are conceptualized with metaphors taken from the

---

2005), 365; Thyen, "Über die Versuche, die sogenannte 'eucharistische Rede' (Joh 6,51c–58) als redaktionelle Interpolation auszuscheiden," in *Studien zum Corpus Iohanneum*, WUNT 214 (Tübingen: Mohr Siebeck, 2007), 539–47; Johannes Beutler, "Zur Struktur von Johannes 6," in *Studien zu den johanneischen Schriften*, SBAB 25 (Stuttgart: Katholisches Bibelwerk, 1998), 247–62; Beutler, "Joh 6 als christliche 'relecture' des Pascharahmens im Johannesevangelium," in *Damit sie das Leben haben (Joh 10,10): Festschrift für Walter Kirchschläger zum 60. Geburtstag*, ed. Ruth Scoralick (Zurich: Theologischer Verlag, 2007). For a detailed discussion, see Heilmann, *Wein und Blut*, 155–61.

[15] Ulrich Busse, *Das Johannesevangelium: Bildlichkeit, Diskurs und Ritual*, BETL 162 (Leuven: Leuven University Press, 2002), 273–402; Ruben Zimmermann, *Christologie der Bilder im Johannesevangelium: Die Christopoetik des vierten Evangeliums unter besonderer Berücksichtigung von Joh 10*, WUNT 171 (Tübingen: Mohr Siebeck, 2004), 407–46; Jan G. van der Watt, *Family of the King: Dynamics of Metaphor in the Gospel according to John*, BibInt 47 (Leiden: Brill, 2000), 111–38; van der Watt, "I Am the Bread of Life: Imagery in John 6:32–51," *AcT* 2 (2007): 186–204. See also Jörg Frey, "Das Bild als Wirkungspotenzial: Ein rezeptionsästhetischer Versuch zur Funktion der Brot-Metapher in Johannes 6," in *Bildersprache verstehen: Zur Hermeneutik der Metapher und anderer bildlicher Sprachformen*, ed. Ruben Zimmermann, Übergänge 38 (Munich: Fink, 2000), 331–61, here 344.

[16] For the following discussion, see further Heilmann, *Wein und Blut*, 144–54, 174–200.

[17] See ibid., 145 n. 198, for numerous references, most notably in the LXX: Gen 1:29, 2:9, Job 33:20, Ps 13:14, etc., Wis 4:5, Isa 55:10, Jer 15:13, 19:17, 41:20. In the New Testament, see Matt 6:19–20, Rom 14:17, 1 Cor 8:4, 2 Cor 9:10; see also Josephus, *A.J.* 1.13.2 §230; 1.20.2 §334; Aristotle, *Eth. nic.* 1118A; Plutarch, *Quaest. conv.* 2.2 (635c).

source domain "war."[18] Similarly, the conceptual metaphor EATING/DRINKING IS ADOPTING TEACHING describes a concept which shapes communication about the reception of teaching (in oral or written form), one that is widely attested in ancient sources.[19]

Close parallels to the imagery of John 6 can be found especially in the Prophets and in Jewish wisdom tradition.[20] For example, Jeremiah says that "your words were found, and I ate them, and your words became to me a joy and the delight of my heart" (Jer 15:16). Even closer to John 6 is the imagery in Isa 55:1–3, 10–11.

> [1]Ho, everyone who thirsts, come to the waters; and you that have no money, come, buy and eat! Come, buy wine and milk without money and without price. [2]Why do you spend your money for that which is not bread, and your labor for that which does not satisfy? Listen carefully to me, and eat what is good, and delight yourselves in rich food. [3]Incline your ear, and come to me; listen, so that you may live. I will make with you an everlasting covenant, my steadfast, sure love for David.... [10]For as the rain and the snow come down from heaven, and do not return there until they have watered the earth, making it bring forth and sprout, giving seed to the sower and bread to the eater, [11]so shall my word be that goes out from my mouth; it shall not return to me empty, but it shall accomplish that which I purpose, and succeed in the thing for which I sent it.

Here one finds the following motifs: coming to the water as someone who is thirsty, eating the word of god that comes down from heaven like bread for sustenance. The book of Sirach explicitly associates eating and drinking with receiving instruction: "She [wisdom] will feed him with the bread of learning, and give him the water of wisdom to drink" (Sir 15:3). Moreover, in chapter 24 one finds the motif that wisdom came down to earth (v. 3), the motif of coming to wisdom (v. 19), and the following personification of wisdom, which is an important pre-text of John 6:35: "Those who eat of me will hunger for more, and those who drink of me will thirst for more" (Sir 24:21). There is also evidence in New Testament, early Christian, early Jewish, and rabbinic sources that drinking metaphorically conceptualizes the receiving of teaching. An impressive example is m. ʾAbot 1:4, where Yose ben

---

[18] See, e.g., George Lakoff and Mark Johnson, *Metaphors We Live By* (Chicago: University of Chicago Press, 1980).

[19] See, e.g., Mark 6–8 (cf. Matthias Klinghardt, "Boot und Brot: Zur Komposition von Mk 3,7–8,21," *BTZ* 19 [2002]: 183–202); Col 4:6; Heb 6:4–5; Rev 2:17; Barn. 10.11, 11.11; Ign. *Trall.* 6.1; Gos. Thom. 28 (P.Oxy. 1.14–17); Acts Paul (P.Bodm. 41.3.14–15; P.Hamb. 4.5); Aristophanes, *Nub.* 523; Philo, *Legat.* 2.86; Quintilian, *Inst.* 2.4.5; 2.5.18; 3.1.5; 10.1.4; 10.6.25, etc.; Seneca, *Ep.* 84.5–6; Aelian, *Var. hist.* 13.22; Ovid, *Pont.* 3.4.53–56; Artemidorus Daldianus, *Onir.* 2.45; Macarius, *Apocr.* 2.12.6; Justin, *Dial.* 120.1–2; Tertullian, *Marc.* 4.7.6; Clement of Alexandria, *Paed.* 1.6.45–46; Gen. Rab. 70.5.

[20] Apart from the sources discussed in the following, see Ezek 2:8–3:11 (cf. the reception of Ezek 2:8–3:3 in Rev 10:9–10), Prov 3:13–20, 9:2–17.

Yoezer says, "May your house be a meeting house for Sages ..., and drink their words thirstily."[21]

In classical sources the evidence in Athenaeus, *Deipn.* 347e, is of particular interest. According to Athenaeus's account, Aeschylus called his tragedies the slices of fish or meat of the great Homeric banquets (τεμάχη τῶν Ὁμήρου μεγάλων δείπνων). Also significant is the striking imagery in Aristophanes's comedy *The Acharnians*. Line 484 uses the metaphor of "gulping" Euripides (καταπιὼν Εὐριπίδην). In all of these examples, the language of eating is used metaphorically to refer to adopting teaching, without reference to an actual meal or physical eating. This suggests that the conceptual metaphor EATING/DRINKING IS ADOPTING TEACHING was well known and therefore could also plausibly be seen as the basis of the imagery in John 6:51–58.

IV. DRINKING THE BLOOD OF JESUS AND EATING HIS FLESH: A METAPHOR?

The majority of exegetes hold that verses 51–58 are primarily sacramental rather than metaphorical due to the concrete language of the passage.[22]

---

[21] Moreover, see 1 Cor 3:1–2; Heb 5:11–14; 1 Pet 2:2–3; 1QH XIII; b. Hag. 3a; m. 'Abot 1:11, 2:8; Justin, *Dial.* 120.2.

[22] For further detail on the following, see Heilmann, *Wein und Blut*, 167–73, 200–240. In contrast, see James D. G. Dunn, "John VI—a Eucharistic Discourse?," *NTS* 17 (1971): 328–38, here 338. My interpretation, however, differs from Dunn's thesis that the imagery of eating the flesh of Jesus and drinking his blood refers to "the believing reception of the Spirit of Christ." Dunn's interpretation constricts the significance of the imagery unnecessarily. See the short evaluation of Dunn's thesis by Silke Petersen, "Jesus zum 'Kauen': Das Johannesevangelium, das Abendmahl und die Mysterienkulte," in *"Eine gewöhnliche und harmlose Speise"? Von der Entwicklungen frühchristlicher Abendmahlstraditionen,* ed. Judith Hartenstein, Silke Petersen, and Angela Standhartinger (Gütersloh: Gütersloher Verlagshaus, 2008), 113 n. 26. In my view, Jesus's correction in verse 63 (the verse forms the basis of Dunn's argument) refers solely to the materialistic misunderstanding of the unbelieving disciples and does not function as an interpretation of the imagery. The interpretation of the imagery is given by Peter in verse 68 (see below). See also David Gibson, "Eating Is Believing? On Midrash and the Mixing of Metaphors in John 6," *Themelios* 27 (2002): 5–15; John Bowman, "Metaphorically Eating and Drinking the Body and Blood," *AbrN* 22 (1983–1984): 1–6; Robert Kysar, *Voyages with John: Charting the Fourth Gospel* (Waco, TX: Baylor University Press, 2005), 200–215.

That the passage must be understood nonmetaphorically is often postulated in biblical exegesis. See, e.g., Paul N. Anderson, *The Christology of the Fourth Gospel: Its Unity and Disunity in the Light of John 6*, WUNT 2/78 (Tübingen: Mohr Siebeck, 1996), 111–12; Jesper Tang Nielsen, *Die kognitive Dimension des Kreuzes: Zur Deutung des Todes Jesu im Johannesevangelium*, WUNT 2/263 (Tübingen: Mohr Siebeck, 2009), 265–66. Although Jane S. Webster emphasizes that "the eucharistic tradition does not necessarily determine the meaning" of John 6:51–58 (*Ingesting Jesus: Eating and Drinking in the Gospel of John*, AcBib 6 [Atlanta: Society of Biblical Literature,

Consequently, they understand Jesus's words to be referring to a meal in which bread and wine are identified with Jesus's body and blood because a literal interpretation is also impossible. In their argument, they refer to the semantics of the verb τρώγω ("munch"). This meaning, in their view, precludes a metaphorical meaning of verses 51–58, though why this should be the case is not explained.[23] It is noticeable that in many cases these exegetes postulate that the section makes sense only against the background of "the Eucharist."[24] The following arguments can be made against this view:

1. Semantically, the Greek verb τρώγω does not at all preclude a metaphorical meaning of the passage. Indeed, there are several sources that attest a metaphoric use of the verb, as Hugo Blümner has shown.[25]

2. The historicity of cultic meals with features such as theophagy, *sparagmos*, and *omophagy*, which are sometimes presented as an analogy to the meal in the background of John 6,[26] is highly controversial. According to Benedikt Eckhardt, it is difficult to prove that such rituals took place.[27] The motif of drinking the blood of humans or the accusation of holding Thyestic meals is a common literary topos used for polemical purposes and therefore may not be a description of a specific ritual that was actually performed.[28]

2003], 84), she still assumes a connection between the ingesting imagery and "the eucharistic tradition" (153).

[23] See, e.g., Peder Borgen, *Bread from Heaven: An Exegetical Study of the Concept of Manna in the Gospel of John and the Writings of Philo*, NovTSup 10 (Leiden: Brill, 1965), 89–93; Helge K. Nielsen, "John's Understanding of the Death of Jesus," in *New Readings in John: Literary and Theological Perspectives; Essays from the Scandinavian Conference on the Fourth Gospel in Aarhus 1997*, ed. Johannes Nissen and Sigfred Pedersen, JSNTSup 182 (Sheffield: Sheffield Academic, 1999), 232–54, here 243.

[24] A particularly striking example can be found in the commentary of Christian Dietzfelbinger, who argues against a noneucharistic reading of John 6:51–58: "Christians of the New Testament period could not understand John 6:51ff. as other than referring to the Lord's Supper" (*Das Evangelium nach Johannes*, 2 vols., ZBK 4 [Zurich: Theologischer Verlag, 2001], 170 [my translation]).

[25] See Hugo Blümner, *Studien zur Geschichte der Metapher im Griechischen: Über Gleichniss und Metapher in der attischen Komödie* (Leipzig: Teubner, 1891), 52–53, with reference among others to Aristophanes, *Ran.* 367; *Vesp.* 158, 586, 672. See also the striking examples in Aristophanes, *Nub.* 924; Aristotle, *Metaph.* 3.1001A; and Sotades, *Lyricus* 15.15.

[26] See, e.g., Petersen, "Jesus zum 'Kauen'"; Esther Kobel, *Dining with John: Communal Meals and Identity Formation in the Fourth Gospel and Its Historical and Cultural Context*, BibInt 109 (Leiden: Brill, 2011), 231–36; Kobel, "The Various Tastes of Johannine Bread and Blood: A Multiperspective Reading of John 6," in *Decisive Meals: Table Politics in Biblical Literature*, ed. Nathan MacDonald, Luzia Sutter Rehmann, and Kathy Ehrensperger, LNTS 449 (London: T&T Clark, 2012), 88–92.

[27] See Leonhard and Eckhardt, "Art. Mahl V (Kultmahl)," 1012–51.

[28] See further Mark J. Edwards, "Some Early Christian Immoralities," *AncSoc* 23 (1992): 71–82; Andrew B. McGowan, "Eating People: Accusations of Cannibalism against Christians in

3. The close connection between wine and blood in the ancient world is a scholarly chimera based mainly on problematic conclusions derived from rhetorical figures in a few literary sources. The occasional rhetorical play with the color of blood and red wine does not mean that blood and wine were always or even often associated in the ancient world.[29] Further, the lexeme σάρξ ("flesh") in John 6:51–58 does not function as a reference to the *meat* of the cooked Passover, as some scholars assume based on the references to the Passover in the Johannine passion narrative (ch. 19).[30] The more common term for such meat would have been κρέας ("meat") as in LXX Exod 16:3, 8, 12, which rather denoted roasted, edible *meat*, while σάρξ is more often used for the "living" flesh.[31] Jesus's invitation to eat his *flesh* (σάρξ) is even more scandalous because he requests his audience to eat and drink him while he is still alive.[32]

4. As shown in section III, both the imagery of drinking and the intensification of the metaphoric language of adopting teaching in the sense of eating flesh have parallels in the ancient sources (see esp. Athenaeus, *Deipn.* 347e; Aristophanes, *Ach.* 484).

5. There are significant differences between the so-called words of institution and the predications in John 6:51–58.[33] Regardless of whether the demonstrative

---

the Second Century," *JECS* 2 (1994): 413–42; Annette Keck, Inka Kording, and Anja Prochaska, eds., *Verschlungene Grenzen: Anthropophagie in Literatur und Kulturwissenschaften*, Literatur und Anthropologie 2 (Tübingen: Narr, 1999); Daniel Fulda and Walter Pape, eds., *Das andere Essen: Kannibalismus als Motiv und Metapher in der Literatur*, Rombach Wissenschaften: Litterae 70 (Freiburg im Breisgau: Rombach, 2001); J. Albert Harrill, "Cannibalistic Language in the Fourth Gospel and Greco-Roman Polemics of Factionalism (John 6:52–66)," *JBL* 127 (2008): 133–58, https://doi.org/10.2307/25610110; Philip A. Harland, *Dynamics of Identity in the World of the Early Christians: Associations, Judeans, and Cultural Minorities* (New York: T&T Clark, 2009), 161–81; Heilmann, *Wein und Blut*, 172 n. 320.

[29] See further Heilmann, *Wein und Blut*, 69–75.

[30] See, e.g., Christine Schlund, *"Kein Knochen soll gebrochen werden": Studien zur Bedeutung und Funktion des Pesachfests in den Texten des frühen Judentums und im Johannesevangelium*, WMANT 107 (Neukirchen-Vluyn: Neukirchener Verlag, 2005), 139–72.

[31] See the sources cited in LSJ, s.v. "σάρξ."

[32] Although the studies of Kobel and Webster are valuable in other respects, they are both based on this presupposition (Kobel, *Dining with John*, 178–86, 231–37, 251–70; Webster, *Ingesting Jesus*, esp. 34, 76–79, 148–49). It is also misleading to interpret Jesus's request to drink his blood in 6:53–56 as a request to drink his blood shed on the cross in 19:34, contra Joseph A. Grassi, "Eating Jesus' Flesh and Drinking His Blood: The Centrality and Meaning of John 6:51–58," *BTB* 17 (1987): 28–30.

[33] A large majority of scholars suggest that John 6:51–58 contains a reference to the words of institution. See, e.g., Rudolf Schnackenburg, *Das Johannesevangelium*, 4 vols., HThKNT 4 (Freiburg im Breisgau, 1965–1984), 2:91; Perry, "Evolution of the Johannine Eucharist," 22–23; Kobel, "Various Tastes," 85–86. A few scholars argue against this: Craig R. Koester, "John Six and the Lord's Supper," *LQ* 4 (1990): 419–37; Donald A. Carson, *The Gospel according to John*, PilNTC (Grand Rapids: Eerdmans, 1991), 296–98; Maarten J. J. Menken, "Joh 6,51c–58: Eucharist or Christology?," *Bib* 74 (1993): 1–25; Mira Stare, *Durch ihn Leben: Die Lebensthematik*

pronoun τοῦτο in Matt 26:26–29, Mark 14:22–26, Luke 22:15–20, and 1 Cor 11:23–26 refers to the physical bread or more likely interprets the narrated acts performed by Jesus,[34] the different order of subject and predicative noun is striking (τοῦτό ἐστιν τὸ σῶμά μου [Mark 14:22 par.] vs. ἐγώ εἰμι ὁ ἄρτος [John 6:51]/ἡ γὰρ σάρξ μου ἀληθής ἐστιν βρῶσις [John 6:55]). As Klinghardt has shown, the subject and predicative noun in the predications of both the words of institution and John 6 are arranged in a fixed order: "the notorious copula 'ἐστι' is not a mathematical equal sign that expresses ontological equivalence."[35] The specification with the adjective ἀληθής in 6:55, which indicates metaphorical language in the Gospel of John,[36] can be explained against the background of the frequent occurrence of the motif of the true testimony in the Gospel of John (3:33; 4:18; 5:31–32; 8:13, 14, 17, 26; 10:41; 19:35; 21:24). There is more evidence, however, for the thesis that the words of institution are not in the background of John 6:51–58.

Exegetes who postulate a literary dependence of John 6:51–58 on the words of institution see in the giving of bread in verse 51e a reference to the *giving* of Jesus's σῶμα. This idea can be countered by the following arguments: The use of the verb δίδωμι in verse 51e develops the earlier use of δίδωμι in John 6 (cf. verse 27 and the citation of Exod 16:15 in verse 31); it does not have to refer to the words of institution. Furthermore, the giving of Jesus's σῶμα occurs only in the longer version of the words of institution in Luke 22:19. Neither 1 Cor 11:24 nor Mark 14:22 nor Matt 26:26 implies that the mention of Jesus's σῶμα is a reference to the giving of Jesus's σῶμα at the cross.[37] If, as numerous scholars agree, the longer version of the Lukan

---

in Joh 6, NTAbh NS 49 (Münster: Aschendorff, 2004), 206–19; Thyen, *Das Johannesevangelium*, 367–70; Meredith J. C. Warren, *My Flesh Is Meat Indeed: A Nonsacramental Reading of John 6:51–58* (Minneapolis: Fortress, 2015), 82–84. Frequently, however, scholars do not clearly differentiate between the question of the intertextual relationship between John 6:51–58 and the words of institution, on the one hand, and the question of whether John 6:51–58 refers to a specific meal ritual labeled "the Eucharist," on the other.

[34] See Wolfgang Schrage, *Der erste Brief an die Korinther*, 4 vols., EKKNT 7 (Zurich: Benziger, 1999), 3:34–38; Ulrich Luz, *Das Evangelium nach Matthäus*, 4 vols., EKKNT 1 (Zurich: Benziger, 2002), 4:116; Luz, "Das Herrenmahl im Neuen Testament," BK 57 (2002): 2–8, here 4–5; Jens Schröter, *Das Abendmahl: Frühchristliche Deutungen und Impulse für die Gegenwart*, SBS 210 (Stuttgart: Katholisches Bibelwerk, 2006), 128–30; Schröter, "Die Funktion der Herrenmahlsüberlieferungen im 1. Korintherbrief: Zugleich ein Beitrag zur Rolle der 'Einsetzungsworte' in frühchristlichen Mahltexten," ZNW 100 (2009): 78–100, here 93; Klinghardt, "Der vergossene Becher," 56.

[35] Klinghardt, *Gemeinschaftsmahl und Mahlgemeinschaft*, 439 (my translation).

[36] See Rainer Hirsch-Luipold, "Klartext in Bildern: ἀληθινός κτλ., παροιμία – παρρησιά, σημεῖον als Signalwörter für eine bildhafte Darstellungsform im Johannesevangelium," in *Imagery in the Gospel of John: Terms, Forms, Themes, and Theology of Johannine Figurative Language*, ed. Jörg Frey, Jan G. van der Watt, and Ruben Zimmermann, WUNT 2/200 (Tübingen: Mohr Siebeck, 2006), 70.

[37] The verb δίδωμι in the narrator's voice in Mark 14:22 and parallels is simply a reference to the common gesture of opening the meal.

words of institution is secondary,[38] it is unlikely that John would have been familiar with Luke's distinctive form of the words of institution, which are absent from the shorter version, which was likely closer to the form that would have circulated prior to the time the Fourth Gospel was written.

Thus, the combination of bread and flesh can be explained by positing an allusion in the Bread of Life discourse to LXX Exod 16, where bread and flesh (vv. 3, 8, 12) occur together. As demonstrated decisively by Gary A. Phillips,[39] the bread in John 6:51e is to be read as a metaphor for Jesus's teaching, which he himself embodies. The future tense δώσω (v. 51e) indicates that John 6:51–58 functions as a proleptic reference to Jesus's teaching in the following gospel text, particularly in the Farewell Discourse (chs. 14–17).[40] Here in the Farewell Discourse, Jesus *teaches* the disciples about his death and its implications for them. In this sense, ingesting the flesh and blood of Jesus means "to be willing to share with him in his sufferings and death as a factor of discipleship faithfulness" and is also a "close parallel to Mark 8[:34–35]."[41] In the Gospel of John, however, "death as a factor of discipleship faithfulness" does not mean martyrdom in the usual sense but the *social death* of the disciples who believe in Jesus and will therefore be hated by the world (see 15:18–16:4). In the Fourth Gospel, as others have shown, the death of Jesus can be interpreted as a consequence of his open (παρρησία) teaching of the *logos* of God (see 7:4, 26; 11:54; 18:19–20).[42] He put his life at risk for his friends by speaking openly to the world (see 15:13).[43]

---

[38] The shorter version of the Lukan words of institution is the *lectio difficilior* and the *lectio brevior*. There is no conclusive argument for the assumption that a scribe has erased τὸ ὑπὲρ ὑμῶν διδόμενον ... ἐκχυννόμενον in Luke 22:19–20. See further Martin Rese, "Zur Problematik von Kurz- und Langtext in Luk. xxii. 17 ff.," NTS 22 (1975): 15–31; Matthias Klinghardt, *Das älteste Evangelium und die Entstehung der kanonischen Evangelien*, 2 vols., TANZ 60 (Tübingen: Francke, 2015), 1019–28.

[39] Cf. Gary A. Phillips, "This Is a Hard Saying: Who Can be Listener to It? Creating a Reader in John 6," *Semeia* 26 (1983): 23–56, here 37–51. I owe this reference to Adele Reinhartz.

[40] The relative clause ὃν ἐγὼ δώσω ("that I will give") refers to the bread. Thus, Jesus does not say that he will *give his flesh* (contra, e.g., Webster, *Ingesting Jesus*, passim; Warren, *My Flesh Is Meat Indeed*, passim). Some older translations are based on textual variants.

[41] Paul N. Anderson, review of *Ingesting Jesus: Eating and Drinking in the Gospel of John*, by Jane S. Webster, *Int* 59 (2005): 432; see also Thyen, *Das Johannesevangelium*, 367–70; J. Ramsey Michaels, *The Gospel of John*, NICNT (Grand Rapids: Eerdmans, 2010), 396, 402.

[42] For further reading, see Michael Labahn, "Die παρρησία des Gottessohnes im Johannesevangelium: Theologische Hermeneutik und philosophisches Selbstverständnis," in *Kontexte des Johannesevangeliums: Das vierte Evangelium in religions- und traditionsgeschichtlicher Perspektive*, ed. Jörg Frey and Udo Schnelle, WUNT 175 (Tübingen: Mohr Siebeck, 2004), 321–63.

[43] The verb τίθημι in 15:13 should not be understood in the passive sense of "lay down his life," as most of the English translations suggest, but—following ancient conceptions of friendship—in the active sense of a person risking his or life, which could include death. See Jens Schröter, "Sterben für die Freunde: Überlegungen zur Deutung des Todes Jesu im Johannesevangelium," in *Religionsgeschichte des Neuen Testaments: Festschrift für Klaus Berger zum 60.*

V. Evidence for a Metaphorical Interpretation of John 6:51–58 from Its Context and from Its History of Reception

The context of John 6 supports the metaphorical interpretation of verses 51–58. Those who argue in favor of a sacramental interpretation refer to the meal setting at the beginning of the chapter, the feeding of the five thousand (vv. 1–15): the setting of the narrative in proximity to the Passover (v. 4), the absolute use of the verb εὐχαριστέω in verse 11, and the analeptic reference by the narrator to "the place where they had eaten the bread after the Lord had given thanks [ἔφαγον τὸν ἄρτον εὐχαριστήσαντος τοῦ κυρίου]" (v. 23). These elements, which have their own text-critical problems,[44] are interpreted as "eucharistic overtones" and are understood to refer to the Synoptic accounts of Jesus's last (Passover) meal with his disciples.[45] At least two arguments, however, speak against this view.

1. The verb εὐχαριστέω refers primarily to the common Jewish practice of thanking (blessing) God for bread prior to eating a meal (see Did. 9:1; 10:1, 7)[46] and should not be interpreted as "eucharistic language" at such an early stage in the history of Christianity. The absolute use of εὐχαριστέω can also be found in Mark 8:6 (cf. also Matt 15:36). To assume the use there as "eucharistic"—that is, referring to a sacramental meal practice in early Christianity—is a circular argument. Moreover, the closest analogy of verse 11 is neither the story of the Last Supper nor the meal at the lake (John 21:13) but "the raising of Lazarus, where thanksgiving

---

Geburtstag, ed. Axel von Dobbeler, Kurt Erlemann, and Roman Heiligenthal (Tübingen: Francke, 2000), 263–87; Zimmermann, *Christologie der Bilder*, 252, 390–95; Thomas Söding, "Einsatz des Lebens: Ein Motiv johanneischer Soteriologie," in *The Death of Jesus in the Fourth Gospel*, ed. Gilbert Van Belle, BETL 200 (Leuven: Leuven University Press, 2007), 363–84. See further Heilmann, *Wein und Blut*, 201–9, 273–78.

[44] Verse 4 is missing in minuscule 1634 and a few other manuscripts; εὐχαριστήσαντος τοῦ κυρίου is missing in the famous Codex Bezae Cantabrigiensis (D 05), in majuscule 092 and a few other majuscules, in some Old Latin manuscripts, and in the Syriac manuscripts—thus a typical Western noninterpolation that can, with good reason, be interpreted as older compared to the "majority text." See, e.g., Michael Wade Martin, "Defending the 'Western Non-interpolations': The Case for an Anti-separationist *Tendenz* in the Longer Alexandrian Readings," JBL 124 (2005): 269–94, https://doi.org/10.2307/30041013, with further references; Klinghardt, *Das älteste Evangelium*, passim.

[45] See, e.g., Perry, "Evolution of the Johannine Eucharist," 23–24; Thomas Popp, *Grammatik des Geistes: Literarische Kunst und theologische Konzeption in Johannes 3 und 6*, ABIG 3 (Leipzig: Evangelische Verlagsanstalt, 2001), 292–93; Schnelle, *Das Evangelium nach Johannes*, 160–62; more carefully: Barrett, *Gospel according to St John*, 237.

[46] See Rudolf Bultmann, *Das Evangelium des Johannes*, 17th ed., KEK (Göttingen: Vandenhoeck & Ruprecht, 1962), 157.

[εὐχαριστέω] works like petitionary prayer.... Here too, 'giving thanks' shows Jesus' dependence on the father, and consequently the five thousand were fed."[47]

2. The Bread of Life discourse in the narrow sense (vv. 25–59) is explicitly marked as a teaching scene in a synagogue (v. 59) and does not take place at a meal or even a paschal[48] meal. Moreover, verses 22–24 clearly demarcate the teaching scene from the feeding of the five thousand both (1) temporally and (2) spatially: (1) The temporal markers in verses 16–17 (ὄψιος ["evening"]; σκοτία)[49] indirectly sets the previous meal scene as a *deipnon* in the late afternoon. In contrast, the temporal marker τῇ ἐπαύριον ("the next day," v. 22) suggests that the reader should imagine an earlier time of day for the teaching scene in the synagogue of Capernaum. (2) The crowd finds Jesus not at "the place where they had eaten the bread [after the Lord had given thanks]" (v. 23) but on the other side of the sea in the synagogue of Capernaum (see vv. 24–25). This means that they searched at the wrong place or for the wrong thing and so misunderstood the real meaning of what had happened to them (see v. 26). Thus, in the context of John 6, the story of the feeding of the five thousand functions as a "prelude" to the misunderstanding of the crowd (later of "the Jews") of the mostly metaphorical statements of Jesus, which is characteristic for the Bread of Life discourse. Evidence for the fact that John 6 deals not with material eating but with teaching would then be found in the connection of chapter 6 to chapter 5: "But if you do not believe what he wrote, how will you believe what I say?" (5:47). Furthermore, the story of the feeding of the five thousand is well suited to function as a prelude to the subsequent misunderstandings of Jesus's metaphorically conceptualized teaching, because the bread in Mark 6–8 (in my view, one source text for John 6) already refers metaphorically to the teaching of Jesus, which John had understood correctly.[50]

Moreover, the sequence of typical Johannine misunderstandings in John 6 verifies a metaphorical interpretation of verses 51–58. According to R. Alan Culpepper's systematization of Johannine misunderstandings, the drastic metaphorical language in verses 53–58 is part of a conscious provocation of the recipients at the level of the narrated world and, therefore, part of a typical Johannine misunderstanding scene:

[47] Michaels, *Gospel of John*, 349.
[48] In my view, the notice "the Passover ... was near"—in connection with the hint that Jesus does stay away from Jerusalem (7:1)—is to be understood as a variant of the motif of the hour (i.e., the Passover of Jesus's death) that has not yet come. (On the narrative function of the motif of the hour in the Fourth Gospel, see Tobias Nicklas, "Wiederholung und Variation: Das Motiv der 'Stunde' im Johannesevangelium," in *Repetitions and Variations in the Fourth Gospel: Style, Text, Interpretation*, ed. Gilbert Van Belle and Michael Labahn, BETL 223 [Leuven: Peeters, 2009], 295–320); Michaels rightly concludes that the notice "should not be allowed to govern the interpretation of the entire chapter" (*Gospel of John*, 343).
[49] See the motif of the night in John 13:30 in the context of the advanced table talk.
[50] See Klinghardt, "Boot und Brot," 191–200.

(1) Jesus makes a statement which is ambiguous, metaphorical, or contains a double-entendre [see esp. vv. 53–58]; (2) his dialogue partner responds or protests which shows that he or she has missed the higher meaning of Jesus' words [see v. 60b–c: 'This teaching is difficult; who can accept it?']; (3) … an explanation is then offered by Jesus … [see v. 62–63: "Then what if you were to see the Son of Man ascending to where he was before? It is the spirit that gives life; the flesh is useless. The *words* that I have spoken to you are spirit and life.]⁵¹

Although Culpepper does not include John 6:51–71 in his list of Johannine misunderstandings, the passage does evince the characteristics he delineates.⁵²

In my view, the main goal of the narration in John 6 is the constitution of the twelve disciples of Jesus. The drastic imagery is part of the narrative strategy of the chapter: The disciples who leave Jesus (see v. 66) (mis)understand his speech literally because of their lack of faith (see v. 64). Yet the answer of Peter in verse 68 ("You have the words of eternal life [ῥήματα ζωῆς αἰωνίου]") shows clearly that the twelve disciples were able to overcome the cognitive dissonance created by the contradictory statements of Jesus in verses 51–58 versus verse 63. The statement of Jesus in verse 63 and that of Peter in verse 68 offer the readers the hermeneutical key to unlock the metaphorical meaning of the motif of eating and drinking in John 6. It is Jesus's teaching (see διδάσκω in v. 59) that has to be incorporated in order to receive eternal life.

To sum up, the imagery in verses 51–58 describes the believers' need to eat, to drink, and to chew—in other words, to incorporate completely—the incarnated *logos* of God that has become flesh and blood (cf. 1:14; 19:34) to have eternal life.⁵³ The acceptance (παραλαμβάνω) of the incarnated *logos* is a key motif of the Gospel of John (see 1:11–12): To accept the *logos* by believing in Jesus and his teaching is the precondition for receiving the eternal life that is expressed in the Gospel of John in many variations (see, e.g., 3:14–21; 5:24, 38; 6:35; 8:34–41; 14:6) often embedded in scenes with misunderstandings. John 6:51–58 is simply one of these variants.

Thus, the motif of drinking the blood of Jesus does not reference the actual act of drinking wine. Nothing in the Bread of Life discourse indicates to the reader that the pericope has to be understood against the background of their own meal practice; the entire discourse is a textual phenomenon that makes use of the imagery of eating and drinking but does not refer to a specific meal practice of early Christians.

---

⁵¹ R. Alan Culpepper, *Anatomy of the Fourth Gospel: A Study in Literary Design* (Philadelphia: Fortress, 1987), 152.

⁵² In contrast, see D. A. Carson, "Understanding Misunderstandings in the Fourth Gospel," *TynBul* 33 (1982): 59–91, here 91; Tom Thatcher, *The Riddles of Jesus in John: A Study in Tradition and Folklore*, SBLMS 53 (Atlanta: Society of Biblical Literature, 2000), 284–87.

⁵³ It has often been seen that σάρξ and αἷμα in John 6 could simply refer to the "humanity" of Jesus in the sense of the traditional merism (see Sir 17:30; 28:5; Matt 16:17; 1 Cor 15:50; Gal 1:16; Eph 6:12; Heb 2:14). Cf., e.g., Webster, *Ingesting Jesus*, 84, with further references.

I would also argue that the imagery of John 6:51–58 is not intended to evoke associations of any form of "sacrificial meal," as proposed by Meredith J. C. Warren.[54] Rather, the imagery is self-referential. It is the words of Jesus in the text of the Gospel of John that are to be "eaten," "chewed," and "drunk."[55] The Gospel of John is not a text for a quick, one-time reading; the Fourth Gospel reveals itself only if readers chew and drink the words of Jesus in the text through an intensive and repetitive reading process.[56]

The early reception history of John 6:51–58 supports the interpretation offered here.

> ... we partake of the flesh of Christ, that is, of the divine Scriptures [*several lines missing*] of the true Lamb, for the Apostle professes that the lamb of our passover is Christ when he says: For Christ, our paschal lamb, has been sacrificed; his flesh [σάρκες instead of κρέα in Exod 12:8] and blood, as shown above, are the divine Scriptures, eating [τρώγω] which, we have Christ; the words becoming his bones, the flesh becoming the meaning from the text, ... and the blood being faith in the gospel of the new covenant. (Origen, *Pasch.* 1.96–97 [Daly, ACW 54:45])

The wording (σάρκες, τρώγω) in this quotation from Origen's *Peri pascha* refers unambiguously to the imagery in John 6:51–58. Origen here interprets the Johannine passage as referring to the text of the Fourth Gospel itself.

In addition, in the *Apocriticus* of Macarius Magnes, one finds a comment on John 6 made by an unidentified "Greek" perhaps from the third century CE. In his *quaestio* regarding "that saying of the Teacher" (ἐκεῖνο τὸ ῥῆμα τοῦ Διδασκάλου) in John 6:53, the Greek (Ἕλλην) shows a complete lack of understanding of the imagery in John 6.

> That saying of the Teacher is a far-famed one, which says, "Except ye eat my flesh and drink my blood, ye have no life in yourselves." Truly this saying is not merely beast-like and absurd, but is more absurd than any absurdity, and more beast-like than any fashion of a beast, that a man should taste human flesh, and drink the blood of members of the same tribe and race, and that by doing this he should have eternal life. For, tell me, if you do this, what excess of savagery do you introduce into life? Rumour does not record—I do not say, this action, but even the mention of this strange and novel deed of impiety. The phantoms of the Furies never revealed this to those who lived in strange ways, nor would the Potidasans have accepted it unless they had been reduced by a savage hunger. Once the

---

[54] See Warren, *My Flesh Is Meat Indeed*, esp. 187–243. I do agree with Warren, however, that John 6:51–58 is to be understood as "nonsacramental," although the description "nonsacramental" is misleading for the New Testament period in that it evokes an anachronistic ritual concept.

[55] For this pragmatic dimension of the text, see Phillips, "This Is a Hard Saying," 51–53.

[56] Cf. the imagery in Ezek 2:8–3:11 and Rev 10:9–10. Incidentally, this has an interesting point of reference in the practice of subvocalized reading in the Hebrew Bible (e.g., Josh 1:8). For more on ancient reading techniques, see A. K. Gavrilov, "Techniques of Reading in Classical Antiquity," *ClQ* 47 (1997): 56–73.

banquet of Thyestes became such, owing to a sister's grief, and the Thracian Tereus took his fill of such food unwillingly. Harpagus was deceived by Astyages when he feasted on the flesh of his dearest, and it was against their desire that all these underwent such a pollution. But no one living in a state of peace prepared such a table in his life; no one learnt from a teacher any knowledge so foul. If you look up Scythia in the records, and go through the Macrobian Ethiopians, and if you career through the ocean girdle round about, you will find men who eat, live, and devour roots; you will hear of men who eat reptiles and feed on mice, but they refrain altogether from human flesh.... Wherefore it seems to me that neither Mark nor Luke nor even Matthew recorded this, because they regarded the saying as not a comely one, but strange and discordant, and far removed from civilized life. (Macarius, *Apocr.* 3.15.2–4 [Crafer, Translations of Christian Literature])

It is significant that "the Greek" neither makes any reference to the meal practice of early Christians nor draws a parallel to the so-called words of institution. Even more important, however, is the response of the Christian Macarius. He explains to the Greek what the verse is about:

Now the flesh and blood of Christ, or of Wisdom (for Christ and Wisdom are the same), are the words of the Old and New Testaments spoken with allegorical meaning, which men must devour with care and digest by calling them to mind with the understanding, and win from them not temporal but eternal life.... Thus did the saints one by one, once long ago, and again and again, by eating the flesh and drinking the blood of Wisdom, that is, by receiving in themselves the knowledge and revelation of her, live for aye with a life that will never cease. (Macarius, *Apocr.* 3.23.11–12; Crafer, Translations of Christian Literature)

Like Origen, Macarius interprets the imagery as referring to the biblical text itself and is thereby aware of the connection of the Gospel of John to Jewish sapiential theology.[57]

VI. Redefining the Relationship between John 6 and the Development of Eucharistic Meals

My concluding remarks address the influence of John 6 on the development of eucharistic meals in later church history. The epistles of Ignatius are frequently

---

[57] For further reading, see Petra von Gemünden, "Weisheitliche Bilderkonstellationen im Johannesevangelium? Einige strukturelle Überlegungen," in *Picturing the New Testament: Studies in Ancient Visual Images*, ed. Annette Weissenrieder, Friederike Wendt, and Petra von Gemünden, WUNT 2/193 (Tübingen: Mohr Siebeck, 2005), 159–82; Angelika Strotmann, "Die göttliche Weisheit als Nahrungsspenderin, Gastgeberin und sich selbst anbietende Speise: Mit einem Ausblick auf Joh 6," in Hartenstein, Petersen, and Standhartinger, *"Eine gewöhnliche und harmlose Speise,"* 131–56.

mentioned as an analogy for a eucharistic understanding of flesh and blood in John 6. But *Eph.* 20.2 does not document a "sacramental realism." Rather, this passage has to be understood in relation to the motif of the unity of the Christian community, which is one of the main themes of the epistles of Ignatius:

> Assemble yourselves together in common, every one of you severally, man by man, in grace, in *one* faith and *one* Jesus Christ, who after the flesh was of David's race, who is Son of Man and Son of God, to the end that ye may obey the bishop and the presbytery without distraction of mind, breaking *one* bread; that [ὅ] is the medicine of immortality and the antidote that we should not die but live forever in Jesus Christ." (*Eph.* 20.2; Lightfoot [slightly modified])[58]

The subordinate clause that is initiated by the neuter pronoun ὅ does not point to the material bread (*masculinum*) but refers to the entire preceding sentence: to break *one* bread harmonious in unity (cf. also Ign. *Eph* 5) that is the medicine of immortality.[59]

The reception by the ancient church of the motif of drinking the blood of Jesus shows that this motif first entered into the *discourse on meals*. Only in a second step did the motif of drinking the blood of Jesus influence and change *the ritual semantics themselves*.[60] (The term "ritual semantics" describes the meaning that is generated within the performance of a ritual through the interaction of the single elements of the ritual.)[61] This observation corresponds with the highly dynamic and complex historical development of Christian meal practice, which Klinghardt, McGowan, and Wallraff, among others, have described.[62] In John 6, one finds the

---

[58] J. B. Lightfoot, ed., *The Apostolic Fathers*, 2 parts in 5 vols. (Hildesheim: Olms, 1973), 2.2:87.

[59] See Lightfoot, *Apostolic Fathers*, 2.2:87.

[60] See Heilmann, *Wein und Blut*, 219–31.

[61] See further Gerald A. Klingbeil, *Bridging the Gap: Ritual and Ritual Texts in the Bible*, BBRSup 1 (Winona Lake, IN: Eisenbrauns, 2007), 127–34.

[62] Klinghardt, *Gemeinschaftsmahl und Mahlgemeinschaft*, 499–522; Andrew B. McGowan, "'Is There a Liturgical Text in This Gospel?': The Institution Narratives and Their Early Interpretive Communities," *JBL* 118 (1999): 73–87, https://doi.org/10.2307/3268225; McGowan, "Rethinking Agape"; McGowan, "Rethinking Eucharistic Origins"; Wallraff, "Von der Eucharistie zum Mysterium: Abendmahlsfrömmigkeit in der Spätantike," in *Patristica et Oecumenica: Festschrift für Wolfgang A. Bienert zum 65. Geburtstag*, ed. Peter Gemeinhardt und Uwe Kühneweg, MThSt 85 (Marburg: Elwert, 2004), 89–104; Wallraff, "Christliche Liturgie." See also Henk J. de Jonge, "The Early History of the Lord's Supper," in *Religious Identity and the Invention of Tradition: Papers Read at a NOSTER Conference in Soesterberg, January 4–6, 1999*, ed. Jan Willem van Henten and Anton Houtepen, STAR 3 (Assen: Van Gorcum, 2001), 203–37; Paul F. Bradshaw, *Eucharistic Origins* (Oxford: Oxford University Press, 2004), 97–115, 139–57; Jason König, *Saints and Symposiasts: The Literature of Food and the Symposium in Greco-Roman and Early Christian Culture*, Greek Culture in the Roman World (Cambridge: Cambridge University Press, 2012), 123–30; Harald Buchinger, "Early Eucharist in Transition? A Fresh Look at Origen," in *Jewish and Christian Liturgy and Worship: New Insights into Its History and Interaction*, ed. Albert Gerhards

well-known innovative capacity of John that has shaped the language of the early Christians,[63] and the influence of this innovation on the evolution of the Christian Eucharist should not be underestimated. To be more specific, within the dynamic process of the ritual evolution of the Eucharist, the metaphors of eating the flesh of Jesus and drinking his blood became *ritualized* in the truest sense of the word. A question for further discussion concerns whether, in terms of the metalanguage of ritual studies, the later eucharistic ritual might result from a conflation of the imagery of John 6 and of the so-called words of institution.[64] In conclusion, the reception of the text of the Gospel of John influenced the development of ritual, but ritual did not influence the text of John 6.

---

and Clemens Leonhard, JCPS 15 (Leiden: Brill, 2007), 207–27; Leonhard and Eckhardt, *RAC* 23:1081–83.

[63] See, e.g., Labahn, "Die παρρησία des Gottessohnes," 363.

[64] For further reading on the application of this concept to the field of early Jewish and Christian rituals, see, e.g., Jonathan Brumberg-Kraus, "'Not by Bread Alone …': The Ritualization of Food and Table Talk in the Passover 'Seder' and in the Last Supper," *Semeia* 86 (1999): 165–91.

Veiling among Men in Roman Corinth: 1 Corinthians 11:4 and the Potential Problem of East Meeting West

PRESTON T. MASSEY
ptmassey@gmail.com
Indiana Wesleyan University, Marion, IN 46953

Close attention to the original meaning of the words κατακαλύπτω (1 Cor 11:6) and κατὰ κεφαλῆς ἔχων (1 Cor 11:4) permits a translation only of a material head covering. These words do not describe the process of letting hair hang down loosely. These words are consistently used in Classical and Hellenistic Greek to describe the action of covering the head with a textile covering of some kind. In spite of sustained efforts by advocates, the long-hair theory still has not succeeded in gaining an entry into standard reference works. The original edition of BAGD in 1957, the revised edition in 1979, and the more recent edition of BDAG in 2000 all support the view that the text of 1 Cor 11:2–16 describes an artificial textile head covering of some kind.

In 1988, Richard Oster published a provocative article detailing the cultural practice of Roman men wearing head coverings in a liturgical setting.[1] His study called attention to the value of the artifactual evidence as well as the many literary texts documenting the widespread use of veiling among Roman men. His purpose was to establish the fact that it was obligatory for elite Roman men in certain ritual settings to wear a head covering. His article did not focus on the element of shame. He followed up this study with a second contribution in 1992, bemoaning the "little concern" that New Testament scholarship had shown with regard to the artifacts of the Greco-Roman world.[2] In a similar vein, David Gill in 1990 registered his own evaluation of Roman portraiture, arguing that texts in 1 Corinthians should be interpreted against the backdrop of Corinth as a Roman colony, not a

---

[1] Richard E. Oster, "When Men Wore Veils to Worship: The Historical Context of 1 Corinthians 11.4," *NTS* 34 (1988): 481–505.
[2] Richard E. Oster, "Use, Misuse and Neglect of Archaeological Evidence in Some Modern Works on 1 Corinthians (1 Cor 7,1–5; 8,10; 11,2–16; 12,14–26)," *ZNW* 83 (1992): 52–73, here 52.

Greek city.³ He applied this model to both male and female head coverings. The ongoing scholarly focus on cultural issues involving the appropriateness of women's dress, however, resulted in the neglect of the work of Oster and Gill. In 2010, Mark Finney took up the question again in a well-argued article.⁴ I believe that Finney's study shifts the interest away from an exclusive attention on veiling practice among women and draws attention to the neglected issue of male veiling. Finney provides scholarly documentation and references to ancient sources that make it difficult to discredit the thesis that some Roman men did, in fact, have the serious obligation of appearing before a deity with their heads covered. Finney acknowledges his debt to the previous work of Oster and Gill, as well as of Anthony Thiselton and Craig Keener.⁵ He takes exception to the works of Jerome Murphy-O'Connor, Richard Hays, and Gordon Fee, who all argued that the text is discussing long hair, not veiling.⁶ Although the issue of women's dress has dominated the discussion of this text, Oster anticipated the discussion of male head coverings by a margin of over twenty-five years. Finney, rather than avoiding the topic, as many have done, has faced the issue.

The present study is based on the foundational work of Oster, Gill, and Finney. These three scholars articulate the view that head coverings for a Roman male were for the specific purpose of prayer and offering a sacrifice to their gods. Finney states

---

³ David W. J. Gill, "The Importance of Roman Portraiture for Head-Coverings in 1 Corinthians 11:2–16," *TynBul* 41 (1990): 245–60, esp. 245. See also his follow-up article, "In Search of the Social Élite in the Corinthian Church," *TynBul* 44 (1993): 323–37, esp. 327: "The Romanness of the colony should not be underestimated." See also Michael D. Dixon, "A New Latin and Greek Inscription from Corinth," *Hesperia* 69 (2000): 335–42, esp. 338 n. 6: "of the 104 inscriptions datable prior to Hadrian's reign, only three were inscribed in Greek." See also the excellent article by R. A. Kearsley, "Women in the Public Life in the Roman East: Iunia Theodora, Claudia Metrodora, and Phoebe, Benefactress of Paul," *TynBul* 50 (1999): 189–211. For the argument that Roman Corinth was neither completely Greek nor completely Roman, see Benjamin W. Millis, "The Social and Ethnic Origins of the Colonists in Early Roman Corinth," in *Corinth in Context: Comparative Studies on Religion and Society*, ed. Steven J. Friesen, Daniel N. Schowalter, and James C. Walters, NovTSup 135 (Leiden: Brill, 2010), 13–35.

⁴ Mark Finney, "Honour, Head-Coverings and Headship: 1 Corinthians 11.2–16 in Its Social Context," *JSNT* 33 (2010): 31–58.

⁵ Anthony C. Thiselton, *The First Epistle to the Corinthians: A Commentary on the Greek Text*, NIGTC (Grand Rapids: Eerdmans, 2000), 825; Craig S. Keener, *1–2 Corinthians*, NCBiC (Cambridge: Cambridge University Press, 2005), 93. For David Gill, see Finney's references, "Honor, Head-Coverings," 35–37.

⁶ Finney ("Honor, Head-Coverings," 36 n. 22, 41 n. 39, and 45 n. 55) cites Jerome Murphy-O'Connor, "1 Corinthians 11.2–16 Once Again," *CBQ* 50 (1988): 265–74, esp. 267; Richard B. Hays, *First Corinthians*, IBC (Louisville: John Knox, 1997), 186; and Gordon D. Fee, *The First Epistle to the Corinthians*, NICNT (Grand Rapids: Eerdmans, 1987), 507, where Fee writes: "There is almost no evidence (painting, reliefs, statuary, etc.) that men in any of the cultures (Greek, Roman, Jew) covered their heads." This is a rather astounding claim, perhaps one that Fee would like now to retract.

the prevalent view: "it may be reasonable to conclude that the *capito velato* is specific to those taking a central and active role in the service and, as such, stands as an unmistakable sign of status and honour."[7] Finney adds the word "specific" to his discussion, indicating that Roman men did not make it a practice to wear head coverings outside of the context of a worship setting.[8] There may have been exceptions to this general practice depending on the particular situation. Although a material textile cloth (a Roman toga) would be the suitable and preferable covering for the head, the example of Julius Caesar shows that a helmet could suffice (Appian, *Bell. civ.* 2.104).

What more can be said that could possibly advance the discussion? In the present study, I will address the following three questions: (1) To what extent would male head-covering ideology in Greek and Roman cultures be at loggerheads with the text of 1 Cor 11:4? (2) To what extent would wearing a veil for a man create tensions of shame and conflict in the church in Roman Corinth? And (3) what is the specific issue regarding male sartorial practice? I will first address the controversial and long-standing issue of whether the verse refers to veils, long hair, or both.

I. Defining the Terms of the Discussion: The Vocabulary of Veiling

The context of 1 Cor 11:2–16 concerns proper dress while at worship. The etiquette of proper head coverings during the act of prayer suggests that veiling is in view, not the everyday styling of hair or the length of hair.[9] Roman liturgical settings would be emotionally charged with specific requirements for ritual dress and behavior. There is little evidence to suggest that hairstyles were a factor in formal sacramental activity. I could find no text involving prayer to Greek or Roman gods in which hairstyles or length of hair was ever a matter of concern.[10]

---

[7] Finney, "Honor, Head-Coverings," 37. See also Bruce Winter, *After Paul Left Corinth: The Influence of Secular Ethics and Social Change* (Grand Rapids: Eerdmans, 2001), 122: "This evidence of the material culture patently demonstrates that the practice of men covering their heads in the context of prayer and prophecy was a common pattern of Roman piety and widespread during the late Republican and early Empire."

[8] Both Oster ("When Men Wore Veils," 501 n. 1) and Finney ("Honor, Head-Coverings," 37 n. 26) cite the text of Lucretius, *De rerum natura* 5.1198: *nec pietas ullast velatum saepe videri* ("It is no piety to show oneself with covered head"). What does Lucretius mean by this? Lucretius is faulting hypocrisy by asserting that the wearing of a proscribed religious dress does not guarantee the true spirit of Roman religion.

[9] Plutarch makes a distinction between the appearance of head and hair by using different verbs and adjectives: ἀπαρακαλύπτῳ τῇ κεφαλῇ for veiling or unveiling the head; καὶ ταῖς κόμαις λελυμέναις for describing the hair (*Quaest. rom.* 13–14 [266F–267A]).

[10] Furthermore, it is rare to find a case among Roman men in which the hair is specifically

For example, a rare exception in which hair is actually mentioned is the text of Vergil's *Aeneid* 3.405: "purpureo velare comas adopertus amictu" ("veil your hair with a covering of purple robe").[11] Most likely the word *comas* ("hair") is poetic metonymy for *caput* ("head"). There is no concern for a proper hairstyle in the devotional rite.

By contrast, head coverings were a critical issue. Care was taken with regard to the fabric used for the head covering: it must have the color purple and it must be capable of blocking out hostile faces.[12] In *Aen.* 3.545, Vergil mentions that the first prayers to Juno were made with heads covered in a Phrygian mantle ("capita ante aras Phrygio velamur amictu"). When a Roman is about to pray, he first draws a cloak over his head before raising his hands to heaven.[13] His hair is typically not mentioned in the ritual, only his head. Even Josephus mentions covering the head as the customary practice for Roman leaders in the act of praying.[14] I argue, therefore, that the occasion of prayer with head coverings is the issue in 1 Cor 11:4. κατακαλύπτω is never used in ancient Greek to describe the covering of either a man's or woman's head with hair; neither is the expression κατὰ κεφαλῆς ἔχων ever

---

mentioned as covered in a nonliturgical context. The only one that I could find was in Vergil's *Aeneid* (11.77), which describes the funeral of Pallas: Aeneas, desiring to give Pallas an honorable burial with the proper last rites ("supremum ... honorem"), covers the hair of the deceased with a mantle ("comas obnubit amictu"). A possible second text is in Livy, *Ab urbe cond.* 24.26.18, where some soldiers, while they eat, are forced to wear their hair fashioned with white woolen headbands ("pilleati aut lana alba velatis capitibus").

[11] In *Aen.* 3.174, the gods (*deorum* in 3.172) have their heads (*comas*, their "hair") covered. It may be that Vergil conceives this in his vision and then transfers it to humans. Perhaps this was to distinguish Roman men from the Greeks, who do not veil their heads. Macrobius states that sacrifice is done with "uncovered head" ("aperto capite") owing to its foreign origin (*Sat.* 1.10.22); he identifies the original rite of Saturnalia as coming from Greece and, therefore, as being administered "aperto capite" (1.8.2). See also *Aen.* 2.721–723, in which a yellowed lion's skin is used to cover a "bowed neck" ("subiectaque colla"); 11.100 states, "Iamque oratores aderant ex urbe Latina, velati ramis oleae veniamque rogantes" ("And now pleaders/ambassadors came from the city of Latin, veiled with olive boughs and pleading for favor"). This seems to be the Roman way: when asking for grace and favor, either from gods or men, you veil your head in some appropriate fashion. Similar texts are found in *Aen.* 7.154 and 8.260–290.

[12] Michael D. Goulder argues just the opposite: the veil or hood is drawn down over the face for both males and females (*Paul and the Competing Mission in Corinth*, Library of Pauline Studies [Grand Rapids: Baker Academic, 2001], 136–37).

[13] See Dionysius of Halicarnassus, *Ant. rom.* 15.9.2: μέλλων δ' ἀπιέναι τήν τε περιβολὴν κατὰ κεφαλῆς εἵλκυσε καὶ τὰς χεῖρας ἀνασχὼν εἰς τὸν οὐρανόν, "As he was about to depart, he drew his cloak down over his head and raised his hand(s) to heaven" (my translation).

[14] In the *Jewish War* (7.128), Josephus describes Vespasian covering most of his head while praying: τὸ πλέον τῆς κεφαλῆς μέρος ἐπικαλυψάμενος εὐχὰς ἐποιήσατο τὰς νενομισμένας, "['with his cloak/mantle'] he veiled most of his head [the greater part] and then prayed the customary prayers" (my translation). Vespasian's prayer is then followed by Titus praying in like manner.

used in ancient Greek to describe hair coming down. On the contrary, these words describe the covering of the head with a material veil.[15]

Turning now to the Latin side, there are four principal verbs to describe the action of covering or uncovering the head of Roman men: *caput obnubere, caput adopertire/apertire, caput obvolvere,* and *caput velare.*[16] Generally speaking, the safe assumption is that the verb alone describes adequately the action of covering or uncovering for men; with women, however, additional nouns normally accompany the verbs. Exceptions may be found for each case.

What can be said other than pedestrian documentation?[17] I begin with the Roman historian Livy. His *Ab urbe condita* contains seven specific references to *caput velare.*[18] Counting up all other alternative terms for veiling, the total number comes to fourteen references to head coverings in Livy,[19] and all of these texts describe only men.[20] This is a striking and important consistency. Not one single text refers to a woman.[21] One clear implication is that head coverings for Romans were not only an accepted part of their culture but also a requirement in ritual settings.

II. The Significance of Head Coverings for Roman Men

What meaning or meanings did Romans attach to the wearing of a head covering by males? The following five rubrics will categorize the various nuances of head coverings for Roman men. The three principal studies mentioned above

---

[15] For detailed discussion of the vocabulary of this text, see Preston T. Massey, "The Meaning of κατακαλύπτω and κατὰ κεφαλῆς ἔχων in 1 Cor 11.2–16," *NTS* 53 (2007): 502–23, esp. 511–12.

[16] For a listing of these terms, see Heinrich Freier, *Caput Velare* (inaugural diss., Tübingen, 1963), 36–38. See also his conclusion (174): "Abschließend darf festgestellt werden: Der Ausdruck *caput velare* ist weithin ein *terminus technicus* für die Verhüllung des Hauptes, wie sie am häufigsten bei Gelübde, Gebet, und Opfer *Romano ritu* zu finden ist."

[17] For documentation not discussed elsewhere in this article, see Valerius Flaccus, *Argon.* 2.254, 5.97; Ovid, *Metam.* 1.382, *Fast.* 3.362; Velleius Paterculus, *Hist. rom.* 2.4.6; Plautus, *Amph.* 1095; Plutarch, *Num.* 7.2; Seneca, *Herc. fur.* 355; Suetonius, *Cal.* 51.1; Vergil, *Aen.* 8.277–279.

[18] Livy, *Ab urbe cond.* 1.18.7; 1.32.6; 1.36.5; 8.9.5; 10.7.10; 23.19.18; 24.16.18.

[19] Livy, *Ab urbe cond.* 1.18.7; 1.26.6, 11, 13; 1.32.6; 1.36.5; 2.39.12; 2.54.5; 8.9.5; 10.7.10; 22.1.4; 23.10.7; 23.19.18; 24.16.18.

[20] Livy, *Ab urbe cond.* 1.18.7 (an augur: *augur*); 1.26.6, 11, 13 (Horatius); 1.32.6 (an envoy: *Legatus*); 1.36.5 (a statue of Attus); 2.39.12 (priests: *sacerdotes*); 2.54.5 (those doomed to death); 8.12.11 (plebeians: *multi ex plebe*); 8.9.5 (Decius); 10.7.10 (a man: *qui*); 22.1.4 (perhaps a wig on Hannibal: *tegumenta capitis*); 23.10.7 (Decius Magius); 23.19.18 (Marcus Anicius); 24.16.18 (soldiers). I have not included the freedman's cap (30.45.5: *pilleo capiti*) as part of this count.

[21] Livy, *Ab urbe cond.* 35.34.7 may be an exception. What undermines confidence and creates doubt is that this family of wife and children are described as "tenentes velamenta supplicum" ("carrying or holding," not wearing). Further, it is not just the wife but also the children who are carrying these objects.

(Oster, Gill, and Finney) focused mainly on the cultural fact of male headdresses; less attention was paid to the specific issue of shame. This section will devote more attention to the various aspects and nuances of shame involving head coverings among Roman males.

A. Voluntary Veiling Can Indicate a Desire to Conceal Feelings of Shame

Whether Greek, Roman, or Jewish, under certain conditions all three cultures would agree that covering the head for a male indicates the intention to conceal personal feelings of shame and embarrassment.[22] From the Roman point of view, but helpfully narrated in Greek, Dio Cassius (*Hist. rom.* 58.27.3) describes Nero as he endeavors to flee for his life: after dressing himself in shabby clothing and covering his head (κατακεκαλυμμένος), he rides off into the night. Having lost his dignity and fearing for his life, Nero dresses himself to both conceal his identity and hide his feelings of shame. In a similar manner, Horace, referring to Damasippus, states, "for after my business failed and I wanted to cover up my head and fling myself into the river" ("nam male re gesta cum vellem mittere operio me capite in flumen"; *Sat.* 2.3.37). Livy describes plebeians who, having lost all hope and in despair, covered their heads (*captibus obvolutis*) and then threw themselves into the Tiber (4.12.11). Here we have the notions of shame, despair, and male veiling. A further case in point is the account of Quintus Curtius in his narrative concerning the wife of Darius who has just been reported as dead (*Hist. Alex.* 4.10.34).[23] Darius, overcome with grief, begins to weep. In order to conceal his misery, he covers his head (*capite*

---

[22] For Greeks, covering one's head out of shame can be traced back to Homer. The Homeric expression κατὰ κρᾶτα καλυψάμενος ("[Odysseus] would again cover his head") is found in *Od.* 8.92. Homer mentions specifically that it was out of shame (αἴδετο) that Odysseus covered his head. Richard John Cunliffe describes the word κάρη as defining the head (κρᾶτα is the accusative singular) ("κάρη," *A Lexicon of the Homeric Dialect* [1924; new ed., Norman: University of Oklahoma Press, 1980], 212). This association of male shame with veiling provides a second bridge to the biblical text. The information from the archaic Greek tradition reinforces the view that κατὰ τῆς κεφαλῆς ἔχων (or its Homeric counterpart κατὰ κρῆθεν) is used to describe male shame when used along with a material head covering.

For Roman tradition, Dio Cassius's account (*Hist. rom.* 42.4.5) of the end of Pompey's life may illustrate the point. Pompey, having suffered heavy losses at the hands of Caesar, flees to Egypt. Here, however, he meets an unfortunate end. Seeing that the Egyptians are going to take his life, he suddenly veils himself (συνεκαλύψατο). Rather than offer resistance, his last act is to veil himself, which suggests feelings of shame.

For Jewish evidence, see Massey, "Meaning of κατακαλύπτω," 502–23.

[23] It is clear from this text that Curtius shows Darius first covering his head while he cries over the loss of his wife. Then Darius, removing his cloak from his face (*veste ab ore reiecta*), lifts his hands to heaven. Curtius records a similar case in 5.12.8 in which Darius veils his head (*capite velato*) in order not to see Artabazus departing.

velato).²⁴ An arresting example further detailing this convention is Plutarch's *Apoph. rom.* 13 (200F):

> τῆς νεὼς ἀποβὰς ἐβάδιζε κατὰ τῆς κεφαλῆς ἔχων τὸ ἱμάτιον, ἠξίον ἀποκαλύψασθαι περιθέοντες οἱ Ἀλεξανδρεῖς καὶ δεῖξαι ποθοῦσιν αὐτοῖς τὸ πρόσωπον
>
> Deboarding the ship, he went on his way with his head covered with a *himation*; the Alexandrians, upon surrounding him, demanded that he unveil himself and show his face to their wishful eyes. (my translation)

Plutarch is describing the notable Roman personality Scipio, who, because of his notoriety as a Roman general, apparently does not want to draw attention to himself and so covers his head by pulling his ἱμάτιον over his head (κατὰ τῆς κεφαλῆς ἔχων τὸ ἱμάτιον). Since Scipio is a Roman of considerable importance, we must assume that Plutarch has substituted the Greek ἱμάτιον for the Roman toga. Scipio may have also drawn his toga up closer around his face, perhaps creating a shadowy and unrecognizable appearance. In other words, he wants to travel incognito. The attempt at concealment does not work; the Alexandrians want a closer look at this famous person. At first glance, this is a puzzling picture. Why would Scipio want to veil himself? This is certainly not a liturgical setting. His behavior appears linked to his wishes to remain unrecognized. But why? In 16 (201C), Plutarch provides a motivation for Scipio's covering of his head: Scipio was going about with a black cloak (σάγον … μέλανα) pinned around him, saying that he is "in mourning over the disgrace of the army" (πενθεῖν τὴν τοῦ στρατεύματος αἰσχύνην λέγων) (trans. Babbitt, LCL).

Tying these two Plutarchean texts together, we note several things. First, the language of κατὰ τῆς κεφαλῆς ἔχων τὸ ἱμάτιον approximates the language of 1 Cor 11:4. The only difference is that Plutarch adds the name of the garment. Second, both texts connect to issues of shame. Scipio, however, exercises the prerogative of voluntarily veiling himself owing to feelings of embarrassment over the performance of his army. This usage has a possible connection to the situation at Corinth. Paul, to the contrary, indicates that such symbolic manifestations of shame are inappropriate for a worship setting. In other words, it is shameful to bring shame into a worship setting by insinuating embarrassment. If a male symbolically

---

²⁴Dio Cassius (*Hist. rom.* 44.19.5) introduces us to a gesture not easy to interpret. In his account of the assassination of Julius Caesar, he records that Caesar was so caught off guard by the surprise attack that he had time to do only one thing before succumbing: veil himself (συγκαλυψάμενον). What is the basis of his reaction? Is this an instinctive defensive measure in order to protect himself, a veiling in order to conceal the shame of the moment, or even a gesture in anticipation of meeting the gods? Similarly, Lucan (*Bell. civ.* 8.614–617), poetically describes the assassination of Pompey as he covers both eyes and head from the assassin's blows ("involvit voltus atque, indignatus apetum fortunae praebere caput"). According to Lucan, Pompey does this in order not to allow any tears to mar his eternal glory. Suetonius (*Jul.* 82.2) offers no commentary on the significance of the head covering.

covered his head in a worship setting owing to feelings of embarrassment, this could be construed as self-righteous displeasure over the behavior of other believers.[25] Or, this covering of the head by a male or males could indicate displeasure and embarrassment in the event of the women removing their head coverings.

There is one other aspect to consider. It is clear that some Roman officials never removed their head coverings.[26] Yet, outside of a religious and liturgical context, Roman men did not traditionally veil their heads.[27] Why would this be appropriate inside such a setting and against custom outside such a setting? An examination of the key word *nupta* and its cognates may help with this question. *Nupta* as a noun conveys the idea of a wife;[28] the cognate *nuptia* describes the wedding ceremony itself.[29] Other derivatives from this root include *pronuba* (an attendant of the bride, perhaps the modern "maid of honor") and *conubium* (the condition of living together but not married). As an adjective, *nupta* defines the status of a woman who is married; it can also be used metaphorically. Martial (*Ep.* 8.12) says, "Uxorem quare locupletem ducere nolim quaeritis? uxori nubere nolo meae." W. Ker in the LCL translates "uxori nubere nolo meae" as "I am unwilling to take my wife as a husband." The translation is more literally, "I am unwilling to veil myself to my wife." *Nubere* by extrapolation suggests the idea of "covering like a cloud," as the noun (*nubes*) is a cloud.[30] (Note: this is my own judgment on the word.) By extension, it means "to veil." By further extension, it means "to marry."[31] The point of Martial's Latin is that, by accepting a veil in marriage, a married

---

[25] Appian, *Bell. civ.* 2.104: "Caesar, lifting his hands to heaven, implored all the gods that his many glorious deeds be not stained by this single disaster. Approaching his soldiers, he exhorted them, removing his helmet and shaming them" (ὁ Καῖσαρ ἱκέτευε, τὰς χεῖρας ἐς τὸν οὐρανὸν ἀνίσχων, μὴ ἑνὶ πόνῳ τῷδε πολλὰ καὶ λαμπρὰ ἔργα μιῆναι, καὶ τοὺς στρατιώτας ἐπιθέων παρεκάλει τό τε κράνος τῆς κεφαλῆς ἀφαιρῶν ἐς πρόσωπον ἐδυσώπει) (trans. White, LCL, adapted). Caesar leaves his helmet on while appealing to the gods, yet he removes his helmet in order to berate his soldiers. If it is possible from this example to make a connection to Roman Corinth, it may be that a Roman believer at Corinth, offended at unacceptable behavior, might remove his head covering at the actual moment of berating.

[26] Appian (*Bell. civ.* 65), states the information as he has received it: the priest of Jupiter alone (μόνος) wore the flamen's cap at all times (αἰεί). Aulus Gellius (10.15.17) supplements this with the additional information that every day is a holy day for the Dialis and, therefore allegedly, he may not go outside his house "without his cap" (*sine apice*). See also Varro, *Ling.* 5.84.

[27] See Cicero, *Sen.* 34: "nullo imbri, nullo frigore adduci ut capite operto sit" ("no rain or cold can induce him to cover his head"), describing ninety-year-old Masinissa, who does not wear a head covering even in bad weather.

[28] Pliny (*Ep.* 6.33.2) describes Attia Viriola as a "femina splendide nata, nupta praetorio viro" ("a woman of fine birth, the wife of a praetorian senator").

[29] Tacitus (*Ann.* 14.63) mentions, "primum nuptiarum dies" ("the first day of marriage"). See also his *Ann.* 12.25: "conciliator nuptiarum" ("a matchmaker"). See also Pliny, *Ep.* 4.2.7.

[30] Thus the word is a fitting poetic metaphor for concealing the face of the sun on a cloudy day (Ovid, *Metam.* 5.570). By extension, the removal of the *nubes* reveals a woman's face and hair.

[31] Livy, *Ab urbe cond.* 1.46.5: his duobus … duae Tulliae regis filiae nupserant ("These two

woman places herself under subjection to her husband and is thereby willing to be submissive to him. Martial's epigram describes, through the metaphor of veiling, a man's unwillingness to be subject to a woman. This would further indicate that under normal circumstances a married man did not veil himself while his wife did.[32]

From a Roman point of view covering the head is a potential symbol of shame for a married man of nonelite status. This would hold true as well for a Greek man. The relationship between 1 Cor 11:4 (πᾶς ἀνὴρ προσευχόμενος ἢ προφητεύων κατὰ κεφαλῆς ἔχων καταισχύνει τὴν κεφαλὴν αὐτοῦ) and 11:5 (πᾶσα δὲ γυνὴ προσευχομένη ἢ προφητεύουσα ἀκατακαλύπτῳ τῇ κεφαλῇ καταισχύνει τὴν κεφαλὴν αὐτῆς) now merits closer scrutiny. Has the behavior described in verse 5 caused the behavior in verse 4? Although the order of actual practice (though not the theological order) is in reverse, is there a cause-and-effect relationship between the two behaviors? If a married woman took the initiative by first uncovering her head independent of her husband's will, this could precipitate a reciprocal response on the man's part to cover his head. He would then be substituting the status of a respected married man for the shame of one who is dishonored. The cumulative effect would be a double dose of shame: the shame of her uncovering would result in the corresponding shame of his covering. Her actions would telegraph a message of immodesty; his actions would signal embarrassment and possible forfeiture of male leadership and respect among male peers. The particular context and sequence would determine how others would interpret the gesture. The key point, however, is the possibility of additional shame intruding into the assembly if a married man placed a covering over his head, provided his wife first removed hers. The associations connoted by Roman and Greek customs on this point would be similar.

Regarding the question whether 1 Cor 11:4–5 emphasizes one gender over the other or whether there is an equal distribution of paraenetic teaching, David E. Garland argues for an emphasis on the woman. He isolates four particular points from the text: (1) "Paul oscillates back and forth with statements about men and women, but this pattern is broken in 11:13 with a statement about the woman but none about the man."[33] (2) After admonishing the woman to cover herself, Paul supplements this statement with additional reasons in verses 5 and 6 but omits these in the application for the man. (3) After mentioning the enigmatic and surprising reference to angels in verse 10, Garland says that there is "no comparable explanation" given for why men should not be covered. (4) Finally, he calls attention to the fact that the only imperatives in the text are addressed to women, one in verse 13 and the other in verse 6. My own judgment supports Garland's exposition. The

---

... married the two Tullias, daughters of the king"). See also Martial, *Epigram* 6.7: et nubit decimo iam Telesilla viro. Quae nubit totiens, non nubit: adultera lege est.

[32] The adjective *nupta* also suggests a continuing condition, at least when out in public. It would make little sense to refer to a married woman as a *nupta* if this description was confined only to the singular moment of a wedding ceremony.

[33] David E. Garland, *1 Corinthians*, BECNT (Grand Rapids: Baker Academic, 2003), 507–8.

text, it may be confidently stated, is concerned primarily with the appropriateness of a married woman's dress at worship.³⁴ *Pace* Jerome Murphy-O'Connor, who argued, "In fact, men figure equally prominently in this section,"³⁵ there is clearly not an equal distribution of concern in the text. Rather, there is an uneven emphasis on women over men. If married women took the first step in removing their veils, this could account for the emphasis on women in the text. This is one possible way of interpreting both conditions of shame.

B. Violation of Ritual Protocols Can Lead to Feelings of Shame and Humiliation

There are further nuances to consider. In some cases shame or embarrassment can be the result of an accident. The Scriptores historiae augustae records Hadrian suffering such an embarrassment when his toga slipped off of his head ("praetexta sponte delapsa caput ei aperuit") in a public ceremony (Hadrian 26.6). Because of the other unfortunate things going on in his life, the embarrassment at this unintended social gaffe gave Hadrian a premonition of his own death. The mere slippage of his toga was perceived as a moment of embarrassing consequence. A similar incident is reported by Livy (*Ab urbe cond.* 5.21.16) regarding Camillus, who, in the act of a public prayer, slipped and fell. Witnesses to this faux pas interpreted the misstep as pointing to the condemnation of Camillus. Although Livy does not mention a veil falling off the head, such must have been the case. Of significance also is the salient fact that Camillus is pictured in the act of praying while wearing a veil. Regarding this incident, Dionysius of Halicarnassus (*Ant. rom.* 12.16.4) states, ὁ Κάμιλλος νόμοις ἐπειδὴ τὴν εὐχὴν ἐποιήσατο καὶ κατὰ τῆς κεφαλῆς εἵλκυσε τὸ ἱμάτιον ἐβούλετο μὲν στραφῆναι ("It was in accordance with the traditional usages, then, that Camillus, after making his prayer and drawing his garment down over his head, wished to turn his back"). These awkward incidents indicate that there were strict protocols attached to the formality of ceremonial prayers by persons of elite status.³⁶

Once again, from a Roman point of view, there are conditions when veiling would be entirely inappropriate and therefore shameful. Dio Cassius (*Hist. rom.* 59.27.5) records the plight of one Vitellius, who was summoned by Gaius to be put to death. In order to save his life, he goes through the following motions: first, he

---

³⁴ See Preston T. Massey, "Gender versus Marital Concerns: Does 1 Corinthians 11:2–16 Address the Issues of Male/Female or Husband/Wife?," *TynBul* 64 (2013): 239–56.

³⁵ Jerome Murphy-O'Connor, "Sex and Logic in I Corinthians 11:2–16," *CBQ* 42 (1980): 482–500, here 483.

³⁶ See also Valerius Maximus, *Mem.* 1.1.5, who mentions a Q. Sulpicius who, allowing his "mitre" (*apex*) to slip off of his head while in the act of sacrifice, suffered the loss of his priestly office. In *Mem.* 1.1.8, Valerius follows up with a commentary that Romans were scrupulous about the smallest matters in religious rite ("tam scrupulosa cura parvula").

dresses beneath his "glory" (σχηματίσας ... καὶ ἐλάττων αὐτῷ τῆς δόξης φανῆναι). Next, Vitellius falls at the emperor's feet and worships him (προσπεσὼν ... καὶ προσκυνήσας). Finally, he promises that if his life is spared, he will offer a sacrifice to Gaius (ἂν περισωθῇ, θύσειν αὐτῷ). Dio ends this humiliating account by attributing to Vitellius the ignoble distinction of surpassing all others in κολακεία, which is an insincere expression of fawning or flattery. Heinrich Freier conjectures that this humiliating act must have involved veiling the head: "wird wohl auch die Verhüllung des Hauptes verstanden werden müssen."[37] Suetonius (*Vit.* 2.5) reports similar details regarding Vitellius. Veiling before men in an insincere act of devotion in order to manipulate others would be considered shameful.

C. Ritual Head Coverings for a Roman Male Indicate a Desire to Shield One's Eyes from Hostile Omens

Vergil's *Aeneid* (3.398–405) evidences several elements that Romans attributed to the original significance of male veiling: "purpureo velare comas adopertus amictu" ("veil your hair with a covering of purple robe" [trans. Fairclough, LCL, modified]). Vergil does not stop there; he adds, "ne qua inter sanctos ignis in honore deorum hostilis facies occurrat et omina turbet" ("lest among the holy fires in worship of the gods no hostile face may occur and disturb the omens"). Here there is a reason for the veiling: to conceal a possible "hostile face" and so upset the ritual. This hostile face is stated in unmistakable terms: it is clearly the "evil Greeks" (*malis ... Grais*). Vergil, picturing Aeneas on hostile Greek soil, devises a means whereby the liturgist could avoid the distraction of a hostile presence whose sudden appearance would then disturb the omens.[38] Since the purpose of the sacrifice was to secure the goodwill of the gods, bad omens would disturb or perhaps offend. In this case, a bad omen could be the sudden appearance of a Greek!

Plutarch was certainly aware of the motive among Romans for wearing a veil. He states in *Quaest. rom.* 10 (266D) that, during an act of worship, Romans pull their togas over their head (τῇ ἐπικρύψει τῆς κεφαλῆς) or their ears (τῶν ὤτων) as a precaution (ἐφυλάττοντο) against bad omens (ἀπαίσιον). A toga coming down from the head would provide covering for both eyes and ears. Protection for the eyes would shield the sacrificant from seeing the unwanted sight; protection for the ears would muffle any approaching undesirable sound. Plutarch further develops this very thought in 266C:

Διὰ τί τοὺς θεοὺς προσκυνοῦντες ἐπικαλύπτονται τὴν κεφαλήν, τῶν δ᾽ ἀνθρώπων τοῖς ἀξίοις τιμῆς ἀπαντῶντες, κἂν τύχωσιν ἐπὶ τῆς κεφαλῆς ἔχοντες τὸ ἱμάτιον, ἀποκαλύπτονται;

---

[37] Freier, *Caput Velare*. 121.
[38] See ibid., 75: "Dies ist auch die übereinstimmende Erklärung für diesen Brauch in der Antike, wenn seine Einführung durch Aeneas erwähnt wird."

> Τοῦτο γὰρ ἔοικε κἀκείνην ἐπιτείνειν τὴν ἀπορίαν. εἰ μὲν οὖν ὁ περὶ Αἰνείου λεγόμενος λόγος ἀληθής ἐστιν, ὅτι τοῦ Διομήδους παρεξιόντος ἐπικαλυψάμενος τὴν θυσίαν ἐπετέλεσε, λόγον ἔχει καὶ ἀκολουθεῖ τῷ συγκαλύπτεσθαι πρὸς τοὺς πολεμίους τὸ τοῖς φίλοις καὶ ἀγαθοῖς ἐντυγχάνοντας ἀποκαλύπτεσθαι.
>
> Why is it that when they worship the gods, they cover their heads, but when they meet any of their fellow men worthy of honour, if they happen to have the toga over the head, they uncover?
>
> This second fact seems to intensify the difficulty of the first. If, then, the tale told of Aeneas is true, that, when Diomedes passed by, he covered his head and completed the sacrifice, it is reasonable and consistent with the covering of one's head in the presence of an enemy that men who meet good men and their friends should uncover. (trans. Babbitt, LCL)

The above text has a number of helpful connections to Roman Corinth. First, Plutarch uses six different expressions to describe either the covering or uncovering of the head with a material garment: ἐπικαλύπτονται τὴν κεφαλήν, ἐπὶ τῆς κεφαλῆς ἔχοντες τὸ ἱμάτιον, ἀποκαλύπτονται, ἐπικαλυψάμενος, συγκαλύπτεσθαι, and ἀποκαλύπτεσθαι. Clearly, veiling of the head with a garment is the subject under discussion. The words τὴν κεφαλήν and τὸ ἱμάτιον leave no doubt that covering the head with a ἱμάτιον is the topic. Second, the context is the worship of the Roman gods, for which it was necessary for a male to cover the head. Third, in the anecdote about Aeneas, Plutarch mentions that, at the moment of sacrificing to the gods, Aeneas was unveiled. But when he saw Diomedes approaching, he covered his head. Diomedes is a Greek, and Aeneas considered him an enemy!

An application to the situation at Roman Corinth would make possible the following connection: if a believer, wearing a purple-bordered toga, suddenly veiled his head during worship or prayer, this act could conceivably send a shame-generating message. The shame would accrue based on the underlying assumption in Roman ritual of a potential *hostile* presence of some kind. In other words, the presumed hostile face in the assembly could be considered to be the Greeks themselves, a visitor, or unveiled women. If the believer was a Roman who suddenly covered his head, the Greeks would undoubtedly take offense.

D. *The Roman* praetexta, *Advertising Rank and Status, Is a Purple-Bordered Toga Used for Covering the Head*

Roman head coverings were often purple, signifying authority and wealth. The Roman *praetexta* and the *toga purpurea*,[39] along with gold and silver, were considered worthy as gifts for kings (Livy, *Ab urbe cond.* 31.11.12). This particular

---

[39] This "robe of state" is often used interchangeably: Livy (*Ab urbe cond.* 34.7.2) indicates a combining of these two designations into one: *praetextis purpura togis*. See also Livy, *Ab urbe cond.* 1.8.3.

garment was also designated as part of the wardrobe of priests (Livy, *Ab urbe cond.* 34.7.2; 33.42.2). According to Louise Revell, a Roman historian,

> Wearing distinctive clothing and carrying special objects set the priests apart, and acting in an authoritative manner and interpreting the will of the gods demonstrated a knowledge not available to the rest of the community.... The right to preside over a sacrifice was limited to those with *auctoritas*, such as the *paterfamilias*, magistrates and priests.[40]

Paul Zanker observes, "It is astonishing how many portraits of Augustus made during his lifetime, both on coins and as honorific statues, show him veiled in a toga. Many such statues were even exhibited in Greece and Asia Minor, where this type of ruler portrait was surely quite alien."[41] According to Zanker, in fact, a veiled statue of Augustus Caesar was discovered at Corinth in 1915 and is now in the museum in Corinth.[42] What was accepted and honored in Rome could be offensive in subjugated Greece. Such portraits could be construed as symbolic monuments to foreign rule and oppression.

Since the Roman toga of elite men was often bordered by the color purple,[43] this was a color of prestige and prominence. This elegant color may have signaled additional notions of rank and status. Ancients clearly valued this color.[44] What is significant, though, is that in certain contexts the color purple was required along with the *capite velato* (Livy, *Ab urbe cond.* 8.9.5).

Gill focuses on this aspect of status in his description of a Roman male in a strategic position of leadership: "Not everybody present at the sacrifice would have to pull their toga over their head. This feature of the so-called *capite velato* was the

---

[40] Louise Revell, *Roman Imperialism and Local Identities* (Cambridge: Cambridge University Press, 2009), 165.

[41] Paul Zanker, *The Power of Images in the Age of Augustus*, trans. Alan Shapiro, Jerome Lectures 16th Series (Ann Arbor: University of Michigan Press, 2000), 127. See also Klaus Fittschen and Paul Zanker, *Kaiser- und Prinzenbildnisse*, vol. 1 of *Katalog der römischen Porträts in den Capitolinischen Museen und den anderen kommunalen Sammlungen der Stadt Rom*, Beiträge zur Erschliessung hellenistischer und kaiserzeitlicher Skulptur und Architektur 3 (Mainz: von Zabern, 1983), pl. 57, no. 51, showing Hadrian veiled; the commentary reads: "die Toga *capite velato* stelle einen Kaiser immer als Pontifex Maximus dar."

[42] See, e.g., Dietrich Boschung, *Gens Augusta: Untersuchungen zu Aufstellung, Wirkung und Bedeutung der Statuengruppen des julisch-claudischen Kaiserhauses*, Monumenta Artis Romanae 32 (Mainz: von Zabern, 2002), pls. 48.1 and 50.1, and commentary on p. 64.

[43] Dionysius of Halicarnassus (*Ant. rom.* 3.60.1) describes the Roman toga in a twofold manner: χιτῶνά τε πορφυροῦν χρυσόσημον καὶ περιβόλαιον πορφυροῦν ποικίλον ("a purple tunic decorated with gold and an embroidered purple robe"). Dionysius identifies this dress as part of the "insignia of sovereignty" (τὰ σύμβολα τῆς ἡγεμονίας). The τε ... καί construction ("not only ... but even") suggests two separate pieces of clothing. This is confirmed by Livy (*Ab urbe cond.* 10.7.9): "toga praetexta, tunica palmate et toga picta."

[44] See Rev 17:4 and 18:16. See also Mark Bradley, *Colour and Meaning in Ancient Rome*, Cambridge Classical Studies (Cambridge: Cambridge University Press, 2009), 189–211.

iconographical mark of a sacrificant presiding over a specifically Roman ritual."⁴⁵ Here the emphasis is on the one "presiding" and the dress that distinguishes such a leadership role—the toga pulled up over the head. Gill develops this thought further: "Paul may be attempting to say that if certain men adopt the form of dress suitable for a select band of people at a religious act, then division would occur."⁴⁶ Gill's emphasis is on "certain men" and "a select band of people" who wear easily identifiable clothing marking them off as notable. Finally, Gill draws an even tighter conclusion: "The issue which Paul is dealing with here seems to be that members of the social elite within the church—the *dunatoi* and the *eugeneis* (1:26)—were adopting a form of dress during worship which drew attention to their status in society."⁴⁷ We return once again to a form of dress. In Gill's reconstruction, it is not that these "certain men" or "band of people" were exercising spiritual gifts within the community of faith but, rather, that they were bringing their outside social status into the fellowship and using dress as evidence of it to elevate themselves over others of less privilege.

As a color, purple conveyed overtones of authority, luxury, and prestige. For example, Dionysius of Halicarnassus describes purple as one of the symbols of power (πυρφύρα ... καὶ ἄλλοις τῆς ἐξουσίας συμβόλοις; *Ant. rom.* 5.29.1). Although Oster declines to view social status as a contributing factor to Paul's concern in this text,⁴⁸ it must be conceded that Roman male ideology regarding veiling on this point would introduce a clash of values. A striking text illustrating how purple can be used to emphasize status and self-importance is Livy, *Ab urbe cond.* 24.5.3–5:

> Hieronymous at his very first appearance showed how different everything was, just as if he wished by his vices to make them regret his grandfather. For, though through so many years they had seen Hiero and his son Gelo not differing from the rest of the citizens [*civibus*] in garb [*vestis*] or in any other distinction, they beheld *purple* and a diadem and armed attendants and a man who came forth from the palace sometimes even in a chariot with four white horses after the manner of Dionysius the tyrant. This haughty state and *costume* were suitably attended by contempt shown towards everyone. (trans. Moore, LCL)

E. The Act of consecratio or devotio to the Wrath of the Gods Requires the Ritual Covering of the Head

Livy records a number of incidents that may be categorized under the heading of *devotio*. Although there is some confusion among Latin writers over the

---

⁴⁵ Gill, "Importance of Roman Portraiture," 247.
⁴⁶ Ibid., 248.
⁴⁷ Ibid., 250.
⁴⁸ Richard Oster, *1 Corinthians*, College Press NIV Commentary (Joplin, MO: College Press, 1995), 253, "This means that social status issues were not what the apostle was striving to counter."

difference between *consecratio* and *devotio*,⁴⁹ I assume that the rite of *devotio* is the original act and that *consecratio* is a later development. The historicity of this rite also has been questioned;⁵⁰ I make use of it even though at times it is likely to have had an imaginary role in Rome's legendary past. Whether based on historical fact or imagination, its potential influence in Corinth cannot be ruled out. Livy's idea of *devotio* predates his own time by some three hundred years. I cite two texts from Livy: the first is from *Ab urbe cond.* 8.9.1–14.

> Decius the consul called out to Marcus Valerius in a loud voice: "We have need of Heaven's help, Marcus Valerius. Come, therefore, state pontiff of the Roman People, dictate the words, that I may devote [*devoveam*] myself to save the legions." The pontiff bade him don the purple-bordered toga [*togam praetextam*], and with veiled head [*velato capite*] and one hand thrust out from the toga and touching his chin, stand upon a spear that was laid under his feet, and say as follows: "Janus, Jupiter, Father Mars, Quirinus, Bellona, Lares, divine Novensiles, divine Indigites, ye gods in whose power are both we and our enemies [*hostium*], and you, divine Manes, I invoke and worship you, I beseech and crave your favour, that you prosper the might and the victory of the Roman People of the Quirites, and visit the foes [*hostes*] of the Roman people of the Quirites with fear, shuddering, and death.... I devote [*devoveo*] the legions and auxiliaries of the enemy [*hostium*], together with myself, to the divine Manes and to Earth." (trans. Foster, LCL)

This tradition chronicles the origin of the *devotio* as Livy has received it. When the consul Decius despaired of victory over the enemy, he summoned the pontifex to preside over a very formal ceremony. First of all, this ritual required that Decius cover his head with a purple-bordered toga. Second, he needed to verbalize a deliberate decision to march out against the enemy so that, with the help of the Roman

---

⁴⁹ For example, L. Annaeus Florus (*Hist. rom.* 1.12.7) states, Decius *more patrio devotum dis minibus optulit caput, sollemnemque familiae suae consecrationem in vitoriae pretium peregit* ("Decius, following the example of his father, offered his life as a sacrifice to the gods below, and thus by performing an act of *devotio*, which was the custom of his family, paid the price for victory" [my translation]). Florus reveals his understanding in a number of critical ways: the rite traces back to Decius; this man devotes himself to the gods of the underworld; this act of *devotio* is further explained as a *consecratio* for the sake of victory. Florus records a similar scene (*Hist. rom.* 1.8.3) in which he describes a Roman consul who, upon veiling his head (*capite velato*), devotes himself to the infernal gods (*dis manibus se devoverit*). This he does in front of the army in order to inspire his troops. This symbolical act of self-sacrifice is reminiscent of the movie *El Cid* (1961), a historical epic film that romanticizes the life of the Castilian knight Don Rodrigo Díaz de Vivar, called "El Cid." At the end of the movie, El Cid, now mortally wounded, is strapped to his saddle as he rides out of the castle and leads his troops in battle. His troops, thinking their leader is still alive, take fresh courage. For another use of *consecratio*, see Cicero, *Dom.* 46–49/122–128.

⁵⁰ For a balanced and generous account of both sides of the issue, see S. P. Oakley, *A Commentary on Livy, Books VI–X*, 4 vols. (Oxford: Clarendon, 1998), 2:477–86. What is significant for our purpose is that the prayer of *devotio* was still extant in Pliny's day (*Nat.* 28.12).

gods, both he and the enemy would be destroyed. According to Livy, who does not question the historicity of this event and who never uses the word *fabula* when discussing the rite,[51] Decius rode out to his anticipated death. His body was found the next day and given an appropriate burial. This sacramental death is clearly calculated to inspire fear in the enemy and provide fresh courage to the Roman soldiers. The second text then follows closely at 8.10.11–14, giving Livy's own understanding of this ritual:

> It seems proper to add here that the consul, dictator, or praetor who <u>devotes</u> [*devoveat*] the legions of the *enemy* [*hostium*] need not <u>devote</u> [*devovere*] himself, but may designate any citizen he likes from a regularly enlisted Roman legion; if the man who has been <u>devoted</u> [*devotus est*] dies, it is deemed that all is well; if he does not die, then an image of him is buried seven feet or more under ground and a sin-offering [*piaculum*] is slain; where the image has been buried, thither a Roman magistrate may not go up. But if he shall choose to <u>devote</u> himself [*sese devovere*] as Decius <u>did</u> [*devovit*], if he does not die, he cannot sacrifice either for himself or for the people without sin, whether with a victim or with any other offering he shall choose. He who <u>devotes</u> himself [*sese devoverit*] has the right to dedicate his arms to Vulcan, or any other god he likes. The spear on which the consul has stood and prayed must not fall into the hands of an enemy.

The above text is loaded with formalities: it limits the rite to specific people (consul, dictator, or praetor) for the purpose of destroying enemies by devoting oneself or a designated alternate, accompanied by an act of prayer, with head veiled (*velato capite*), and with supplementary provisions for a sacrificial substitute in the event of a nondeath. Furthermore, this text clearly states that the entire ritual is connected to the Roman gods. This act of *devotio* anticipates the death of the one making such a vow, and its sole purpose is to bring about the destruction of the enemy. It appears, however, that Livy may be interpreting the original event as it may have evolved over time. Livy inserts the information that the leader of such a ceremony has the discretion to make a substitution. This may be an innovation.

H. S. Versnel breaks down the *devotio* into the following components: (1) The essence of apotropaic prayer is "the tendency to avert imminent disaster by transferring it to others."[52] (2) This prayer, requesting such a transference to the enemy, shows that "the gods or demons of death are entitled to a victim."[53] (3) Therefore, a substitution must be made: the idea embodied in the term *vicarios* is probably

---

[51] Tacitus (*Ann.* 2.69) is noncommittal about the historicity of this ritual. He simply says, creditur animas numinibus infernis sacrari ("it is believed that souls are devoted or consecrated to the gods of the underworld"). For the unquestioned practice of this ritual in the historical tradition, see L. Annaeus Florus, *Hist. rom.* 1.12.7; Livy, *Ab urbe cond.* 5.41.3; Valerius Maximus, *Mem.* 1.7.3; 5.5; Cicero, *Nat. d.* 2.3.10; for its use in poetry, see Juvenal, *Sat.* 8.254–259. For the tradition that the devotee is to appear *capite velato*, see Florus, *Hist. rom.* 1.8.3.

[52] H. S. Versnel, "Two Types of Roman *devotio*," *Mnemosyne* 29 (1976): 365–410, esp. 389.

[53] Ibid.

based on a widespread belief that in order to avert evil a substitute must be indicated to whom the evil can be transferred.[54] The intended result of this kind of prayer and *devotio* would be the destruction of the enemy.

Such a prayer in the Corinthian assembly would have significant repercussions, depending on the identification of the enemy. If a believer showed up for worship wearing a Roman toga with a purple border and then prayed *velato capite* for the destruction of Rome, of a personal enemy, or even of someone else in the assembly (such as a woman), this action could potentially be considered shameful.

III. Conclusion

Greek culture has a limited purpose for male head coverings. Romans, by contrast, have numerous nuances for this male accoutrement. I have documented a total of five potential scenarios in which the notion of shame and male head coverings could possibly intersect. These multiple aspects involving the practice of *capite velato* make it difficult to isolate solely on a single dimension of this symbolism. Regarding the particular situation at Roman Corinth, the demeanor of a man covering his head in worship may have afforded more than one opportunity for manifestations of shame. Since Corinth was a Roman colony, we cannot dismiss the possibility that several different Roman veiling practices may have played a role in the injunction in 1 Cor 11:4. Depending on the degree of Roman infiltration and assimilation, multiple applications may have influenced the congregation. At least at the theoretical level, such influences may have been possible.

---

[54] Ibid., 395.

New and Recent Titles

THE RHETORIC OF ABRAHAM'S FAITH IN ROMANS 4
Andrew Kimseng Tan
Paperback $44.95, 978-1-62837-208-3   348 pages, 2018   Code 064822
Hardcover $59.95, 978-0-88414-289-8 E-book $44.95, 978-0-88414-290-4
Emory Studies in Early Christianity 20

THE FIRST URBAN CHURCHES 3
Ephesus
James R. Harrison and L. L. Welborn, editors
Paperback $46.95, 978-0-88414-234-8   382 pages, 2018   Code: 064209
Hardcover $61.95, 978-0-88414-236-2 E-book $46.95, 978-0-88414-235-5
Writings from the Greco-Roman World Supplement Series 9

READING AND TEACHING ANCIENT FICTION
Jewish, Christian, and Greco-Roman Narratives
Sara R. Johnson, Rubén R. Dupertuis, and Christine Shea, editors
Paperback $40.95, 978-1-62837-196-3   338 pages, 2018   Code: 064212
Hardcover $55.95, 978-0-88414-261-4 E-book $40.95, 978-0-88414-260-7
Writings from the Greco-Roman World Supplement Series 10

PEDAGOGY IN ANCIENT JUDAISM AND EARLY CHRISTIANITY
Karina Martin Hogan, Matthew Goff, and Emma Wasserman, editors
Paperback $49.95, 978-1-62837-165-9   424 pages, 2017   Code: 063548
Hardcover $64.95, 978-0-88414-208-9 E-book $49.95, 978-0-88414-207-2
Early Judaism and Its Literature 41

SACRIFICE, CULT, AND ATONEMENT IN EARLY JUDAISM AND CHRISTIANITY
Constituents and Critique
Henrietta L. Wiley and Christian A. Eberhart, editors
Paperback $56.95, 978-1-62837-155-0   434 pages, 2017   Code: 060393
Hardcover $76.95, 978-0-88414-191-4 E-book $56.95, 978-0-88414-190-7
Resources for Biblical Study 85

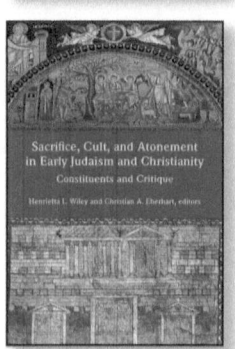

SBL Press • P.O. Box 2243 • Williston, VT 05495-2243
Phone: 877-725-3334 (toll-free) or 802-864-6185 • Fax: 802-864-7626
Order online at www.sbl-site.org/publications

The Rider on the White Horse, the Thigh Inscription, and Apollo: Revelation 19:16

JAMES R. EDWARDS
jedwards@whitworth.edu
Whitworth University, Spokane, WA 99218

This article proposes a solution to the puzzling thigh inscription of Rev 19:16, beginning with an examination of seven thigh inscriptions from antiquity, both statuary and literary. All but one of the inscriptions are dedicated to Apollo. I treat the thigh inscription of Rev 19:16 in light of possible images and allusions to Apollo in the Apocalypse. The saga of the celestial woman, the child, and Satan in Rev 12 emerges as a primary allusion to the Leto–Apollo–Python myth of antiquity. I consider secondary allusions to Apollo in relation to the defeat of Satan, the function of doxologies, oracle and revelation, and the imagery of the sun in the Apocalypse. I conclude that the inscription on the thigh of the rider on the white horse recapitulates the various terms and images reminiscent of the Apollo cult in the Apocalypse, which are perfected and fulfilled in Jesus Christ, who is "King of kings and Lord of lords" (19:16).

Revelation 19:11–16 introduces a vision of a rider on a white horse in heaven. The rider is faithful and true, and he judges and wages war in righteousness. His eyes are flames of fire, and he is crowned with many crowns and clothed in a garment dipped in blood. He rides forth to execute the judgment of Almighty God, leading an army in heaven also riding white horses and clothed in white linen. A sharp sword issues from his mouth, which is interpreted in light of Ps 2:9, "he will shepherd them with an iron rod." The rider bears a name known only to himself (19:12),[1] but he is called "the word of God" (19:13) and "upon his garment and upon his thigh is written the name, 'King of kings and Lord of lords'" (19:16).

I wish to thank Jonathan Moo, Roger Mohrlang, Will Kynes, Josh Leim, Margaret Schatkin, Christopher Synodinos, and two anonymous reviewers for their counsel in the preparation and publication of this article.

[1] Biblical citations without a book name refer to Revelation. Unless otherwise noted, translations of inscriptions, original sources, and biblical material are my own.

The images of this descriptive collage were applied to Jesus earlier in the Apocalypse, including "Lord of lords and King of kings," used with reference to him as the victorious Lamb of God (17:14). The rider is manifestly Jesus Christ. The one new image in this collage—an image that appears nowhere else in the New Testament—is the reference to the thigh inscribed with "King of kings and Lord of lords" (19:16). The thigh image is "an exegetical puzzle"[2] to interpreters of the Apocalypse, many of whom pass over it without comment. The lack of evidence with reference to the thigh has led to various speculations regarding its meaning. Patristic writers often interpret "thigh" allegorically as a reference to the posterity of Jesus, analogous to "all the souls that came with Jacob into Egypt, who came out of his thighs" (Gen 46:26).[3] Modern scholars generally agree that the meaning is literal rather than allegorical but without consensus on the meaning of the image. Some suggest that the name is written at the place where the garment covers the thigh.[4] Others take "thigh" as a metonym for "sword," that is, the place where the sword is kept (Homer, *Il.* 1.190; *Od.* 11.231; Vergil, *Aen.* 10.788; Exod 32:27; Judg 3:16, 21; Ps 45:3; Cant 3:8).[5] Somewhat similarly, David Aune suggests that thigh might refer to the haunch or hip of the horse rather than of its rider.[6] These explanations largely dismiss thigh as a meaningful descriptive element in 19:16.

Interpreters who discuss thigh as a meaningful descriptive element differ widely. Ernst Lohmeyer thinks thigh is inspired by the Egyptian custom of inscribing the royal name on every limb.[7] H. B. Swete speculates that the thigh inscription may imitate an "equestrian statue at Ephesus similarly inscribed."[8] G. K. Beale suggests that the name is hidden by the rider's garment, invisible until the garment is "blown aside" as he rides past.[9] Edmondo Lupieri acknowledges that a name on a

---

[2] So described by G. R. Beasley-Murray, *The Book of Revelation*, NCB (London: Oliphants, 1974), 281.

[3] Arpingius of Beja, *Tract. Apoc.* (19:15–16), CCSL 107:74; Oecumenius, *Commentarius in Apocalypsin*, ed. Marc de Groote, TEG 8 (Louvain: Peeters, 1999), 244–45 on 19:15–16; Primasius, *Comm. Apoc.* (19:16), CCSL 92:268–69. See William C. Weinrich, *Revelation*, ACCS 12 (Downers Grove, IL: InterVarsity Press, 2005), 313–14.

[4] E.g., Henry B. Swete, *The Apocalypse of St John: The Greek Text with Introduction, Notes, and Indices* (London: Macmillan, 1906; repr., Grand Rapids: Eerdmans, 1951), 255; Robert H. Mounce, *The Book of Revelation*, rev. ed., NICNT (Grand Rapids: Eerdmans, 1997), 356.

[5] Among many others, G. B. Caird, *A Commentary on the Revelation of St. John the Divine*, HNTC (New York: Harper & Row, 1966), 246–47.

[6] David E. Aune, *Revelation 17–22*, WBC 52C (Nashville: Nelson, 1998), 1044. Julius Wellhausen (*Analyse der Offenbarung Johannis* [Berlin: Weidemann, 1907], 30) proposed a conjectural textual emendation of ἱμάτιον to ἵππον in 19:16 in support of such an interpretation.

[7] Ernst Lohmeyer, *Die Offenbarung des Johannes*, 2nd ed., HNT 16 (Tübingen: Mohr Siebeck, 1953), 159–60. By way of analogy, Lohmeyer likens the thigh inscription to the indelible colored mark left by the impregnating serpent on the body of Atia, mother of Augustus (Suetonius, *Aug.* 94.4).

[8] So Swete, *Apocalypse of St John*, 255.

[9] G. K. Beale, *The Book of Revelation: A Commentary on the Greek Text*, NIGTC (Grand Rapids: Eerdmans, 1999), 963.

thigh "evokes Hellenistic statuary" and tentatively posits that the inscription may be a *gemmadia*—mysterious letters that sometimes appear in paleo-Christian portraiture.[10] Other commentators declare that ancient thigh inscriptions contain the name of the person represented.[11] In a recent article on Rev 19:16, Sheree Lear proposes that the thigh inscription recalls Gen 49:10.[12]

To date, no consensus has emerged regarding the meaning of thigh in 19:16.[13] I propose a new solution to this puzzle. I begin by considering seven thigh inscriptions that have not previously been discussed in relation to 19:16. This evidence, both statuary and literary, reveals that thigh inscriptions, though rare, are dedicated to Apollo. Following examination of epigraphic evidence, I will consider Apollo

---

[10] Edmondo Lupieri, *A Commentary on the Apocalypse of John*, trans. Maria Poggi Johnson and Adam Kamesar, Italian Texts and Studies on Religion and Society (Grand Rapids: Eerdmans, 1999), 306–7.

[11] So Mitchell G. Reddish, *Revelation*, SHBC (Macon, GA: Smyth & Helwys, 2001), 369: "John is reflecting the custom mentioned in some ancient inscriptions of statues that have on the thigh of the person the name of the individual represented"; and David Andrew Thomas, *Revelation 19 in Historical and Mythological Context*, StBibLit 118 (New York: Lang, 2008), 140: "it was typical practice to write the names of heroes and gods on the thighs of statues that were cast in their image."

[12] Sheree Lear, "Revelation 19.16's Inscribed Thigh: An Allusion to Gen 49.10b," *NTS* 60 (2014): 280–85. The thesis of Lear's article is, as its title indicates, that Rev 19:16 is an allusion to a Hebrew version of Gen 49:10. In her words, "it would appear that John was reading a text similar to the MT. The translation 'inscribed on his thigh' is a legitimate translation of the consonants we find represented in the MT" (284). The chief appeal of the argument is the translation of רגל as μηρός in Gen 49:10. The term μηρός occurs in Rev 19:16, but this agreement with Gen 49:10 is insufficient to prove a correlation between the two texts. Although μηρός is a *hapax legomenon* in the New Testament, it occurs some thirty-five times in the LXX. The remainder of Lear's article falls short of proving the proposed thesis. With reference to Gen 49:10b (ומחקק מבין רגליו), which Lear translates "Nor the commander's staff from between his feet"), she argues that John "chose to interpret the participle מחקק with the meaning 'inscribe'" (283). This seems extremely doubtful. In v. 10, מחקק, a masculine *polel* participle, functions as a noun, not a verb. Its use as a *qal* verb for "inscribe" occurs only four times in the MT by my count (Isa 30:8, 49:16, Ezek 4:1, 23:14), whereas its nominative form (חק), whose function the participial form of the word fulfills in Gen 49:10, occurs 130 times in the MT in the sense of "rule" or "law." This argues against John's choosing to translate מחקק by a rare verb form, "inscribe." If "inscribe" were admitted, a straightforward translation of 49:10b (MT) would be: "inscribed between his feet/legs." Whatever the precise meaning of that phrase may be, it differs substantially from the LXX of Gen 49:10b (καὶ ἡγούμενος ἐκ τῶν μηρῶν αὐτοῦ, "and a ruler from his thighs"), which Lear admits "also offers a legitimate Greek equivalent of what we see in the MT" (284). The LXX version of Gen 49:10b thus refers to procreation, and its MT version to legitimacy of rule, but neither approximates a name written on a thigh, which is the clear meaning of Rev 19:16.

[13] The substitution of "forehead" (μέτωπον) in 19:16 for "garment" (ἱμάτιον) in minuscules 1006 (eleventh century) and 1841 (ninth/tenth century) attempts, ostensibly, to harmonize the verse with the frequent references (eight times only in Revelation) to names written on *foreheads*. The paucity and lateness of textual witnesses for "forehead" do not commend this variant for serious consideration.

imagery and allusions in the Apocalypse. Apollo was the most famous son of Zeus, the most Greek of the gods, and one of the only Olympians to retain the same name in both Greek and Latin. From a moral perspective he was the most exemplary member of the Greek pantheon. His epithets as "Helper," "Sun God," "Oracle Giver," and "Beneficent Revealer," and above all his victorious conquest over Python correspond in various ways to attributes of Jesus Christ in the Apocalypse.[14] On the basis of epigraphic evidence from ancient thigh inscriptions and the Apollo imagery in the Apocalypse, I conclude that the thigh inscription of 19:16, although enigmatic to subsequent readers and interpreters of the Apocalypse, would have signaled to John's readers that the virtues enshrined in the cult of Apollo are consummated in Jesus Christ as the victorious rider on the white horse.

I. Evidence of Thigh Inscriptions from Antiquity

Miletus Statue

In the newly completed museum at Miletus a life-sized torso (chest to knees) of realistic style and proportion, identified as Apollo, bears an inscription on its left thigh (fig. 1). The orthography of the inscription, with Π formed approximating an English "P" (Ր), for example, dates the inscription to no later than the fifth century BCE.[15] Only a limited number of words of the inscription can be read with any degree of certainty. This is due, first, to the fact that the left leg of the statue is broken off at mid-thigh, which results in the loss of the inscription between the break and the knee. The complete text of the inscription is thus lost. Several extant letters are also too faint or corrupted to be deciphered with certainty. The inscription is further complicated by the fact that it is written from right to left. The inscription begins at the knee and reads leftward up toward the hip, at which point it makes a U-turn and continues leftward down toward the knee. The preserved letters thus represent the middle part of the inscription, with loss of the beginning and end of the inscription at the break above the knee. In order for the backward-written script to appear in proper Greek orthography, the inscription must be read from its reflection in a mirror.

---

[14] Apollo's favorable comparison with the Greek pantheon did not render him faultless, however. He, too, was complicit, if to a lesser extent, in the wrongdoings of the pantheon. Homer's *Iliad* records Apollo delivering a cowardly blow to Patroclus from behind, wounding him so he could be slain by Hector (*Il.* 16.915–960); Oedipus blames Apollo for bringing "these my woes to pass, these my sore, sore woes," which resulted in the misfortune of Thebes (Sophocles, *Oed. tyr.* 1329–1330); and Euripides recounts Apollo's rape of helpless Creusa and abandonment of both her and the child born of his violation (*Ion*, 384–90).

[15] For the formation of Greek letters prior to the fifth century BCE, see Herbert W. Smyth, *Greek Grammar*, rev. Gordon Messing (Cambridge: Harvard University Press, 1984), §2.

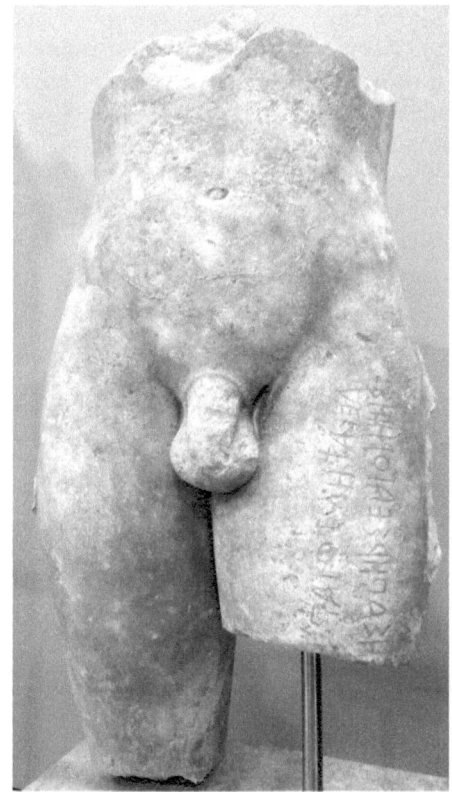

FIGURE 1. A life-sized torso (chest to knees), marble, lifelike in motif, identified tentatively by the museum as Apollo, inscribed on left thigh in only partially legible Greek, written right to left. Fifth century BCE. Miletus Museum, Turkey. Photograph by James R. Edwards, January 2014.

The inscription is transcribed and translated as follows:

...ΗΞΑΠΗΡΞΕΑΤΟ????
ΔΕΚΑΤΗΝΤΩΙΑΠ[ΟΛΛΩΝΙ]

...η ξ ά π ή ρ ξ (ε) α τ ο ? ? ? ?
δ ε κ ά τ η ν τ ῷ Ἀ π [ό λ λ ω ν ι]

... made an offering of ... a tithe to Ap[ollo].

The name of the putative donor of the offering and statue likely appeared in the lost letters. The votive nature of the inscription is evident from ἀπήρξ(ε)ατο and δεκάτην, and its dedication to Apollo, though not certain, is probable.

Claros Statue

A second thigh inscription appears on a statue at Claros (fig. 2), less than fifty miles north of Miletus. Like Didyma, to which Miletus was tethered by a ten-mile

Sacred Way, Claros was a celebrated oracle center of Apollo (Tacitus, *Ann.* 2.54). The statue under consideration is one of two at Claros, both dated to the sixth century BCE. The statue with the inscribed thigh is also only a torso (navel to knees). The Claros statue is elongated, stylized, and less lifelike than its counterpart in Miletus. Two complete lines of text, and a remnant third, run from just below the waist down the left thigh to the knee. The orthography of the text is conventional—each line is written left to right, and each begins anew at the top of the inscription.

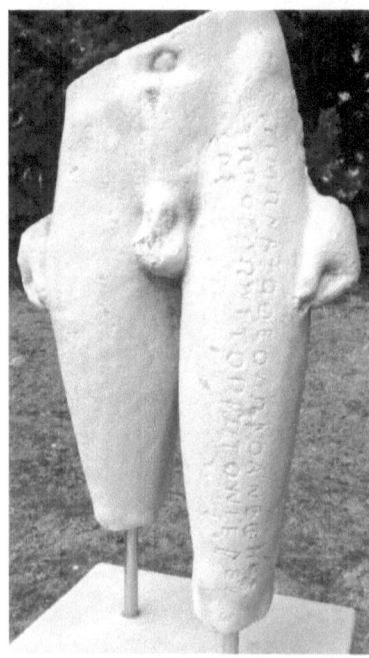

FIGURE 2. The Claros statue is a marble torso (navel to knees), elongated and stylized rather than lifelike, with clearly legible Greek lettering written conventionally from left to right. Sixth century BCE. Claros, Turkey. Photograph by Aydin Aygun, July 2015.

The inscription is transcribed and translated as follows:
ΤΙΜΩΝΑΞΟΘΕΟΔΩΡΟΑΝΕΘΗΚΕ
ΤΩΠΟΛΛΩΝΙΤΟΠΡΩΤΟΝΙΕΡΕΥ
ΣΑΣ

Τιμῶναξ ὁ Θεοδώρο ἀνέθηκε
τῶ (Ἀ)πόλλωνι τὸ πρῶτον ἱερεύ
σας.

Timonax, son of Theodorus, offered to Apollo the first sacrifice.[16]

---

[16] According to Smyth, *Greek Grammar*, §1301, the "genitive of belonging" appropriately translates the first two names in the sense of ὁ [υἱὸς τοῦ] Θεοδώρο[υ] ("the son of Theodorus"). It is unclear whether τὸ πρῶτον intends *the* first sacrifice, or *his* (Timonax's) first sacrifice. See again

Unlike its Miletian counterpart, the thigh inscription of Claros is complete and undamaged. Its donor is identified as Timonax, the name of Apollo (though contracted with its article) is assured, and ἱερεύσας signifies a votive or priestly offering at the cult of Claros.

Mantiklos Statue

A third thigh inscription exists in the Boston Museum of Fine Arts (fig. 3, p. 524). The statue on which it is inscribed was discovered in Thebes (Greece) in the 1890s, and is dated to 700–675 BCE.[17] Unlike the previously mentioned statues, the MFA figure is not a life-sized marble torso remnant but a nearly complete bronze statuette of a standing nude male, twenty centimeters (eight inches) in height. W. Froehner knows no sculpture as old that equals the excellence of its artistry.[18] The right arm of the statuette is missing, but the left arm is raised as if to hold a bow. The inscription, written in archaic Boeotian characters, appears on the front of both legs. The inscription begins at the right knee and reads up the thigh toward the waist, where it makes a broad U-turn down the left thigh to the knee. At the left knee, the inscription makes a sharp U-turn back up the left leg where another broad U-turn at the waist returns the inscription down to the right knee, where it ends. The inscription is thus a boustrophedon, that is, it "snakes"[19] into an outer and inner horseshoe: the outer one written conventionally left to right, but the inner horseshoe, like the inscription on the Miletus statue, written in Greek letters facing and reading from right to left.

The inscription preserves the chief elements present in the Claros inscription—the name of the donor and a votive offering to Apollo, here signified by "Archer of the Silver Bow" (Homer, *Il*. 2.766) and his ancient epithet Φοῖβος, "Bright One."[20]

Smyth, *Greek Grammar*, §1611. I am indebted to Dr. Christopher Synodinos for both of these references, as well as for references to secondary literature on the following Mantiklos inscription.

[17] W. Froehner, *Monuments et mémoires*, 2 vols. (Paris: Ernest Leroux, 1894–1895), 2:137–43; Paul Friedländer, *Epigrammata: Greek Inscriptions in Verse from the Beginnings to the Persian Wars* (Berkeley: University of California Press, 1948), 38–39.

[18] Froehner, *Monuments et mémoires*, 140: "De tous les ouvrages archaïques qui nous sont connus, aucun, il faut l'avouer, ne répond exactement au type que je viens de decrire."

[19] The German word for "boustrophedon" is *Schlangenschrift*, "serpentine script."

[20] See LSJ, s.v. "φοῖβος."

The inscription is transcribed and translated as follows:[21]

ΜΑΝΤΙΚΛΟΣΜΑΝΕΘΕΚΕϝΕ
ΚΑΒΟΛΟΙΑΡΓΥΡΟΤΟΧΣΟΙΤ
ΑΣΔΕΚΑΤΑΣΤΥΔΕΦΟΙΒΕΔΙ
ΔΟΙΧΑΡΙϝΕΤΤΑΝΑΜΟΙ

Μάντικλός μ' ἀνέθηκε ϝεκαβόλοι ἀργυροτόχσοι τᾶς δεκάτας, τὺ δὲ φοῖβε δίδοι χαρίϝετταν ἀμοι[ϝάν].[22]

Mantiklos donated me as an offering to the Archer of the Silver Bow; now you, Phoebus, grant a reward in return.

FIGURE 3. *Mantiklos "Apollo."* Greek. Late Geometric or Early Orientalizing Period, about 700–675 B.C. Place of Manufacture: Boiotia, Thebes, Greece. Bronze. Greek, Etruscan, & Roman Bronzes (MFA), no. 015; Sculpture in Stone and Bronze (MFA), p. 118 (additional published references); Highlights: Classical Art (MFA), p. 047. Height: 20.3 cm (8 in.) Francis Bartlett Donation of 1900. 03.997. Photograph © 2018, Museum of Fine Arts, Boston.

[21] Following the transcriptions of Froehner, *Monuments et mémoires*, 138; and Friedländer, *Epigrammata*, 39. The MFA web site (www.mfa.org/collections/object/mantiklos-apollo-152660) mistakenly doubles the *mu* in the final word.

[22] Τύ is the Doric second-person singular nominative pronoun for σύ (Smyth, *Greek Grammar*, §132 D). The first digamma (ϝ) is a reduplication of augmented ἐκαβόλοι (ibid., §122.b). Froehner seems right in rendering τᾶς δεκάτας as an indefinite offering, from spoils in war, for example (*Monuments et mémoires*, 139). Δίδοι (ibid.) is an imperative form employed by Pindar. The last two words pose the chief problem of the inscription. Χαρίϝετταν is without analogy in ancient Greek. Since half the words in the inscription are known from Homer, Froehner (138–39) emends the reading to χαρίϝεσσαν, and the final word to ἀμοι[ϝάν], in conformity with *Od.* 3.58, δίδου χαρίεσσαν ἀμοιβήν ἀμοιβήν, "grant a reward." Froehner's emendation has been adopted by most classical scholars.

Statue Mentioned by Cicero

In his second speech prepared for the prosecution of Verres, a first-century BCE proconsul of Sicily, Cicero accuses his opponent of sacrilege and of crimes of theft, corruption, and extortion against the Roman people (*Verr.* 2). Verres had succeeded in remaining in office by evading similar charges on earlier occasions, but he was unable to withstand the speed and forensic skill of Cicero's case against him, which resulted in his conviction and banishment.[23] Among Cicero's charges against Verres was the "impious and abominable theft ... from the much-venerated temple of Aesculapius at Agrigentum, ... of a beautiful statue of Apollo, on whose thigh was inscribed the name of Myron in small silver letters" (scelus illud furtumque nefarium ... Agrigento, ... signum Apollinis pulcherrimum, cuius in femore litteris minutis argenteis nomen Myronis erat inscriptum, ex Aesculapii religiosissimo fano sustulisti; *Verr.* 2.4.93).[24] Like the three statues considered above, the figure referenced by Cicero was a statue of Apollo with an inscribed thigh, although which thigh is not specified. Cicero describes the statue as "a memorial of Scipio," which implies its votive nature. Cicero does not specify whether the inscription contained more than the name "Myron."[25]

Statue Mentioned by Pausanias

A second literary reference to a thigh inscription comes from the second century CE. In approximately 175, the Greek traveler and geographer Pausanias, a native of Lydia, wrote what we today would call a travel guide on the history, topography, religions, mythologies, and monuments of important cities in Greece, as well as of some cities in Palestine, Egypt, and Italy (especially Rome). Pausanias's descriptions show a preference for the religious significance and associations of a site. In book 5 of his *Graeciae descriptio*, Pausanias discusses Elis, the main sanctuary of Zeus in Greece, in the northwest region of the Peloponnese that was dominated by Mount Olympia. The discussion of Elis contains a reference to "Apollo of Delphi" (5.27.1), who is subsequently called "the god of Delphi" (5.27.10). The ascription to Apollo is followed by mention of a statue of a fallen warrior "with an elegiac couplet written on its thigh: 'To Zeus, king of gods: the Mendeans, who overpowered Sipte by the might of their hands, placed me here as a first-fruit'" (ἐλεγεῖον δὲ ἐπ' αὐτὸ γεγραμμένον ἐστὶν ἐπὶ τοῦ μηροῦ· Ζηνὶ θεῶν βασιλεῖ μ'

---

[23] For a description of Cicero's spectacular defeat of the lawyers and orators marshaled by Verres, see Mary Beard, *SPQR: A History of Ancient Rome* (New York: Liveright, 2015), 253–54.

[24] Text and translation from L. H. G. Greenwood, *Cicero: The Verrine Orations*, LCL (Cambridge: Harvard University Press, 1935), 396–97.

[25] The suggestions of Reddish and Thomas (see n. 11 above) that thigh inscriptions contained only names of individuals may derive from a generalization based on Cicero's report. My survey demonstrates that thigh inscriptions (including perhaps the one referenced by Cicero) typically contained text as well as names.

ἀκροθίνιον ἐνθάδ' ἔθηκαν Μενδαῖοι, Σίπτην χερσὶ βιασσάμενοι) (*Descr.* 5.27.12).[26] This is the only known thigh inscription that appears on a statue other than of Apollo, although, as noted, it occurs in the context of Apollo's oracular activity at Delphi. Like the other statues in its genre, the figure at Elis is a votive statue (referred to as ἀκροθίνιον rather than δεκάτας).

References to Thigh Inscriptions in Secondary Literature

Two further thigh inscriptions are referenced in Froehner's discussion of the Mantiklos statuette.[27] Similar to the Mantiklos inscription, the two are inscribed on both thighs of bronze statuettes. The first was located by Froehner in the "Museum of Berlin" (Pergamon?) and inscribed, [Δ]ειναγό[ρ]ης μ' ἀνέθηκεν ἑκηβόλωι Ἀπόλλωνι ("Deinagores donated me to the Archer Apollo"). The second, provenanced from the Temple of Ptoos in Egypt, bears the inscription [ἀργ]υρόχσοι ("To the Silver Bow [Bearer]") on the right thigh, and the names of its donors on the left, Πυθίας ὠκραιφ[ιεὺς] καὶ Ἀσχρίων (ἀν[ε]θ[έταν] ("Donated by Pythia, the defender(?), and Aschrius"). The epithets "Archer" and "Silver Bow," as in the Mantiklos statuette, designate Apollo. "Pythia" in the second inscription likely designates the Pythian priestess of Apollo at Delphi.

Summary of Inscriptional Evidence

The foregoing summarizes all known thigh inscriptions from antiquity. The testimony of Cicero (*Verr.* 2.4.93) is frequently the lone evidence from Greco-Roman antiquity cited with reference to Rev 19:16. The conclusion typically drawn —that "names were inscribed in the thighs of statues of antiquity"[28]—is, as the foregoing survey demonstrates, inaccurate. Thigh inscriptions are relatively rare in antiquity,[29] and they contain text in addition to names. A characteristic template

---

[26] See the text of W. H. S. Jones and H. A. Ormerod, *Pausanias II, Description of Greece*, LCL (Cambridge: Harvard University Press, 1977), 548–51.

[27] Froehner, *Monuments et mémoires*, 139–42.

[28] *EDNT* 2:425, s.v. "μηρός"; similarly, Lohmeyer, *Die Offenbarung des Johannes*, 159–60; Reddish, *Revelation*, 369; Thomas, *Revelation 19*, 140.

[29] The source most commonly referenced by commentators in support of the frequency of thigh inscriptions in antiquity is J. J. Wettstein, Η ΚΑΙΝΗ ΔΙΑΘΗΚΗ: *Novum Testamentum Graecum*, 2 vols. (Amsterdam: Ex Officina Dommeriana, 1752), 2:834. An examination of Wettstein with reference to 19:16 does not affirm the frequency of thigh inscriptions in antiquity, nor his intention to demonstrate such. Of Wettstein's seven references, one (Plutarch, *Per.* 21.2) refers not to a thigh inscription but rather to the Lacedaemonians who engrave on the forehead (μέτωπον) of a wolf their privilege of consulting the oracle of Delphi. Another (Musonius Rufus [first century CE], *T. 1. Tab. XIV.1* [as cited by Wettstein]), also not a thigh inscription, refers to lettering on the cloak of a Roman officer that runs from the area covering the thigh down to that covering the shin. Of sources that refer to the leg, two (Anacreontea [first?/sixth century CE], mistaken by

of thigh inscriptions contains (1) the name of a donor, (2) who offers a "tithe" or "first sacrifice," (3) in fulfillment of a vow to Apollo.

II. Apollo Imagery in Revelation

If the thigh inscription of 19:16 were the only allusion to Apollo in the Apocalypse, it would be of doubtful significance for John's readers. In order to be meaningful, the thigh inscription, like images of a similar nature such as "Jezebel" (2:20), "root" (5:5, 22:16), or various combinations of "twelve" (21:12, 4:4, 21:17, 7:4), would need either to be independently recognizable or to recapitulate prior elements in the narrative. In this section I wish to demonstrate that the thigh inscription of 19:16, which, as I have demonstrated above, typically referenced Apollo in Greco-Roman antiquity, recapitulates earlier allusions to Apollo in the Apocalypse.

Revelation 12

The most significant Apollo prototype in Revelation is the depiction in chapter 12 of the heavenly woman, who gives birth to a child and who is subsequently pursued to earth by a dragon. Chapter 12 is distinguished in the Apocalypse by its independent and "patently mythological narrative" structure.[30] It also repeats signature elements of the Hellenistic myth of Leto–Apollo–Python, which belonged to the common cultural stock of John's readers in Roman Asia.

The celestial woman arrayed with the sun, whose footstool is the moon and whose head is crowned with stars, is in birth pangs. A powerful red dragon, its seven heads bedecked with diadems and its violent tail capable of sweeping a third of the stars from the sky, crouches before the woman to devour the child at birth. The woman gives birth to a son, whose destiny is to shepherd the nations with a rod of iron (Ps 2:9). Before the dragon can kill the boy, however, he is seized by God to his throne, and the woman flees to earth, where God has prepared a place for her in the desert. Michael and his angels defeat the dragon in battle and banish it from heaven, whereupon it flees to earth in pursuit of the woman, who is aided and

---

Wettstein for Anacreon [fourth century BCE], *Carmina Anacreontea* 50.1 and the scholia on Lucian [second century CE], *Ind.* 5) refer to the branding of horses on their haunches or hips. (These two references may account for the favoring of this interpretation by Wellhausen and Aune; see n. 6 above.) A single reference in Aristophanes (*Nub.* 122) refers to a crescent (σῖγμα) around the thigh (not an inscription on the thigh) of the Sapphorai. Wettstein also cites the report of Marcus Junianius Justinus (third century CE) 15.4.5, 9, of a figure of an anchor that appeared on the thighs of certain Seleucids from birth through childhood. This is not technically a thigh inscription, however, for it concerns a figure rather than letters. Only one of Wettstein's sources refers to a thigh inscription, the citation from Pausanias discussed above.

[30] David Aune, *Revelation 6–16*, WBC 52B (Nashville: Nelson, 1998), 674–75.

defended by the forces of nature. The cosmic drama ends with the dragon, frustrated in its schemes, plotting revenge against both woman and child. Revelation 12 is, of course, an allegory that is understandable and successful without reference to a mythic prototype. The woman is God's people in the churches of Asia Minor, the dragon is Satan, and the child is the Messiah.

Nevertheless, the warp and woof of Rev 12—the mortal struggle between the divine woman and evil dragon—preserve the same two mythic elements that are widespread in ancient mythology, especially in the Near East: two primordial beings and their allies—a protagonist representing order, virtue, and fertility and an antagonist representing chaos, destruction, and sterility—are locked in combat from the moment of creation. Creation myths throughout the ancient Near East preserve similar cosmic struggles: between Marduk and Tiamat or Gilgamesh and Humbaba in Babylonian mythology; between Baal and Yam (the sea) or Baal and Mot (Death), or YHWH and Rahab/Leviathan in Canaanite mythology; between Osiris and Set, or the sun god Re, to whom Pharaoh was assimilated in Egyptian mythology; and between Ouranos and Kronos, or between Zeus and Kronos, the Titans, and Giants in Greek mythology. Zoroastrianism, one of the oldest surviving religions of the ancient Near East, is defined by such cosmic dualism—good and wise Ahura Mazda in combat with a lying and evil archrival, the Druj.

The primordial dualism of light and darkness, good and evil, order and chaos was adopted, adapted, and adorned throughout ancient Near Eastern mythology. The dramatic *theomachies*—battles of the gods—depicted on the friezes of the Temple of Zeus at Pergamon or at the Sebasteion of Aphrodisias, for example, are visual tapestries of this same genre. A similar motif is present also in the Old Testament in the figure of YHWH as the divine warrior who executes just vengeance.[31] A version of the "combat myth" that depicts many of the essentials of Rev 12 was preserved by the second-century Latin mythographer Hyginus in the myth of Leto–Apollo–Python.[32] Although Hyginus postdated the Apocalypse by approximately

---

[31] Among many texts, see Exod 15, Deut 33, Judg 5, Isa 24–27, Hab 3, Ps 68. On YHWH as divine warrior, see Gerhard von Rad, *Holy War in Ancient Israel*, trans. and ed. Marva J. Dawn (Grand Rapids: Eerdmans, 1996; German original, 1965); Ben C. Ollenburger, *Zion, the City of the Great King: A Theological Symbol of the Jerusalem Cult*, JSOTSup 41 (Sheffield: JSOT Press, 1987); and, most recently, Andrew R. Angel, *Chaos and the Son of Man: The Hebrew* Chaoskampf *Tradition in the Period 515 BCE to 200 CE*, LSTS 60 (London: T&T Clark, 2006).

[32] Nothing is known of Hyginus's personal life (not even his full name). His *Fabulae*, written in approximately 200 CE, is an anthology of Greek and Roman myths in a low-quality Latin translation or paraphrase. The critical edition of Mauricius Schmidt, *Hygini Fabulae* (Jena: Libraria Maukiana, 1872) is based on a single manuscript copied and edited in Basel in 1535, which itself derived from a single manuscript of the same work dated to the ninth or tenth century. The Latin edition of Schmidt is translated and edited by Mary A. Grant, *The Myths of Hyginus*, University of Kansas Publications: Humanistic Studies 34 (Lawrence: University of Kansas Publications, 1960). For assessments of Hyginus and his *Fabulae*, see Grant, *Myths of Hyginus*, 1–24; and H. J. Rose, "An Unrecognized Fragment of Hyginus' *Fabulae*," *ClQ* 23 (1929): 96–99.

a century, he preserved in writing a version of the myth that contained earlier elements with which John would have been familiar.³³

> Python, offspring of Terra, was a huge dragon who, before the time of Apollo, used to give oracular responses on Mount Parnassus. Death was fated to come to him from the offspring of Latona (Leto). At that time Jove (Zeus) lay with Latona, daughter of Polus (Coeus). When Juno (Hera) found this out, she decreed (?) that Latona should give birth at a place where the sun did not shine. When Python knew that Latona was pregnant by Jove, he followed her to kill her. But by order of Jove the wind Aquilo (Boreas) carried Latona away, and bore her to Neptune (Poseidon). He protected her, but in order not to make void Juno's decree, he took her to the island Ortygia, and covered the island with waves. When Python did not find her, he returned to Parnassus. But Neptune brought the island of Ortygia up to a higher position; it was later called the island of Delos. There Latona, clinging to an olive tree, bore Apollo and Diana (Artemis), to whom Vulcan (Hephaestus) gave arrows as gifts. Four days after they were born, Apollo exacted vengeance on his mother. For he went to Parnassus and slew Python with his arrows. (Because of this deed he is called Pythian.) He put Python's bones in a caldron, deposited them in his temple, and instituted the funeral games for him which are called Pythian.³⁴

The skeletal structure of Rev 12 is preserved in this myth. A virtuous woman at the point of giving birth is attacked by a powerful dragon intent on killing her and/or her son. A superior power enlists the forces of nature to aid the woman in escaping the machinations of the dragon. The abortive schemes of the dragon are thwarted, and the endangered child survives birth to fulfill his divine fate to slay the dragon.³⁵

---

³³ See Debra Scoggins Ballentine, *The Conflict Myth and the Biblical Tradition* (Oxford: Oxford University Press, 2015), 139: "The conflict between the mother and dragon in Rev 12 most likely depends upon the Greek myth of Leto and Python.... However, as a whole the conflict between the dragon and divine figures in Revelation is an articulation of the ancient West Asian conflict topos, and these traditions were obviously compatible."

³⁴ Hyginus 140 "Python," in Grant, *Myths of Hyginus*, 115–16. Joseph Eddy Fontenrose documents eight versions of the Python myth prior to Hyginus (Homeric Hymns, Simonides, Pseudo-Julian, Ovid, Euripides, Servius, Lactantius Placidus, and Lucan) (*Python: A Study of Delphic Myth and Its Origins* [Berkeley: University of California Press, 1959]).

³⁵ Fontenrose offers a tenfold summary of his exhaustive study of ancient combat myths: The enemy (1) was of divine origin, (2) had a distinctive habitation, (3) had extraordinary appearance and properties, (4) was vicious and greedy, and (5) conspired against heaven; (6) a divine champion appeared to face and (7) fight the enemy; (8) the champion nearly lost the battle but (9) finally destroyed and (10) disposed of the enemy and celebrated his victory (*Python*, 9–11). Adela Yarbro Collins (*The Combat Myth in the Book of Revelation* [HDR 9; Missoula, MT: Scholars Press, 1976], 57–83), following the lead of Fontenrose, correlates the chief features of the Leto–child–Python myth with Rev 12 as follows: (1) dragon (v. 3), (2) chaos and disorder (v. 4a), (3) attack (v. 4b), (4) champion (v. 5a), (5) champion's "death" (v. 5b), (6) recovery of the champion (v. 7a), (7) battle renewed and victory (vv. 7b–9), (8) restoration and confirmation of order (vv. 10–12a), (9) dragon's reign (vv. 12b–17). Collins concludes, "The striking similarities between

The cult of Apollo flourished in the region to which John addressed the Apocalypse. On the southern circumference of the circuit of churches to which John wrote in Asia lay Didyma, home to the most important oracular cult of Apollo outside Delphi. A sacred area of Apollo had existed at Didyma from at least the eighth century BCE, prior to the first Ionian settlement there (Pausanius, *Descr.* 7.2.6). But in the third century BCE the Apollo cult in Asia grew to unprecedented proportions with construction of an immense Hellenistic temple at Didyma. Comprised of 120 columns sixty-five feet high and six-and-a-half feet in diameter, the temple (though never fully completed) was the third largest religious edifice in the Hellenistic world.[36] The Temple of Didyma attracted military and political luminaries of the Greco-Roman world, including Lysimachus, Augustus Caesar, and Trajan. Its spectacular construction nourished the memory of the Apollo cult throughout the Roman period, particularly in Asia. As noted earlier, a ten-mile Sacred Way linked the Temple of Apollo at Didyma to another Apollo cult site, the sanctuary of Apollo Delphinos in Miletus, which lay even closer to John's circuit of churches.

John's seven churches in Asia were in the immediate vicinity of the powerful purveyors of the Apollo cult at Didyma and Miletus. The inscribed thigh on a victorious rider of a white horse recapitulated in a single image the fuller narrative of the birth of the Messiah in Rev 12. The explicit citation in Rev 12 and 19 of Ps 2:9, "he will shepherd his people with a rod of iron," a text cited elsewhere in the Apocalypse only in 2:27, appears clearly to identify the messianic king born of the celestial woman in 12:5 with the rider on the white horse in 19:15.

Vanquisher of the Serpent Foe

Although chapter 12 is the fullest allusion to the Apollo myth in the Apocalypse, several further descriptions or images associated with Jesus Christ appear to recall particular characteristics of Apollo and his cult. The feat for which Apollo was most renowned was the slaying of Python, the dragon guardian of the sacred oracle at Delphi. The dragon was frightful and the contest grueling, but Apollo's unerring arrows won the victory. Importantly, δράκων, "dragon," which occurs nowhere else in the New Testament, appears thirteen times in the Apocalypse with

---

Revelation 12 and the Python–Leto myth led to the conclusion that Revelation 12 is an adaptation of that myth" (83). Aune (*Revelation 6–16*, 660–93) rightly finds some of Yarbro Collins's correlations forced but also rightly, in my judgment, affirms that "the version of the combat myth found in Rev 12 is closest to the Greek Leto–Apollo–Python myth" (712).

[36] The Temple of Didyma was only slightly smaller than the Artemision in Ephesus and the Heraion on the island of Samos west of Ephesus. For a complete description of the history, plan, and archaeology of the Temple of Didyma, see Ekrem Akurgal, *Ancient Civilizations and Ruins of Turkey: From Prehistoric Times until the End of the Roman Empire*, trans. John Whybrow and Molly Emre, 10th ed. (Istanbul: Net Turistik Yayinlar San. Tic. A.S., 2007), 222–31.

reference to Satan. Seven of the occurrences are clustered in chap. 12. Christ as the rider on the white horse seizes the beast and false prophet who lead the world astray and hurls them into the lake of fire and burning sulfur (19:19–21), after which "the old serpent, who is the devil and Satan" (20:2) is "cast into the lake of fire and sulfur, where the beast and false prophet are, and they shall be tormented day and night forever and ever" (20:10). The reference to "the old serpent, the devil, and Satan" (20:2) repeats the description of the dragon in 12:9 and is thus a distinctive link between the defeat of Satan in chapter 12 and the rider on the white horse in chapters 19–20. The Apollo–Python myth appears as a pilot analogy native to John's Asian readers of the greater cosmic victory over Satan by Jesus Christ, "the King of kings and Lord of lords" (19:16).

Doxologies

A principal characteristic of the Apollo cult was music and adoration. Apollo was the great musician of the Greek pantheon, entertaining the gods with his lyre or harp (κιθάρα). He was frequently depicted in art with a laurel crown on his head and either stringed instrument or strung bow in hand. The crown and lyre are likewise associated with Jesus in Revelation. The Son of Man seated on a heavenly cloud wears a golden crown (στέφανος) on his head (14:14), and, as the rider on the white horse in chapter 19, there are "many crowns [διαδήματα] on his head" (19:12). Others also, such as the twenty-four elders, wear crowns, though not of gold. But they cast their crowns before the throne of God and the Lamb, singing, "You are holy, our Lord and God" (4:10–11). As the Lamb standing on Mount Zion, Jesus is extolled in thunderous praise, approximating "the sound of many waters and great thunder, and the sound I heard was the sound of harpists playing their harps" (14:2; further, 15:2–4). The triple repetition of κιθάρα in 14:2 accentuates the adoration rendered the Lamb.

Processions to the temple or holy site of a Greek deity were typical of Greek festivals. Among the most prominent destinations of processions were oracular shrines of Apollo, the most esteemed oracular god of the Greek pantheon. The great festal processions "before the throne and the Lamb" (7:9) repeat on a grander scale the scenes of pagan choirs that processed annually to Apollo sanctuaries.[37] The processions of choirs before the Messiah are no longer localized at Didyma or Miletus or Claros, however, but now include "every nation, tribe, people, and tongue (4:7–11, 7:9–17, 13:7). They swell with "myriads of myriads and thousands of thousands" (μυριάδες μυριάδων καὶ χιλιάδες χιλιάδων) who sing a *new* song to the Lamb, the Christ of God (5:8–13, 15:3–4). The hymn and ritual associated with

---

[37] See, e.g., the description in Robin Lane Fox, *Pagans and Christians* (New York: Knopf, 1989), 180–82.

the cult of Apollo are in the Apocalypse devoted to Jesus Christ in fuller chorus and in universal scope.

Oracle and Revelation

Several offices of Apollo are likewise applied on a grander scale to Christ in the Apocalypse. Apollo's most important divine endowment was his oracular power, shunted through his cult sites and priestesses at Delphi, Didyma, Claros, and Miletus. As the son of Zeus, Apollo was the *magna vox* of the Greek pantheon—and as such second only to Zeus. Apollo's prophecies were communicated chiefly via oracles and music. John likewise assures readers that Jesus Christ is the unique and all-sufficient revealer of God. Jesus's prophecies, however, are communicated primarily in writing, as indicated by the sealed book in the right hand of the One who sits on the heavenly throne. This book cannot be opened by any mortal in heaven or on earth or under the earth. Only the Lion of Judah, the Root of David, is able to open the book and its seven seals (5:1–5). Two references immediately prior to the thigh inscription in 19:16 are relevant in this regard. The description of the witness of Jesus Christ as "the Spirit of Prophecy" (19:10, τὸ πνεῦμα τῆς προφητείας) is particularly reminiscent of Apollo's office as oracular revealer of the Greek pantheon. But, unlike Apollo, Jesus is not simply the revealer of God. He is the "Word of God" itself (19:13, ὁ λόγος τοῦ θεοῦ).

Light of the Sun

From the earliest days of the cult, Apollo was correlated with the sun, which was deemed an appropriate symbol for his purity and moral earnestness. This correlation frequently appears in numismatic images of Apollo. Sunlight, likewise, symbolizes the purity and holiness of Jesus Christ. In an opening description in the Apocalypse, the face of the celestial Christ "shines as the sun in its brilliance" (1:16). The concluding description of the new heaven and earth in the Apocalypse reports no need of the sun, for "the Lamb is its light" (21:23, 22:5), "the bright morning star" (22:16). Both of these descriptions are particularly reminiscent of "bright Apollo ... great god of glorious light" (Ovid, *Metam.* 1.450–453). Similarly, Φοῖβος, "Bright One," was a common epithet of Apollo. Further correlations of Christ with the sun/brightness occur in 10:1, 12:1, 14:14, and 21:23, and most importantly in 19:17, immediately following the thigh inscription in the preceding verse.

Summary of Apollo Imagery in Revelation

The thigh inscription in 19:16 can be seen as a capstone image for a variety of Apollo allusions in the Apocalypse. Even if Apollo imagery is secondary to the load-bearing symbolism that draws on the history of Israel, it is not insignificant.

The primary locus of Apollo imagery is the saga of the celestial woman, messianic child, and dragon in chapter 12. Secondary allusions occur in the defeat of the dragon, doxologies, festal processions, prophecy and oracular powers, and references to the sun and light. All these images were associated with the Apollo cult. These same images are repeatedly transferred to Jesus Christ in the Apocalypse. Three of the images—prophecy, thigh inscription, and sun—are linked consecutively in 19:15–17. Further, the quotation of Ps 2:9 in 19:15 and 12:5 links Christ as the rider on the white horse with the vanquisher of Satan in chapter 12. Finally, the emphatic epithet—"the great dragon, the age-old serpent, who is called Devil and Satan and who leads the world astray" (12:9)—is repeated with similar emphasis in the context of the rider on the white horse in 20:2.

III. Conclusion

The thigh inscription of 19:16 is not an isolated and disconnected image in Revelation, but an apparent symbol recalling the Apollo cult prevalent in first-century Asia. The inscription on the thigh of the triumphant Christ, "King of kings and Lord of lords" (19:16), is the divine rejoinder to the inscription on the forehead of the great harlot and antichrist, "Babylon the great, the mother of the earth's whores and abominations" (17:5). Although a forehead inscription is more prominent than a thigh inscription, it is not more significant, for the thigh is where a warrior's sword was hung.[38] In her hubris, the great harlot attacks the Lamb, but the Lamb triumphs because he is "Lord of lords and King of kings" (17:14). This is the name the rider on the white horse bears on his thigh (19:16). "King of kings and Lord of lords" is the ultimate epithet of the Messiah, for only where the Messiah is acknowledged as ruler of all kings, and of all lords and gods, is the Messiah properly glorified.[39]

The Apocalypse is a graphic narrative drama in which the power of the crucified and resurrected Jesus, the Lamb and Messiah of God, overcomes sin, evil, and death in order to restore fallen and captive creation to a new heaven and earth. The new creation is symbolized by the descent of the new Jerusalem, into which are ushered the people, wealth, and glory of all history and nations (21:22–27). The new Jerusalem, which signifies the particular fulfillment of Israel's salvation history, remarkably is empty of the temple, for the Lord Almighty and the Lamb are

---

[38] Homer, *Il.* 1.190; *Od.* 11.231; Song 3:8. On "sword" and "rod of iron" as symbols of masculine sexual domination, see Christopher Frilingos, *Spectacles of Empire: Monsters, Martyrs, and the Book of Revelation*, Divinations (Philadelphia: University of Pennsylvania Press, 2004), 85–92, who rightly concludes that in 19:15 eroticism is "entirely absent" from the symbols.

[39] See Steven J. Friesen, *Imperial Cults and the Apocalypse of John: Reading Revelation in the Ruins* (New York: Oxford University Press, 2001), 209.

themselves the temple (21:22). Nor is there a sun in the new Jerusalem, for the Lamb is the source of light (21:23). The new Jerusalem equally signifies the universal scope of the redemption wrought by Jesus Christ, for John repeatedly includes "every nation and tribe and tongue and people" in the purview of the Apocalypse (5:9, 7:9, 10:11, 11:9, 14:6). The gentiles are now guided by the same light of the Lamb that guides Israel, for "the nations will walk by the light [of the Lamb], and the kings of the earth will bring their glory into [the city]" (21:24). The inscription on the thigh of the rider on the white horse appears as a graphic illustration of the Lamb-turned-victorious-Warrior fulfilling his sovereignty over the nations.[40] The various terms and images reminiscent of the Apollo cult that are preserved in the Apocalypse are perfected and fulfilled in Jesus Christ, who is "King of kings and Lord of lords" (19:16).

[40] Similarly, ibid., 172.

CORE BIBLICAL STUDIES
New this Spring!

Wisdom Literature
Samuel E. Balentine | ISBN: 9781426765025

For the wisdom writings of the Old Testament, the pursuit of wisdom calls for the ongoing attainment of instruction, insight, shrewdness, knowledge, prudence, learning, and skill. And persons who attain wisdom think more deeply, are more discerning, and have a keener insight into the complexities and nuances of decision making. For a world-perspective that assumes the power and reality of divinity, being wise means living ethically - and to live ethically, one must be in a constant intellectual pursuit of meaning.

The book details the structure, themes, and contribution to both ancient and modern society of Job, Proverbs, and Ecclesiastes. The chapters on Sirach and the Wisdom of Solomon will discuss the consonance and dissonance with canonical wisdom, giving special attention to the development of their core ideas. The book concludes with a chapter on Wisdom's abiding legacy.

Samuel E. Balentine is Professor of Old Testament at Union Presbyterian Seminary.

See all current and forthcoming volumes at
AbingdonAcademic.com/Core

www.ingramcontent.com/pod-product-compliance
Lightning Source LLC
Chambersburg PA
CBHW021821300426
44114CB00009BA/271